Sharing the Burden

OXFORD STUDIES IN INTERNATIONAL HISTORY

JAMES J. SHEEHAN, SERIES ADVISOR

Sharing the Burden

The Armenian Question, Humanitarian Intervention and Anglo-American Visions of Global Order

CHARLIE LADERMAN

OXFORD
UNIVERSITY PRESS

OXFORD
UNIVERSITY PRESS

Oxford University Press is a department of the University of Oxford. It furthers
the University's objective of excellence in research, scholarship, and education
by publishing worldwide. Oxford is a registered trade mark of Oxford University
Press in the UK and certain other countries.

Published in the United States of America by Oxford University Press
198 Madison Avenue, New York, NY 10016, United States of America.

Library of Congress Cataloging-in-Publication Data
Names: Laderman, Charlie, author.
Title: Sharing the burden : the Armenian question, humanitarian intervention,
and Anglo-American visions of global order / Charlie Laderman.
Description: New York, NY : Oxford University Press, 2019. |
Series: Oxford studies in international history | Includes bibliographical references and index.
Identifiers: LCCN 2019006333 (print) | LCCN 2019017260 (ebook) |
ISBN 9780190618612 (updf) | ISBN 9780190618629 (epub) |
ISBN 9780190618605 (hardcover)
Subjects: LCSH: Armenian massacres, 1915–1923. | Armenian question. |
World War, 1914–1918—Territorial questions—Armenia. |
Intervention (International law) | United States—Foreign relations—20th century. |
Great Britain—Foreign relations—20th century.
Classification: LCC DS195.5 (ebook) | LCC DS195.5.L33 2019 (print) |
DDC 956.6/20154—dc23
LC record available at https://lccn.loc.gov/2019006333

1 3 5 7 9 8 6 4 2

Printed by Integrated Books International, United States of America

CONTENTS

Sharing the Burden

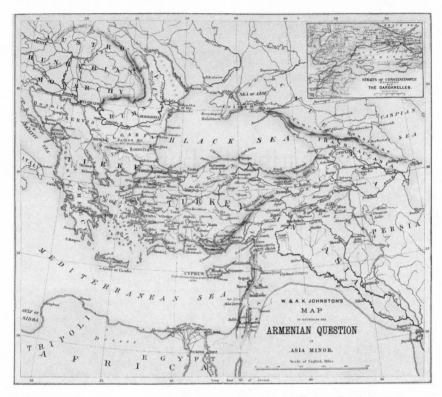

Figure 0.1 The Armenian question in Asia Minor, 1895, Bodleian Library, D30 114.

Introduction

The Armenian Question

> Probably Armenia was known to the American school child in 1919
> only a little less than England. The association of Mount Ararat and
> Noah, the staunch Christians who were massacred periodically by the
> Mohammedan Turks, and the Sunday School collections over fifty
> years for alleviating their miseries—all cumulate to impress the name
> Armenia on the front of the American mind.
>
> —Herbert Hoover, *The Memoirs of Herbert Hoover: Years of
> Adventure* (1951)

> The Armenians and their tribulations were well known throughout
> England and the United States. This field of interest was lighted by the
> lamps of religion, philanthropy and politics. Atrocities perpetrated
> upon Armenians stirred the ire of simple and chivalrous men and
> women spread widely about the English-speaking world. Now was the
> moment when at last the Armenians would receive justice and the right
> to live in peace in their national home. Their persecutors and tyrants
> had been laid low by war or revolution. The greatest nations in the hour
> of their victory were their friends, and would see them righted.
>
> —Winston Churchill, *The World Crisis: The Aftermath* (1929)

The First World War was the foundational crisis of the twentieth century. It was
the "calamity from which all other calamities sprang," as historian Fritz Stern put
it.[1] The conflict precipitated the collapse of international order, prompting the
downfall of empires and provoking the displacement of entire populations. The
world had never before witnessed death and destruction on this scale. Almost
ten million combatants were killed and millions more were permanently dis-
abled. Yet even among this carnage, Theodore Roosevelt was adamant that one
atrocity was unique in its horror. The former president would declare unequivocally in 1918 that "the Armenian massacre was the greatest crime of the war."[2] On
the other side of the Atlantic, Lord Robert Cecil, the British undersecretary for
foreign affairs, went even further, stating, "without the least fear of exaggeration,
that no more horrible crime has been committed in the history of the world."[3]

Roosevelt and Cecil encapsulated the attitude of their fellow countrymen to the wartime annihilation of around one million Armenian Christians in the Ottoman Empire.[4] Indeed, the plight of the Ottoman Armenians had long been a humanitarian cause célèbre in the United States and across the British Empire, since earlier massacres of over 100,000 Armenians by the Ottoman Sultan Abdul Hamid's forces and Kurdish irregulars between 1894 and 1896. The Armenians' staunch Christian faith, their distinctive national culture, and their position as downtrodden subjects of an Islamic Empire that many Americans and Britons considered despotic gave them a unique hold on the public imagination in both countries. This appeal was strengthened by the Armenian claim to be descended from Noah, whose ark, according to the Book of Genesis, came to rest on Mount Ararat—in the heart of the Armenian homeland. American affinity for the Armenians was further bolstered by the preponderant influence of their Protestant missionaries in the Armenian provinces of the Ottoman Empire. Yet prior to the 1894–1896 massacres, the US government had largely avoided any political entanglement in the so-called Armenian question—the diplomatic term for the issues that arose from the insecurity of the Armenians in the Ottoman Empire—retaining its traditional policy of aloofness from events in the Near East and Europe more generally. As American power grew at the turn of the twentieth century, however, so did the sense of responsibility felt by leading Americans for preventing the kind of atrocities to which the Armenians had fallen victim.

In 1896, the US Congress adopted an unprecedented resolution that called for US diplomatic intervention on behalf of the Armenians to "stay the hand of fanaticism and lawless violence" in the Ottoman Empire.[5] This marked a major turning point in the nation's international humanitarianism and signaled a fundamental departure in American foreign policy. Throughout the nineteenth century, private charities and churches had taken the lead in marshaling relief efforts for humanitarian catastrophes around the world, while the federal government declined to involve itself diplomatically in any such crises occurring outside its traditional sphere of interest in the Western hemisphere. In its response to the Armenian massacres, however, the US government was drawn for the first time toward outlining a political solution to a humanitarian problem occurring elsewhere.[6] Legislative agitation did not ultimately lead to executive action in 1896, but it did reveal a bold new spirit in US diplomacy that grew stronger over time. This spirit was evident when the United States intervened militarily to address a humanitarian problem closer to home in 1898, that of Spanish oppression in Cuba, establishing a Pacific and Caribbean empire in its wake. It was also discernible in US diplomatic interventions under President Theodore Roosevelt on behalf of Eastern European Jews and in the Congo during the opening decade of the twentieth century. John Quincy Adams's famous warning that Americans should not go overseas "in search of monsters to destroy," a dictum that shaped the nation's foreign policy for much of the nineteenth century, no longer appeared to deter American activism.[7]

When renewed massacres broke out in the Ottoman Empire in 1904, however, Roosevelt recognized that the country lacked the instruments and inclination to engage in a large-scale military intervention to protect the Armenians, despite widespread public sympathy. Nor were most Americans prepared to maintain a consistent engagement in global affairs after Roosevelt left office; the Armenian question was left to Britain and the other European powers to try and resolve. Only with the upheaval and turmoil of the First World War did the potential for US intervention on behalf of the Armenians emerge as a realistic possibility. In the shadow of the unprecedented wartime destruction of the Armenian people, Americans initiated an unparalleled relief effort to save the survivors. But for some Americans, impassioned expressions of private philanthropy were insufficient. Out of office, Roosevelt led calls for the US government to use its power to protect the Armenians, but the official response under his rival President Woodrow Wilson was initially characterized by restraint. No official protest was made when the wartime massacres began in 1915 and despite declaring war on Germany and Austria-Hungary in 1917, the first deployment of US power in Europe, the country remained at peace with the other great Central Power, the Ottoman Empire, for the duration of the conflict. Yet Wilson's apparent inaction in the face of the massacres belies the outsized role that the Armenian question would come to play in his own vision of reforming global politics. At the end of the war, Wilson hoped Americans would take the lead in establishing a new world order, guaranteeing "justice to all peoples and nationalities, and their right to live on equal terms of liberty and safety with one another, whether they be strong or weak."[8] And in this new order the United States would have a special role to play in Armenia. In addition to urging US membership in the new League of Nations he had outlined, Wilson hoped that it would accept a mandate for the nascent Armenian state. The mandate would not only resolve the Armenian question, therefore, but also secure and symbolize the United States' new global role.

This work traces the story of the US response to the Armenian question as an essential but neglected window onto the rise of the United States to world power. It sets the United States' Armenian diplomacy within the broader context of a public debate in American society and politics over the nature and purpose of the nation's newly established power at the turn of the twentieth century. In doing so, it explores the controversy over the role of humanitarian intervention in US foreign policy during this period. More broadly, it examines the significant impact that the Armenian question exerted on American ideas about international order and explains why this question came to assume such importance to so many Americans, particularly Roosevelt and Wilson.

In order to fully understand the American response to the Armenian question, it is necessary to consider it in tandem with the British response. American and British policies on this issue offer a critical, yet overlooked, perspective on the evolution of Anglo-American relations in this period, and particularly Britain's response to the rise of the United States to world power at a time when its leaders were worried about their own nation's international position. Growing US involvement in international politics at the turn of the twentieth century encouraged British dreams of an Anglo-American alliance, and this book shows how Britain's statesmen attempted to use shared sympathy for the Armenians to help advance that goal. It also explores why a number of prominent American advocates of intervention for the Armenians, most notably Roosevelt, were determined supporters of the United States assuming a leading international role in partnership with Britain. Furthermore, it explains why an American mandate for an independent Armenia, through the League, emerged as a central tenet of Britain's strategy for the postwar world. Woodrow Wilson and British Prime Minister David Lloyd George both came to see American protection of the Armenians as key to the establishment of a reformed international system. However, they had very different visions of the new international organization, and an appreciation of their respective policies on the question of an American mandate for Armenia illuminates the thinking behind their peace plans after the First World War.

***

The unprecedented scale and destruction of the war and its aftermath would instigate a revolution in the conduct of international relations and inspire new thinking about global political reform. Ideas about restructuring the world order proliferated in many societies but were particularly pronounced in the United States and across the British Empire.[9] While France, the other principal victorious power, was primarily concerned with the threat posed by its German neighbor, the relative distances of Britain and the United States from the European continent afforded them different degrees of latitude in addressing the problems presented by the war.[10] Furthermore, the two powers had greater capacities to shape world affairs than other countries, and this enabled its policymakers to pursue a wider range of options. There was a fundamental disparity, though, between the global positions and strategic outlooks of the two nations. An awareness of this is crucial to understanding their positions on the Armenian question specifically and on the postwar international order more generally.

By the end of the First World War, American economic strength was on a vastly different scale than Britain's. This economic dominance combined with the pivotal US role in the Allied victory meant the world was now forced to come to terms with "America's new centrality" in the international system.[11]

Unlike Britain and France, the great power status of the United States was less dependent on its acquisition of overseas possessions. The geostrategic foundation of its position in the world remained its dominance of the Western hemisphere, which helps explain why the nation's initial enthusiasm for establishing a colonial empire after the 1898 war with Spain rapidly abated. On the other hand, Britain possessed a worldwide empire and its interests were tied up in its imperial system. This made it more vulnerable to the geopolitical and economic consequences wrought by the war. Britain's victory in the conflict came at a huge financial cost and, coupled with the breakdown of the prewar global order, in which Britain was the leading power, this meant that its capacity to exercise a hegemonic role in the postwar international system was increasingly constrained.[12] As a result, a number of British policymakers looked to a cooperative relationship with the United States as the basis for a postwar order, after its intervention in the war on the Allied side had fueled dreams of an Anglo-American combination.[13]

The League of Nations was envisaged as the mechanism to convert the wartime Anglo-American association into a postwar partnership.[14] More specifically, it was the League's mandate system that was seen by British statesmen as the means to achieve this goal. This initiative was designed to allow the allied nations, under "mandate" from the League, to assume responsibility for administering the former German colonies and new states that had emerged after the wartime collapse of the Ottoman, Austro-Hungarian, and Russian empires. American acceptance of a protectorate over one of these territories was central to British visions for the new organization, ensuring that the United States became an active player in international politics outside its traditional sphere of influence, and helping to forge the Anglo-American alliance that was so important to many British policymakers. This idea of an Anglo-American "colonial alliance," as one of its leading proponents, British Colonial Secretary Lord Milner referred to it, is one of the most intriguing of the forgotten ideals of the World War I period.[15] What has not been fully appreciated by historians is the significance of the United States assuming a mandate in order to cement that partnership or the importance of the Near East as the crucible where that new order would be forged, after Wilson agreed to accept mandates, subject to Congressional assent, for Armenia and the Ottoman capital Constantinople. Wilson's commitment to assuming a mandate came not from his desire to establish an Anglo-American colonial alliance, however, but from his determination for the United States to play a hands-on role in establishing a different form of world order. For Wilson, the mandates were a manifestation of this new order, providing an American alternative to Europe's imperial practices and, more importantly, ensuring that the United States assumed a position of global leadership. Which mandates the United States would assume and the struggle over them are crucial to understanding British and American strategies for an international organization and their competing conceptions of global order. Furthermore, the controversy over the mandates would serve as the culmination of more than two decades of debate in the United States and Britain over whether—and, if so, how—to resolve the Armenian question.

That period witnessed such enormous global upheaval that the Armenian issue is often little more than a footnote in most accounts of US foreign affairs or Anglo-American relations.[16] Conversely, there are a number of excellent, more focused studies that explore the American and British responses separately across this period or, in the case of Britain, within the context of imperial politics and with regard to wider European geopolitics.[17] But considering the American response alongside the British shows the connections between them, and reveals something broader about the historic debates over the United States' growing power, its evolving relationship with Britain, and the development of ideas on humanitarian intervention and global order at the turn of the twentieth century.

This book charts how the idea of an American solution to the Armenian question evolved from the mid-1890s, when the plight of the Armenians first imprinted itself on the American consciousness just as the United States began its rise to world power.[18] It explores why the 1894–1896 massacres led to the emergence of a public and political discourse on America's responsibility to aid the survivors and punish the perpetrators, and how US government officials grappled with the legal and geopolitical implications of intervention in the Armenian question. It examines the intersection between US activism on behalf of the Armenians and its intervention over Cuba in 1898, as well as the complex interplay between humanitarianism and empire in the nation's conception of its "civilizing" role in international affairs at this time. It also uncovers how these initial Armenian atrocities led to the first serious discussion of a joint Anglo-American intervention in the Near East and the first proposal for an American protectorate over the Ottoman Empire, one that would safeguard the Armenians and ultimately stimulate a regional, and potentially global, entente between the two powers. It explores Roosevelt's thinking on an alliance with Britain, a significant but neglected feature of which was a shared responsibility to censure humanitarian atrocities that offended the civilization of the age, and the protection of peoples such as the Armenians. It traces the genesis of Roosevelt's doctrine of American responsibility to intervene in response to "crimes against civilization," a set of principles that was profoundly shaped by the 1894–1896 massacre of Ottoman Armenians, along with the actions that he took in support of this.[19] And it explains why, by the end of Roosevelt's presidency, he had come to regard American missionaries as the best chance of achieving a long-term solution to the Armenian question. It sketches out this "missionary solution" by exploring the missionaries' informal "civilizing mission" in the Ottoman Empire, their developing relationship with US government officials and business leaders, and the ties they forged with their international peers, particularly in the British Empire, as they sought to build support for a campaign to transform the Near East.[20]

After this ambition was brought to a catastrophic halt when the Armenians were threatened with wholesale destruction amidst the turmoil of World War I, American missionary leaders, despite pioneering a vast relief effort that "quite literally kept a nation alive," insisted that the United States refrain from declaring war on the Ottomans.[21] In uncovering the motivations behind missionary policy, this book also explores Woodrow Wilson's pragmatic decision not to declare war on the Ottoman Empire after US entry into the conflict in 1917 and sheds light on the US relationship with its wartime partners, of whom Wilson insisted the United States was an "associate" rather than an "ally." The Armenian question grew in significance in Wilson's own mind once he was freed from the constraints of war and set to establish a reformed international system, in which the Ottoman Empire would be dismembered and the security of its subject peoples guaranteed.[22] This study reveals why Wilson believed his new global order, led by the United States and centered on the League of Nations, was the only permanent way of protecting peoples such as the Armenians and maintaining world peace. In explaining why the Armenians were the only people for whom Wilson specifically asked Americans to assume a mandate, it shows how their independence struggle, more directly than that of any other people during the League fight, forced Americans to confront the extent of global responsibilities that they were willing to assume.[23] Based on research in the papers of the Armenian National Delegation, the Ottoman Armenians' representatives to the cabinets of the great powers, it divulges how the Armenians themselves and the diaspora community in the United States, which numbered just 100,000 by the time of the First World War, sought to appeal to Americans to safeguard their security and for help in determining their future. Furthermore, it analyses how leading British statesmen attempted to entice the United States into assuming a mandate and helping to construct a system of international governance, built around Anglo-American collaboration and based on shared political responsibilities in the Near East.

The book concludes by discussing why the question of an Armenian mandate, although generally overlooked in studies of the League fight, is so significant to understanding American attitudes to this organization. It explores the findings of the two investigative groups that Wilson sent to the Near East—the King-Crane and Harbord Commissions—to assess conditions in the region and ascertain whether the United States should accept a mandate. It explains why the debate in the US Senate over a mandate ultimately reached its conclusion in

June 1920, more than two months after the defeat of the Versailles Treaty. And it highlights how the lingering American mistrust of British imperialism, as well as the growing British disillusionment with American indecision over whether to commit to a new role in the Near East, profoundly impacted the postwar relationship between the two countries with significant consequences for regional and global order.

As Herbert Hoover and Winston Churchill recalled, the fate of the Armenians was of special concern to the peoples of the English-speaking world at the outset of the twentieth century. The aim of this book is to show why the survival of one of the world's smallest nations became so entangled with the foreign policies of the two most powerful states, the relations between them, and their search for a new global order.

***

While a century ago many Americans and Britons were aware of the rough contours of Armenian history and their position in the Ottoman Empire, most contemporary readers are unlikely to be so familiar with the issue. To understand the larger story, therefore, requires setting it against the historical backdrop of the Armenian question itself and its place within the larger Eastern question. Prior to falling under Ottoman rule, the Armenians had developed a distinctive national culture. Around the sixth century B.C. they had emerged as an identifiable people, occupying lands between the Black, Caspian, and Mediterranean seas. In A.D. 301, twelve years before Constantine's Edict of Toleration legalized Christian worship in the Roman Empire, the Armenians became the first people to embrace Christianity as their state religion and they held resolutely to their faith over the succeeding centuries.[24] By 1400, however, most of the territory that had historically belonged to them, in what is today referred to as Eastern Anatolia and Transcaucasia, had fallen under Ottoman control, with a separate Eastern section occupied by Persia. In the Ottoman Empire, the Armenians were members of a multiconfessional and multiethnic polity but, as an Orthodox Christian minority, they were considered second-class citizens and forced to pay special taxes. Nevertheless, while the Empire thrived, most Armenians lived peacefully in their historic homeland, working as tenant farmers for feudal Muslim landlords. A significant number prospered in international commerce or entered the skilled professions. However, by the eighteenth and nineteenth centuries the Empire was in decline and the Armenians' position had deteriorated. The Empire's administrative, economic, and military infrastructure was beset by internal corruption and it was increasingly difficult to compete with its dynamic European rivals. The Armenians labored under the weight of growing official discrimination and their tax burden became more oppressive as the Empire's finances came under greater strain.[25]

As the Ottoman state struggled to adapt to the challenges of the nineteenth century, many of its subject minorities, influenced by romanticist ideologies that were spreading from Europe, underwent a cultural and political revival. A number of these groups successfully fought for political independence, occasionally supported by particular European states, causing the Ottomans to lose most of their Balkan provinces. As the Empire contracted, the European powers grew increasingly concerned. Sprawled over an area of pivotal strategic significance, the Empire lay at the crossroads of three continents, a critical component in the European balance of power. Its decline threatened to destabilize the continent and gave rise to the Eastern question in European diplomacy, of what should be done about the moribund Empire. At the same time, Ottoman liberal elites, painfully aware of the Empire's precarious condition, enacted the Tanzimat edicts of 1839 and 1856 in an attempt to establish a modernized, centralized state and stave off the prospect of military and economic decline. This extensive series of reforms failed to convince the European powers that the condition of the "Sick man of Europe" was improving.[26] While eager to capture any territorial spoils, they were equally determined that none of their rivals should profit if the Empire collapsed. Following the Crimean War, they pledged to maintain the Empire's territorial integrity. Yet this did not prevent them from seeking to advance their geopolitical and commercial objectives in Ottoman territories. Nor were they averse to exploiting the growing nationalist ambitions of the Empire's minority peoples for their own ends.[27]

During the early to mid-nineteenth century, Britain emerged as the Ottoman Empire's principal supporter among the European powers. This had less to do with any great affinity for the Ottomans and was more a reflection of the British government's concerns about Russia, particularly the threat that Russian expansion posed to Britain's lines of communication to its imperial possessions in the East. In particular, British leaders were determined to prevent Russia from seizing control of the Ottoman capital, Constantinople, which was situated on the Dardanelles Straits, the strategic nexus that linked Europe and Asia. If Russia occupied Constantinople then its fleet would have access to the Mediterranean Sea and could cut British links to its territories in Asia, while denying Britain's navy access to the Black Sea, where it could threaten Russia's own coastline. As a result, successive British governments supported the Ottoman Empire as a buffer against Russia. Lord Palmerston, who dominated British foreign policy for much of the period from 1830 to 1865, was a key figure in devising this strategy. While in office as both prime minister and foreign secretary, he worked to develop closer ties with Constantinople despite criticism from opponents, who condemned the Ottomans for their corruption and treatment of Christian minorities. In particular, Palmerston and his successors were determined to keep Russia from exploiting its claim to be the defender of Ottoman Christians to justify any intervention in the Empire. As a result, Britain's diplomats in the Near East acted to deter hopes among the Empire's minority populations that they would receive British support for any separatist aspirations.

As the Armenians had spread throughout the Empire and no longer comprised a majority in their historic territories, they were initially less susceptible than other communities to visions of national independence. Nevertheless, Armenians also experienced a cultural revival in the nineteenth century. Thousands enrolled in schools run by European and American missionaries, while hundreds traveled to Europe for higher education. They subsequently established schools and newspapers for their conationals across the Empire. Gradually there built up a network of literate Armenians imbued with a sense of national self-consciousness. This cultural awakening was accompanied by Armenian disillusionment with the effects of the Tanzimat reforms. Furthermore, Armenians were increasingly concerned about their economic and physical security, which was threatened by corrupt government officials and growing lawlessness in the eastern provinces of Anatolia, where most still resided. The Armenians' desire to ensure the security of their communities and property, within an increasingly unstable and illiberal Empire, led to the emergence of the Armenian question as part of the larger Eastern question.[28]

Between 1875 and 1878 multiple insurrections erupted in the Ottoman Empire, in what came to be known as the Great Eastern Crisis. In 1876, the outbreak of a rebellion in Bulgaria was brutally repressed by the Ottomans and resulted in an international outcry. Britain's Liberal leader William Gladstone, then in opposition, denounced the "Bulgarian Horrors" and condemned Benjamin Disraeli's Conservative government for its support of the Ottomans. In doing so, he captured the mood of the outraged British electorate. While recognizing that Britain's public had turned viscerally anti-Ottoman, Disraeli continued to favor them, supporting the new young sultan, Abdul Hamid II, who took the throne in 1876 and granted the Empire's first constitution that year. Disraeli's major fear was that Russia, convinced that Britain would be prevented by public opinion from opposing a Russian intervention, intended to exploit the Bulgarian atrocities to expand its own territory. In 1877, Russia did invoke its position as the guardian of the Empire's Orthodox Christians to declare war on the Ottomans. After advancing deep into Ottoman territory, the Russian forces pressured the defeated Ottomans into signing the Treaty of San Stefano in March 1878, which diminished Ottoman possessions in Europe still further.[29] Moreover, this treaty, and the Berlin Treaty that revised it later that year, signaled the internationalization of the Armenian question.

The Russians, who in 1829 had annexed the eastern provinces of historic Armenia, occupied most of Ottoman Armenia at the end of the 1877–8 conflict. Ottoman Armenian leaders appealed to victorious Russian commanders for the peace terms to make provisions for their protection. Consequently, the Russians inserted a clause in the Treaty of San Stefano, making withdrawal of their troops contingent on the Ottomans introducing reforms in the territories and ensuring the Armenians were protected from marauding bands of Kurds and Circassians, their principal tormentors. However, Britain and Austria-Hungary were alarmed that San Stefano's terms allowed Russia to expand its influence toward the Mediterranean and called a Congress in Berlin to revise the treaty. In particular, Disraeli regarded Russian domination of the area from the Caucasus to Eastern Anatolia, where the historic Armenian homeland was situated, as a critical threat to the British passage to India. In Berlin, Disraeli worked to limit Russian territorial gains in Eastern Anatolia.[30] To the disappointment of the Armenians, the Berlin Treaty stipulated that Russian forces should immediately withdraw from Eastern Anatolia. Although the Treaty instructed Constantinople to carry out reforms in the Empire's Armenian provinces and "to guarantee their security," under the supervision of the European Powers, the nature of that oversight was left undefined and no mechanism was provided for its enforcement.[31] The Cyprus Convention of 1878, under which the Ottomans accepted Britain's occupation and administration of Cyprus as a base for preventing Russian seizure of Ottoman territory, also provided imprecise instructions to the sultan to implement reforms in the Armenian populated regions of the Empire. The Armenians were nonetheless hopeful that the Treaty and the presence of British troops in Cyprus would enable the European powers to intervene on their behalf and protect them from repression by imperial authorities. The presence of Western officials and missionaries within their communities only heightened these expectations. The Great Powers initially cooperated to pressure the Ottomans to fulfill their treaty obligations but soon became distracted by imperial interests elsewhere, and the issue of Armenian reforms slipped down the diplomatic agenda.

The Russo-Turkish War led to the Ottoman Empire losing one-third of its territory and 20 percent of its inhabitants.[32] It also exposed the Empire's precarious economic position and led to the establishment of the Ottoman Public Debt Administration, under which Britain and France took control over Ottoman fiscal policy, further undermining Constantinople's sovereignty. Armenian appeals to the Europeans for intervention were another source of humiliation for the tottering Empire, and raised the specter of a potential enemy within. In this context, the Sultan placed a greater emphasis on Islamic solidarity to reinforce his fragile regime, in the process helping to inculcate anti-Christian sentiment and a sense of their subordinate status in the Empire. He was committed to securing the loyalty of Kurdish tribes in Eastern Anatolia and using his fellow Muslims to maintain regional order. Consequently, the Kurds were allowed, and often encouraged by local Ottoman authorities, to terrorize Armenian villages. Now convinced the Ottoman government was tyrannical and complicit in their oppression, and despairing of outside aid from the powers, growing numbers of Armenians began organizing in self-defense groups. Inspired by the struggles of Balkan Christians, many believed that they needed to take up arms to protect themselves. In addition, several secret political societies had been established by the 1890s. Unlike their Balkan counterparts, however, most of these organizations were not yet prepared to champion national independence. Instead they emphasized regional autonomy, cultural freedoms, civil liberties, greater economic opportunity, and the right to bear arms.[33] In 1894, members of one of these political groups, the socialist Hunchak Party, organized local farmers in the village of Sasun to resist attempts by local Kurdish tribal chiefs to collect feudal dues in exchange for vows of protection. In the resulting confrontation several Kurds were killed. Determined to check any suggestion of revolution, Sultan Abdul Hamid's forces descended on Sasun and the surrounding villages. The ensuing destruction led to the deaths of at least 3,000 Armenians, provoked outrage across Europe and North America, and ensured the Armenian question was once more a live issue in international diplomacy.

There was widespread support for the Armenians in Britain, where prominent liberals, led by former Prime Minister Gladstone, had continued to rail against the condition of Eastern Christians in the Ottoman Empire. Furthermore, hostility to the Ottomans now cut across party lines and the Armenian massacres ensured that anti-Ottoman feeling became entrenched even among Conservatives.[34] The Sasun massacre encouraged Lord Rosebery's Liberal government to pressure France and Russia to revive the issue of Armenian reform. In May 1895, the three powers issued a joint proposal to the Ottoman government that recommended consolidating the six Anatolian provinces with the largest Armenian populations into a single administrative unit, the release of political prisoners, reparations for the people of Sasun and surrounding villages, and the establishment of a permanent commission to ensure reforms were implemented. As the sultan procrastinated, 4,000 Armenians, led by the Hunchaks, marched in protest in Constantinople and were again met with violence. Alarmed at the prospect of a mass Armenian insurrection in Anatolia, and concerned that Armenian revolutionists were already colluding with Macedonian insurgents in the western provinces of the Empire, Ottoman authorities unleashed a campaign of terror in a bid to maintain the status quo. Government troops and regional notables incited mob violence across Eastern Anatolia, while Kurdish militias were given free rein to attack Armenian communities. By the end of 1896, systematic pogroms had claimed the lives of between 100,000 and 200,000 Armenians, in a series of atrocities that came to be known as the Hamidian massacres.[35]

The brutality of this crackdown would inspire renewed debate in Europe over a nation's responsibility to intervene on behalf of a persecuted people. While there was a long history of European states intervening in each other's internal affairs for a combination of strategic reasons, the protection of coreligionists and the advancement of political liberties, by the beginning of the nineteenth century the practice of nonintervention in the domestic politics of another sovereign state had been largely established as a norm in European diplomacy.[36] However, this principle did not fully extend to the Ottoman Empire, which the European powers did not believe was "civilized" enough to be immune from outside intervention, and which they were increasingly convinced could not or would not reform itself. Under the special status that the Eastern question occupied in European politics, the powers gave themselves permission to intervene if large-scale disturbances occurred, for instance if the Ottoman authorities violently suppressed a revolt and massacres resulted.

While European diplomats debated what criteria—such as the number of people massacred and the nature of the killing—needed to be met to provoke action, the principal determinant for sanctioning an intervention was whether it enhanced or endangered European peace. As a result, the interventions that did occur in the nineteenth century were largely carried out in concert, such as when Britain, France, and Russia joined together to intervene in Greece in 1827 or when France secured permission from the other powers to occupy parts of Greater Syria in 1860 after the massacre of thousands of Maronite Christians. In these cases the intervening states were hardly motivated by pure humanitarian concerns, with each acting to secure clear, discernable interests, but they were, for the most part, careful to assure the other European powers that their military actions were not primarily intended for their own economic or territorial self-aggrandizement. As such, these were practical, if imperfect, examples of "humanitarian intervention", a term that entered the international diplomatic vocabulary during the 19th century, though its contours remained imprecisely defined and its validity intensely debated by contemporary legal theorists.[37] These interventions were often precipitated by pressure from an outraged public opinion, particularly in powers with parliamentary systems of government and a relatively free press like Britain and France. By the late nineteenth century, eyewitness reports of atrocities from foreign correspondents and accounts from missionaries were relayed at previously inconceivable speed thanks to the recently invented telegraph, arousing indignation and demands for action.[38] Undoubtedly, certain victims attracted a far greater degree of support for action than others. The campaigns for intervention in the Ottoman Empire were predominantly directed at protecting Ottoman Christians (and occasionally Jews), while violence against Muslims, notably in Crete or against the Druze in Lebanon, was largely ignored. However, as Davide Rodogno, a leading scholar of these interventions, has argued, although "selective and biased" they can still be termed "humanitarian" when their principal motive was to "save strangers from massacre." Nevertheless, the fact that they were aimed at the Ottoman Empire, chiefly on behalf of Christians, reflected an inclination to contrast Europe's "civilization with that of a 'barbarous,' 'uncivilized' target state, prone to inhumanity, incapable of reforming itself and whose sovereignty and authority they contested."[39] Consequently, interventions were intended initially to save fellow Christians, subsequently to spread European ideas of civilization to the Ottoman Empire and, most importantly, were only undertaken after evaluating the consequences for continental order.

The Hamidian massacres occurred on a larger scale than previous bloodshed that had prompted outside intervention and provoked widespread public outrage and denunciation of Ottoman "barbarity" across Europe. The bipartisan support for the Armenians in Britain, encouraged the Conservative Lord Salisbury, who replaced Rosebery as prime minister in June 1895, to seek support from the other European powers in order to coerce the sultan into bringing an end to the massacres. However, by the mid-1890s, the configuration of European geopolitics had shifted. No power was willing to risk continental stability, or their own interests, to intervene on behalf of the Armenians and, to Salisbury's exasperation, the only collective action that the European powers could agree upon was an ineffectual naval demonstration in 1895.

Unlike the European powers, the United States had no substantial material or geostrategic interests at stake in the issues surrounding the massacres. Its government had traditionally avoided involvement in the diplomatic disputes arising out of the Eastern question, regarding it as an extension of European affairs and therefore an inappropriate sphere for political involvement. The United States was not a signatory to the Berlin Treaty and therefore did not share with the European powers the responsibility for overseeing the Armenian reforms. In addition, its regional economic interests were minimal. Yet the United States did have a significant longstanding link to the Ottoman Empire that ensured public and governmental interest in Near Eastern affairs. American missionaries had been proselytizing in the Empire since the beginning of the nineteenth century and had established the most wide-ranging mission field of any nationality group, with Armenians as their principal wards. Within American society, their expertise was unparalleled and they proved instrumental in shaping public perceptions of the Empire and its inhabitants. Missionaries represented the most active American involvement in the Near East during an era of limited political engagement.[40] As American power expanded in the last decade of the nineteenth century, however, and turmoil in the Ottoman Empire deepened, missionary leaders would urge their government to adopt a more assertive regional role, protecting not only them and their institutions but the Armenians too. The ensuing debate over the appropriate response to the Armenian atrocities would encourage many leading Americans to question the continued relevance of their most revered diplomatic shibboleths and to contemplate a new world role.

1

The Origins of a Solution

On July 4, 1821, Secretary of State John Quincy Adams declared that while the United States "is the well-wisher to the freedom and independence of all, she is the champion and vindicator only of her own." In defining his vision of the United States' world role, Adams was dismissing the demands of domestic opponents for the United States to intervene in the Ottoman Empire in the cause of Greek independence. Echoing George Washington's warning to avoid entanglement in foreign affairs, Adams proclaimed that the United States would continue to "abstain from interference in the concerns of others, even when conflict [was] for principles to which she clings."[1] Two years later, Adams helped draft the Monroe Doctrine to prevent European powers from interfering in the Western hemisphere by defining it as an American sphere of influence. In return, the United States would avoid political involvement in the Old World, such as the ongoing Greek-Ottoman conflict.

In 1823 the United States was a fledgling republic but, as the century closed, its power increased rapidly. In the decades after the American Civil War, the US population grew dramatically, making it the second-most populated power after Russia, and it emerged as a leading economic force.[2] In 1889, the US Navy still ranked twelfth in the world. Within a couple of years, however, Congress appropriated funds for a fleet that, once completed, would make the US Navy equivalent to that of Germany and surpass those of Austria-Hungary, Italy, and the Ottoman Empire.[3] At the same time, the nation expanded its territory westward across the continent, reasserted its intention to assume a hegemonic role in the Western Hemisphere, and expanded its commercial presence in the Pacific.

In the last decades of the nineteenth century, a network of American missionaries also spread out across the globe, including the Near East. While the presence of missionaries in East Asia helped stimulate American commerce and encouraged a more assertive government policy to protect the rights and privileges of US citizens in the region, the United States continued to abstain from official involvement in the Near East, maintaining its pledge to avoid European entanglements. Yet when the Ottoman Empire again descended into violence in 1894, many Americans argued that Adams's cautionary approach was no longer suitable if the nation aspired to great power status. The response to the Armenian massacres would reveal that Americans were increasingly conscious of their nation's rising power and that some were determined to dispense with its self-imposed commitment to confine itself to the New World. Moreover, by demonstrating a greater assertiveness in safeguarding its citizens and their interests from the repercussions of the disorder, even at the risk of embroiling itself in Old World disputes, it raised the possibility that the United States might intervene to protect the rights of others.

American Perceptions of the Near East

During the Gilded Age, even though US policymakers were focused on their own hemisphere and US–Ottoman commercial ties were limited, American elites did take an interest in the region. This was evident in coverage devoted to the Empire in the new mass-circulation magazines that explored international developments in considerable depth, reflecting their middle and upper class readers' intellectual interests and desire for travel. Many exploited new tourism opportunities to take grand tours of Europe and the Near East. While visitors marvelled at the Ottoman Empire's ancient sites, the prevailing attitude to the territory's current condition and the nature of its government was overwhelmingly negative. The *Nation* castigated Ottoman rule as a "tyranny more blighting than any ever known in Europe," while a columnist for *The Galaxy* declared no governmental system could be "worse than that which exists in European Turkey."[4] Many commentators accredited the state of the Empire to its Islamic foundation.[5] While some writers reminded their readers that, historically, many Muslim rulers had shown greater tolerance for religious minorities than their Christian counterparts in Europe, far more shared the view of *The Nation's* editor Edwin Lawrence Godkin that, whatever its past virtues, Islam as a political creed was "wholly out of harmony with the needs and aspirations of modern society."[6] This perception was only strengthened in the mid-1870s by accounts of atrocities against Christian insurrectionists in Ottoman controlled Bosnia, Herzegovina and Bulgaria. These reports were regarded as confirmation of the Empire's essential "incapacity for civilization."[7] By contrast, American observers celebrated the revolutionary spirit of the insurgents. George F. Herrick, a long-time missionary in the region, urged Americans to recognize that the Christian nations of the Empire were fighting for the "recovery of long lost human rights."[8] The widespread American perception of the Ottoman Empire was that of a retrograde and repressive polity that was resistant to reform, maltreated its downtrodden Christian communities, and was destined to collapse.

When Russia joined with its ally Serbia to support the Christian Slavic rebels and declared war on the Ottomans in 1877, most American pundits predicted that the Ottoman Empire's demise was imminent and the Tsarist Empire would subsequently dominate the region. Some American liberals, echoing the view of the British Liberal leader William Gladstone and his followers, looked forward to a Russian victory. Godkin and his staff at *The Nation* argued that Russia, despite its illiberal political system, was "a civilising agent of extraordinary effectiveness" and contrasted that with the Ottomans, who had reduced "the fairest portions of the earth's surface to degradation."[9] However, other analysts countered that Russia's meddling in the Balkans had contributed to the declining relations between the Ottoman Empire and its Christian subjects. Furthermore, the editor of *Appletons* argued that Russia's own record of oppressive imperial rule meant "the cause of civilization [would] not be advanced one iota" by its victory.[10] While American columnists weighed up possible solutions to the Eastern question, they recognized that the matter was of little concern to their government or to the majority of their fellow citizens. As President Rutherford B. Hayes declared in his inaugural address, at the height of the Russo-Turkish War, "we are reminded by the international complications abroad threatening the peace of Europe that our traditional policy of noninterference in the affairs of foreign nations has proved of great value in past times, and ought to be strictly observed."[11]

Despite its official policy of noninvolvement in the region, the United States did have an important national interest in the Ottoman Empire, one that was increasingly drawing its government into the complexities surrounding the Eastern question. American missionaries had been active in the Ottoman Empire since the early 1800s. Initially, Muslims and Jews were the target of proselytizing American Protestants. Experiencing little success, they switched their efforts to regenerating Near East Christianity to provide a beacon of Christian devotion in the Islamic world. In the Empire's Armenian provinces, the missionaries encountered the world's oldest Christian community. American missionaries believed these Gregorian Christians required spiritual renewal and flocked to the Empire, determined to re-educate "the degenerate churches of the East" and spread the gospel of New World Protestantism and Enlightenment values.[12] Missionaries proceeded to develop a more extensive network in the Near East than any other nationality group. While British, French, and Russian missions were prominent in the Empire's Arab provinces, Americans predominated in the Turkish territories, with their strength most evident in Anatolia among Armenians.[13] The American Board of Commissioners for Foreign Missions (ABCFM) was pre-eminent among the American groups. With 114 organized churches serving over 13,000 converts, and 1,500 evangelical schools catering for 60,000 students, the Board's operation accounted for almost 75 percent of all

Western Protestant enterprises in Asia Minor and European Turkey at the end of the nineteenth century.[14]

The Russo-Turkish War confirmed the faith of American missionaries that their teachings could bring spiritual and social sustenance to the people of the Ottoman Empire. The ABCFM had been active among adherents of the Bulgarian Orthodox Church in the Ottoman Empire since the 1850s, and its missionaries and educators had helped lay the cultural foundations for Bulgaria's national awakening. Its press produced seventy-five of the first hundred books printed in modern Bulgarian. During the Bulgarian uprising, American missionaries helped promulgate their cause in Europe and North America, publicized the atrocities and promoted the idea of an independent Bulgarian state.[15] After Bulgaria achieved its autonomy at the close of the Russo-Turkish conflict in 1878, the ABCFM's annual report proclaimed that the Bulgarian people had now been "emancipated from Muslim domination."[16] Alumni of the ABCFM's schools and colleges were active in the new Bulgarian government. Graduates of Robert College of Constantinople, which became the first American center of higher learning outside the United States when it opened in 1863, were so prominent that the college's President George Washburn claimed the King of Bulgaria had informed him that the institution was "a nursery of Bulgarian statesmen."[17] Other Ottoman subjects also experienced a revived interest in their native language and culture under the tuition of American missionaries. The early Christian Arab nationalist leader, Butrus al-Bustani, worked with American missionaries in the mid-nineteenth century to produce an Arabic translation of the Bible. While the missionaries proved unsuccessful in this bid to convert the Middle East to American Protestantism, the collaboration between Americans and Arabs ultimately produced an outpouring of Arabic texts during the 1870s and 1880s, helping to stimulate a literary revival that would contribute to the development of an Arab nationalist movement.[18] The Armenians, who remained the ABCFM's principal wards, accounting for around 90 percent of the organization's work, also experienced their own cultural renaissance during this period.[19] Missionaries helped stimulate this revival through the publication of a modern Armeno-Turkish translation of the Bible and the establishment of schools, populated almost exclusively by Armenians. Enhanced literacy and education encouraged the emerging Armenian national, political movement. As Edwin Pears, a British author and barrister in Constantinople who had worked with US missionaries to arouse international awareness of the "Bulgarian atrocities," recalled: "In a very real sense it may be said that fomenters of political agitation in Armenia, as in Bulgaria, were the schoolmasters and the missions."[20] The ABCFM's representatives, unwilling to risk endangering their position in the Empire by arousing the hostility of Ottoman authorities, refrained from officially supporting the Armenian nationalist cause. However, they were not oblivious to the effect that their teachings were having on the Empire's subject peoples. The ABCFM's Annual Report declared in 1881 that the Ottoman Empire, "a problem that is the puzzle of statesmen . . . is perhaps waiting its solution at the hands of American missionaries, through the infusion of a new moral and intellectual life."[21]

American missionaries retained their independence from the State Department to avoid the implication that they were merely agents for advancing their government's political and economic interests in the Empire. In fact, US officials were so detached from the region that missionary leaders often felt they were forced to serve as their own diplomatic representatives. In the aftermath of the Russo-Turkish War, however, Ottoman officials were increasingly suspicious of all foreign missionaries, concerned that their institutions had become centers for political intrigue and convinced that they were actively encouraging nationalist aspirations among the Empire's Christian minorities. As tensions rose between imperial authorities and religious minorities, civil disorder grew. US missionaries increasingly looked to Washington for protection, and launched a campaign to educate the American public on the deteriorating situation for the Armenians.

One group that was already familiar with the situation in the Near East was the tiny Armenian American community, which numbered 10,000 by the beginning of 1894. Many were young men who had come temporarily to the United States in search of work. Some were Protestant converts, whose passage was arranged by their missionary sponsors, while others were thriving merchants.[22] Armenian immigrants to the United States were able to take advantage of their new homeland's exceptional naturalization laws, which enabled them to return to the Ottoman Empire under protection of the American flag (Armenians naturalized in European states did not enjoy the same rights.) A number of naturalized Armenian Americans went back to the Empire to distribute money, propaganda and occasionally even arms to their conationals. Although US diplomats sympathized with Ottoman determination to exclude "objectionable aliens" from their territory, they were also committed to providing equal protection to all American citizens, whether naturalized or native born. The revolutionary activities of these naturalized Armenian Americans presented US officials with a dilemma and embroiled them in the increasingly fraught relations between the Armenians and the Ottoman authorities.[23]

A Blot Upon the Civilization of the Age

When firsthand reports from missionaries filtered into the United States of the mass killing of Armenians in 1894, Americans were horrified. A number of newspapers initially also reported the official Ottoman account—that Armenian revolutionaries had initiated hostilities in order to encourage reprisals and invite European intervention in the Empire. However, by the end of the year, the American press was virtually unanimous in denouncing the Ottoman authorities for the violence. The *New York Times* carried emotionally charged headlines of "Holocaust" and "Slaughter of Innocents."[24] Secular and religious publications nationwide featured front-page articles, reports, and editorials condemning the massacres.[25] Mass rallies were held to protest the bloodshed. Civic organizations raised money for relief. The National Armenian Relief Committee, spearheaded by leading American financiers and with support from John D. Rockefeller, amassed more than $300,000 in 1896–1897. The aid was distributed by the seventy-four-year-old founder of the American Red Cross, Clara Barton, who led a mission to the Ottoman Empire, which was a signatory to the Geneva conventions and therefore obligated to allow her to conduct relief operations.

Fervor for the Armenian cause transcended religious denomination. The priest R. M. Ryan penned an article in the *Catholic World*, titled "Why We Catholics Sympathize With Armenia."[26] Rabbi Stephen Wise and the industrialist Jacob Schiff were at the forefront of American Jewish relief efforts. Baptists, Congregationalists, and Methodists united in horror at this "atrocious crime against Armenian Christians."[27] Invoking religious imagery, the Armenians were portrayed as ancient Christians under threat of destruction by "unspeakable Turks" in biblical lands. The Catholic editor, John J. O'Shea, claimed that the underlying cause of the carnage was "the experiment of trying to reconcile the Oriental barbarism which Turkey represents with the social life and the Christian systems of Eastern Europe and transCaucasia."[28] An appeal printed in the *San Francisco Call* insisted that "a quarter of a million souls are destitute and helpless through the fanatical fury of Mohammedan mobs and the soldiers of the sultan, whose constant thirst is for the blood of Christian men, women and children."[29] The language used in these protests, the struggle of civilization against barbarism, resonated in an American political and cultural environment saturated with moralism and religiosity.

A number of activists rejected this rhetoric. Former abolitionist William Lloyd Garrison Jr. argued for aid, "not because they are Armenians and Christians, but because they are human beings with rights and liberties as precious as my own," and asserted that he would have acted similarly "were the case reversed and Christian Armenians were butchering and violating Mohammedan Turks and Kurds."[30] As the leader of an organization that was committed to neutrality, and aware that her own safety was at stake if she appeared too partisan, Clara Barton urged Americans to recognize that "by the obligations of the Geneva Treaty, all national controversies, racial distinctions, and differences in creed must be held in abeyance, and only the needs of humanity considered." She criticized the

Christian relief groups in the United States for ignoring "the international and neutral character of the Red Cross" and declaring their "discordant opinions" about Muslims.[31] However, most activists conflated the language of Christianity, civilization, and humanity. As Julia Ward Howe, the author of "The Battle Hymn of the Republic" and president of the Friends of Armenia Society, declared in her rallying cry, "the spirit of civilization, the sense of Christendom, the heart of humanity—all of these plead for justice."[32]

For some, protests and relief were insufficient. In December 1894, during a Senate debate on the appropriate American response to the massacres, Democratic Senator Newton Blanchard of Louisiana denounced them as "a blot upon the civilization of the age, meriting the severest condemnation of mankind."[33] That month, the Senate passed a resolution calling on President Grover Cleveland to work with the European powers to press for the Ottoman government to put a stop to the massacres and to provide the chamber with information on injuries suffered by US citizens. While Cleveland expressed concern for the safety of American missionaries in his 1895 Annual Message to Congress, he declined to involve the United States in the Armenian question, on the basis that it was not a signatory to the Berlin Treaty that ended the Russo-Turkish War and had no legal right to interfere in Ottoman affairs. However, as the violence continued, American missionaries stepped up their lobbying efforts. As popular outrage grew, petitions containing thousands of signatures poured into Congress. The majority pressed for greater security for American missionaries but a substantial number also demanded assistance for the Armenians, with some calling for the United States to commit its warships to the region.[34] Condemning the "brutal murders" of Armenian innocents, who they claimed were being massacred "for no other or better reason than because of their devotion to the Christian religion," the Ohio General Assembly petitioned Congress to extend to Armenians "such protection and material aid as is within the power of this Government."[35]

In December 1895, Democratic Senator Wilkinson Call of Florida introduced a joint resolution urging the United States to join with "civilized governments" in the name of "humanity and religion and the principles on which all civilization rests," to ensure the massacres ceased and to establish for the Armenians "a government of their own people," through "peaceful negotiations, or if necessary by force of arms."[36] This resolution was watered down by the Senate Committee on Foreign Relations. In January 1896, its chairman, Republican Shelby Cullom of Illinois, introduced a revised resolution that urged those European powers, which were party to the Treaty of Berlin, to recognize their "imperative duty in the interests of humanity" to end the violence and secure for the Armenians "all the rights belonging to them, both as men and as Christians and as beneficiaries . . . of the treaty." Cullom also promised the president that Congress would support him in taking the "most vigorous action" to protect US citizens in the Empire and to secure an indemnity for any missionaries injured or property damaged during the massacres.[37] Call regarded Cullom's resolution as insufficient, providing neither relief nor protection for the Armenians. However, the Republican Senator George Frisbie Hoar of Massachusetts urged his colleagues to remember the security of Americans residing in the Empire and to refrain from violently denouncing the Ottomans. Ultimately, Cullom's resolutions decisively passed the Senate and moved to the House, where they were subjected to a vigorous four-hour debate.

Like Senator Call, Republican representative Charles Henry Grosvernor of Ohio regarded the resolutions as ineffective. Invoking Biblical imagery, Grosvernor inveighed, "[The Armenians] have asked us for bread, and we are giving them a stone. They have asked us for the fish of a Christian nation's powerful protest, and we have given them the serpent of an abject falling down and apology at the feet of the Turkish government." Another Republican, Williams Hepburn of Iowa, called for the Ottoman representative in Washington, Mavroyeni Bey, to be expelled.[38] His colleague from Iowa, David Henderson, proclaimed that "if need be, I am ready to have the two-edged sword of civilization pierce the cruel heart of the Ottoman Empire." Others urged prudence. Robert Adams, a Republican from Pennsylvania, cautioned his colleagues against violating the Monroe Doctrine. Democrat Henry Turner of Mississippi warned against discarding the "great precedent established by Washington himself" and wondered whether Americans wished to "constitute ourselves universal guardians of mankind."[39] Eventually, the Cullom resolutions passed the House by 143 votes to 26. Their passage served as a landmark in the history of US international humanitarianism. As the esteemed historian Merle Curti has declared, during these debates and in the resolutions reached by Congress, "the emphasis for the first time . . . was not on temporary relief" but "rather on political action to remove the causes of a great and continuing disaster."[40]

As a result of the resolutions, Cleveland dispatched two US navy cruisers, the *San Francisco* and *Marblehead*, to the Eastern Mediterranean to guard against further threats to American missionaries. However, the president resisted appeals by missionary leaders for the United States to employ more assertive gunboat diplomacy to end the violence and to force the sultan to pay the indemnity for their losses. When New York businessman and missionary benefactor William E. Dodge and educational leader Andrew D. White led a delegation to Washington to demand Cleveland act more decisively on the Cullom resolutions, he demurred. Despite the unprecedented Congressional intervention, the president remained determined to avoid entangling the United States any further than was necessary in the Near East.

Standing with England for a Great Cause

In London, policymakers cautiously observed the growing American public and political engagement with the Armenian cause. In their coverage of the massacres, American publicists and politicians had lambasted the European powers for failing to prevent the violence but had reserved particular fury for Britain. As a *New York Times* editorial affirmed, "England's policy has been the chief obstacle to the settlement of the Armenian question, as it has been, for twenty years, the chief obstacle to the settlement of all the questions arising out of Turkish misgovernment and savagery."[41] When Cullom introduced his resolutions in the Senate, he had denounced the "indifference" of all the European powers but especially blamed Britain, for its "double obligation" to act under the Berlin Treaty and the

JOHN BULL'S DILEMMA.
"It 's 'ard to 'ave to Disturb 'im — 'e 's Such a Good Customer!"

Figure 1.1 1895 cartoon reflecting a popular American perception of Britain's self-interested response to the Armenian massacres. *Puck*, John Bull's Dilemma, Library of Congress, LC-DIG-ppmsca-29072.

Cyprus Convention. Senator Frye went further, castigating Britain, "the stead-fast enemy of the United States," which had aided the Confederate cause during the American Civil War and had now "stood idly by when it had the power to stop these barbarities" against the Armenians.[42]

While Frye's speech illustrated the enduring legacy of Anglophobia and the continued bitterness felt by Americans for Britain's conduct during the Civil War, a more recent incident was responsible for the resurgence of anti-British hostility.[43] In 1895, a long simmering boundary dispute between Venezuela and British Guiana had threatened to embroil the United States and Britain in conflict. Having invoked the Monroe Doctrine and demanded that Britain agree to arbitration of the dispute, Cleveland and his Secretary of State Richard Olney further antagonized London by proclaiming US predominance in the Western Hemisphere. When Prime Minister Lord Salisbury questioned the applicability and the legal validity of the Monroe Doctrine, Cleveland urged Congress in his Annual Message of December 1895 to establish a commission to determine a just boundary, which the United States would use "every means in its power" to enforce.[44] Cleveland's response led to a brief war scare. The fervor of American jingoes shocked the British public and even the Liberal *Daily News*, normally a vehement critic of the Conservative government, saw the US challenge as "an intolerable pretense."[45] Conservative publications were more vociferous in condemning the United States. The premier conservative journal *The Spectator* even suggested that Cleveland's "sensational Message" served as a "death-warrant of Armenia," because it made it "impossible for Great Britain, with such a menace from the West hanging over her, to break loose from the concert of Europe, or to risk the outbreak of a European war in which, owing to American hostility, she might be powerless to interfere, or might even live to find a widespread coalition threatening her scattered dominion on many points at once."[46] In both Britain and the United States, responsibility for the fate of the Armenians was used to indict the conduct of the other.

While the Venezuelan dispute stirred passions, both sides quickly agreed to submit the matter to arbitration and in its aftermath, Salisbury's Conservative government was eager to establish a rapprochement with the United States. Some of its leading figures raised the possibility of a joint intervention for the Armenians as way to further that goal. This would distract attention from dissension between the two countries in Latin America and undercut charges, both at home and abroad, that Britain's government was not doing enough to stop the massacres. After becoming prime minister and foreign secretary in June 1895, Salisbury had initially proceeded cautiously in his response to the massacres. He was unwilling to destabilize the precarious balance of power in the Near East and risk a wider European conflict by intervening unilaterally. He was also opposed to convening a conference on the model of the Congress of Berlin, concerned that France would raise Britain's occupation of Egypt, which was still nominally part of the Ottoman Empire. Furthermore, Salisbury was skeptical that Europeans shared British humanitarian sympathies, doubting that "from Archangel to Cadiz there is a soul who cares whether the Armenians are exterminated or not."[47]

Britain's Colonial Secretary Joseph Chamberlain reminded Salisbury that a popular movement on behalf of the Armenians akin to the British one had emerged in the United States. He urged him to appeal to Washington to join Britain in a naval demonstration in the Eastern Mediterranean. This would resolve the immediate danger to the Armenians. It would force the Ottoman Sultan to call off his troops and implement reforms, while discouraging the French or Russians from provoking "a combination of the two Anglo-Saxon nations." A joint intervention would erase memories of the Venezuelan dispute and revolutionize American attitudes to Britain. This position was supported by *The Spectator*, which suggested that if Britain took the initiative on behalf of the Armenians, "such a movement made in the interests of humanity would conciliate American opinion more than any amount of despatches."[48] Ultimately, Chamberlain counseled Salisbury, a joint intervention would help realize the "proper destiny" of the two nations: establishing an Anglo-American alliance to bring "irresistible force to bear in defence of the weak and oppressed."[49]

While Salisbury agreed to consider Chamberlain's proposal, he was privately scornful, confiding to his nephew Arthur Balfour that it was hard to imagine a "madder suggestion."[50] In any case, the government's attention was soon diverted to a crisis in South Africa. However, after a group of Armenian revolutionaries seized the Ottoman Bank in Constantinople in August 1896 and renewed massacres of Armenians broke out in reprisal, agitation for a British intervention resumed. It was led by the eighty-seven-year-old Gladstone, who outlined a comprehensive program for intervention in his final great political speech in late August. Gladstone demanded that Salisbury's government break off diplomatic relations with Constantinople and issue a "self-denying ordinance," promising to forgo British gains from any humanitarian venture. He was convinced that this would prevent European interference and enable Britain to coerce the Ottomans without triggering war.[51] Gladstone's proposal exerted intolerable pressure on the leader of his own party, Lord Rosebery, who took the occasion to resign. Despite his pro-Armenian sympathies, Rosebery was not as ardent an interventionist as the majority of Liberals and was definitely opposed to unilateral interference.[52] He informed Gladstone that he did not see why Britain "should bear the whole burden of this astute if pious race."[53] On the Conservative side, Chamberlain remained convinced that the United States could be induced to share this burden. He again pressed Salisbury to work for a joint intervention. Chamberlain stressed that the Anglo-American alliance that would result from this intervention would be "the greatest coup ever made in English politics," allowing the Conservatives to trump the Liberals as the main pro-American party.[54] Chamberlain resolved to raise the Armenian issue with Cleveland's Secretary of State Richard Olney.

Olney, like Cleveland, had initially seen no reason to involve the United States in the Armenian question, cleaving to the dictates of the Monroe Doctrine. He argued that if "Europe were to suddenly fly to arms over the fate of Turkey" then it would be "preposterous that any American state should find itself inextricably involved in the miseries and burdens of the contest."[55] Initially, as domestic pressure had grown on the administration to safeguard American missions in the Empire, Olney dismissed any suggestion of sending a US warship as entirely impracticable and preferred to rely on Britain's naval presence in the Mediterranean to protect US citizens.[56] However, after the Venezuelan dispute, Olney became increasingly convinced that the United States should work more closely with Britain in world affairs. When Chamberlain proposed a joint intervention for the Armenians, the secretary implied the administration might consider it. Under pressure from Congress and the missionaries to vigorously assert American rights in the Ottoman Empire, Cleveland gave Olney cautious backing to explore the British proposal. The president reminded his secretary that the United States' responsibilities should be focused on safeguarding its citizens. He made no mention of protecting the Armenians, informing Olney that Chamberlain should have no "excuse for saying that we are in the least unmindful of the duty that rests upon us—even if his country is backward in doing hers."[57] Cleveland's belief that Britain had shirked its duty in the Near East was reinforced by a pamphlet that Olney had shared with him.[58] Written by a British Liberal and former Cabinet minister, the Duke of Argyll, it argued Britain had a special responsibility to aid the Armenians, having prevented Russia from interfering unilaterally on behalf of Ottoman Christians since the Crimean War but refusing to intervene itself.[59]

Olney drew a different conclusion. He was conscious that Britain would not act alone as its fleet could not pressure Constantinople without co-operation from the other European powers.[60] However, if Britain was bolstered by US support then it could intervene without fear of arousing a European coalition, as well as advance an entente that Olney was increasingly convinced was vital to US interests. Taking Cleveland's tepid approval as a green light, Olney wrote to Chamberlain:

> Because of our inborn and instinctive English sympathies, proclivities, modes of thought and standards of right and wrong, nothing would more gratify the mass of the American people than to stand side by side and shoulder to shoulder with England in support of a great cause—in

a necessary struggle for the defence of human rights and the advancement of Christian civilization.

This was a blueprint for a joint intervention based on shared values, but Olney
continued to prioritize American interests as justification for action. He declared
that if Britain should "set about putting the Armenian charnel-house in order"
then the Cleveland administration would "consider the moment opportune for
vigorous exertion on behalf of American citizens and interests in Turkey." The
United States would back up these demands with all the "physical force at its
disposal," which would necessarily "strengthen the hands of England."[61] To protect US regional interests and advance the rapprochement, Olney was prepared
to reverse one of the most cherished tenets of US foreign policy and intervene
outside the Western Hemisphere in support of a cause that only the previous
year he had dismissed as "preposterous."

Prior to approaching Olney, Chamberlain laid the groundwork by circu-
lating the idea of a joint intervention among his friends in the British press.[62]
Furthermore, he alluded to it in a speech on Anglo-American collaboration,
proclaiming: "Would it were possible that, instead of wasting breath in a petty
South American boundary dispute, we could count on the powerful support of
the United States in enforcing the representations which hitherto we have fruit-
lessly made in behalf of those who are suffering by Turkish tyranny and Turkish
fanaticism."[63] The proposition of a joint intervention attracted US interest, particularly among American missionaries.[64] Reliance on British naval power to
protect them and their institutions during the massacres had strengthened their
"consciousness of a worldwide Anglo-Saxon community" and led them to argue
that the United States should expand its global role so that it could work with
Britain to maintain order in the Near East.[65] In *The Nation*, Godkin declared
that "the spectacle of the two great Anglo-Saxon Powers acting together, not
for aggrandizement but for order and civilization, would be one of the finest
the modern world has ever seen." However, he sarcastically reminded his "Jingo
brethren" that this "would involve the abandonment of the sacred Doctrine of
'the immortal Monroe,' and it would commit you to the cares and responsibilities and dangers of European politics and—harder than all—it would compel
you be to be civil to the odious 'Britishers.'" If Americans were unwilling to
make those sacrifices, then Godkin advised his countrymen that the "less you
vapor and threaten, the more the civilized world will respect you."[66]

At Harvard in October and November 1896, students debated whether
"the United States should propose an alliance with England for the protection of the Christians in Turkey." Those in favor of an Anglo-American intervention argued this would be the "most reasonable and effective means of
restoring order," justifying the concord on the grounds of race, language, laws,

religion, and common humanitarian sentiments. They were certain that this would be "universally recognized as a moral alliance" as Britain's government was motivated by popular humanitarianism and the United States could not be accused of territorial ambitions in the Near East. The students opposing doubted that British motives would be free from European suspicion, even if allied to the United States. Americans were under no obligation to act and should avoid an intervention that might "cause greater evils" and "involve us in dangerous and unnatural complications." The appeal for noninterference won out by thirteen to nine.[67]

In the country at large opposition to an intervention, with or without an alliance with Britain, was even stronger. The *New York Times* observed that "there is a curious persistence in the minds of some Englishmen . . . that the United States is intimately connected with the Armenian question." While "as a sentiment [Chamberlain's suggestion] cannot, of course, be condemned . . . it would be contrary to all our traditions of the past, all our present interests and a grave peril for the future were we to join such a conflict, however noble the cause."[68] Protestant publications continued to express outrage but the humanitarian coalition that coalesced in 1895 failed to re-emerge. Relief contributions declined and only the missionary organizations continued to agitate for US military action.[69] In Britain, *The Spectator* lamented that while "we should welcome anything which brought American and English fleets into action side by side," this remained out of the question, "in spite of Mr. Chamberlain's vague hopes," because "the tradition that their business is with their own hemisphere is almost immovable in American minds."[70] However, while the intervention did not materialize, the massacres had initiated a debate over the nature and purpose of US power that would continue to animate the American public, press, and politicians, and affect its relations with Britain, into the next century.

In his final Annual Message to Congress, Cleveland placed the "disturbed condition in Asiatic Turkey" at the forefront of his discussion of US foreign relations. As the humanitarian catastrophe "so mars the humane and enlightened civilization that belongs to the close of the nineteenth century," it was inconceivable that "the earnest demand of good people throughout the Christian world for its corrective treatment will remain unanswered." Nevertheless, Cleveland maintained that the United States would not provide the solution, urging Americans not to let their passions so "blind their reason and judgement as to lead them to demand impossible things." American attempts to exert effective military pressure would be resisted by the Ottomans and might interfere with the European powers, who had the right under treaty to act.[71] At the close of Cleveland's administration, the possibility of the US government providing a solution to the Armenian question or joining with Britain in the type of alliance outlined by Olney and Chamberlain remained remote.

Armenian Affairs and American Interests

American missionaries continued to pressure Cleveland's successor to intercede with the Ottoman Empire on their behalf. They lobbied the new administration to employ aggressive gunboat diplomacy to collect indemnities for thousands of dollars worth of ABCFM property destroyed by the Ottomans during the massacres. President William McKinley, however, was preoccupied with events closer to home. On the Caribbean island of Cuba, around a hundred miles from the Florida coast, Spanish colonial rulers had responded to a fearsome insurgency by instituting a brutal "reconcentrado" policy that forced the peasant population into fortified camps where the squalid conditions resulted in the deaths of 95,000 people. Faced with growing domestic pressure to intervene in Cuba, McKinley was even less inclined than his predecessor to entangle the United States in the Near East.[72] Nevertheless, as the *New York Times* warned the incoming president, the United States had "rights and duties in Turkey" and Americans expected reparations for the damaged missionary property.[73] Under increasing pressure to protect US interests in the Near East but with demands also growing for the administration to drive Spain from the New World, McKinley was determined to resolve the indemnity issue peacefully. In his search for a solution, he turned to Jewish New York attorney and former Minister to the Ottoman Empire Oscar Straus.[74]

Straus had served in Constantinople between 1887 and 1889 during Cleveland's first administration. Henry Ward Beecher, the noted abolitionist and Congregationalist clergyman, proposed Straus's appointment to show disdain for European anti-semitism, illustrate the United States' exceptional religious tolerance, and recognize the Jewish contribution to American prosperity. The US government already sent "Danes to Denmark and Germans to Germany . . . why should we not make a crowning testimony to the genius of our people, by sending a Hebrew to Turkey?"[75] Although Beecher regarded this as a natural fit, considering the Jewish presence in the Empire's Palestinian province, Straus's suitability to protect the interests of so many Christian missionaries was questioned in some quarters. However, he proved himself a zealous supporter of the missionaries and their institutions, establishing a relationship that would endure for decades. During his time in Constantinople, Straus first became acquainted with the Armenian question. After a number of Armenian teachers in missionary schools were arrested for promoting revolutionary activities, Straus was forced to dispel Ottoman suspicions about American institutions. However, he privately warned the missionaries not to expose their interests to any accusation of collusion with the Armenians, as the US government had "assumed no obligation toward any creed or race in this empire."[76] Yet when massacres broke out in

1894, the Ottomans blamed international missionaries, Americans included, for arousing Armenian aspirations of independence, just as Straus had feared.

From New York, Straus kept abreast of events. While he deplored Armenian suffering, he was less willing than other Americans to condemn the Ottoman government outright.[77] Adamant that there was no justification for the atrocities, he was nonetheless convinced that Russian agents were responsible for fomenting unrest in the Empire, to hasten its breakup and stake Tsarist claims to the prime spoils in the Ottoman succession.[78] He was already hostile to Russia for pogroms against his coreligionists in the last decades of the nineteenth century.[79] Straus's conviction that the "cause of civilization" would not be advanced by Russian domination of Constantinople strengthened his already firm philo-Turk impulse.[80] He had maintained correspondence with many leading Ottoman officials, including the sultan, with whom he had developed warm relations. The massacres had led to Abdul Hamid's vilification throughout Europe and North America, but Straus was not convinced the sultan was responsible.[81] While Straus was sympathetic to the Armenians, he was persuaded by his geopolitical perspective and personal acquaintances in the Empire that the situation was more complex than the state sanctioned terror portrayed by the American press.

Straus also did not believe diplomatic protests would serve the US national interest. The United States should abide by its traditional commitment not to involve itself in the internal affairs of other sovereign states unless it affected US citizens. He remarked to Henry Otis Dwight, an American missionary in Constantinople and correspondent for the *New York Tribune*, "We should carefully discriminate between Armenian affairs and American interests." While the latter should be "followed with official energy and perseverance," the former should only be "handled unofficially, and with great discretion, so as not to involve our interest in what may result in a European turmoil."[82] Straus himself was particularly discreet with his public pronouncements on the massacres. Although he received hundreds of invitations to speak and publish his opinion on the "Turkish-Armenian Question," he declined, convinced that as a former US representative in the Empire, he should maintain official neutrality so as not to endanger American missionaries.[83]

Nevertheless, Straus was aware that failure to secure compensation for the missionaries was encouraging American belligerence. Disconcerted by growing American jingoism, Straus saw suggestions that the country should commit itself militarily in the Near East as part of a worrying trend. Americans were in danger of departing from their hallowed foreign policy traditions. At the time of the Venezuelan dispute, Straus reminded Cleveland of the Monroe Doctrine's "bilateral significance." While the United States would regard European interference in the Americas as unfriendly, the United States, for its part, should reaffirm its policy of noninterference in the internal affairs of other nations, such as the "disturbed conditions in Turkey." Straus felt the Doctrine's bilateral basis had been forgotten. He urged Cleveland to publicize this bilateralism to counteract those jingoes who, in their "misguided zeal" for the Armenians, had overlooked "the moral weight of the wise limitations of our foreign policy."[84] It was Straus who helped shape Cleveland's response to the congressional resolutions on the Armenian massacres, advising the president not to attempt to influence the internal affairs of the Ottoman Empire and to instead focus on the facilitation of relief as the only effective and appropriate US response.[85]

"Cuba is our Armenia"

For all his calming influence on government policy, Straus remained concerned by the popular passions that the Armenian massacres aroused.[86] These emotions were again evident as tensions with Spain over Cuba escalated. Straus was alarmed by the combative rhetoric of American legislators and publicists.[87] Proponents of US intervention, moreover, explicitly linked Cuba and Armenia. Wilkinson Call, who had led the campaign in the Senate for intervention in the Near East, declared that "we have right here an Armenia at our own doors."[88] His Democratic colleague, John Daniel of Virginia, condemned Spain as "the Turk of the West."[89] The analogy was also employed by journalists, not least in the mass-circulation New York newspapers of William Randolph Heart, who, like his rival Joseph Pulitzer, sensationalized the Cuban issue to boost sales and contributed to the increasingly belligerent public mood. Hearst's New York Journal asserted, "The American people will not tolerate in the Western Hemisphere the methods of the Turkish savages in Armenia, no matter what the cost of putting an end to them might be." His San Francisco Examiner urged Americans to recognize that "Cuba is our Armenia, and it is at our door."[90]

Proximity was used to justify why the United States could and should intervene for the Cubans as it had been unable to do for the Armenians. The New York Times declared: "The slaughter of the Armenians never disturbed our peace or threatened to disturb it" but the Cubans "are so much nearer to us" and their "afflictions sharply disturb our tranquillity."[91] Moreover, having condemned European inaction over the Armenian massacres, advocates of intervention argued that the United States had an added responsibility to act. The Minneapolis Journal reminded its readers that "Americans have damned Great Britain and Russia for not interfering to stay the red hands of the Turkish butchers in Armenia and yet a worse [condition] than Armenia piteously pleads to us almost at our own shores. This great nation cannot avoid its duty."[92] Americans were cautioned that they could not afford to have their conduct exposed to charges of hypocrisy by Britain. "We blame England for abandoning the harmless and peaceful Armenian Christians to massacre by the Moslems," admonished William E. Chandler, a Republican Senator from New Hampshire, but "England retorts that we dare not stop the methods of uncivilized warfare applied at our very doors."[93] Hearst's *Examiner* declared: "Cuba must not stand in the relation to us that Armenia does to England."[94] US intervention for the Cubans would illustrate its moral superiority over the European powers who had failed to protect the Armenians.

Demands for war with Spain became increasingly frenzied after the sinking of the USS *Maine* in suspicious circumstances in Havana harbor in February 1898. McKinley had consistently sought to resolve the clash between Spain and the Cuban insurrectionists without resorting to US military intervention. However, when a Naval Board of Inquiry reported that the *Maine* had been destroyed by an external mine, attributed to Spain, the stampede to war became irresistible.[95] On April 11, 1898, McKinley asked Congress to sanction a US declaration of war against Spain to protect vital national interests and advance the "cause of humanity." This was imperilled by a "constant menace to our peace" in a territory "right at our door."[96] During the ensuing conflict, Spain was banished from the New World. After the war Talcott Williams, a nationally renowned journalist for the *Philadelphia Press* and son of Ottoman Empire missionaries, reflected on the new spirit that infused US diplomacy. In an article titled "Cuba and Armenia," Williams observed that for the first hundred years of its existence the United States had exhibited "a habitual disavowal of international obligations or duties, except as derived from national interests." However, European inaction over Armenia "brought us to the public recognition of a new national duty and obligation" and "we drew the sword for Cuba, when Europe stood with sheathed sword before worse and more brutal deeds in Armenia."[97] Proponents of intervention in Cuba justified the US action by commending Americans for vindicating their duty to a people suffering under imperial oppression, a responsibility they believed Europeans had shirked in Armenia.

Many Americans were uncomfortable with their country's expansion after the war, however, above all its annexation of Spain's former colony, the Philippines. Straus was among them. He was concerned that the United States' acquisition of an empire would undermine its democratic institutions and exceptional position in global affairs. Following US Commodore George Dewey's decisive victory over the Spanish squadron in Manila Bay, Straus warned McKinley that "nothing but entanglement and embarrassment" would result from American occupation of the Philippines. Dismissive of Philippine capacity for self-government, he warned it would be impossible for American troops to withdraw after intervening without resulting in "anarchy and slaughter." He was equally concerned that entrusting the Philippines to another major power would involve the

United States in "European complications" during an age of intense imperial competition. Instead, he urged McKinley to resist the temptation to occupy the Philippines and show that this was not a war of American aggrandizement.[98]

Straus's suggestion did not discourage McKinley, who soon announced that "acceptance of the archipelago" was the United States' "duty."[99] McKinley was more inclined to seek Straus's counsel on the Ottoman Empire. In the days leading up to war with Spain, he informed Straus that US Minister to Constantinople James Angell, backed by American missionaries, was urging the administration to send warships "to rattle the Sultan's windows" as the only way to finally settle the unpaid indemnity. With the *Maine*'s destruction fresh in his mind, McKinley was concerned that dispatching a warship to the Near East would risk a similar incident. He asked Straus to return to Constantinople as minister to help resolve the issue, assuring him that "no vessels will be sent to Turkey unless you demand them, and then, only then, will they be sent."[100] McKinley hoped this would not be necessary and Straus could smooth over US–Ottoman relations, while the president focused on more pressing issues arising out of the war with Spain. The conflict had signaled that the United States was emerging as an international power but its focus remained on the Caribbean and the Pacific rather than the Mediterranean.

An Alliance of the Anglo-Saxon Race and a Shared "Civilizing" Mission?

In Europe, the great powers recognized the rise of a new competitor. Even before the 1898 war, there had been widespread continental concern at the United States' burgeoning economic strength and unrivalled industrial output. The McKinley administration's imposition of new and higher tariffs on imported goods had further intensified European fears. As conflict loomed between the United States and Spain, the powers considered participating in a démarche to register disapproval of American actions. The other European powers only agreed to cooperate if Britain joined them, as British naval supremacy ensured that it would be responsible for making any demands effective. Salisbury's natural conservatism led him to regard the Cuban revolution with suspicion. He sympathized with Spain's predicament but wished to avoid any impression of opposition to US policy, particularly as British interests in Cuba were relatively insubstantial. Britain's ambassador in Washington, Sir Julian Pauncefote, had worked tirelessly for an Anglo-American rapprochement but was eager to avoid a Spanish-American war. He urged his superiors to allow him to dispel the impression among Americans that their action commanded the support of the "civilized world."[101] With Salisbury ill, his nephew, Arthur Balfour, presided over the Foreign Office and initially gave Pauncefote tentative approval to explore a joint missive. But after consulting Chamberlain, who opposed any interference, Balfour restrained Pauncefote, warning that an appeal was unwise and unlikely to succeed. In any case, Germany and France also rejected the plan, and the démarche collapsed.[102] Although Britain's government was not entirely sympathetic to US intervention, rumors abounded in the United States that Britain had prevented a hostile European coalition. This perception was inaccurate, but convinced many Americans that Britain was the only friendly European power. During the conflict, Britain proclaimed neutrality but imperial officials interpreted this in a manner that favored the United States. British officials in Hong Kong allowed Dewey's Asiatic Squadron to refuel in Mirs Bay, while Spain's fleet was denied passage to the Philippines through the Suez Canal by British-controlled Egypt. A myth also arose that British commander Captain Edward Chichester had protected Dewey's vessels from a large German fleet in Manila Bay. The fact that Chichester saluted the raising of the American flag over Manila and his German counterpart did not only added to the legend, strengthening American feelings of fellowship for its former colonial ruler.[103]

Above all, Americans regarded Britain as more supportive than other powers principally because government policy was reinforced by the only public opinion consistently favorable to the US cause. While press organs in continental Europe condemned American actions and sympathized with Spain, the British press largely welcomed the US intervention.[104] Like American proponents of the war, a number of British observers drew an analogy between Armenia and Cuba to justify US actions. Prominent journalist Sidney Low reminded his countrymen that "we went wild over atrocities in the remote recesses of the Armenian hills," and asked Britons to imagine "if we had an Armenia in the English Channel." Low had no doubt that "we should not have endured it. The Spaniard would have been cleared out bag and baggage from Cuba long ago."[105] The use of "bag and baggage," the famous phrase that Gladstone used in his *Bulgarian Horrors* pamphlet to call for the removal of the Ottomans from Bosnia, Herzegovina, and Bulgaria, only enhanced this comparison. Leopold Maxse, the editor of the conservative British publication *National Review*, assured his readers that "there is no more land-grabbing in the Cuban agitation in America than there is in the Armenian agitation in England."[106] And *The Spectator* expressed its sympathy with the American claim that "they are intervening to stop the perpetration of horrors in Cuba which are as bad as, or worse than, anything which took place in Armenia," emphasizing "that the real, as well as the nominal, cause of the war is Spain's inhuman treatment of Cuba," which was "Turkish in [its] cruelty and horror."[107]

Figure 1.2 1898 cartoon showing Britannia (Great Britain) embracing Columbia (the United States) as a new imperialist partner and celebrating the rapprochement between the two nations. The United States emerged as a great power with its victory in the "Spanish-American War" (written in the clouds on the right). Behind Britannia, the storm clouds labeled "Eastern Question" depict the growing turmoil and instability in the Ottoman Empire. *Puck, After Many Years*, Library of Congress, LC-DIG-ppmsca-28710.

Mutual concern for the Armenians, and a commitment to their security, was widely viewed in both Britain and the United States as deriving from a common Anglo-American notion of "civilization." In the English-speaking world at this time, the concept of civilization was so widely referenced and assumed that its rationale was only occasionally explained systematically or explicitly. It was generally understood, however, as the promotion of international trade on the basis of respect for property rights and contract, progress toward political democracy and a law-governed, predominantly Christian culture.[108] Britons and Americans shared a devotion to these liberal ideals in their domestic affairs and a transatlantic network of campaigners had developed in the nineteenth century in pursuit of common humanitarian causes, most notably that of anti-slavery.[109]

For many in the English-speaking world, the advance of civilization was also tied to a racially rationalized, idealistic belief in the providential mission of the Anglo-Saxon peoples to collaborate and ensure the spread of global progress.[110] The language of Anglo-Saxon unity had developed on both sides of the Atlantic during the latter decades of the nineteenth century. It was stimulated by the social, familial, and literary network that existed among Anglo-American elites, which flourished during an era of advances in communications and transport links between the two countries.[111] British statesmen were eager to stress these shared ideals to further Anglo-American relations. They had become concerned that their Empire's resources were overstretched, and might not continue to support its global commitments.[112] The dominant international position that Britain had enjoyed since the Napoleonic Wars was vulnerable, confronted by numerous military, economic, financial, and strategic challenges. The rise of the United States posed less of a threat to Britain's core interests than its European rivals.[113] Although the 1895 Venezuelan boundary dispute aroused Anglo-American tensions, and the Salisbury government initially had misgivings over the 1898 war with Spain, the increasing British willingness to accept the Monroe Doctrine and cede dominance in the Western hemisphere to the United States served American interests.[114] In addition, many American policymakers were concerned by the influx of new immigrants to the United States; 23 million new immigrants arrived between 1880 and 1914, mainly from eastern and southeastern Europe, regions that had not traditionally been sources of large-scale migration to the New World. Consequently, American elites embraced the language of Anglo-Saxonism and welcomed closer ties with Britain. An avowed shared belief in Anglo-Saxon supremacy was bolstered by the adherence of the majority of the population in both countries to Protestantism and a revived evangelical commitment to its values. This was seen as bringing with it a responsibility to enlighten others and underpinned popular conceptions of "civilizing missions" in both countries.[115]

As a consequence, many British writers celebrated not only what they saw as the noble causes of the US conflict with Spain, but also its imperial consequences. Like American proponents of expansion, their British counterparts regarded the establishment of a US overseas empire as in keeping with the nation's destiny and the inevitable manifestation of its growing strength. Furthermore, they believed US expansion would be beneficial to Britain's interests. The former editor of the liberal Sunday newspaper *The Observer*, Edward Dicey, expressed the prevailing British opinion when he declared US expansion gave "promise of gain rather than loss to our own country."[116] These potential benefits were not necessarily material. Although it was frequently assumed that the United States would adopt free trade policies amenable to British interests, the commercial advantages were rarely articulated. Indeed, purely prosaic considerations could have been—and occasionally were—used to arouse concern at US expansion. More practical advantages would arguably have accompanied closer association with Germany but that country's rise resulted in antagonism with Britain instead of the co-operative relationship recommended with the United States.

Rather, the US adoption of an imperial role was viewed as inevitably stem-ming from "the Anglo-Saxon desire for expansion."[117] Americans were urged to imitate their racial brethren in the Eastern Hemisphere by assuming their his-toric destiny in the Western, a responsibility they were charged with hitherto neglecting. Rhetorical references to blood linkages and a shared heritage were prevalent in British commentary during and after the US conflict with Spain. Britons beseeched Americans in numerous articles to join them in a divinely inspired "civilizing" mission to uplift "backward" peoples.[118] As Dicey main-tained, Britons and Americans must "carry out that manifold destiny which is the birthright of the Anglo-Saxon race."[119] These racial characteristics were seen as the basis for Britain's pre-eminence in imperial administration; therefore it was believed that as Americans were of a similar stock they would prove equally adept at colonialism, after gaining the necessary experience. The Spectator declared that Britons hoped Americans would succeed in developing their overseas empire and would exhibit no jealousy if, as expected, the United States expanded "into a dominion as great as our own."[120] Both nations were "fellow-laborers in the work of the better ordering of the world."[121] Indeed, there was widespread relief that Britain no longer needed to labor alone as the only power with the capacity to share the imperial burden had seemingly embraced empire. The mission of the Anglo-Saxon nations extended beyond conferring the blessings of civiliza-tion on their colonial dependencies. They would also need to ensure that other professedly civilized nations abided by ethical precepts of justice, humanity, and altruism in the conduct of their external affairs. The Spectator asserted that an Anglo-American combination could "guarantee that civil and religious liberty shall be firmly established in the world."[122] The Fortnightly Review went further in declaring "the English speaking nations, if they act in harmony, and if they prove worthy of their high destiny, hold the fate of the world in their hands" and "can introduce an era of peace and prosperity such as has been unknown in history." For its British supporters, US expansion carried the promise that the two peoples would ultimately unite to advance the spread of their ideals, for the benefit of their mutual relations and the progress of mankind.

Some American exponents of expansion also drew on Anglo-Saxon tropes to justify imperialism.[123] The arch imperialist Indiana Senator Albert Beveridge shrugged off suggestions of American inexperience in overseas colonialism by stating that "the sovereign tendencies of our race are organization and govern-ment," and it was inevitable that the United States would expand to become "a greater England with a nobler destiny."[124] However, expressions of Anglo-Saxon unity did not go unchallenged. Anti-imperialists emphasized the exceptionalism of the race that had evolved in the United States, stressing that British blood had fused with that of other peoples to create a distinctly American type with its own unique political culture and national destiny.[125] Moreover, Anglophobia remained a potent factor in American public life. Historic resentments had been aggravated by economic competition, and were further fuelled by Irish Americans who despised Britain for its continued subjugation of their homeland.[126] They took the lead in establishing an Anti-British Alliance Society, while the German-born anti-imperialist Carl Schurz scorned the proposal that "the American Republic must imitate the example of England" by acquiring colonies.[127] These lingering anti-British feelings, reinforced by the prejudices of recent immigrants, rendered talk of any type of formal association politically inexpedient.

Despite these obstacles, advocates of an Anglo-American understanding continued to champion its merits. Once out of office, former Secretary Olney felt free to publicly promote the combination that he had privately proposed at the time of the Armenian massacres. In a speech at Harvard in March 1898, subsequently published in *The Atlantic*, he urged the United States to throw off its "international isolation" and assume a more active international role. Olney argued that this would help Americans advance their material interests, particularly the nation's commerce, but he also stressed that if they wished to enjoy these advantages then they had a duty to "forego no fitting opportunity to further the progress of civilization practically as well as theoretically, by timely deeds as well as by eloquent words." To support his argument, Olney declared that in response to the "Armenian butcheries . . . to any power that will send its fleet through the Dardanelles and knock the Sultan's palace about his ears, we boldly tender our 'moral support' [and] we loudly hark Great Britain on to the task of achieving that result, but come to the rescue ourselves with not a gun, nor a man, nor a ship, with nothing but our 'moral support.'" Consequently, he suggested that the rest of the world saw the United States as a "nation of sympathizers and sermonizers and swaggerers—without purpose of power to turn our words into deeds and not above the sharp practice of accepting advantages for which we refuse to pay our share of the price." Olney stressed that if the United States was going to adopt a more assertive global position and assume the responsibilities that accompanied its growing power, then it needed allies. He recalled that even Washington, in his "Farewell" Address, had allowed for "temporary alliances for extraordinary emergencies." As an example of such an emergency, Olney pointed to the maltreatment of American missionaries and the destruction of their property in the Ottoman Empire. In an instance like this, Olney suggested that "by joining hands with some competent Power, having perhaps similar grievances, the government could assert its rights and could obtain redress for American citizens." This was, of course, exactly the arrangement that he had previously discussed confidentially in his correspondence with Chamberlain. Now, Olney was prepared to openly call for the "Anglo-American" people to join in a "patriotism of race," arguing that "in that same community, and in that cooperation in good works which should result from it, lies, it is not too much to say, the best hope for the future not only of the two kindred peoples but of the human race itself."[128]

However, the new Republican Secretary of State John Hay knew that such an arrangement was currently impossible. The most Anglophile of American statesmen, Hay had spoken of mutual imperial missions and hinted at an alliance while he was ambassador in London.[129] Nevertheless, soon after becoming secretary of state, he noted that "an alliance must remain, in the present state of things, an unattainable dream."[130] The British politician most publicly committed to this ideal also came to recognize this reality. Chamberlain had proclaimed to his Birmingham constituents during the Spanish-American War that "terrible as war may be, even war itself would be cheaply purchased if in a great and noble cause the Stars and Stripes and the Union Jack should wave together over an Anglo-Saxon alliance."[131] In an article in *Scribner's* magazine in December 1898, Chamberlain expanded on this theme. He proclaimed that he "would not shrink even from an alliance *contra mundum* [against the world], if the need should ever arise, in defense of the ideals of the Anglo-Saxon race—of humanity, justice, freedom, and equality of rights." As an example of such a necessity, Chamberlain claimed that if the US fleet could have co-operated with the British navy to intervene during the Armenian massacres, "it is almost certain that the other Powers would have held aloof, in presence of such a combination, and a great and bloodless service might have been rendered to humanity." In a case like this, "the co-operation of the two English-speaking nations might be the only means of obtaining peacefully results equally desired by both." Nevertheless, Chamberlain recognized that any co-operation between Britain and the United States would have to be on an informal basis, based on an appreciation of common interests on a particular international issue, rather than an open agreement. He was aware that both nations continued to adhere to traditions of isolationism and, despite his vision of a closer connection between them, he knew that a formal alliance was unattainable in the immediate future.[132] The young Winston Churchill was also skeptical. He confided to his American mother that while the rapprochement appealed to him, as a "representative of both countries," he believed "no alliance is possible until a community of interest is established." While "an Anglo-Saxon alliance may delight or alarm Editors, jingos and idiots of various countries," it remained "unlikely that the cute Uncle Sam will pick our Asiatic, African and European chestnuts out of the fire for us."[133]

Stead's Dream: An Anglo-American Alliance and a Solution to the Eastern Question

While policymakers dismissed plans for any kind of formal Anglo-American alliance as impractical and unrealizable, idealistic thinkers continued to dream. The most ardent advocate was W. T. Stead, famed editor of the British evening newspaper the *Pall Mall Gazette* and a zealous campaigner for moralistic causes. An investigative report into child prostitution had earned him great renown across the British Empire.[134] Stead's investigations into immorality eventually took him to Chicago. The trip led to a scathing attack on the city's corruption, spawned a bestselling book, and made him a bona fide celebrity in the United States.[135] In 1890 Stead established the *Review of Reviews*, which soon became the most widely read monthly periodical of the day, and the following year, a US subsidiary, the *American Review of Reviews*, appeared. Stead's goal with these publications was to encourage "inter-communication" among the component parts of the "English-speaking world."[136] Stead had entertained this vision since the 1880s, when he first became fascinated with the concept of imperial federation.[137] However, the establishment of a federal British Empire was only the first step in Stead's program to unite the English-speaking peoples. As Stead informed his US editor, Albert Shaw, the journal's purpose was to advance the "cause of Anglo-American reunion."[138] Stead also encouraged his friend, South African mining magnate turned imperial statesman Cecil Rhodes, to include Americans in the Oxford scholarships programme that were provided by his will and which were originally intended solely for students from the colonies. Like Rhodes, Stead considered the American Revolution a tragedy and a setback for Anglo-Saxon unity.[139] Stead also found a kindred spirit in the Scottish-born American capitalist, Andrew Carnegie, whose treatise on philanthropy, "The Gospel of Wealth," he published in his *Pall Mall Gazette*.[140] Throughout the 1890s, they conspired to devise "arguments we can advance to influence the American Republic to enter into an alliance with Britain."[141] Carnegie deferred to Stead in this campaign, lauding him as the pre-eminent "missionary militant for the British American Union."[142] Both men believed this alliance was a necessary precursor to peace on earth. Stead was convinced the "English speaking race" was "one of the chief of God's chosen agents for executing coming improvements in the lot of mankind."[143] For Carnegie, Anglo-American union would be the harbinger for "The Brotherhood of Man, the Federation of the World."[144]

Unlike Carnegie, who came to oppose American colonialism, Stead cautiously embraced it as likely to advance their common goal. When US victory over Spain was followed by a circular appeal from the Russian government to the other powers to meet to discuss the reduction of armaments, Stead saw it as an auspicious sign of the advent of international harmony. He embarked on a tour around Europe in the autumn of 1898 to explore the prospects for continental peace and, most significantly, to ascertain attitudes to US imperialism. Across Europe, Stead discovered that there was renewed disquiet at the growth in US commerce. American manufactured goods were flooding European markets, adding to fears already aroused by the dominance of US agricultural exports.

He also heard concerns from policymakers and publicists alike that the United States was embarking on a new career of overseas conquest and territorial annexation and that American professions of disinterested humanitarianism over Cuba were seen as insincere cant masking longstanding territorial ambitions. Stead contrasted this with the British belief in the sincerity of the American cause, which he put down "not so much [to] community of language as the instinct of race." He suggested that there was a close analogy between the "American movement for the liberation of Cuba and the great agitations which from time to time had swept over this country in favour of the liberation of Christian provinces from the Sultan."[145]

Stead's own interest in the Ottoman Empire, and its Christian subjects, was first piqued by the Bulgarian atrocities of the 1870s. The British campaign for the Bulgarians appealed to Stead's fervent Puritanism and moralistic bent.[146] It also aroused in him the image of "the Turk" as despotic, domineering, and licentious.[147] Stead employed his gift for sensationalism to stimulate British support for Bulgaria's independence struggle, denouncing Ottoman misgovernment and accusing Benjamin Disraeli's Conservative Cabinet of complicity in the crimes through indifference and inaction.[148] Unlike his political hero Gladstone, who limited his plea to Ottoman removal from Bosnia, Herzegovina, and Bulgaria, Stead believed the atrocities were grounds for "the expulsion of the Turk from Europe."[149] He retained little confidence in the will or capacity of the Concert of Europe to restrain the Ottomans, a belief confirmed by the outbreak of the Armenian massacres in the 1890s.

Initially, Stead focused on rousing Britain to its responsibility to protect the Armenians. To awaken sympathy, he published *Political Papers for the People: The Haunting Horrors of Armenia*, featuring a map of the sites of Armenian massacres, with places named as they were in the New Testament.[150] This was intended to imprint on the public imagination the interconnection between Ottoman Armenia and its Biblical heritage. It also reminded readers of the relationship between Roman era Armenia and the development of early Christianity, and illustrated that the massacres were occurring in the region around Mount Ararat, where Noah's Ark was supposed to have landed.[151] While he had denounced the "devildom" of Disraeli, Stead was slightly more supportive of Salisbury, whom he knew had been sympathetic toward the Bulgarians and was therefore considered more trustworthy.[152] Nevertheless, while refraining from demanding the downfall of Salisbury's government, Stead accused Conservative and Liberal leaders, including Gladstone, of not doing enough to resolve the Eastern question or to prevent the Armenian outrages. Above all, he condemned the Conservatives for allowing longstanding jealousy of Russia to prevent the Russians from occupying the Christian provinces of the Empire and providing a remedy for the wrongs committed.[153] Stead was a Russophile and his sympathies had been strengthened by Russia's military response to the "Bulgarian Horrors," which he contrasted with Britain's inertia. However, on this occasion, with Russia reluctant to act for the Armenians, Stead invested his hopes in the United States.

As a young man, Stead had been captivated by the writings of the radical liberal statesman and free trade advocate Richard Cobden. In particular, he embraced Cobden's suggestion that the administration of the Ottoman Empire should be transferred to an American syndicate or trading company. American management would ensure the region realized its commercial and industrial potential, benefiting international society in general and British trade in particular.[154] In subsequent years, the establishment of the substantial American missionary community in the Near East encouraged Stead to remark to his many prominent American correspondents, "half in jest and half in earnest, that there was no better solution of the Constantinople problem than that which planted the Stars and Stripes on both sides of the Bosphorus." They dismissed the idea of an American protectorate in the Near East as delusional. However, as he observed the increasing attention that the US press, led by his own franchise, paid to the region, Stead grew more certain that his prognosis would prove accurate. He informed his British readers that Americans had taken "more interest in the wrongs of the Armenians than has been shown in this country."[155] US engagement with events in the Ottoman Empire convinced Stead that a revolution was imminent in the nation's foreign policy and Americans would soon enter upon a "career of expansion."[156] When the situation in Cuba deteriorated, Stead consistently referred to it as "the American Armenia," noting that "Cuba is to the United States what Armenia is to the European Concert." For Stead, therefore, US intervention in Cuba not only revealed the nation's military strength but also offered Europeans an example of the assertive, humanitarian spirit required in the Near East.[157] Furthermore, he was convinced that the United States was destined to assume a greater role in the Eastern Mediterranean, after the acquisition of the Philippines showed that it had renounced its self-denying commitment to confine itself to the Western Hemisphere.[158]

In the book Stead produced about his trip, there was a section on the "Possible Outcomes" that would result from the "immense events" of 1898. Stead dedicated a chapter to his visit to Constantinople. He informed his readers that the American achievements during its war with Spain paled in significance compared with the "peaceful campaign which America is waging in the Ottoman Empire." Stead praised the record of American missionaries in the Empire, claiming they were "the chief hope of the future of the millions who inhabit the Sultan's dominions" and would "supply the personnel of the civilized administration which must some day supersede the barbaric horror that is at present misnamed the Government of Turkey." He suggested the Ottoman authorities had every reason to contemplate the conduct of the American missionaries with misgivings. They were already responsible for the success of Bulgaria's nationalist struggle, having introduced ideas of independence to Bulgarian students at Robert College and then trained them to become statesmen. Indeed, Stead saw the Americans as at present "the only people who are doing any good for humanity in Asiatic Turkey." Britain's salutary work was confined to its consuls, backed by British naval power, helping defend American missionaries when they confronted difficulties with Ottoman authorities. Yet in this collaboration Stead discerned the fulfilment of the Anglo-American partnership about which he had long dreamed. While others spoke as if "the Anglo-American alliance was a peaceful dream to be realized in the remote future," Stead proclaimed that "if they lived in Asia Minor they would discover that it is a very practical working factor in the daily life of millions of men." Foremost among the groups affected by this alliance were the Armenians who, he maintained, were being trained by American missionaries for eventual independence under the protection of British consuls.[159]

Although US policymakers were preoccupied with the Philippines, Stead was convinced that with the US rise, particularly the development of its fleet, and Ottoman decline, his vision of an American protectorate in the Ottoman Empire that would safeguard the Armenians would soon be realized. In fact, while in Constantinople, Stead had happened to meet Straus, who was still trying to secure Ottoman compensation for the missionary property destroyed in the massacres. Stead sensed that American patience was wearing thin and that the United States would soon warn the sultan of the dangers to the Empire if the missionaries remained uncompensated and Armenian massacres reoccurred. He viewed growing American assertiveness in the region as a clear indication that there were "few things more probable than that it may be reserved for the United States to achieve results in the Near East far greater even than those which Admiral Dewey effected when he destroyed the Spanish fleet at Manila." Furthermore, his own visit to the region convinced him that British authorities would not oppose a US intervention in the Ottoman Empire or the "indefinite occupation of Constantinople by the Americans" and their assumption of a protectorate over the Armenians. He proclaimed that relations between the "Embassies of Britain and America at Constantinople . . . could hardly be closer and more cordial if there had been a hard-and-fast, cut-and-dried, signed, sealed and delivered treaty of alliance, offensive and defensive, between the two Powers." Stead viewed Anglo-American co-operation in the Near East as a sign that his larger dream, of a union between the English-speaking peoples, would soon be fulfilled.[160]

Americanizing the Ottoman Empire
and the World

Stead was correct that Straus had grown increasingly frustrated with the Ottoman failure to pay the indemnity, despite the sultan's repeated promises to do so.[161] During his second posting, Straus had become disturbed by the sultan's authoritarianism. By December 1899, he had had enough and asked Washington's permission for leave to return home. He notified the Ottoman minister of foreign affairs that as the sultan had procrastinated over the payment for over a year, he was returning home to consult with his government. Leaving the chargé d'affaires, Lloyd Griscom, in control, he traveled back to Washington where he pressured his Ottoman counterpart to lobby the sultan to indemnify American losses.[162] Straus initially attributed his failure to resolve this issue to the sultan's tyrannical rule and the perilous position of Ottoman public finances.[163] However, after re-examining the timeline of his negotiations with the sultan, Straus came to think that his difficulties stemmed from Stead's visit to Constantinople. Straus believed that the sultan had made his first promise to pay the indemnity in good faith, but Stead's publicity of his "chimerical idea" that "America would solve the Eastern question" through its missionary stations had alarmed him and American expansion in the Philippines added to this anxiety. Straus heard that Stead had also visited the Russian Embassy in Constantinople, and outlined his argument about American missionary stations being "political centres," engaged in "Americanizing Turkey." Straus was certain the Russians had subsequently influenced the sultan to "obstruct in every way English and American interests." Regardless of whether these ideas actually played any role in delaying payment of the indemnity, Straus's dismissal of Stead's vision revealed that an American solution to the Armenian and larger Eastern question was still regarded as mere fantasy by its key regional official.[164]

Despite his irritation with Stead, Straus's experiences in Constantinople instilled in him the belief that the United States and Britain should co-operate to advance their common interests around the world. After leaving Constantinople, he advised Griscom to collaborate with Britain's ambassador, "because their diplomatic affairs run very much on the same lines which I cannot say for any other power represented at Constantinople." Despite his German heritage, Straus stated this included the Germans, who "are not in sympathy with us" as they prioritized material interests over humanitarian endeavors.[165] Straus went even further in a letter to his former British colleague in Constantinople, declaring that he was "one of those who believe that by an historical destiny England and America must confront the problems of the world together; as they have substantially the same aims and the same enemies."[166] Despite his scorn for any suggestion of US control over Constantinople, Straus confirmed Stead's belief that the informal Anglo-American alliance in the Near East could progress to a broader entente.

By the spring of 1900, American patience with the sultan had run out. The McKinley administration leaked a story to the press about the "grave" situation and that the president was considering dispatching a strong US fleet to the Mediterranean to back up its demands. The story was taken up nationally and also widely publicized throughout Europe. The Vienna correspondent of the London *Times* warned the sultan that if he expected protection from any European power, then "let him remember Spain," while the *Pall Mall Gazette* cautioned that "these Americans so far from playing a game, are positively talking of seizing Smyrna." The American threats roused the Ottoman minister in Washington to action. He informed Hay that the sultan would purchase a warship from the United States, with the compensation for the missionaries included as part of the deal.[167] Consequently, Griscom took up negotiations with the sultan and the premier American shipbuilding firm, Cramp & Sons Company.[168] When discussions dragged on through the winter of 1900, it was arranged that the new US battleship, the *Kentucky*, would stop off at Smyrna en route to the Philippines. This had the desired effect of speeding up the transaction. When a contract was eventually signed between the Cramps and the Ottoman government, with an indemnity of $83,000 included, Straus attributed it to "the presence of an American man-of-war."[169] The settlement of the indemnity completed Straus's own evolution from a conservative opponent of American expansion into one who was willing to use the instruments of the nation's newly manifest power to advance its interests. Moreover, this demonstration of strength in support of its missionaries illustrated that the US government was increasingly prepared to intervene on behalf of its citizens, even in regions far removed from its traditional sphere of influence.

It also raised the possibility that the United States might one day intervene in the Near East to safeguard other people in need of protection. The USS *Kentucky's* captain, "Red Bill" Kirkland, warned Smyrna's governor that "if these massacres continue I'll be swuzzled if I won't someday forget my orders . . . and find some pretext to hammer a few Turkish towns." Kirkland's translator interpreted this outburst more diplomatically but the original threat filtered back to an approving American public.[170] Over the coming decade US warships would return to the region to protect American missionaries, again raising the hopes of Armenians and their supporters that the United States might intervene on their behalf.

Stead's *American Review of Reviews* responded to this exercise of gunboat diplomacy by suggesting that the USS *Kentucky* should serve as the "sheriff" of the Eastern Mediterranean, maintaining American mandated law and order in the region and protecting the Armenians.[171] Stead himself was more convinced than ever that the United States was destined to solve the Armenian, and larger Eastern question, as part of the wider global mission that it would undertake in partnership with the British Empire. In his bestselling book *The Americanization of the World*, published in 1902, Stead declared that the US rise to become the greatest of world powers, in political, social, and commercial terms, was the most important trend of the twentieth century. He warned his fellow Britons that unless they succeeded in "merging the British Empire in the English speaking United States of the World" then their island would "descend slowly but irresistibly to the position of Holland and of Belgium." He consoled those Britons who resented the thought of the United States refashioning the world in its image by stating that the US global vision reflected the shared racial and religious ideals that it derived from Britain. This kinship was particularly evident in the Near East, where Stead again looked forward to the inevitability of US intervention to protect the Armenians and "solve the hitherto insoluble problem of the ownership of Constantinople."[172]

The frontispiece of *The Americanization of the World* carried a notable image— a portrait of the broad-shouldered, bespectacled Theodore Roosevelt, the new president of the United States. Having assumed office after McKinley's assassination in 1901, Roosevelt came to symbolise the US rise to world power. He would emerge as the preeminent American supporter of an alliance with Britain, albeit initially in private, and the most prominent advocate of US intervention in the Armenian question.

2

The Rooseveltian Solution

No American statesman more embodied the new spirit in US diplomacy at the turn of the twentieth century than Theodore Roosevelt. Drawing his familial heritage from the North and South, Roosevelt symbolized the reunification of the United States after the Civil War. A naturalist, editor, and historian, he epitomized the nation's cultural and intellectual growth at the beginning of the century. As Colonel Roosevelt of the "Rough Riders," he helped drive Spain out of Cuba and initiated the US surge to great-power status. His assumption of the presidency at forty-two, making him the country's youngest president, coincided with the United States assuming a new world role.

Roosevelt also exemplified the peculiar humanitarian mood that animated American society at the outset of the twentieth century. He preached to Americans a gospel of moralism, righteousness, and global duty. From his "bully pulpit" Roosevelt articulated a doctrine which stressed that the advance of "civilization" required US expansion overseas and the corollary that it must use its power, where possible, to prevent atrocities that violated contemporary civilized norms. The Armenian massacres of the 1890s, and the failure of any power to intervene to prevent them, made a profound impression on Roosevelt. He would frequently invoke Armenian suffering as a symbol of man's inhumanity to man and the clearest justification for righteous wars to advance civilization and overcome barbarism. He would reference the Armenians when defending war with Spain and subsequent expansion, protesting anti-Jewish pogroms in Eastern Europe, intervening diplomatically against King Leopold's regime in the Congo, and even reflecting on the treatment of minorities in the United States. During his presidency he was cautious in his crusading overseas, conscious that his policy required the support of the American people to be successful and aware that they were less willing than him to assume an active role in international affairs. While often eager to protest abuses by other nations, they were reluctant to develop the instruments of power that Roosevelt insisted were essential to make such protests effective.

Figure 2.1 Portrait of Theodore Roosevelt. Library of Congress, LC-DIG-ppmsca-36041.

Roosevelt was conscious of the United States' dread of "entangling alliances," but strived to act in concert with other powers that he considered civilized when intervening in humanitarian causes overseas. Above all, he believed that the United States should work together with the British Empire.[1] His ardent nationalism had initially encouraged him to challenge Britain when its interests conflicted with American ones. His hostility was directed less toward Britain itself than against American "Anglo-maniacs" who retained an attitude of colonial dependency and were not prepared to fight for US interests. By the time he assumed the presidency, however, Roosevelt had come to regard the British Empire as the one power that most closely shared the United States' interests and its conception of civilization. He viewed US expansion in the Philippines as in keeping with the civilizing mission Britain was undertaking in its Empire, although his patriotism led him to refute any suggestion that British colonialism was superior. Diplomatic interventions protesting anti-Jewish pogroms and Leopold's tyranny in the Congo were undertaken in co-operation with Britain. Yet the majority of the American public did not share Roosevelt's readiness to assume overseas responsibilities and colonial dependencies, nor his belief in the desirability of an alliance with the British Empire. Consequently, he was forced to promote closer Anglo-American relations and what he viewed as a shared civilizing mission, including humanitarian causes, through largely unofficial channels. Not until the US intervention in the First World War would an opportunity arise for Roosevelt to formally pursue both of these long-held goals.

Roosevelt's correspondence provides a crucial insight into his foreign policy thought and conduct. While his private letters often embellish his achievements, exaggerate the moral principles that motivated his actions, and denigrate those of his opponents, they are also notable for their clarity and candidness.[2] Conversely, Roosevelt's public addresses, despite his carefully cultivated reputation for blunt speaking, were generally tempered by a concern for political considerations, particularly when he occupied high public office. Roosevelt established a network of diplomatic confidants, including the naval theorist Alfred Thayer Mahan, Senator Henry Cabot Lodge, his Secretaries of State John Hay and Elihu Root, and Oscar Straus, who Roosevelt appointed as the first Jewish member of a US Cabinet in 1906. Roosevelt also forged links with like-minded British statesmen, most notably the diplomat Cecil Spring Rice and historian-statesman James Bryce. These men helped shape what the historian William Widenor has referred to as "the Rooseveltian Solution" to the problems of conducting foreign policy under the unique circumstances faced by a US government.[3] It was in dialogue with them that Roosevelt developed his ideas about America's responsibility to protest "crimes against civilization" and, in extreme cases, intervene to protect the oppressed, a belief that formed a significant but underexplored component of the Rooseveltian Solution.

National Power and Civilizational Ideals

One of the most perceptive scholars of Roosevelt, John Morton Blum, argues that his diplomacy was above all geared toward ensuring stability and a desire to accumulate power.[4] He praised Roosevelt for a detailed understanding of global affairs and an appreciation of great-power rivalries but confesses that his belligerent tone ensured "the awful suspicion ever lingered that he cared as much for fighting as for right."[5] This observation did little to dispel concerns, first voiced by Roosevelt's political opponents, that he was a warmonger for whom the call to arms was a first, rather than last, resort.[6] In part, this interpretation was a consequence of Roosevelt's oft-quoted aphorism, "Speak softly and carry a big stick." Indeed, for his critics, Roosevelt spoke so softly that the more nuanced aspects of his diplomacy were barely audible. Instead they chose to focus on the "big stick" wielded by a man infatuated with power.

Yet Roosevelt was conviced that power could not be divorced from the duty to exercise it responsibly and his diplomacy sought to reconcile idealism with self-interest.[7] As one analyst of his statecraft emphasizes, Roosevelt's "instinct to approach issues in terms of right and wrong" inevitably resulted in him adopting a "moralistic approach to international relations."[8] His diplomatic outlook was not confined to conventional power politics and geopolitics: ideals and values also helped shape his philosophy. Chief among them was a commitment to what historian Frank Ninkovich has labeled an "ideology of civilization." This creed encompassed his Lamarckian racial framework and led Roosevelt, unlike many other Anglo-American statesmen who were adherents of Social Darwinism and regarded certain races as irredeemably inferior, to maintain that although there was a hierarchy of races, all peoples were capable of progress. It also incorporated his desire to prevent wars between nations that he considered civilized and his conviction that expansion by great powers led to order and stability.[9] Yet another critical aspect of Roosevelt's civilizational framework was his belief that a government that officially sanctioned the maltreatment of its own people threatened the advance of civilization.

Roosevelt's commitment to these ideals was underpinned by an assertive nationalism. By the time he first began to take an active interest in America's global role in the late 1880s and early 1890s, he was convinced that the United States was superior to all other countries and determined to implant this sense of patriotism in his fellow countrymen.[10] Roosevelt's nationalism did not allow for any "strained humility towards foreigners, . . . especially toward Englishmen."[11] He enjoyed close friendships with a number of leading British figures, and admired Britain's national achievements and its contribution to American culture. Yet he urged Americans to cast off all vestiges of colonialism and stand up for their country, even when it came into conflict with Britain.[12] Roosevelt felt that only through an assertive nationalism could the United States play an active role in world affairs. While stressing that Americans should first look to their own nation's rights and security, however, he invariably stated that in exceptional cases, they should also stand for the rights and security of others. For Roosevelt, true humanitarianism was inseparable from patriotism. He maintained that it was only the "nation which is most thoroughly saturated with the national idea" that would have a "scrupulous regard for the rights of other nations or a desire to remedy the wrongs of suffering peoples."[13]

Roosevelt was concerned, above all, that his country should be militarily and physically prepared and willing to protect its security and interests against all rivals. This inspired his first work of history, *The Naval War of 1812*; it remained an obsession throughout his career.[14] He embraced Alfred Thayer Mahan's doctrine of sea power and employed it to urge the buildup of the American navy.[15] He was intent on taking his own part in turning this preparedness creed into action and hardly a diplomatic disagreement arose that did not arouse his trucu-lence. Roosevelt's principal foreign policy preoccupation in the 1890s was "ulti-mately driving every European power off of this continent," including Britain's presence in Canada.[16] He was especially determined to stop European nations acquiring new territory in the Western Hemisphere and to prevent them from engaging in the type of imperialistic expansion in the Americas that they were pursuing in Africa and East Asia. In this spirit, he celebrated Cleveland's message on Venezuela to Salisbury in 1895. He did not shrink from the possibility of an Anglo-American war, even envisaging his own participation in a US conquest of Canada.[17]

Social and domestic, more than international, factors argued for an assertion of American nationalism and an affirmation of its independence from its former colonial ruler. Roosevelt railed against "the men who put monetary gain before national honor, or who are still intellectually in a state of colonial dependence on England."[18] Influenced by the writings of his friends, Henry and Brooks Adams, Roosevelt sensed that excessive materialism inculcated a timidity that weakened civilized nations and left them vulnerable to attack from less advanced, more warlike nations.[19] However, inspired by his own transformation from an infirm child into a paragon of American manhood and strengthened by his supreme belief in "character" to offset any weakness that accompanied an advanced civ-ilization, he refused to share the pessimism of the Adams brothers.[20] Instead, he strove to find an arena in which to showcase his and the nation's virility and to prove that his vision of its destiny as the greatest of great powers was more compelling than one based on materialism. As he wrote to Lodge during the Venezuelan crisis, "The clamor of the peace faction has convinced me that this country needs a war."[21]

That war would arise with Spain over Cuba. Roosevelt regarded the conflict as a necessity from the standpoint of "national self-interest" and "in the name of humanity."[22] It would divert Americans' attention from mere moneymaking and enable the nation to remove Spain from the hemisphere, offering a lesson to any other power that might try to advance its position in America's vicinity, notably Japan and Germany.[23] Roosevelt also hoped that a Spanish war would result in the United States securing naval bases in the Caribbean and Pacific, acquisitions dictated by Mahan's naval strategy.[24] However, Roosevelt's con-ception of the national interest was not the limited one employed by interna-tional relations scholars, that of purely promoting US interests over and above those of other nations, but a more traditional and all-encompassing notion of the public interest that embraced both nationalism and idealism.[25] His confidence in the nation's destiny as the leading global power reinforced his conviction that the United States could advance its own position in the world and ameliorate the ethical standards of international affairs. Consequently,

Roosevelt consistently placed the humanitarian justification for war with Spain alongside the war's benefits to the United States. He emphasized atrocities committed by Spanish troops against women and children in Cuba, evidence to him of Spain's barbarism, and lamented that Americans could "allow this hideous welter of misery at our doorsteps" for so long.[26] He was restrained from speaking out by his position as assistant secretary of the navy but urged intervention on the Cabinet and President McKinley, whose initial unwillingness to intercede led Roosevelt to privately complain that he had the "backbone of a chocolate éclair."[27] Above all, Roosevelt viewed the Cuban crisis as a test of America's "national honor." This stance was only strengthened by the destruction of the *Maine*.[28]

Correspondingly, he saw the American response, and his own, as a trial of personal honor. As he informed James Bryce in early 1898: "I feel that we have been derelict in not interfering on behalf of Cuba for precisely the same reason that I felt you were derelict in not interfering on behalf of Armenia—and I never preach for others what I don't, when I have the power, advocate doing myself."[29] Roosevelt had referred to the Armenian massacres, and "the upholding of the Turk by certain Christian powers," as the "great crime of this century against civilization" in an essay on the Monroe Doctrine published in 1896. Like British liberals, he charged Britain with primary responsibility for the Armenian plight by propping up Ottoman rule during the Crimean War and after the Russo-Ottoman War. He condemned Britain for having "looked on motionless while the Turks perpetrated on their wretched [Armenian] subjects wrongs that would blast the memory of Attila." He also stated that the Monroe Doctrine did not remove the American right or responsibility to intervene for the Armenians, and it was "to be regretted that our representatives do not see their way clear to interfere for Armenia."[30]

Roosevelt would discover the difficulties that attended interference for the Armenians when, as McKinley's assistant secretary of the navy, he was responsible for deciding which ships should be sent to protect US missionaries in the Near East. He concluded that it was impossible to dispatch a flotilla formidable enough to fight the Ottomans if required while simultaneously maintaining a squadron on the Atlantic coast strong enough to act in Cuba if necessary. Concerns closer to home trumped those in the Near East.[31] In 1898, with the fate of the Armenians still in mind, he declared that "Spain and Turkey are the two powers I would rather smash than any in the world."[32] There was still little prospect of America interfering in the Near East at this time, but he felt that Americans had sole responsibility to intervene in their neighborhood. In doing so, he believed America was providing Europeans with an example of "American ideals" by fulfilling a "duty to humanity" and emphasizing what should have been done for the Armenians.

Expansion and Peace

Roosevelt welcomed the expansion that followed war with Spain.[33] Although he had not had a premeditated plan for the Philippines and initially opposed annexation, preferring to limit America's presence to a coaling station, after the United States erected its flag and the Filipinos rose up in revolt, Roosevelt's nationalism was aroused.[34] He was determined to defeat Emilio Aguinaldo's rebels and committed to establishing a US empire that would serve as a model for other nations and, more importantly, uplift the American character.[35] While economic and strategic considerations were not absent from his calculations, Roosevelt's imperialism was a mix of national prestige, racial supremacy, his civilizational creed, and American moralism.[36] Roosevelt recognized that he and his fellow expansionists would first need to overcome their anti-imperialist opponents. He argued that US colonialism overseas was a continuation of its ongoing continental expansion. In 1900, while campaigning for vice president, Roosevelt repeatedly stressed that if Americans "were morally bound to abandon the Philippines, we were also morally bound to abandon Arizona to the Apaches."[37]

US expansion overseas was also consistent with a larger manifest destiny. Roosevelt had already referred to this vision in 1890, in his history of the settling of the nation's western frontier, as "the grandeur of the movement by which the English speaking race was to spread over the world's waste space until a fourth of the habitable globe was in its hands, and until it became the mightiest race on which the sun ever shone."[38] Despite his determination to challenge Britain when it encroached on the United States' sphere of influence, he had long regarded the British as coworkers in the spread of civilization. When his friend and correspondent Rudyard Kipling sent him his poem "The White Man's Burden," written to encourage US colonialism in the Philippines, Roosevelt remarked to Senator Henry Cabot Lodge that it was "rather poor poetry, but good sense from the expansion stand-point."[39] Roosevelt believed the English-speaking peoples were at the forefront of that expansive movement. At this time, however, he was prepared to celebrate almost any extension of European control over the rest of the world, except in the Western Hemisphere. He viewed US expansion in the Pacific as part of this larger dissemination of European peoples and their principles. He considered the US role in the Philippines alongside that of "England when she took Egypt and the Sudan; by France when she took Algiers; and by Russia when she expanded over Turkestan," regarding each as "for the immeasurable benefit of civilization."[40]

Roosevelt envisioned Americans serving as political mentors in their overseas territories, training their subjects in "orderly liberty" and entrusting them with a measure of self-government unequalled by any other colonial power.[41] As he informed an anti-imperialist correspondent, "every consideration of honor and humanity" required Americans in the Philippines to "establish order and then give a constantly increasing measure of liberty and self-government while ruling with wisdom and justice" before withdrawing.[42] He regarded the anti-imperialists as hopelessly naïve and wrongheaded in their belief that immediate American withdrawal from the Philippines would be more beneficial for both countries.[43] Rather, he believed that that spreading civilized values was the most realistic way to achieve pacific ambitions.

He outlined this conviction in an article titled "Expansion and Peace" in December 1899. In defending American expansion, he again invoked the example of the Armenians. Roosevelt began his essay by referring to Alfred Mahan's denunciation of those who espoused "peace at any price" and who dismissed "war as so entirely wrong that beside it no other tolerated evil is wrong. Witness Armenia and witness Crete. War has been avoided; but what of the national consciences that beheld such iniquities and withheld the hand."[44] Roosevelt again stated that "the great blot upon European international morality in the closing decade of this century has been not a war, but the infamous peace kept by the joint action of the great powers, while Turkey inflicted the last horrors of butchery, torture and outrage upon the men, women and children of despairing Armenia." Ottoman "barbarism" was illustrated by emphasizing that atrocities were committed on women and children. He contrasted this "human misery" with the "immense and permanent increase of happiness" that accompanied the Russo-Ottoman War. This earlier conflict resulted in Bulgaria, Serbia, and Bosnia-Herzegovina becoming independent or passing under the rule of the Austro-Hungarian Empire, which Roosevelt regarded as more civilized. This was proof that it was "only the warlike power of a civilized people that can give peace to the world" and provide "law, order and righteousness" to the territories into which they expanded.[45]

The paradox of Roosevelt condemning Ottoman rule over the Armenians while simultaneously celebrating European and US imperialisms, with their accompanying atrocities, was apparent to his contemporaries. In response to reports of a massacre by American troops in the Philippines, the leading anti-imperialist Moorfield Storey stated that if "the Turks had so attacked and slaughtered Armenians" then Americans would have been outraged. How was it then possible, Storey asked, that "this is all the greatest and freest nation in the world, as we like to believe ourselves, can do for a people over whom we insist on extending our benevolent sway?"[46] Roosevelt regarded the two instances as incomparable. If he had answered Storey's inquiry, he would undoubtedly have stated that American atrocities in the Philippines, unlike Ottoman actions against the Armenians, were not official government policy and that the perpetrators of the most egregious abuses on the US side were, for the most part, punished by the authorities. With less justification, he also regarded the cruelties committed in the Philippines as a regrettable but necessary consequence of conflict with a people that he regarded as "savages" unlike the Armenians whom he considered pacific remnants of Christian civilization in a region dominated by militaristic Muslims. Furthermore, he argued that the attendant benefits of US rule in the Philippines outweighed individual brutalities. When one correspondent confronted him with a crime committed by American soldiers in the Philippines, Roosevelt responded that it should be "punished with merciless severity; but to withdraw from the contest for civilization because of the fact there are attendant cruelties, is, in my opinion, utterly unworthy of a great people."[47]

In subsequent years, Roosevelt would strive to balance his belief that the exercise of "warlike power by a civilized people" was morally desirable and sometimes necessary to advance peace with his awareness that many Americans were uneasy about these interventions and that even those who supported them were unwilling to bear the cost of the responsibility.

The Advance of the English-Speaking Race

The war with Spain also had profound consequences on Roosevelt's perception of Britain. He informed his British and American correspondents that previously he had been "rather anti-British," but Britain's conduct during this war "worked a complete revolution" in his perspective while the behavior of other European powers alerted him to potential danger from that quarter.[48] From 1898 onward, Roosevelt was convinced that if "the British Empire suffer a serious disaster . . . in five years it will mean war between us and some one of the great continental European military nations, unless we are content to abandon the Monroe doctrine."[49] US security and geopolitical interests argued for improved relations with Britain. This was reinforced by Roosevelt's increasing conviction that Britain and the United States were superior to other powers and their interests should take precedence when either came into conflict with another nation. This was not based on racial sentiments. He reminded British correspondents that "this country is not by blood at all purely English" and that he himself had "practically no English blood."[50] His disregard for purely racial considerations was confirmed by his support of Britain during the Boer War, despite his own Dutch descent and membership in the Dutch Reformed Church. Although he admired the Boers and their fighting ability, he was convinced that "even from the standpoint of their own ultimate good, no less than from the standpoint of the advance of civilization, which to my mind is wrapped up in the advance of the English speaking race, it was best that the English should triumph."[51]

Although American impressions of Britain had improved since the war with Spain, the Boer War led to a resurgence of anti-British feeling.[52] Roosevelt was aware that many German and Irish immigrants had an ingrained hostility to Britain but his faith in the American "melting pot" convinced him that in time, they would become "absolutely Americanized and become part of the great English speaking race and regard America's friends as their friends, her foes as their foes."[53] He reserved his greatest disdain for American anti-imperialists, who proposed anti-British and pro-Boer resolutions in Congress just as they had condemned US imperialism and supported insurgents in the Philippines.[54] Despite his disgust, Roosevelt recognized that these resolutions were byproducts of continued American opposition to his ideal of a US civilizing mission overseas in cooperation with the British Empire. Roosevelt realized that overeffusive championship of Anglo-American kinship would backfire. He would need to work gradually to achieve this goal. Nevertheless, his temperament did not condition him to quietly wait for circumstances to change. After assuming the presidency in 1901, Roosevelt worked cautiously but assiduously to subtly alter those conditions and advance Anglo-American cordiality.

Diplomacy of Humanity

One of the first foreign-policy crises that Roosevelt faced, just a few days after taking office, involved the kidnap of a female missionary, Ellen Stone, in the Ottoman Empire.[55] The kidnappers were a band of Christian Macedonian mountaineers, suspected of having political motives to unite the Macedonian province of the Ottoman Empire with independent Bulgaria. They demanded $100,000 in gold to finance their rebellion. America's regional officials suspected the main aim was to demonstrate Ottoman incapacity to police its territory and bring about foreign intervention to secure Macedonian detachment from the Empire.[56] In Washington, State Department officials were initially suspicious of the Ottomans, convinced that they were in cahoots with the kidnappers in an amateurish attempt to gain reimbursement for the indemnity.[57] Roosevelt was no more inclined to trust the Ottomans. Just before assuming the presidency he privately expressed hope that "the Bulgarian or the Rouman, or someone of that type could take Constantinople."[58] However, as it became clear that it was Christian bandits with links to Bulgaria who were responsible for the kidnapping, Roosevelt found himself having to work with the Ottomans. Inundated with letters from concerned Americans, he was determined that "everything that can be done must be done to try to rescue Miss Stone."[59] His natural pugnacity was checked, by warnings that dispatching American gunboats to the region or landing troops would likely result in Stone's death.[60] Further hamstrung by the executive's inability to appropriate funds, a privilege exclusively enjoyed by Congress, he was forced to wait for the public to raise the ransom. Roused by a press campaign that portrayed Stone as an image of American innocence, Americans quickly raised $65,000.[61] American missionaries managed to secure Stone's release for the reduced sum in February 1902. US officials in the region informed Washington that the Ottoman government had rendered valuable aid in liberating the captives.[62] Nevertheless, Roosevelt—like Stone herself, who blamed the Ottomans for her prolonged captivity due to their continued subjugation of Balkan Christians—retained his prepresidential conviction that the Empire was "uncivilized."[63]

Later in 1902, Roosevelt was confronted with another diplomatic difficulty in Europe. On this occasion, the people whose security and rights were violated were not US citizens. Since the nineteenth century, oppression of Jews in Eastern Europe, particularly Romania, had been increasing and Jews responded by fleeing to the United States.[64] US government officials were horrified at religious persecution and infuriated that the oppression prompted waves of newcomers to American shores, at a time when unprecedented levels of immigration, largely from Southern and Eastern Europe, were already arousing concerns among old-stock Americans.[65] The largely German-born leaders of the American Jewish community, including Oscar Straus, expressed similar concerns. They were appalled at the treatment of their coreligionists but privately disturbed that the flood of Yiddish speaking newcomers would incite the kind of anti-Semitism that they hoped they had escaped in Europe.[66] When Romanian authorities passed legislation further restricting Jewish rights in the spring of 1902, Straus led efforts by American Jews to lobby the Roosevelt administration to issue an official protest.[67] Although the United States was not a signatory to the Treaty of Berlin, Straus stressed that an American remonstrance would follow the precedent established by Presidents Ulysses Grant and Benjamin Harrison at the end of the nineteenth century. They had protested to Russia about its treatment of Jews.[68] In August 1902, Roosevelt directed Hay to issue a strong protest against these "wrongs repugnant to the moral sense of liberal modern peoples," objecting on both humanitarian grounds and its impact on the United States, the "only refuge" for these downtrodden communities. At Hay's instigation, American diplomats urged London, Paris, Berlin, and Vienna to help the United States right this "international wrong."[69]

Straus worked with prominent British Jews, including Lord Rothschild and Sir Joseph Sebag Montefiore, to put pressure on Britain's government to join the United States in a démarche.[70] Prominent non-Jewish figures, including Joseph Chamberlain and Edward Dicey, were also sympathetic to the plight of Eastern European Jews as well as proponents of closer Anglo-American relations. This concerted pressure helped ensure the Foreign Secretary, Lord Lansdowne, responded favorably to Hay's plea. The *Daily Telegraph* declared that the "significant co-operation of the two Anglo-Saxon Powers will go far to put an end to a condition of things which is a scandal of modern civilization itself." The co-operative action would be the "first instance of the English-speaking countries working together upon an issue of this kind." Ultimately, however, Britain declined to act officially after the other European powers refused to do so.[71] Lansdowne did make unofficial representations to Romania, but neither his remonstrations nor Hay's note had much effect on Romanian policy.[72] Despite insignificant results, Hay's diplomatic intervention had lasting consequences. It enabled Roosevelt to advance Anglo-American relations by again revealing that the two nations were more willing to protest gross violations of religious liberty than any other powers. At the same time, as Straus proclaimed, Roosevelt's government had publicly set a precedent in formulating "the ethical principle that where wrongs extend beyond national boundaries, so also does the right for their redress."[73]

The Romanian diplomatic intervention was followed by a more significant one for Russian Jews. Between 1881 and 1911 the population of Jews in the United States multiplied tenfold, from about 200,000 to around 2,000,000, with the bulk of immigrants from Russia. Jews constituted an important electoral constituency with communities concentrated in politically pivotal states, including New York and Massachusetts. Moreover, Russian restrictions on Jewish liberties also applied to foreign Jews, including US citizens returning to Russia. Roosevelt regarded discrimination against Americans on the grounds of religion as a national insult and a violation of fundamental American principles.[74]

Prior to becoming president, Roosevelt regularly expressed concern about Russia's autocratic government and its treatment of minorities, including Finns and Poles as well as Jews. In a letter to Cecil Spring Rice in 1896, Roosevelt concluded that "Russia seems bound to develop in her own way, and on lines that run directly counter to what we are accustomed to consider as progress."[75] Roosevelt may have welcomed Russian expansion over Turkestan, but he was opposed when its advance encroached on the interests of the English-speaking peoples.[76] The writings of Brooks Adams and Mahan again exerted decisive influences on Roosevelt's outlook, impressing on him that Russian expansion in East Asia was not for "the immeasurable benefit of civilization" as it undermined Anglo-American influence in the region.[77] Russian forces had been entrenched in Manchuria since 1900, threatening America's "open door" policy in China and arousing Roosevelt's belligerence, albeit with the recognition that the United States was powerless to protect its interests.[78]

It was in this context that Roosevelt heard of anti-Jewish pogroms in Kishineff in April 1903.[79] Forty-seven Jews had been massacred, over four hundred others suffered injury, and damage to property amounted to an estimated 2.5 million rubles. Before receiving a delegation of prominent American Jews, demanding a vigorous response from their government, Roosevelt asked Hay, "would it do any good for me to say a word in behalf of the Jews or would it do harm?"[80] Hay objected to Roosevelt responding in any fashion. He believed that criticizing the internal policy of Russia, a great power unlike Rumania, did not serve US interests or help Russia's Jews.[81] However, Roosevelt was unwilling to let the issue rest. He cabled an official petition to the tsar, aware the Russians would refuse to accept it. However, they would have to file the cable as a formal message, while American Jews could publicize his action in any manner they wished.[82] Furthermore, Roosevelt issued a strongly worded public statement condemning both Russia's oppression of Jews and its policy in Manchuria.[83] By linking Kishineff and Manchuria, Roosevelt believed he was condemning a system of government that was an affront to American values and a threat to its interests.

Straus's public praise of his actions as the "Diplomacy of Humanity" delighted Roosevelt.[84] He was mindful that American Jews might reward him with their votes in the 1904 presidential election, but he was also genuinely appalled by the massacres.[85] He asked the explorer George Kennan, foremost American critic of Russia's autocracy (and distant cousin of the future diplomat) to investigate the tsar's complicity in the pogrom. Kennan confirmed Roosevelt's belief that the Russian government "permitted that outbreak and that some of its high officials instigated it."[86] Roosevelt regarded Russian pogroms as government-sanctioned atrocities akin to those perpetrated by the Ottomans against the Armenians.

Protesting Every Wrong that Outraged the Civilization of the Age

Most Americans shared Roosevelt's horror at the Kishineff pogrom. Demonstrators came out at seventy seven public protests nationwide.[87] At one such event at Carnegie Hall, former president Grover Cleveland condemned this "wholesale murder" of the vulnerable and defenseless "under the protection of a professedly civilized government."[88] The New York Times declared that no such government "can be called civilized, or can ask the respect of decent governments," while the Philadelphia Ledger agreed that the "Russian Government has no title to the respect of civilized Powers, and deserves to be dealt with as are barbarous nations when they outrage humanity." However, Roosevelt was also conscious that many disagreed with the way he had responded. Prior to his intervention, the Literary Digest reported that only one paper that it had surveyed, the Des Moines Register and Leader, advocated the government sending a protest to Russia.[89] After Roosevelt's actions, Cleveland's former Secretary of State Richard Olney led accusations that Roosevelt's stance was disingenuous and merely a ruse to secure Jewish votes for his re-election.[90] In a speech in New York, Olney condemned Roosevelt for his willingness to "lecture a foreign state upon the management of its own internal affairs and to call upon it to mend its ways." He had

Figure 2.2 Cartoon illustrating Roosevelt's diplomatic protest after the 1903 Kishineff pogrom. In his 1904 Address to Congress, Roosevelt would cite this massacre and the oppression of Ottoman Armenians as examples of atrocities that would justify American intervention. *Judge*, Stop Your Cruel Oppression of the Jews, Library of Congress, LC-DIG-ppmsca-05438.

planned to go further in his denunciation. In a thinly veiled attack on the influence of the Jewish lobby, Olney claimed "the Jews, for reasons not wholly inscrutable, to be especial administration pets," and stated that he knew "of nothing more extraordinary in international intercourse than the round-robin . . . complaining of Roumania." This section of the speech was removed at the request of the National Democratic Committee, who recognized that attacking overbearing Jewish influence in a speech in New York was poor politics. However, Olney did ask his audience to "imagine the wrath, the tempest of rhetoric, that would be evoked if any foreign nation retaliated in kind—should, for instance, suggest that lynchings in this country were disgracefully frequent and that the Washington government would do well to bestir itself and put a stop to them."[91]

Others shared Olney's concern that Roosevelt's protest would focus international attention on humanitarian abuses at home. In 1903 there were ninety-nine recorded lynchings in America, with the overwhelming majority perpetrated against black Americans.[92] This frenzy of mob-executed ritual violence led novelist Mark Twain to label his country "The United States of Lyncherdom" and lambast an "epidemic of bloody insanities."[93] Twain was not alone in enquiring how a nation in which lynchings were rife could brazenly condemn other states for their humanitarian abuses or engage in civilizing missions overseas when its own citizens were committing such uncivilized acts at home. The *Chicago Tribune* suggested that if a foreign government protested against lynchings in the United States then it "would create a whirlwind of indignation in this country [and] Americans would resent bitterly what they would call an insolent interference with their internal affairs." The Massachusetts based *Springfield Republican* concurred, stating that "until our own skirts are cleaner, this should be a cardinal feature of our policy—to mind our own Kishineffs, and pray that other nations may be saved from the brutal and passionate excesses of mankind."[94] Even within the administration, Hay had expressed concern to Roosevelt: "What would we do if the Government of Russia should protest against mob violence in this country?"[95] This paradox was encapsulated in a cartoon in the *Literary Digest* that showed the tsar tearfully rejecting the petition against the Kishineff pogrom because he was too busy weeping over reports of a lynching in the United States.[96]

Foreign diplomats gleefully exposed this paradox. The Russian ambassador in Washington, Arturo Cassini, responded to Roosevelt's protest by issuing his own objection to American lynchings.[97] That summer, the Ottoman ambassador in Washington, Chekib Bey, also highlighted American domestic abuses. Bey's comments came after reports that the US vice consul in Beirut, William Magelssen, had been assassinated. Magelssen had previously protested to the Sublime Porte about renewed Ottoman attacks against Armenians. His reported murder impelled Roosevelt to dispatch three US warships to the Eastern Mediterranean. Even after hearing that the diplomat was actually alive, having been merely brushed by a bullet fired by revellers at an Arab wedding, Roosevelt was determined to make a demonstration of American power. The US cruisers, with five hundred armed Marines on board, blockaded Beirut in order to pressure the Ottomans into guaranteeing the safety of US missionaries working in the Syrian province of the Empire.[98] Upon hearing of the threatened assault, Bey complained to Hay that the missionaries enjoyed "great liberties" and responded by provoking Armenians to rebellion. Bey demanded to know what would happen if he established "a school for [American] Negroes, and my teachers should tell the Negroes ... that they ought not to submit to lynching and should rebel?"[99] Roosevelt eventually succeeded in securing the sultan's informal commitment not to discriminate against American missionary schools after sending gunboats back to the Mediterranean the following year.[100] However, Roosevelt was discomfited by the continued counteraccusations of racial violence in the United States and well aware that it hindered America in "taking the lead on behalf of humanity." As he lamented to New York congressman Lucius Nathan Littauer, after the Kishineff intervention: "I wish to Heaven our course were clearer in the lynching business!"[101]

Roosevelt's own position on race questions was complex and he was by no means immune to the racial ideas of his time.[102] Although he declared his commitment to treat "each black man and each white man strictly [according to] his merits as a man, giving him no more and no less than he shows himself worthy to have," Roosevelt did not always adhere to the spirit of this principle.[103] During his presidency the structure of the segregationist regime took shape in the South, sanctioned by the Supreme Court and with few protests from the White House. Roosevelt made fewer black appointees than his predecessor and was engulfed in a scandal when he dishonourably discharged an entire all-black infantry regiment after unproven allegations of an assault on white residents in Brownsville, Texas. Nevertheless, Roosevelt won the allegiance of the majority of blacks, and became for a time the most unpopular president since the Civil War among Southern whites, because of his high-profile violations of the "color line" and outspoken condemnation of racial violence. He experienced the violent backlash of Southern racists when he entertained the African American educator, Booker T. Washington, for lunch at the White House just months after assuming the presidency.[104] Above all, Roosevelt deplored lynchings, which he considered acts of unmitigated "evil" that corrupted any white person that participated. He made headlines with his public condemnations of the practice.[105] However, he did not see how the federal government could intervene.[106]

When a British humanitarian organization protested against American lynchings, Roosevelt seized the opportunity to combine his rejection of race violence at home and his commitment to protecting persecuted minorities abroad.[107] John St. Loe Strachey, editor of *The Spectator*, defended Roosevelt's response to lynchings to his readers, claiming the president "is quite as indignant at those outrages as he can be, and that the wretched victims are constantly defended by all the armed force available."[108] While he appreciated Strachey's vindication of his record, Roosevelt was more concerned about educating Americans on their responsibility to hold a "resolute attitude of protest against every wrong that outraged the civilization of the age, at home or abroad."[109] He decided to outline this commitment in his 1904 Address to Congress, written with the help of a "kitchen cabinet." His confidants included Straus, who helped to draft the section outlining the administration's "humanitarian" actions overseas.[110]

Roosevelt's Second Corollary to the Monroe Doctrine

On December 6, 1904, Roosevelt's Annual Message was delivered to Congress. He urged Americans to focus first on "striving for our own moral and material betterment" before seeking to improve conditions in other nations. Americans should prioritize dealing with their own "sins," most damningly "violent race prejudice," over protesting against "wrongdoing elsewhere." Nevertheless, there were "occasional crimes committed on so vast a scale and of such peculiar horror as to make us doubt whether it is not our manifest duty to endeavour at least to show our disapproval of the deed and our sympathy with those who have suffered by it." Roosevelt stressed that abuses would have to be extreme to justify intervention, reiterating that "there must be no effort made to remove the mote from our brother's eye if we refuse to remove the beam from our own." Despite America's "very obvious shortcomings," Roosevelt maintained that the nation had a duty to censure international wrongdoing because it had, on the whole, demonstrated its commitment to "principles of civil and religious liberty and of orderly freedom." Roosevelt suggested that in the United States, even "the worst crime, like the crime of lynching, is never more than sporadic, so that individuals and not classes are molested in their fundamental rights." In fact, lynchings were far from "sporadic," but as he had insisted to Straus, while "unlawful, unjustifiable acts," they were not comparable "with the coldblooded wholesale murder under official recognition, if not at the instigation of the ruling powers, such as the Kishineff massacre."[111] Roosevelt regarded atrocities sanctioned and abetted by central government authorities as graver crimes against civilization than abuses committed by disorderly mobs.[112] Having justified, to his own satisfaction, the grounds for US intervention overseas, Roosevelt outlined how the government should respond. He argued that American actions depended on "the degree of the atrocity and upon our power to remedy it," and suggested that "the cases in which we could interfere by force of arms as we interfered to put a stop to conditions in Cuba are necessarily very few." Yet Roosevelt insisted that the United States would inevitably "desire eagerly to give expression to its horror on an occasion like that of the massacre of the Jews in Kishineff, or when it witnesses such systematic and long-extended cruelty and oppression as the cruelty and oppression of which the Armenians have been victims, and which have won for them the indignant pity of the civilized world."[113]

Roosevelt's set of principles on America's "manifest duty" to intervene in response to crimes against civilization has been overshadowed by another Rooseveltian credo outlined in the same speech: the Roosevelt Corollary to the Monroe Doctrine. This declared that if "chronic wrongdoing" or "impotence" caused breakdowns in "the ties of civilized society" in the Western Hemisphere then it would require intercession by "some civilized nation." Under the Monroe Doctrine, the United States, "however reluctantly, in flagrant cases" must assume the obligation of carrying out "the exercise of an international police power."[114] It was sparked by the threat of European intervention against Latin American states to collect unpaid international debts and also intended to defend interventions in which the United States had already engaged, most notably the protectorate over Cuba it assumed after the Spanish war and its acquisition of the territory surrounding the US-controlled Panama Canal. This corollary explicitly transformed the Monroe Doctrine into a more interventionist instrument of US policy in the Western Hemisphere.[115]

But Roosevelt offered a second corollary to the Monroe Doctrine that has been neglected, in which he declared his principles of intervention in response to crimes against civilization, regardless of whether they occurred within America's sphere of influence. These principles subtly inverted the Monroe Doctrine as it was originally conceived, based on separate spheres of influence and America's self-denying commitment, with regard to Europe, not to "interfere in the internal concerns of any of its powers."[116] Roosevelt had laid out a concise rationale for US interference in a nation's internal affairs, whether they occurred in the Western Hemisphere or not, and illustrated his argument with examples of European misgovernment. In some ways, Roosevelt's second corollary was motivated by similar concerns to his first: a dislike for disorder, a belief that America's newly acquired power brought with it fresh responsibilities and a commitment to spreading civilization, of which he considered the United States to be the principal agent. However, there were also important differences. While the Latin American corollary was described as being in America's "own interest as well as in the interest of humanity at large," Roosevelt stated that the corollary on extreme humanitarian atrocities covered "cases, in which, while our own interests are not greatly involved, strong appeal is made to our sympathies." Furthermore, while the first corollary ranked the United States alongside the great European states as "civilized" powers policing the Caribbean, as Europe did Africa and Asia, the second corollary revealed that even among the "civilized" nations, there were some that Roosevelt considered less "civilized" and whose despotic practices required regulation by a higher power. In fact, both corollaries had already been alluded to in Roosevelt's 1896 article on the Monroe Doctrine, but the 1904 Annual Message publicly proclaimed that the Monroe Doctrine would not restrict the United States from intervening against abuses outside the Western Hemisphere, as Cleveland's administration had been during the Hamidian massacres.

Roosevelt's second corollary made an impression on Roosevelt's contemporaries, albeit not necessarily on his primary audience. A few US publications expressed surprise at Roosevelt's language, with the *Philadelphia Press* noting that it "will send a cold shiver down the backs of the chancelleries of the great capitals" and the *Buffalo Express* acknowledging that "it can hardly be other than offensive to both Russia and Turkey." Both the *Press* and the Boston *Herald* also noted the significance of Roosevelt's decision to place his recommendation that the United States should construct more battleships in the passage immediately after.[117] However, Roosevelt's comments on extreme humanitarian atrocities were largely ignored by the American press. The *New York Times* observed that the president's discussion of foreign affairs "created very little excitement" among Americans, who were more concerned by the sections on domestic affairs.[118] The address did arouse strong emotions abroad, however. The *Outlook*, an American publication, reported that numerous foreign sources had complained that "the President's language is unprecedented in state papers of this character; it indicates a desire to meddle in foreign affairs."[119] Unsurprisingly, the sharpest objections emanated from Russia. The popular daily newspaper and government mouthpiece, *Novoe Vremya*, decried the "New Monroe Doctrine of America." While not objecting to America's "hands off policy" in the Western Hemisphere, the paper denounced Roosevelt for not wanting "to confine the doctrine to South America, but to have a finger in every European pie."[120] The St. Petersburg periodical, *Birzheviya Viedomosti*, also pointed to Roosevelt's pressure on the Ottoman Sultan over his treatment of the Armenians to emphasize that growing US interference in European affairs posed a threat to the wider continental order rather than just Russia alone.

In Germany, the nation that Roosevelt considered the principal challenger to the Monroe Doctrine, there was also alarm at what many observers labeled the "Roosevelt Doctrine." German journalists had regularly denounced the United States as hypocritical for protesting against abuses overseas while lynchings occurred within its own borders. *Kreuz Zeitung*, one of the most anti-American publications, claimed that ever since the United States "unfurled the banner of expansion and imperialism, it had become more and more the custom [to] devote [its] time and attention to the affairs of foreign countries, even when, those affairs happen to be purely internal in character." Its editors were particularly vexed by Roosevelt, an "idealist who considers that he and his country are commissioned by the Almighty to bring about 'freedom and equality' for as much of mankind as possible."[121] There was particular hostility toward Roosevelt for his treatment of the Ottoman Empire. Since 1881 Germany had been sending military missions to the Porte to secure a strategic partnership with the sultan. Following his accession to the throne in 1888, Kaiser Wilhelm II had twice visited Constantinople in an attempt to expand Germany's influence in the Near East and establish it as a world power. As part of his charm offensive, he had even sent a signed photograph of himself to the sultan shortly after his suppression of the Armenian uprising in 1896, while the rest of Europe and the United States was broadly united in its condemnation of "Abdul the Damned."[122] The Kaiser's overtures eventually paid dividends as German engineers began constructing the Berlin to Baghdad railway in 1903. The Kaiser envisaged the railway extending Germany's economic ties to Asia and loosening the British Empire's control over the path to India. However, Roosevelt's gunboat diplomacy in the Near East alarmed German publicists, who were concerned that it could threaten their nation's ambitions by undermining the stability of the sultan's government. The right-wing *Hamburger Nachrichten* was adamant that "a nation which, like the American, itself perpetrates the most shameless atrocities, lynching and burning negroes, has no right to get morally excited over the barbarities of other nations, even were the American people a European one with a right to a voice in European affairs." The editor expressed hope that the Ottoman Empire would show the Americans "her fist," which was "the only language that the Yankee finally understands and appreciates."[123] Even the more liberal Berlin-based journal, accused US missionaries of stirring up sedition among the Armenians by inculcating them with "American republican views."[124] With the Kaiser committed to establishing a warm relationship with Roosevelt at this time, there was little chance that events in the Ottoman Empire would threaten harmonious relations between the two countries. However, the treatment of Armenians in the Ottoman Empire would resurface as a point of tension in US–German relations once the German-Ottoman alliance was cemented.

In France, there was condemnation of Roosevelt's censure of its Russian ally, with *Le Temps* complaining that Roosevelt had "indulged in the spreadeagleism which the more sober traditions of Washington, Jefferson and Lincoln had systematically avoided."[125] *Journal des débats*, a Parisian weekly, condemned Roosevelt for believing that "the presence of United States war-ships was as necessary at Panama as at Beirut, Tangier and Smyrna."[126] The conservative daily *Le Figaro* complained that Roosevelt's "policy of excessive expansion, of militant intervention a little bit everywhere, is not very much in harmony with the strict application of the Monroe Doctrine."[127] The prevalence of such sentiments led the distinguished French historian Henri Hauser to observe in early 1905 that "one hears nothing spoken of in the press, at meetings, in parliament, except the American peril." Hauser set out to provide a dispassionate study of *l'Impérialisme Américain* that went beyond traditional economic and military factors. He noted that American claims that theirs was a "humanitarian imperialism" were not necessarily false. He pointed to Roosevelt's interventions on behalf of Romanian and Russian Jews while the Europeans "did not lift a finger," and the work its missionaries were doing for Armenians. Roosevelt's second corollary to the Monroe Doctrine had merely confirmed what was already obvious: that "times had changed since 1823; the United States has acquired new powers and responsibilities." Hauser warned his countrymen, and the rest of Europe, that "henceforth government of the globe will no longer be a matter for Europe alone."[128]

The country that most enthusiastically greeted Roosevelt's Annual Message was Britain. In 1823, British Foreign Secretary George Canning initially hoped Britain and the United States would make a joint declaration preventing any nation from further colonizing territory in the Western Hemisphere, but John Quincy Adams persuaded his cabinet colleagues to issue the Monroe Doctrine

unilaterally. Due to the weakness of the US fleet, responsibility for upholding the Monroe Doctrine in fact devolved to the British navy, which shared
American concerns for maintenance of open markets and free trade in the
hemisphere. As American power grew in the 1890s and British policymakers
began to sense that their country was becoming overburdened with imperial
commitments, statesmen in London looked to Washington to relieve Britain's
responsibility for maintaining the Doctrine. Roosevelt's 1904 message was
regarded as confirmation that America was prepared to assume that burden.
Soon after its announcement, Britain's naval strategists withdrew its major vessels from its Atlantic stations.[129] *The Economist* voiced the majority sentiment
when it declared that Britain "cannot fail to regard with satisfaction" Roosevelt's
announcement that the United States would now police the Americas.[130] The
president's principles of humanitarian intervention, however, met with a mixed
response. The *Daily Telegraph* approved Roosevelt's call for a "peace of justice,"
while the *Daily Chronicle* asserted that "we may see in this message, the words of
Police Constable Roosevelt of the International Police."[131] However, *The Times*
countered that righteousness was in the eye of the beholder and America's own
failings, which Roosevelt himself had freely admitted, meant it could not "command the universal respect the international policeman would need." *The Times*
correspondent in New York remarked that "it seems never to occur to him that
the rest of the world may not like being lectured."[132] The editors of *Blackwood's
Magazine* were particularly allergic to Roosevelt's moralizing and suggested that
if the president would "look nearer home than Armenia . . . he will find not a
few crimes of which it is his manifest duty to show his disapproval."[133] Despite
Roosevelt's best rhetorical efforts, the perception was still widespread, even in
Britain, that America's humanitarian pretensions overseas were not matched
by its conduct at home. While most Britons were happy to allow Americans to
police the Western Hemisphere, few were yet willing for the United States to
extend its beat to Europe.

Never Draw Unless You Mean to Shoot

Roosevelt's 1904 annual message raised hopes among Armenians, Russian Jews
and their supporters that the United States would interfere more strenuously on
their behalf. Throughout 1903 and 1904, Armenian revolutionary groups had
rebelled against Ottoman rule. A major confrontation between Armenian guer-
rillas and the Ottoman army in Sasun in July 1904 led to reports of renewed
massacres and again aroused widespread American sympathy.[134] Aware of
Roosevelt's personal support for their cause, Armenian insurgents made
repeated requests to the president for intervention.[135] These solicitations were

reinforced by appeals from Armenophiles in the United States. Eminent French lecturer Anatole Beaulieu addressed a mass meeting of recent Armenian immigrants in Boston and urged intervention by the United States, on the grounds it could do so "without jealousy of other powers." Beaulieu advised Roosevelt that "what you did in the Roumanian affair . . . you can do now with the same justification as regards the Armenians."[136] However, the muted American response to his principles of intervention chilled Roosevelt's ardor for action. As Roosevelt informed his close confidant, the Protestant clergyman and *Outlook* editor Lymann Abbot, while he was "entirely satisfied to head a crusade for the Armenians . . . the country has not the remotest intention of fighting on such an issue." He had tried to rouse Americans to their responsibilities but accepted that they had no desire "to back up words by deeds." For the rest of his presidency Roosevelt was far more cautious in his calls for intervention. He was determined to avoid using language or attempt interference, "which would only be justified if, and could under no circumstances do good unless, there was intention to back up the words by an appeal to arms." In response to appeals from others, Roosevelt repeatedly invoked a dictum that he had learned as a rancher: "Never to draw unless you mean to shoot."[137]

Roosevelt had also learned from previous British experiences. He remarked to the British statesman and author George Otto Trevelyan that Britain had rendered a great service by championing Italian independence in the 1860s; correspondingly, the United States had accomplished "a little, a very little" for Eastern European Jews by his actions. Nevertheless, Roosevelt felt that Americans, like the governments of Lords Palmerston and Russell, which protested on behalf of Poles in Russia and Danes in Germany, were "too apt to indulge in representations on behalf of weak peoples which do them no good and irritate the strong and tyrannical peoples to whom the protest is made" unless backed by force. He again stated his desire "to go into a crusade against the Turk" but as the American people did not back him he vowed never again to express publicly, while president, his "sympathy and indignation, lest harm and not good result."[138]

Although Americans were not prepared to act as policemen in the Eastern Mediterranean, Roosevelt hoped that another "civilized" nation would. In response to an appeal from the anti-imperialist Carl Schurz for the United States to support proposals for multilateral disarmament, Roosevelt made his habitual reference to the Armenians to emphasize that peace was often dependent on the "armed interference of a civilized power." If the European powers disarmed, then instances like the Armenian massacres, in which "the moral degradation, the brutality inflicted and endured, the aggregate of hideous wrong done, surpassed that of any war of which we have record in modern times," would continue to occur.[139] Schurz noted the flaw in Roosevelt's argument: "Admitting all you say of the Armenian atrocities—have we not to face the fact that the Powers stood by, without lifting a hand, although they were armed to the teeth?"[140] Russian statesman Serge Witte reinforced Schurz's point. When in the United States negotiating the end of the Russo-Japanese War, Witte remarked to Roosevelt that it was in Russia's interest for the Ottomans to retain control of the Balkan Peninsula as "it would be a very bad thing for Russia to have the Bulgarians, for instance, substituted for the Turks, for the very reason that they might give a wholesome, reputable government and thereby build up a great Slav state to the south." Witte's display of realpolitik disgusted Roosevelt. The president believed that "practical politics are a most sordid business unless they rest on a basis of honesty and disinterested sentiment," albeit with an appreciation that with this "must also go intelligent self-interest."[141] It was evident, though, that no power was prepared to intervene for the Armenians for either sentimental or self-interested reasons.

When renewed anti-Jewish pogroms erupted in 1906 in Russia, in the midst of revolution, Roosevelt again revealed his newfound resolve not to "threaten aimlessly." He rejected a request from the Jewish banker Jacob Schiff to intercede with the Russian government on the grounds it would make the United States look "ridiculous" and do nothing to help Russian Jews. Roosevelt explained to Straus that he wished he were able to act against "the dreadful massacres in Russia" but refused to issue a protest "which might sound well here and have just an opposite effect there."[142] Roosevelt was convinced that destabilization in Russia had rendered the tsarist authorities impotent to control their territory. Any protest would thus be futile. For Roosevelt, the most important factor in justifying intervention was government complicity. The revolutionary upheaval meant Roosevelt was not convinced that the Russian government was accountable for the "dreadful outrages." He contrasted this with the Armenian massacres of the 1890s, when the "Turkish Government was responsible and was able to enforce whatever was desired." However, Roosevelt was now convinced that the Cleveland and McKinley administrations were right not to have threatened war with the Ottomans. This change in attitude stemmed from the recognition, after his own unproductive efforts to change public sentiments, that as "our people would not go into such a war, at least with the determination for the lavish outlay of blood and money necessary to make it effective, it would have been worse than foolish to have threatened it, and not the slightest good would have been or was gained by any agitation which it was known would not be backed up by arms." Roosevelt still personally wished the American public would accept the responsibilities that accompanied its newly acquired power. However, while he was in office, practicalities overrode his idealism. He refused to act on his ideals unless he could do so effectively and while maintaining American dignity, by backing up words with actions.[143]

England and America Acting Together

By this time, another humanitarian cause had aroused Americans. In April 1906, Roosevelt observed that in addition to continued petitions to aid Armenians and Russian Jews, "large numbers of people [were] asking that we interfere about the Congo Free State."[144] Europeans and Americans had initially welcomed its creation in 1884–1885. It was administered by Belgium's King Leopold, independent of the country's parliament, to avoid the African territory becoming a site of great power rivalry and the Belgians being enmeshed in imperial politics.[145] However, by the early years of the twentieth century, reports of atrocities morally outraged people on both sides of the Atlantic. In Britain, E. D. Morel's Congo Reform Association (CRA) publicized the horrors and stirred the conscience of the British public. With Morel's assistance, branches of the CRA sprouted up across Europe. Yet outside Britain, Congo reform only become a truly mass movement in America following Morel's visit in 1904.[146] Morel urged a joint Anglo-American intervention "on behalf of the oppressed and persecuted peoples of the Congo, for whose present unhappy condition you, in America, and we, in England, have a great moral responsibility from which we cannot escape."[147]

At the start of his trip, Morel met with Roosevelt at the White House.[148] Like other Westerners, Roosevelt originally celebrated Leopold's regime as part of the larger European "movement" to colonize Africa and Asia. In 1902, he remarked on the "extraordinary" part Belgium had played in the "international development of Africa."[149] There were tales of atrocities to be sure, but these emerged from many imperial missions, including America's own. However, after Morel and his associate, diplomat Roger Casement, began to reveal the systemic nature of Belgian abuse, Roosevelt privately expressed concern.[150] Roosevelt's response confirmed that his embrace of European imperialism was never unconditional. Expansion was only justified when it advanced Roosevelt's conception of civilization. Increasingly, he was convinced that Leopold's rule did not promote that larger goal. Nevertheless, while Roosevelt received Morel cordially and expressed interest in the cause, he made no definite commitment beyond promising to pass the issue on to Hay.[151]

Morel believed that Roosevelt's subsequent inaction was due to concerns about the political consequences of Anglophobia. His visit coincided with the closing month of election season in 1904, and Hay informed him that if America did anything about the Congo, "it can only be after the presidential election." Morel believed this was a consequence of the administration "spreading a specially attractive bait for the Catholic vote" and having no interest in doing anything that might incur hostility from Irish Americans, who opposed anything that enhanced the Anglo-American rapprochement.[152] Morel was correct. After his ambassadorship in London, Hay was the US official most closely associated with rapprochement. This exposed him to opprobrium and he once complained: "All I have ever done with England is to have wrung great concessions out of her with no compensation. And yet, these idiots say I'm not an American because I don't say, 'To hell with the Queen,' at every breath."[153] His sensitivity to this criticism was reflected in his handling of the Congo issue and he grumbled to Roosevelt that it was "a well-meant impertinence, after all, for Englishmen to come to us to take up their Congo quarrel." Preoccupied with his re-election campaign, Roosevelt passed on Hay's complaint to a prominent Irish American lawyer, Eugene Philbin, who was concerned that the United States might take up the cause of Congo reform.[154]

Morel also recognized that alienating American Catholics would hinder his objective of securing US involvement in a Congo intervention. Belgium was a largely Catholic country. Furthermore, Leopold's patronage of Catholic missionaries, together with the perception that he was the victim of a conspiracy of Protestant missionaries, won him the support of the Vatican and its adherents, including American Catholics.[155] Francis B. Loomis, US Assistant Secretary of State, expressed concern about "sectarianism" in the Congo reform issue when Morel was in Washington.[156] Conscious that a sectarian split would antagonize Washington and hinder efforts to promote a joint intervention, Morel worked, both in Britain and the United States, to prevent Congo reform being identified as a Protestant crusade.[157]

However, the ramifications of Anglophobia and sectarianism only partially explained the Roosevelt administration's response. Hay informed Morel that the legal case for intervention by the United States was weak, as it was not a signatory to the Berlin Act that brought the Congo into existence. The secretary pointed to the "absence of any American interest directly threatened" and stressed the administration could not "take up every humanitarian question which is put before us, otherwise we should be doing nothing else." Furthermore, he reminded Morel that the United States lacked the power to investigate conditions in the Congo as it had no diplomatic representatives there. As a consequence, it had to balance accusations against the denials of Leopold's regime.[158]

This equilibrium became more difficult to sustain after November 1905, when the findings of a commission of inquiry, set up by Leopold himself under Belgian judge Emile Janssens, were published. The Janssens report confirmed that abuses existed, completely undermining the regime's defense that the campaign was simply an English conspiracy to acquire territory or a plot by unscrupulous Protestant missionaries.[159] Furthermore, by this time Morel had helped establish a large-scale American CRA, which made considerable progress in winning over American public opinion.[160] Both Booker T. Washington and Mark Twain wrote popular pieces condemning Leopold and visited Washington to urge Roosevelt to intervene.[161]

In early 1906 Morel sent two British missionaries, Reverend John Harris and his wife Alice, on an American tour to build on his work.[162] They addressed nearly two hundred public meetings. As a result, petitions poured into Washington demanding that the administration put a stop to the atrocities in the Congo.[163] The recipient of these requests was the new Secretary of State Elihu Root. He later complained that "the very people who are most ardent against entangling alliances insist most fanatically upon our doing one hundred things a year on humanitarian grounds, which would lead to immediate war." Root's exasperation was reflected in his reply to a request from Indiana Congressman Edwin Denby for the United States to call for an international inquiry into conditions in the Congo. Root took the opportunity to issue a public statement outlining the administration's position. The secretary denied that the Berlin Act offered any grounds for legal intervention for any nation and certainly not for the United States, which was not even a signatory. Furthermore, he expressed sympathy for Leopold's position, suggesting that "if the United States had happened to possess in Darkest Africa a territory seven times as large and four times as populous as the Philippines, we too might find good government difficult and come in for our share of just or unjust criticism." However, Root's statement did little to stem the flow of petitions, as he noted, "people kept piling down on the Department demanding action on the Congo."[164] Consequently, Root was forced to reverse his claim that the United States had no responsibility for what was going on.[165] Harris reported to Morel that "the ever increasing pressure from the humanitarian public" made American action now "practically certain and at no distant date."[166]

However, while Roosevelt was especially attuned to popular opinion, and his own sympathy for Congo reform had grown, he did not yet envision American intervention. He privately noted to Andrew Carnegie, "It would be an advantage to justice if we were able to interfere in the Congo Free State to secure a more righteous government," just as it would be if Americans "were able effectively to interfere for the Armenians in Turkey, and for the Jews in Russia."[167] But as in those cases, he did not see how America could intervene at present. Like Root, he remained disdainful of "professional international humanitarians" who urged diplomatic protests without recognizing the consequences.[168] Rather than an indication of Roosevelt's lack of sympathy, this was a reflection of his frustration with the activists' lack of realism.[169] As he confided to Straus, his irritation stemmed from their inability to understand that it was "a literal physical impossibility to interfere . . . save in the most guarded manner, under penalty of making this nation ridiculous and of aggravating instead of ameliorating the fate for whom we interfere."[170]

Nevertheless, the surge in popular support increased Roosevelt's inter-est in the Congo, and he began to cautiously explore whether an intercession was possible. In November 1906, the *London Morning Post* announced that the Roosevelt administration was prepared to co-operate with Britain and attend any international conference convened to discuss affairs in the Congo.[171] It was immediately seized upon by Morel, whose pressure had moved Sir Edward Grey, the new British foreign secretary, to come out in favor of the "Belgian solu-tion"—annexation of the Congo by that country's parliament.[172] Morel had long believed that if the United States chose to act it would first explore the issue through unofficial channels. This would ensure action appeared to Americans as an "independent and spontaneous initiative, and not as the outcome of a previ-ous entente with England," which could be exploited by "anti-British sentiment in the States."[173] Regarding the *Morning Post* article as a potential feeler, he con-tacted the US State department and was informed that while Roosevelt could not "announce or even forecast . . . his policy or future course," the United States had previously participated "in conferences concerning the well-being of the natives of Africa" and "should a similar occasion arise, it would doubtless have appropriate consideration."[174]

An occasion for intervention arose the following month. Colonel Henry Kowalsky, a California lawyer hired as a lobbyist for Leopold, sold his complete correspondence with the Belgian King to the *New York American*. The newspa-per exposé revealed how the Belgian Crown had paid agents to subvert members of Congress and even successfully bribed a staff member of the Senate Foreign Relations Committee.[175] In seeking to counter the CRA's conquest of American public opinion, Leopold and his agents overextended themselves and provided an opportunity for American interference. Roosevelt's close confidant Henry Cabot Lodge introduced a Senate resolution, pledging support for any action deemed necessary to secure reforms in the Congo. The Roosevelt administra-tion pre-empted its passage by communicating directly with the British govern-ment its desire to cooperate "towards the realization of whatever reforms may be counselled by the sentiments of humanity."[176]

The news that the United States was willing to co-operate with Britain proved a critical turning point for Leopold's rule. The subsequent downfall of Leopold's administration in 1908 and the annexation of the Congo by a Belgian govern-ment considered more susceptible to international public opinion were largely a consequence of this joint British and American intervention.[177] Morel cer-tainly believed that "England and America acting together" had secured this "triumph."[178] The joint act proved critical in forcing Leopold to yield control over his African possession, even if the ultimate improvement of the territory's administration took several more years.[179] Furthermore, the Congo interven-tion, like that over Romania, bolstered the Anglo-American rapprochement and strengthened perceptions in both countries, not least for Roosevelt himself, that the English-speaking people could best advance their shared civilizing mission by working together.

Retreat from Colonialism and Rejection of an Alliance

Leopold's misgovernment did not diminish Roosevelt's confidence in colonialism and the civilizing missions of European powers.[180] It was increasingly evident, however, that his criteria for determining whether a state was civilized depended on characteristics other than color and that these attributes were not confined to Europe and America. When Japan waged war with Russia in 1904–1905, Roosevelt privately celebrated Japanese victories, convinced they were playing "the game of civilized mankind."[181] Roosevelt welcomed Japan's occupation of Korea, believing that Koreans were incapable of governing themselves and preferring Japanese occupation to Russian.[182] Unlike many European statesmen, Roosevelt did not believe that Russia represented the civilized West and Japan the backward East.[183] He continued to regard the Russian government as despotic and expansionist, oppressing its own people and threatening American economic interests.[184] He claimed, "I should hang my head in shame if I were capable of discriminating against the Japanese because they have different shades of skin."[185] To illustrate his argument that physiology did not determine a nation's level of civilization, Roosevelt compared the Japanese favorably to the Ottomans. In a letter to Spring Rice, he stated the "modern Turks" were "just as much white people" as other European nations that spoke an "Aryan tongue." However, he considered the Ottomans "absolutely alien because of their creed, their culture, their historic associations, and inherited governmental and social tendencies." Although "the Turks are ethnically closer to us than the Japanese, they are impossible members of our international society, while the Japs may be desirable additions."[186] Cultural factors rather than purely biological ones designated a nation's position in Roosevelt's civilizational hierarchy.

Roosevelt still maintained that the British Empire was superior to any other European or Asian imperial power.[187] However, he also retained his strong sense of national pride. Upon hearing that a British Governor of a Malay province had criticized American administration of the Philippines, Roosevelt snapped: "We have had more difficult work to do than the English have had to do in the Malay Settlements, and it has been done better."[188] Roosevelt resented unfavorable comparisons of American to British colonialism, especially when Americans made that critique. On hearing that American anti-imperialist Charles Francis Adams had praised British rule in Egypt, Roosevelt scornfully remarked to

Lodge: "If Mr. Adams had been willing to look at what his own countrymen did he would not have had to wait for seven years and go to Egypt in order to find deeds to admire." On the whole, Roosevelt greatly admired British rule in Egypt but disdained Britain's broken promise to leave after intervening in 1882. He believed it was necessary to break this pledge to advance civilization but foolish to have made it in the first place.[189] Conversely, he was proud that the United States had upheld a similar pledge in Cuba after the war with Spain and again when he reluctantly intervened to quell disorder in 1906. On both occasions American forces and officials withdrew after the initial intervention. In reality, as Roosevelt himself admitted, Cuba's sovereignty remained heavily compromised even after the departure of American troops.[190] For Roosevelt, though, the perception was important. "The good faith of the United States," he insisted, "is a mighty valuable asset and must not be impaired."[191] He was proud that the United States, unlike Britain in Egypt, had kept its promise to give up formal control of the territory. Furthermore, while Roosevelt admired the British proconsul in Egypt, Lord Cromer, he considered him inferior to leading American colonial administrators: William Howard Taft, Governor General of the Philippines, and Leonard Wood, his counterpart in Cuba.[192] Roosevelt celebrated Britain's contribution to the larger "movement" of civilizing the world but his patriotism prevented him from championing it over American colonialism.

Nevertheless, Roosevelt's sensitivity to criticism of America's colonial administration is explained less by chauvinism and more by his awareness that there was some truth to the charges. During his presidency, he became increasingly disillusioned with the attitude of his countrymen toward their overseas territories. For Roosevelt, US expansion brought with it attendant duties to ensure the people of its possessions prospered. He was appalled by American unwillingness, particularly in Congress, to recognize that practical responsibilities (especially tariff advantages) should accompany occupation. Worse still was the failure, despite his repeated attempts, "to awaken any public interest in providing any adequate defence of the islands." He was convinced that the United States could not defend the Philippines "without fortifying them and without building up a navy second only to that of Britain." After the Russo-Japanese War, Roosevelt became increasingly concerned that Japanese aggression would encourage attempts at further expansion in East Asia. He regarded the Philippines as America's defensive "heel of Achilles" and its unfortified defenses as a persistent temptation for Japan. Roosevelt had previously mocked demands that the Philippines be given immediate independence. His "wish" had always been that Americans would be "prepared permanently, in a duty-loving spirit, and looking forward to a couple of generations of continuous manifestation of this spirit, to assume the control of the Philippine Islands for the good of the Filipinos." However, his ideals were tempered by the practical realization that the government must "accommodate ourselves to conditions as they actually are and not as we would wish them to be." It was clear that Americans would refuse to provide the Philippines with commercial benefits or suitable protection and would not "permanently accept the Philippines simply as an un-remunerative and indeed expensive burden." This realization led him in 1907 to write to Taft, as secretary of war, that the United States would have to give the islands independence much sooner than he thought advisable from their own standpoint. Americans were clearly unwilling to assume the military and economic responsibilities required to keep them.[193] He had long since recognized that Americans were more interested in domestic reform than imperial projects or even policing their own neighborhood. There was no question of further colonial expansion, and Roosevelt asserted that he had "about the same desire to annex" another island "as a gorged boa constrictor might have to swallow a porcupine wrong end-to."[194] Public unpreparedness to embrace expansion had sated his appetite for colonialism.

Observers in Britain had long since become disillusioned with US colonialism. Attempts to transfer democratic principles of government to the Philippines were dismissed as naïve.[195] Like Roosevelt, many British writers were horrified by the American refusal to extend tariff benefits to its colonies. They regarded it as unethical and a calculated violation of colonial duty, serving sugar and tobacco lobbyists in America while being "murderous" to the Philippines.[196] Despite initial hopes that constructive criticism could make American colonial conduct more like Britain's, British commentators increasingly expressed misgivings about the capacity of the American political system to produce a cadre of high quality colonial administrators, believing American politics to be corrupted by nepotism, the "spoils system" and domineering party bosses.[197] By the end of Roosevelt's presidency, it had become apparent to analysts on both sides of the Atlantic that an association in colonial projects was not an appropriate instrument for advancing a larger alliance. Moreover, it had become evident that even the most limited compact with Britain was impossible in the current American political climate.

Roosevelt recognized that the overwhelming majority of Americans would not entertain an alliance with Britain. Few of his contemporaries felt that the United States had much of a stake in international affairs.[198] Furthermore, it was injudicious for any national political leader to expose himself to accusations of sacrificing American interests to another power, especially Britain.[199] Roosevelt's own strident nationalism made him uncompromising on the fortification of the US-built interoceanic canal and over the Alaskan boundary dispute. Both issues generated diplomatic tensions before Britain decided to further friendly relations and accept settlements favorable to America. Once Britain had acceded to US supremacy in the Western Hemisphere, Roosevelt set about strengthening the rapprochement through informal means and outside the public eye.[200] His

role in ensuring Japan's military victories against Russia were confirmed by diplomatic success at the American-brokered peace talks was intended to advance
the Anglo-Japanese alliance in East Asia, to which he considered America an
unofficial partner. He also helped bring about a conference over the Moroccan
crisis between France and Germany, which upheld the interests of Britain and
its French ally.[201] Yet he recognized the limitations of Anglo-American co-
operation. When George Kennan suggested formalizing the East Asian understanding with Japan and Britain as an alliance, Roosevelt responded that the
explorer obviously had not followed his difficulties with getting treaties ratified
by the Senate.[202] Equally, in order to get the Senate to pass the Moroccan treaty,
Lodge was forced to defend Roosevelt by asserting that "in entangling alliances,
of course, no man wants to engage this country; we have no concern with the
wars of Europe."[203]

As Lodge well knew, Roosevelt was increasingly concerned with the potential
impact of European events and regarded the Royal Navy as a "distinct help in
keeping the peace of the world," although he continued to insist that the United
States must rely first and foremost on its own strength.[204] Roosevelt informed
his closest American and British correspondents that he regarded "the nightmare of a possible contest between the two great English-speaking peoples [as]
practically impossible now, and that it will grow entirely so as the years go by."[205]
Nevertheless, he objected to formalizing this relationship in a treaty. When his
successor, Taft, attempted to negotiate an arbitration treaty with Britain in 1911,
Roosevelt, along with Lodge and Mahan, led the opposition.[206] Roosevelt maintained that he would have supported arbitration if it was limited to Britain but
objected to Taft's intention to extend the practice to America's relations with
other nations. Furthermore, he was unconvinced that Americans would abide by
an agreement, even with Britain, if they sensed national prestige was at stake.[207]
As with his position on interventions, Roosevelt regarded it as particularly dishonorable to promise to do something and then fail to do it. While retaining his
faith in future harmony between Britain and America, Roosevelt informed his
British friends that "harm and not good is caused by attempting to hurry unnatu-
rally a natural process." Roosevelt was particularly dismissive of W. T. Stead, who
was at the forefront of the arbitration movement, viewing him as "the type that
makes a good cause ridiculous." He also revealed his contempt for Chamberlain's
earlier public advocacy of an Anglo-American alliance. While Roosevelt privately shared the commitment of Chamberlain and Stead to an alliance, he was
convinced that "when things are going satisfactorily, to try to make them go too
fast is of course often the surest way of making them come to a halt."[208] Roosevelt
had done much to strengthen Anglo-American relations during his presidency
and remained personally attracted to an eventual alliance. Yet his sense of what
was practically possible continued to discipline his dedication to this ideal.

As Roosevelt's presidency drew to a close, he recognized that there was no possibility of formally realizing an Anglo-American alliance, and certainly not its most ambitious aspect of a common civilizing mission. He had accepted that the American people were not prepared to commit to a colonial role in the Philippines or anywhere else. Moreover, he had privately acknowledged the American public would not support the solution to the Armenian question that he had previously suggested was necessary, a military intervention on their behalf. However, through his 1904 Second Corollary and his diplomatic interventions in the Congo and Eastern Europe, Roosevelt had gone as far as he felt was politically feasible to educate Americans on their global responsibilities. Within ten years, after renewed massacres erupted in the Ottoman Empire, Roosevelt's vision of America's duty to vindicate victims of crimes against civilization, in concert with Britain, would provoke a public debate over the responsibilities Americans were willing to assume. The possibility of the United States solving the Armenian question through a protectorate for part of the Ottoman Empire would force Americans to decide whether they were willing to share the burden of policing the Near East with the British Empire.

3

The Missionary Solution

Just before leaving office, Roosevelt conducted his most public presidential celebration of Britain's Empire. The stimulus was requests from his British correspondents to defend Britain's dominion over India after its authorities had inflicted violence against Indian rebels unseen since the Mutiny of 1857. Roosevelt's speech, delivered at the Methodist Episcopal Church in Washington, DC on January 18, 1909, extolled the benefits of European colonialism in general and lauded Britain's rule as for "the immeasurable advantage of India, and for the honour and profit of civilization." Roosevelt's British friends, Britain's government, and much of its press welcomed these sentiments.[1] Equally significant was the more nuanced interpretation of America's own civilizing mission that Roosevelt outlined. Despite his private misgivings, Roosevelt continued to celebrate America's record in the Philippines. In this speech, he stressed the role of American missionaries, who "for over a century" had been "trying to carry civilization and Christianity into lands which have hitherto known little or nothing of either." In part, this emphasis reflected Roosevelt's awareness of his evangelical audience. However, even before his presidency Roosevelt had regarded the missionary, alongside the merchant and soldier, as "human instruments" for "destroying barbarism . . . [and] the advance of civilization." Roosevelt insisted that for any intervention by a "civilized power" to be justified, commercial advantages for the dependent society must be accompanied by nonmaterial benefits. He stressed that "civilization can only be permanent and continue a blessing to any people if, in addition to promoting their material well-being, it also stands for an orderly individual liberty, for the growth of intelligence, and for equal justice in the administration of law: Christianity alone meets these fundamental requirements." With his confidence in America's formal colonial mission diminishing, Roosevelt looked to missionaries to serve as the vanguard of the US contribution to spreading "the ideals of civilization and Christianity."[2]

Roosevelt informed his Methodist audience that he had always been especially interested in the "extraordinary work done by the American schools and colleges in the Turkish Empire . . . a work which has borne fruit among the Bulgarians, among Syrian and Armenian Christians, and also among the Mohammedans." Roosevelt claimed the purpose of missionary work among this last group was not conversion, but "to make them vie with their fellow citizens who are Christians in showing those qualities which it should be the pride of every creed to develop." Overcoming his habitual dislike of revolutionary upheaval, he welcomed the Young Turk Revolution. This had begun in 1908 when a group of junior army officers launched a coup leading to the reinstitution of the Constitution of 1876, suspended for the majority of Abdul Hamid's reign, and the resumption of parliamentary politics. Roosevelt believed the revolution had the potential to transform Ottoman society and enable all its citizens to develop the characteristics that he identified with a civilized people. Roosevelt proclaimed: "The present movement to introduce far-reaching and genuine reforms, political and social, in Turkey, an effort with which we all keenly sympathize, is one in which these young Moslems, educated at the American schools and colleges, are especially fitted to take part."[3]

The American Board of Commissioners for Foreign Missions' (ABCFM) leaders were more confident than ever that their work enjoyed the support of the US government and American people.[4] The nation's expansion had enhanced their role as international guides responsible for interpreting the wider world for ordinary Americans and policymakers.[5] Missionary expertise was especially in demand when revolutions occurred in nations in which they were the most prominent American presence, be it Persia in 1905, China in 1911–1912, or the Ottoman Empire. These revolutions, at least initially, were interpreted in the United States as those nations refashioning their cultural, political, economic, and religious values in the American image. The missionaries, often the only Americans active in many regions of those countries, were widely credited by their countrymen as agents of reform.[6] Editor Talcott Williams best summarized majority opinion on the Young Turk Revolution. During an address in New York, Williams declared that while there were a number of causes of the revolution:

> If we ask ourselves what the governing and final factor is which has brought about the first of the world's bloodless revolutions, which has seen a people divided and dissevered by creed, by race, by language, by every conceivable difference which can separate the sons and daughters of men, suddenly act together—we do ill if we forget that for eighty years the American missionaries have been laying the foundations and preaching the doctrine which makes free governments possible.[7]

Previously, many American observers had stressed the incompatibility of Christians living under Muslim rule, blaming Islamic theology for the Armenian massacres and claiming they would only be safe outside the Ottoman Empire. In the immediate aftermath of the Young Turk Revolution, however, Roosevelt and Williams captured a widespread American hope that its missionaries could help construct a constitutional government that would provide security and prosperity to all the Empire's communities, including the Armenians. They believed their missionaries were bringing the blessings of civilization to the Empire and helping to build a reformed Ottoman polity in which the Armenians were protected. This "Missionary solution" to the Armenian question was part of a larger global mission. Strengthened by increased support from their domestic constituencies, missionary leaders looked to exploit the unrivalled opportunities presented by an increasingly interconnected international system and the corresponding breakdown of the established order in non-Christian nations, epitomized by the Young Turk Revolution. They sought to inspire all Protestant missionaries to unite for the urgent spread of Christian ideals around the world. However, these aspirations were checked by the outbreak of World War I. When renewed Armenian massacres broke out in 1915, Roosevelt and the missionaries disagreed over how best to respond.

Missionaries and Merchants

In 1909 missionaries shared Roosevelt's conviction, expressed at the Methodist meeting, that the "change in sentiment in favor of the foreign missionary in a single generation has been remarkable."[8] This shift in attitudes was reflected in the greater financial contributions that missionary organizations received from American businessmen at the turn of the century. The outstanding example was John D. Rockefeller Sr., founder of Standard Oil, and his son John D. Jr, who had been making donations to evangelical and ecumenical causes since the 1880s.[9] From the late 1890s onward, the family's financial contributions to missionary operations became increasingly generous under the guidance of its principal philanthropic and business adviser Frederick T. Gates. The Rockefellers were already making sizeable donations to the YMCA when Gates was approached in 1905 by James Barton, the new foreign secretary of the ABCFM and a former missionary in the Armenian provinces of the Ottoman Empire. After meeting with Barton, Gates recommended the Rockefellers donate at least $100,000, a huge sum at the time, to the ABCFM. Gates justified this largesse by emphasizing the unprecedented opportunities to extend to all nations "the light which English speaking peoples can give." The Rockefellers' agent was a passionate believer in the vision of an Anglo-American mission to govern global affairs and he viewed religious missionaries as the means to help achieve it.

Gates suggested to his patrons that funding missions was also good business. He pointed to the massive increase in American imports and exports from "heathen lands" to illustrate that "missionary enterprise viewed solely from a commercial standpoint is immensely profitable." Furthermore, the fruits of missionary labors were only beginning to mature and, with further techno-logical advances, stimulated by American missionaries and educational institu-tions, these lands would become increasingly fertile fields for US commerce. Yet the economic benefits only partly explained why foreign missions should command American support. Gates declared that the ultimate "effects of the missionary enterprise of English speaking peoples will be to bring to them the peaceful conquest of the world." He insisted this was "not political dominion, but dominion in commerce and manufacture, in literature, science, philosophy, art, refinement, morals, religion." On his advice, the Rockefellers furnished the funds to the ABCFM. An additional donation was made to the Ottoman mis-sion, a territory in which Standard Oil was beginning to take an interest as an export market for its products.[10]

The US government, under William Howard Taft, also recognized that com-mercial advantages could be gained from exploiting markets in territories that American missionaries had already penetrated. In 1906, the US Congress had finally agreed to raise the US legation in Constantinople to an embassy. Taft sought to take advantage of this enhanced diplomatic leverage to extend his "dollar diplomacy" to the Ottoman Empire. In his first annual message, he applauded "the quick transition of the Government of the Ottoman Empire from one of retrograde tendencies to a constitutional government," describing it as "one of the most important phenomena of our time." Taft emphasized the opportunity that it offered Americans to "obtain a greater share of the com-merce of the Near East."[11] Improved trade relations also appealed to the new Ottoman regime, desperate for economic aid to modernize their failing state and hopeful that closer relations with the United States could provide diplo-matic leverage against the European powers.[12] Taft's Secretary of State Philander Knox established a Division of Near Eastern Affairs in 1909 and businessmen opened the American Chamber of Commerce for the Near East in 1911. US–Ottoman trade doubled under the Taft administration, from $12.7 million in 1908 to $25.5 million in 1913.[13]

However, America's economic commitments in the Ottoman Empire were inconsequential when compared with Germany's proposed Berlin-to-Baghdad railway, and with British, French, Italian, and Russian investments. By the end of Taft's administration, Americans dispatched a mere 0.17 percent of their yearly exports to the Ottoman Empire while Ottoman exports to the United States amounted to only 1 per-cent of the full volume of American imports.[14] Oscar Straus, whom Taft appointed to a third mission in Constantinople in 1909–1910, was skeptical of dollar diplomacy. Straus informed the State Department that any substantial American commercial expansion in the Ottoman Empire would be opposed by the European powers and could only be successful if backed by "the strong arm of the Government." As there was no possibility of Washington investing sufficient political or military capital in the Near East, there was little chance of American businesses gaining any large concessions in the Empire. Furthermore, Straus insisted that by angling for commercial contacts, American capitalists would only undermine attempts to protect the legal status and rights of American educational and missionary institutions under the new Ottoman regime.[15] By the time the Chester Project, a proposed railroad and mining scheme, collapsed in 1911, the Taft administration had accepted Straus's analysis and retreated to its traditional stance of "non-involvement in the Eastern Question."[16] Throughout the second decade of the twentieth century, missionaries rather than merchants remained America's most significant interest in the Ottoman Empire.

The Evangelization of the World in This Generation

By the turn of the century, American missionaries in the Ottoman Empire had joined Protestant evangelists in many other countries in an ecumenical commitment to disavow denominational rivalries and work for the worldwide spread of Christianity. The charismatic American missionary leader John R. Mott epitomized this new and expansive global strategy. He impressed on all Protestants that "the gospel can and should be brought within the reach of every creature within this generation."[17] Mott spread his evangelical message in speeches globally and in various texts, including his hugely popular 1900 publication *The Evangelization of the World in This Generation*. He informed his congregants that "in several countries, notably in the United States, Canada, Great Britain and Ireland" the missionary movement has adopted this slogan as their "watchword."[18] The Student Volunteer Movement for Foreign Missions, in which Mott was a leading light, had helped stimulate an upsurge in missionary activities and encouraged thousands of American college students to commit to spreading the gospel across the world. American missionary leaders saw themselves as part of a larger transatlantic evangelical movement but they were determined to establish the United States as its leader. They proved highly successful. In the late 1880s the United States had only nine hundred missionaries abroad. By the end of the century this number had tripled. In 1900 the United States produced 27.5 percent of the world's Protestant foreign missionaries; within ten years, this figure had grown to 38.35 percent. The only other country that compared was Britain, which remained the leading missionary nation up to the twentieth century.[19]

The Anglo-American preponderance in missions had not escaped the attention of W. T. Stead, who noted that "the missionaries of the English-speaking
world exceed in number those of all the other Protestant nations put together."
Stead invoked a Gladstonian phrase, originally referring to Britain and its
dominions, to declare that the entire English-speaking race "may almost claim
to constitute a kind of universal Church in politics." The co-operation between
British and American missions would serve as a precursor to a compact between
the two countries. Stead observed that there were more communicants, more
native adherents, and more Sunday schools attached to churches founded by
American missionaries than those connected to institutions established by their
British counterparts. He consoled his countrymen by reminding them that the
missionaries of the British Empire, as a whole, had still raised more money in
1900 than the Americans.[20]

The primacy of the English-speaking nations was evident at the 1910 World
Missionary Conference in Edinburgh, a gathering of over twelve thousand
Protestant missionaries. Delegates represented Protestant and Anglican foreign missionary societies and, of the 1,215 official representatives, 509 were
British and 491 were North American.[21] The expanded role that American missionaries had established in the global organization of Protestant missions was
symbolized by Mott's election as chairman of the Conference. Mott used this
influential position to argue for the creation of a Continuation Committee of
the Conference under his leadership. Until it was interrupted by the outbreak of
World War I, this Continuation Committee became a de facto secretariat for the
international missionary movement.[22] It established a mechanism for continued
co-operation among the missionary societies and strengthened the association
between the two nations most committed to Mott's goal of evangelizing the
world in this generation.[23]

Mott declared to the delegates at Edinburgh that this was "a decisive hour of
Christian missions." He insisted: "Never before has there been such a conjunc-
tion of crises and of opening of doors in all parts of the world as that which char-
acterizes the present decade." Expanded railway networks enabled missionaries
to interact with millions of people in hitherto inaccessible territories. Moreover,
the vast majority of non-Christian communities were administered by Western
colonial powers or by governments less hostile to Christian missions than their
predecessors. Mott believed that these nations were on the verge of a radical
religious transformation as the traditional orders in these societies broke down.
This new situation offered great opportunities for missionaries. With greater
financial investment from their domestic constituencies, they could advance
political, educational and spiritual reform in the "Non-Christian World," and
thus introduce these people to the gospel. Such conditions also presented grave
dangers. The potential existed for hostile ideologies to fill the vacuum and mold

these societies in an image antithetical to Christian missions. In addition, Mott was concerned by the "corrupt influences of our so-called western civilization" that accompanied colonial occupation and commercial penetration of these countries, a fear increasingly shared by his British missionary counterparts.[24] Mott warned that "if the tide is not set toward Christianity during the next decade both in the Far East and the Near East, it may be turned against us in the decade following." There was an urgent necessity for missionaries to work for the triumph of Christian ideals before it was too late.[25]

The Most Remarkable Revolution

The Young Turk Revolution, which had erupted only two years before the World Missionary Conference opened, was at the forefront of many delegates' minds. At the conference's first morning session, Mott asserted, "In some respects the recent Turkish revolution has been the most remarkable which has ever taken place in any nation." He claimed, "the whole population is awake and thinking as never before;" members of different religions were fraternizing freely, and it was "clear that Turkey has set her face toward modern civilization."[26] The considerable number of ABCFM representatives present at Edinburgh shared Mott's perception. The Board's leaders and its missionaries in the Near East greeted the revolution as a "nation's sudden conversion."[27] Missionary relief at the demise of autocratic government and their excitement for the future was reflected across Ottoman society. Armenian revolutionary groups had worked with the Young Turks as part of a broad movement that re-established constitutional government and promised rights for the Empire's minority subjects.[28] Liberal-minded Armenians and Turks looked forward to greater liberties under the new political system. While some Armenian leaders, notably the Social Democratic Hunchakian Party, were suspicious of this "Young Turkey" "if it proposes to establish the rule of one nation or race over the others," the other leading faction, the Armenian Revolutionary Federation (ARF), was more hopeful. Its leader Aknuni, after returning to Constantinople from exile in August 1908, reported to his colleagues: "You cannot imagine I am to be able to write you from this city without the slightest censorship or control. After thirty-two years of silence, the city is chanting 'Freedom'; the crowds are drunk with joy."[29] From the Turkish perspective, Ahmed Emin Yalman, a journalist, recalled that "everyone was inclined to celebrate the end of the nightmare of despotism and oppression."[30] Halide Edib, a renowned Turkish author and the first female graduate of an American missionary college, declared: "There had never been a more passionate desire in the peoples of Turkey to love each other, to work for the realization of this new Turkey . . . it looked like the millennium."[31] The Ottoman Empire's

Muslim majority did not subscribe to the millenial vision of the Christian missions. Nevertheless, the ABCFM embraced the new "Ottoman nation" and, in their schools and publications, employed a secular message that advocated "modern Ottoman citizenship" to advance coexistence between all its communities.[32] As Roosevelt had celebrated in his 1909 address to the Methodists, most missionaries in the Ottoman Empire emphasized social, educational, and medical improvements over purely spiritual and religious factors. American missions in other countries, and indeed the social gospel movement in the United States itself, were engaged in similar work. Missionaries had certainly not abandoned their ultimate goal of converting non-Christians and "evangelizing the world in this generation," but they believed that social work and promoting good governance was the best way to spread the gospel.[33]

The archetype of this new trend was the ABCFM Foreign Secretary James Barton. He championed the social role of American missionaries, who, by going beyond their initial focus on saving souls, had "set in operation forces which are . . . remaking the national life of the world." For Barton, the clearest indication of this phenomenon was the profound changes occurring in the Near East. He was convinced that American missionaries and their educational institutions in the Ottoman Empire had played an important if indirect role in the revolution by teaching "men and women to think in harmony with our Western ideals and to long for a new day for Turkey herself." Barton proudly proclaimed: "If that is revolution, the missionaries have been revolutionists; if that is the privilege and function of modern education, they have been educationalists; and if it be the highest ideals of the Kingdom of God, they have been true Evangelists."[34] The Edinburgh Conference endorsed his interpretation of the ABCFM role in the Young Turk Revolution. The Conference's Anglo-American commission on Education in Relation to the Christianization of National Life declared that the ABCFM had done "more towards the settlement of the Eastern Question than the joint action of all the European powers."[35]

The line that the ABCFM had traditionally maintained between religious uplift and political involvement was becoming increasingly blurred. There were members of the American missionary community who disagreed with these departures from tradition and protested that the focus should be on evangelization rather than reorganizing native societies.[36] However, Barton was imbued with the optimism of the period and, with his belief in "progress" reaffirmed by the revolution, he was too enthused by the new developments to worry much about dissenters. Shortly after the revolution, he asserted: "Never before in the history of Moslem and Christian intercourse have believers in these two religions so drawn together and publicly demonstrated their purpose to exalt patriotism above creed and love of country above religious hatreds." If constitutional government proved successful then it would ensure the protection of Barton's former wards, the Armenians, within a larger Ottoman polity. Furthermore, if the revolution established a "free Turkey" that safeguarded missionary institutions and allowed them to proselytize with the permission and protection of the authorities, the ABCFM would have prime access to one of the most promising mission fields in the world.[37]

The hopes of the ABCFM, and the visions of Armenian and Turkish coexistence, were threatened by a counterrevolution in April 1909 that brought renewed violence against the Armenians in the Cilician region of the Ottoman Empire. Reactionaries, resentful of the prominence of Armenians and their proclaimed equality under the new regime, initiated a series of pogroms. Around twenty thousand people were murdered, the overwhelming majority being Armenians, but up to two thousand Muslims were killed in reprisals by the Armenian resistance. While local Ottoman authorities were complicit in the brutality against the Armenians, it was not clear that the Young Turk government in Constantinople was directly responsible for the massacres.[38] Moreover, evidence of Armenian revolutionaries and Young Turk leaders working together to protect the constitution, and the decision by the governing Committee of Union and Progress (CUP) to depose the sultan after the counterrevolution, convinced the ABCFM to keep faith with the new regime. Nevertheless, while missionary leaders continued to emphasize the opportunities, the 1909 massacres were an indication of the dangers that would also be present in this new revolutionary era.

Complete Political Disinterestedness

Conditions in the Near East threatened to grow more hazardous after Italy declared war on the Ottomans over Libya in 1911, followed by the Balkan Wars of 1912–1913 during which Serbia, Montenegro, Greece, and Bulgaria conquered Macedonia before clashing with each other over the spoils. After Bosnia-Herzegovina was formally annexed by Austria-Hungary and Crete was confiscated by Greece in 1908, these latest wars signaled the loss of almost all the European provinces of the Ottoman Empire. In addition, the conflicts were accompanied by the brutal cleansing of Balkan Muslims, provoking an influx of refugees into the Empire's Anatolian heartland. These conflicts signified the emergence of a more assertive Turkish nationalism. This trend became even more pronounced after the CUP, which had earlier lost electoral power to the more pluralist İtilâf party, launched an internal coup and instituted a new dictatorial government.[39] Barton had initially hoped that the Ottoman defeat in the Balkan Wars would discredit the state religion in the minds of many Muslims and encourage them to turn to Christianity.[40] Instead, many missionaries noticed a rise in anti-Christian feelings after the overthrow of the constitutional system. William Peet, the treasurer of Bible House in Constantinople, the ABCFM headquarters in the Ottoman Empire, informed Barton that the missionaries were "evidently confronted with an era of fresh opposition in the attitude of the Government, which is strongly pro-Turk and anti-foreign."[41] However, Barton remained optimistic that the opportunities continued to outweigh the dangers. He was convinced that the "Progressives [who] have been foremost in the organization of new Turkey" would ultimately prove victorious over the "fanatical Conservatives," and that this would strengthen the position of the missionaries in the Empire.[42] His confidence was enhanced by the reports he received of fellowship between the different nationalities in ABCFM institutions.[43] Barton believed that these American institutions were showcasing what "true Christianity means" in contrast to the "nominal Christian states" of the Balkans which had waged war under the banner of advancing Christendom.[44] Prominent missionary leaders were becoming convinced that evangelization was better served by adopting pacific language and tactics rather than aggression. Howard S. Bliss, the president of the Syrian Protestant College, declared: "We shall not talk about 'modern crusades'; we shall not speak of Islam as a 'challenge to faith.' Except indeed as applied to our struggle against weakness and temptations common to humanity, we shall drop the whole vocabulary of war."[45]

The ABCFM joined a number of other religious organizations, peace societies and prominent individuals, including former Ambassador Straus, in urging the Taft administration to mediate the Italo-Turkish War. Across the Atlantic, W. T. Stead was at the forefront of British efforts to arbitrate the conflict. He condemned the Italian invasion, regarding it as a threat to his own efforts to convince the great powers to advance world peace by submitting their disputes to international arbitration. Stead was unconvinced by the Young Turks but he still believed the new regime was preferable to Abdul Hamid's autocracy. He even traveled to Constantinople in October 1911 to aid the Ottomans in gaining support for mediating an end to the war.[46] However, this would be his last campaign. Stead drowned in the middle of the Atlantic Ocean in April 1912, a victim of the *Titanic*. An obituary remarked: "His grave is where he might have chosen it, midway between England and America, under the full stream of their intercourse."[47] Despite his death, Stead's ideas on an Anglo-American alliance, and his original conception of an American solution to the Armenian, and larger, Eastern question, would be kept alive during the decade that followed and his vision would resurface after US intervention in the First World War.

Stead's final voyage would have taken him to New York to address a conference on the "World's Peace" at the invitation of President Taft.[48] Even if he had reached New York it is highly unlikely he could have convinced Taft to arbitrate the conflicts in the Near East. Assistant Secretary of State Huntingdon Wilson advised the president that the region was a European sphere. Any American meddling there might offer Europeans an excuse to interfere in the Western Hemisphere.[49] Evidently, despite Roosevelt's attempts to stretch the remit of the Monroe Doctrine, the State Department continued to adhere to a conservative interpretation of that shibboleth, stressing separate spheres of influence. When the Ottoman government itself requested American mediation during the Balkan Wars, the State Department instructed its new ambassador in Constantinople, William W. Rockhill, to refuse the request.[50] The Taft administration did send two US warships to the Eastern Mediterranean, joining the Europeans in protecting their own nationals in the Near East. However, the US government was indifferent to the outcome of the conflicts. In his last annual message of December 1912, Taft announced that the United States was "involved neither directly nor indirectly with the causes or questions incident to any of these hostilities" and "maintained in regard to them an attitude of absolute neutrality and of complete political disinterestedness."[51] Despite a brief flirtation with Near Eastern affairs through his dollar diplomacy, the Taft administration reaffirmed the traditional US policy of political noninvolvement with Europe.

America's True Mission in Turkey

Taft's successor as president was the Democrat Woodrow Wilson, whose 1912 election campaign focused little on foreign policy. As an academic expert on the American political system, Wilson's studies had focused primarily on domestic policy. However, since 1898 Wilson had taken a growing interest in US foreign relations, perceiving it as a "year of transformation." Initially uncertain about US expansion, he came to celebrate Americans' willingness to become "apostles of liberty and self-government" in their overseas possessions.[52] He insisted that America had "risen to the first rank in power and resources" and its "isolation" was over.[53] Wilson did not believe the main purpose of US expansion was to serve its economic interests.[54] Accepting the Democratic nomination for governor of New Jersey in 1910, he declared: "America is not distinguished so much by its wealth and material power as by the fact that it was born with an ideal, a purpose to serve mankind."[55] This service would be its example to the rest of the world, and a selfless foreign policy would act as a beacon to other nations. As his biographer John Thompson emphasizes, Wilson had a fundamental belief "in the virtue and power of his own country" and "in the nation's historic mission to lead the world on to a higher plane."[56] Wilson envisioned an expanded role for the United States in world affairs but knew his foreign policy required domestic support to be successful. In 1890 he had written that "the ear of the leader must ring with the voices of the people," and this conviction continued to shape his conduct in office.[57]

Missionary influence in Washington appeared likely to increase under Wilson, who enjoyed strong personal ties with the movement, sharing their devout Christian faith, commitment to world service, and belief in America's beneficent example. The president was a personal friend of Mott. After declining Wilson's offer to become ambassador to China, so as not to compromise his global leadership role in the evangelical movement, Mott later accepted government appointments as a special envoy to Mexico in 1916 and on a diplomatic mission to Russia in 1917.[58] Wilson's closest personal connection to the missionary community was the New York industrialist Cleveland Dodge. Dodge's family had long been benefactors of missionary institutions. After meeting at Princeton, Dodge supported Wilson financially during his New Jersey gubernatorial campaign and made the largest contribution to his presidential campaign. Passing up a government position, Dodge maintained an informal association with the administration, hoping to advise the president on foreign matters, particularly regarding the Near East. Two of his four children were involved in missionary educational institutions there and Dodge himself was Chairman of the Board of Trustees at Robert College in Constantinople. With his background and close personal ties to the president, Dodge would help shape Wilson's perspective on the region.[59]

As president, Wilson planned to retain control over his administration's most important foreign policy decisions. William Jennings Bryan, three times the Democratic presidential nominee, was appointed secretary of state as "a purely political necessity."[60] The first Democratic president since 1897, Wilson shared Bryan's suspicion that the Republican-appointed professional diplomats they inherited were preoccupied with commercial interests rather than "moral and public considerations."[61] However, Wilson struggled to find ambassadors with the qualities he required and was forced to resort to the traditional pool of campaign contributors and party stalwarts.[62]

Wilson appointed Henry Morgenthau, chair of the Democrats' Election Finance Committee, as ambassador to the Ottoman Empire. To reward Morgenthau's loyalty, but unwilling to appoint him to the cabinet, Wilson offered him the Constantinople ambassadorship. Wilson's rationale was similar to that of Beecher in advising Straus's ministerial appointment in the 1880s. Wilson assumed that because of Morgenthau's Jewish faith, he would be attentive to an empire containing Jerusalem and coreligionists in Palestine. Wilson had little faith in the survival of the crumbling Ottoman Empire and considered the ambassadorship relatively unimportant. When Colonel Edward M. House, the president's unofficial chief adviser, suggested Morgenthau for Constantinople, Wilson quipped, "There ain't going to be no Turkey," to which House responded, "Then let him go look for it."[63] As an area of limited political interest, Wilson delegated the routine conduct of Near Eastern affairs to Bryan who, as Morgenthau observed on his appointment, "knew no more about our relations with Turkey than I did."[64] On becoming president, Wilson did not expect to have to depart from the traditional US policy of noninvolvement in the region.

Missionaries sought to ingratiate themselves with the new ambassador. Barton accompanied Morgenthau to Constantinople in November 1913, impressing on him the exceptional position that American missionaries had developed in the Ottoman Empire.[65] His counsel helped change Morgenthau's perspective. The ambassador recalled that he had "hitherto had a hazy notion that missionaries were sort of over-zealous advance agents of sectarian religion" but was now convinced that they were actually "advance agents of civilization." Soon after his arrival, in a speech to the Constantinople Chamber of Commerce, Morgenthau proclaimed that America's commercial interest in the region was "small" and its "true mission in Turkey . . . was to foster the permanent civilizing work of the Christian missions."[66] ABCFM representatives were delighted. After another speech, Peet excitedly wrote to Barton that Morgenthau had paid a "high compliment" to American missionary work by stating, "that while the business of Turkey is being parcelled out among the several European Nations . . . it has been left to America to do the work of education in Turkey!" Missionaries were convinced that the new ambassador was committed to advancing their interests.[67]

The Board's leaders were particularly grateful for increased support from the US embassy as they discerned growing hostility from Ottoman authorities toward missionary institutions, as well as Christians and foreigners in general.[68] Amid heightened tensions between Muslims and Christians in Anatolia, Armenian leaders appealed to the principal European powers to ensure the implementation of reforms guaranteed by the 1878 Berlin Treaty. The Ottoman government was forced to sign a reform plan by the European powers in February 1914. This program, authored by Russia and substantially revised under German pressure, established two zones out of the provinces with large Armenian populations in Eastern Anatolia and Trebizond on the Black Sea coast, each administered by two European inspectors selected from neutral nations and approved by the Ottomans. Leading CUP figures took a dim view of Armenian requests for outside intervention, particularly as these appeals came in the immediate aftermath of the Empire's defeat in the Balkan Wars, in which the powers evinced little concern about violence against Muslims. The Ottomans denounced the Armenians reform proposals as an invitation for Russian invasion.[69] The following month, Peet reported to Barton that "the race feeling, especially between the Turks and Christians, is running at the present time on a pretty high key" and "the anti-foreign feeling on the part of the Turk is specially strong."[70]

The disturbed conditions in the Near East were a precursor to the complete destabilization of the European balance of power that summer. In August 1914, Mott alerted Americans to the urgent need to press ahead with global evangelization, warning: "We are living in the most dangerous time in the history of the world."[71] That same month, World War I engulfed Europe.

The Eastern Question Is Now Before Us For Solution

At the outbreak of hostilities the Wilson administration immediately declared neutrality, seeking to maintain cordial relations with both the Entente and Central Powers. In doing so, the president was respecting America's traditional noninvolvement in European affairs and pursuing a policy consonant with his own political objectives. In 1914, there was no question of the United States involving itself in the war; the American people had no desire to become entangled in European affairs, particularly when no national interests appeared at stake. Wilson needed to ensure his policy would command popular support if he was to win re-election in 1916. His 1912 victory was secured without an overall majority in the popular vote.[72] Wilson's concept of neutrality was also intended to "preserve the foundations on which peace may be rebuilt."[73] He therefore urged Americans to be "impartial in thought as well as in action" so that when the time came, the United States could fulfil its "duty as the one great nation at peace, the one people holding itself ready to play a part of impartial mediation and speak the counsels of peace and accommodation, not as a partisan, but as a friend."[74]

The Ottoman Empire also proclaimed neutrality when the war broke out. However, American missionaries in the Near East were immediately affected by the conflict. That summer, there were bank runs and asset crashes in countries around the world. Almost every international stock exchange was closed throughout August and the London Stock Exchange, the center of the global financial system, remained shut for five months. Business operations across Europe ground to a standstill.[75] In Constantinople the banks had immediately declared and maintained a moratorium, preventing the secure transfer of funds from the ABCFM's financial bases in the United States to its missionaries in the Empire. In addition, the Board's treasurer in Constantinople William Peet was cut off from his principal financial reserves in London. Even the balances to his foreign credit were useless as no one was prepared to accept bank bills or cheques under such uncertainty. While every international business house and bank in Constantinople was affected by the breakdown in international transactions, missionary operations were particularly crippled. When the war began, the ABCFM employed 151 missionaries, assisted by 1,200 local workers, and ran nine hospitals, eight colleges, forty-six secondary schools, 369 elementary schools, and 137 organized native churches. No other group had so many dependent individuals or institutions in such far-flung provinces. Morgenthau furnished some funds that enabled Peet to meet the immediate crisis. More sustained relief over the coming months was provided by local agents of Rockefeller's Standard Oil Company, who transmitted funds by cable from the United States until gold became more easily attainable.[76] The close relations that the ABCFM had established with the US government and private capitalists helped see them through the crisis and strengthened the bonds between them. Amid the financial turmoil, Peet observed that the Ottoman Empire "though nominally neutral is rapidly mobilizing her forces and this mobilization exceeds anything we have ever known before." He informed Barton that the "real contest with which we are now confronted is one between England and Germany on the question of the hegemony of Europe," and consequently "the eastern question . . . is now before us for solution."[77]

Leading Young Turks sought to exploit the international instability to improve the Empire's strategic position and consolidate their own power. Convinced that the Empire required a powerful European ally to ensure its survival, they had explored alliances with a number of great powers prior to July 1914, even reaching out to Russia, but with little success. However, they seized the initiative during the European crisis and secured a secret alliance with Germany in early August.[78] On September 27 they closed the Dardanelles straits, blockading the Russian fleet, though not before allowing two German cruisers into the Black Sea. The United States and the Allied powers protested this closure without success.[79] Following the Ottoman declaration of war against the Entente on October 30, a proclamation of jihad was issued throughout the Empire. Morgenthau warned the imperial authorities that violence against non-Muslims would impair Ottoman–American relations and might even lead to the United States siding with the Entente.[80] The State Department cautioned Morgenthau not to threaten US entry in the war.[81] The administration was unwilling to compromise neutrality by interfering in Ottoman internal policy.

Although neutrality remained official American policy, anti-Ottoman sentiment, engendered by the earlier Armenian massacres, endured. Ahmed Rustem, the Ottoman ambassador to Washington, denounced the hostility of the American press and public in an interview with the *Washington Evening Star*. He accused Americans of hypocrisy for condemning the Ottomans over their treatment of the Armenians while ignoring the crimes committed by France in Algeria and Britain in India as well as America's own lynching culture and its abuses in the Philippines. Explaining his conduct to Secretary Bryan, Rustem complained, "Turkey has been the object of systematic attacks on the part of the press of the United States," and public opinion "poisoned . . . to such an extent that a member of that race is seldom thought of or spoken of otherwise than as the 'unspeakable.'" Rustem claimed the Armenian massacres were "an inextinguishable theme of violent denunciation of [Turkey]."[82] The State Department offered Rustem the chance to apologize, but he refused and asked his government to relieve him.[83] His outburst was not unfounded. In January 1915, a *New York Times* opinion piece titled "How Turkish Empire Should Be Made Over After the War" dismissed the Turks as "sensuous, lustful, indolent, deceitful and incorrigible."[84] American opinion remained hostile to the Ottomans despite official neutrality.

New Crimes Against Humanity and Civilization

For the CUP leaders, the Ottoman entry into the war provided an opportunity to assert greater control over the Empire's territory and to reduce the influence of foreign forces. The Franco-British-dominated Ottoman Public Debt Administration was abolished as the CUP sought to regain control over the Empire's fiscal policy. The government canceled the Armenian reform plan and abrogated the capitulations, which provided foreigners with economic privileges within the Empire and exempted them from trial in Ottoman courts.[85] Morgenthau joined the Allies in protesting the illegality of the unilateral repudiation of these concessions, but to no avail. Unwilling to compromise neutrality, the State Department advised the ambassador against pressing the issue after Ottoman officials assured Morgenthau that they had no intention of interfering with American missionary activity or commercial operations.[86] While trade with the Ottomans was relatively inconsequential for Americans, the United States accounted for 23 percent of all Ottoman exports by 1914.[87] Unwilling to damage relations with a significant trade partner and one that was also the most powerful noncombatant, Ottoman leaders informed Morgenthau that they regarded the United States as the "only great power with no ulterior motive toward them" and promised to protect the privileged position of its citizens.[88]

Despite these assurances, the missionaries soon found their institutions subjected to heavier taxes and their mail censored.[89] For some time, they were even forbidden from corresponding in English after it was outlawed as a language of the Empire's enemies. Morgenthau's intercession led the Ottoman authorities to issue an edict giving full permission for use of the "American language."[90] Grateful for the ambassador's support, the missionaries adjusted themselves to the new conditions. As the war consumed Ottoman society, the missionaries found opportunities amidst the dangers. At the beginning of 1915, the ABCFM reported to its members that attendance at mission schools and churches in the Empire was up on previous years. In particular, it claimed the number of Muslims attending mission schools was "unprecedented." Board leaders attributed this phenomenon, in part, to a feeling among parents that missionary institutions were the safest place for their children. Above all, however, they suggested that evangelical work had received a "new impulse" as "the fear of some pending disaster seemed to drive the people closer to God." In spite of the hardships of wartime conditions, the majority of the missionaries decided to stay in order to maintain their present operations and possibly use the new circumstances to expand their field.[91]

Following the departure of the Entente ambassadors, Morgenthau remained the only ambassador of a major power not aligned with the Empire represented at the Porte. In early 1915, the Allies launched the Dardanelles campaign to neutralize the Ottomans and capture Constantinople. However, the campaign failed in March, as did the subsequent assault on the Gallipoli peninsula.[92] Morgenthau feared the withdrawal of the Allied fleet from the Dardanelles would awaken Ottoman ethno-nationalism and lead to renewed Armenian massacres.[93] The Armenians were spread across the mountainous border territory between Russia and the Ottoman Empire, which witnessed some of the heaviest fighting on the Eastern Front. The tsar's emissaries had urged Ottoman Armenians to join their Russian brothers in a war of liberation against Islam. Even though the vast majority of Ottoman Armenians were loyal to the Ottomans and many fought alongside them against the Russians, Young Turk leaders feared a potential fifth column and this was heightened in early 1915 after a major defeat on the Caucasian front at Sarikamish, which they blamed on Armenian perfidy.[94]

In April, Morgenthau learned of atrocities against Armenian civilians following their deportation from areas in Anatolia close to the fighting and cabled Bryan about these events.[95] With the secretary's approval, he urged Ottoman authorities to protect the Armenians and joined the Italian ambassador in protesting to the Porte.[96] On May 24, the Entente powers asked for Morgenthau to deliver a public threat on their behalf: those culpable for "these new crimes of Turkey against humanity and civilization" would be held "personally responsible." Bryan forwarded the declaration to Morgenthau but the Wilson administration did not issue its own protest.[97] The Entente was already at war with the Ottomans but the United States remained neutral. An official government protest to a German ally over treatment of its own subjects would have undermined the US position as a neutral nation.

The Entente threat made the front page of the New York Times, but the attention of the country and Wilson was focused on the sinking of the Lusitania and the 1,200 lives lost, including 128 Americans, on May 7.[98] Neutrality still had public support, but pressure was mounting for the president to affirm American rights and issue a strong protest. On May 13 Wilson sent a diplomatic note to Berlin, demanding disavowal of the sinking, reparations for the casualties, and an end to submarine warfare against passenger and merchant ships. Germany's response that the Lusitania was armed and a legitimate target prompted a second note on June 9 reaffirming the demands. Believing that Wilson's response was inconsistent with neutrality and dangerously inflammatory, Bryan refused to sign the second note and resigned. For Wilson, his response had been a matter of American honor; American lives had been lost and the nation's neutral rights challenged. He received broad support from an American public that demanded its government uphold the nation's prestige while keeping it out of the conflict. Nevertheless, while Wilson remained hopeful that he could satisfy the public's "double wish," his language raised the possibility of US intervention in the war if Germany did not adhere to America's demands. On this occasion, after a third note and private pressure from the Wilson administration, Germany agreed to issue a pledge abandoning and repudiating submarine warfare against passenger ships.[99]

With Wilson's attention on events in the Atlantic, it was the new Secretary of State Robert Lansing who shaped the administration's response to Morgenthau's increasingly frantic warnings that "persecutions of Armenians [were] assuming unprecedented proportions." The ambassador reported that his own "unofficial efforts" with the Young Turk leaders had "failed to dissuade them [from] their course which they attempt to justify on the ground of military necessity." Informed by Ottoman authorities that he had no right to interfere in internal affairs, he beseeched the State Department for instructions.[100] Lansing had some sympathy for the Ottoman justification. In a personal memorandum titled "Cruel and Inhuman Acts of War," written the day after the Entente threat, Lansing wrote, "No nation at war, whose national safety is menaced, will permit or should be expected to permit obligations of justice, morality, or honour to interfere with acts which it considers necessary for its self-preservation."[101] House observed, "Lansing believes that almost any form of atrocity is permissible provided a nation's safety is involved."[102] Lansing adhered to a legalistic definition of sovereignty; the US government was obligated to protect American citizens but its purview did not extend to safeguarding other nationalities. His principal concern was whether any native-born or naturalized American citizens had been injured. As he had received no such reports, he informed Morgenthau that the Department could offer no additional suggestions and he should continue with his own unofficial efforts.[103] When Barton forwarded his concern on behalf of the ABCFM, Lansing replied he was doing all he could to pressure the Ottomans, but the Ottoman government claimed it was only taking action "necessary for its own protection against the members of this race."[104] With the president preoccupied with the German threat, and Lansing overseeing Near Eastern affairs, it was the secretary's opinion that was relayed to Morgenthau and Barton.

Massacres and deportations were now taking place all over the Armenian provinces, with many dying of starvation and disease. Morgenthau continued to report on the escalating violence throughout 1915, asking Lansing "to give the matter urgent and exhaustive consideration," with a view to checking Ottoman policy.[105] Morgenthau asked the German ambassador to appeal to the Ottomans but, although a German protest was made, the violence continued.[106] Morgenthau was frustrated by his powerlessness but recognized that "nothing short of force, which obviously the United States is not in a position to exert, would adequately meet the situation." He had accepted the United States must abide by the principles of sovereignty and "unless it directly affected American lives and American interests, it was outside the concern of the American government." Morgenthau even suggested that protests and threats might worsen the situation, as they would "probably incite the Ottoman government to more drastic measures."[107] However, with Armenians still dying in great numbers, the issue of relief became his most pressing concern and the only practical way to improve the situation.

As the leaders of the American Red Cross (ARC) had taken responsibility for distributing aid during the massacres of the 1890s, Armenian American organizations approached the organization to undertake the task again. Writing to the ARC secretary, Mabel T. Boardman, one Armenian American leader declared that Armenians "want to feel that humanity has not forsaken them in their crosses of martyrdom" and "particularly look towards the American noble and great nation, whose former salutary assistance they remember with the warmest gratitude." However, Boardman was forced to respond that the ARC was "simply overwhelmed with the suffering that seems to prevail throughout the world" and had decided to focus on providing relief for combatants, leaving the responsibility for aiding noncombatants to other organizations.[108] As the chairman of the Constantinople chapter of the ARC, Morgenthau was aware of the pressures and constraint on the organization. Through the State Department, he asked his influential friends, including Dodge and Barton, to form a committee to raise funds for Armenian relief.[109] Morgenthau also offered to arrange for the emigration of thousands of Armenians to the United States if sufficient resources were made available.[110] While the emigration plan did not ultimately materialize, in September 1915 the Committee on Armenian Atrocities was founded and quickly raised $100,000.[111] To meet the growing need for relief the Committee expanded, incorporating nearly every Protestant group in the Near East and changing its name to the American Committee for Armenian and Syrian Relief (ACASR).[112] In 1916 donations totalled over two million dollars, and this amount doubled in 1917.[113] With James L. Barton chairing this new organization, the connection between the missionary movement and Armenian relief was clear. The presence on the Committee of Dodge and Charles Crane, another major contributor to Wilson's election campaign and benefactor of Near East educational institutions, is further evidence of its missionary links and influential political connections.[114] The Committee received access to confidential

State Department communications. Drawing on the ties that the missionary movement had forged before the war, the group also received substantial financial backing from the Rockefeller Foundation. Since the Committee's main objective was to raise money for relief, it remained politically neutral and did not call for the United States to make an official protest over the massacres.[115] As Dodge confided to Barton, "It is of course a most difficult problem for our Government to handle, but I feel they are doing all they can wisely do under the circumstances."[116]

To raise awareness and relief, the ACASR prepared communiqués for the press, reinforcing the image of the unspeakable Turk of the 1890s.[117] The *New York Times* ran 145 articles on Armenia in 1915 alone, featuring titles such as "A Policy of Extermination" and "Slain in Cold Blood in Asia Minor."[118] Recalling the earlier massacres, one editorial stated that the perpetrators of these previous crimes "now assume an aspect of moderation compared with those of the present Governors of Turkey."[119] Indeed, newspapers and journals across the country publicized the massacres, with even small town publications embracing the issue. The *Montevideo Leader* disclosed, "One of the most horrible things connected with the war, is the wholesale massacres of Armenian Christians," while the *Red Wing Daily Republican* declared the Turks are planning "to end the Armenian problem by ending the Armenians."[120] Coverage was conspicuous for the same religious and Social Darwinist tone as in the 1890s. A headline in the *Los Angeles Times* read "Crucifixion is Revived," and *The Independent* asserted that the Armenians were an "ancient and proud people, Christian in its religion, and eager for progress."[121] Religious organs such as the *Christian Science Monitor* also brought the plight of Armenians to public attention, as they had in the 1890s. Armenia was presented as a symbol of Christian civilization, an image that resonated with both secular and religious readers.

As Barton intended, there was a widespread public response. Religious and civic organizations across the country staged mass meetings and petitioned Washington to extend aid.[122] Armenian Americans made their own appeals. Thousands had fled to America after the earlier massacres; although there had been only two thousand Armenian immigrants in America before 1895, the Armenian American population of 1915 numbered some one hundred thousand.[123] This was insufficient to afford the community much political influence, but American legislators responded to the public mood. Republican Congressman Richard Austin of Tennessee was just one of the representatives who protested to the State Department that it was "in harmony with the noble traditions of the Land of the Free to raise its voice" and prevent "the extinction of a whole people."[124]

The president and his advisers were not immune to the public outrage. As early as October 1915, Colonel House had written to Wilson speculating "whether

Figure 3.1 Campaign Poster of the American Committee for Relief in the Near East. Library of Congress, LC-USZC4-1343.

this Government should not make some sort of protest over the Armenian massacres."[125] They do not appear to have discussed this further and, in a letter to Morgenthau soon after, the president praised the ambassador for his performance under difficult circumstances but added, "I have nothing special to write about."[126] Wilson, however, shared the people's sympathy. In response to the appeals of a prominent Armenian American, Wilson affirmed his "deep interest in the whole subject" and pledged his administration would continue to use its influence to aid the Armenians.[127] When a former Princeton classmate serving as a Near Eastern missionary sent him a firsthand account of the massacres, Wilson replied that the situation was "nothing less than appalling" and the government had been doing "everything diplomatically possible to check the terrible business."[128] Morgenthau's dispatches left Wilson "sick at heart," and at the request of Congress and the missionary lobby he designated two official relief days for the people of the Near East.[129] However, he did not believe there was anything the government could do beyond facilitating relief. He was not prepared to issue a public protest to one of the Central Powers and risk inciting further massacres. It could also undermine American neutrality.

Lansing, too, recognized the extent of public outrage.[130] In response to the weight of protests, he generated a form letter for the White House to distribute to those requesting information. This stated the government would "continue to use [its] good offices, to the fullest extent consistent with the position of the United States as a neutral country, in behalf of the Armenians in the Turkish Empire."[131] Lansing warned the Ottomans that their persecution of the Armenians was "increasing the horror and indignation which the people of this country feel."[132] On February 16, 1916, he felt compelled to send a note to the German ambassador to Washington, Count von Bernstorff, to appeal on behalf of the Armenians.[133] With a presidential election looming, Lansing was anxious to contain public pressure on the government. He cautioned Morgenthau not to publicize the matter on his return to America "in view of the international situation" and warned him to avoid newspaper reporters, "who may misrepresent you" with "unhappy results."[134] Lansing was not completely insensitive to Armenian suffering, but he feared that responding to public pressure might force America into a diplomatic dispute that would be inimical to American interests.[135]

Going to War For Humanity's Sake?

Although neutrality still enjoyed majority support, Theodore Roosevelt had long denounced Germany's "breach of international morality" in invading Belgium and had campaigned for military preparedness for war.[136] In his first extended public meditation on the conflict in September 1914, Roosevelt returned to the subject of a "righteous" war and the Armenian massacres of the 1890s as he took issue with Wilson's policy of neutrality, which he regarded as ethically dishonorable. Just as there was little "value in the 'peace' which was obtained by the concert of European powers when they prevented interference with Turkey [in 1894–1896] while the Turks butchered some hundreds of thousands of Armenian men, women and children," there was nothing moral about "a neutrality so strict as to forbid our even whispering a protest against wrong-doing, lest such whispers might cause disturbance to our ease and well-being."[137] Roosevelt quickly came to identify with the Allied cause. He wrote to a British friend that he wished he and his four sons "would now be in an army getting ready to serve with you in Flanders or else to serve against Constantinople."[138] The sinking of the *Lusitania* only strengthened his belief that the United States must challenge Germany and its allies.[139]

When the Armenian massacres began in 1915, Roosevelt wrote an open letter to the Committee on Armenian Atrocities that was published in the *New York Times*. He declared: "If this people through its government had not shirked its duty . . . in connection with the world war for the last sixteen months, we should now be able to take effective action on behalf of Armenia."[140] It is not clear what Roosevelt meant by "effective action"—diplomatic or military—but it would seem he genuinely believed that the US government had a duty to the Armenians, which it had refused to fulfil because of neutrality. Roosevelt charged that failure to make an effective protest over Germany's invasion of Belgium now prevented action in response to the "crowning iniquity of the wholesale slaughter of the Armenians."[141]

Roosevelt may well have been using the opportunity to criticize the policy of Wilson, the man who had defeated his third party presidential challenge in 1912, but he knew he did not represent majority sentiment in his opposition to neutrality.[142] Senator Henry Cabot Lodge, Roosevelt's political ally and fellow advocate of preparedness, denounced the "evil plight" of the Armenians and proposed legislation to raise funds for Armenian relief. However, he did not publicly call for America to act on the atrocities or blame neutrality for a failure to do so, despite the large Armenian American population in his home state of Massachusetts and a long-held commitment to their security.[143] Nor would it appear that Roosevelt was merely adopting the Armenians as a new popular cause out of political expediency; although he would have been aware of the extent of public sympathy, he had consistently railed against the oppression of the Armenians. He dismissed "the professional pacifists and praisers of neutrality" who "have ventured to form committees and speak about—not act about—the 'Armenian atrocities.' "[144] Roosevelt was aware that missionary leaders were prominent on those committees. He regarded their conduct as unChristian and declared: "If this nation had feared God it would have stood up for the Belgians and Armenians." Instead, those opponents of war, including the missionaries, who were unwilling "to denounce and antagonize the wrongdoer," be it the Germans or Ottomans, became "not merely passive, but active agents of the devil." Roosevelt had looked to the missionaries to help provide a solution to the Armenian question while formal government intervention was not possible. However, he now believed that by endorsing neutrality, in the face of the latest and most brutal atrocities, the missionary lobby had enabled those crimes and prevented America from "righting the wrongs of the Armenians." For the rest of the war, he would attack Wilson and his missionary supporters for America's failure to do its "duty by Armenia."[145]

For Morgenthau, his own "failure to stop the destruction of the Armenians" had made Turkey "a place of horror." He was convinced only the "moral power of the United States" could save the Armenians, and only President Wilson could exercise that power. Morgenthau left Constantinople in early 1916 and returned to work for Wilson's re-election.[146] On his visit to Washington, the day after he arrived home, he noted Wilson talked "at some length about the Armenian matters, and said that if necessary Americans should go to war for humanity's sake." Unlike Roosevelt, Wilson did not believe the Armenian massacres made this a necessity and there is no evidence they explored this further at the meeting.[147] The president approved Morgenthau's recommendation that a Jewish lawyer, Abram Elkus, be his replacement.[148] In the interim period, Hoffman Philip, the US chargé d'affaires, advised the State Department that the only effective policy in the face of ongoing deportations and massacres was to threaten to withdraw diplomatic representation from "a country where such barbarous methods are . . . carried out by order of the existing government."[149] On his arrival in Constantinople in September 1916, Elkus reported that the Young Turks were continuing an "unchecked policy of extermination through starvation, exhaustion and brutality of treatment hardly surpassed even in Turkish history" and suggested the president publicly appeal to the leaders of Germany and Austria-Hungary to restrain their ally.[150] The State Department rejected all suggestions. Lansing saw no reason to break relations over an Ottoman internal policy and was confident the administration had done all it could, or should, within diplomatic protocol, to stop the massacres.

Lewis Einstein, a career diplomat at the Constantinople embassy, felt the United States could and should have done more. In 1913 Einstein had published an article anonymously in an English magazine (after it was rejected by numerous American publications) that a major war was imminent, and that US security was dependent upon a British victory and a favorable European balance of power.[151] These views had little influence on the incoming Wilson administration, and Einstein was not considered for diplomatic service until his posting to Constantinople in early 1915. Einstein had previously resided at the Constantinople embassy during the Young Turk revolution and was optimistic about a "regenerated Turkey," but the German-dominated Empire he found on his return in 1915 disappointed him. He perceived it as little more than a vassal state and characterized the policy of the Young Turk leaders as "Deutschland über Allah."[152] When the Armenian massacres broke out soon after Einstein's arrival in the Empire, he, like Roosevelt, advocated direct and immediate intervention. Roosevelt was a family friend of Einstein and had given the young diplomat his first appointment in 1903. Both men believed that Wilson's response to the Armenian question was utterly inadequate. Einstein shared Roosevelt's opinion that the Armenian massacres were the "crowning" horror of the war and the missionaries, despite their previous good work in the Empire, were impediments to American action. While Einstein did not think that official US protests could stop the massacres, he believed that US–Ottoman relations should be terminated, and the reasons publicized to the world, "instead of carrying on friendly relations with a government of murderers."[153]

Einstein and Roosevelt were both passionate believers in the Allied cause and ardent defenders of the Armenians. However, neither was in a position to act on their views. Roosevelt privately confessed to the British Foreign Secretary Sir Edward Grey in early 1915, "I have no influence whatever in shaping public action and, as I have reason to believe, very little influence indeed in shaping public opinion."[154] In Constantinople, Einstein resembled a "telephone operator," passing on messages "to a central exchange, which in our case was the State Department." He "felt an inward rage at one's powerlessness."[155] Despite their sense of impotence, Roosevelt and Einstein offered an alternative solution to the Armenian question to that of Wilson and the missionaries, which would come into conflict with America's entry into the war.

British propaganda and American opinion

In Britain, Gladstone's example had continued to inspire liberals to take up the Armenian cause in the years after the 1894–1896 Armenian massacres. A number of his former admirers had established the Balkan Committee in 1902–1903, and after the Balkan Wars of 1912–1913 this group turned their attention to Armenia. The British Armenian Committee was established to lobby for the enforcement of Article 61 of the Berlin Treaty. Led by a group of prominent MPs, it sought to exert pressure on government policy through personal contacts with ministers, parliamentary addresses, and articles in elite publications.[156] Prior to 1914, Herbert Asquith's Liberal government listened politely to the committee's representations but took little action. While Asquith and Foreign Secretary Edward Grey both shared Gladstone's hostility to the Ottomans, the Cabinet regarded the maintenance of Ottoman rule in Asia Minor as the "only safe policy." Britain's government was unwilling to interfere in Ottoman internal affairs, save in the most limited manner, lest it lead to the Empire collapsing in "anarchy and confusion" and cause a European conflict over the spoils.[157] However, when war came in 1914 and the Ottomans joined the Central Powers, the Cabinet resolved to "abandon the formula of 'Ottoman integrity,' whether in Europe or Asia."[158] Asquith and Chancellor of the Exchequer, David Lloyd George, publicly committed the government to overthrowing Ottoman dominion on both continents.[159] In order to galvanize the British war effort, the government encouraged the vilification of the Central Powers and worked closely with British Armenophiles to publicize Ottoman misgovernment. Exposing Ottoman oppression could also convince Muslim subjects of the British Empire, drafted to fight against their coreligionists in the Near East, that the war was being waged against the Porte's misrule rather than against Islam itself. Above all, the British government hoped revelations of Ottoman tyranny would win over neutral opinion in the United States.[160]

When the massacres and deportations of Armenians began in 1915, there was a nationwide relief effort akin to the American one, albeit smaller in scale. The Armenian Refugees (Lord Mayor's) Fund was set up in October 1915, and the British Armenian Committee was active in relief operations.[161] The evangelical revival of the late nineteenth century had stimulated Christian compassion for the Armenians and British church organizations were active in raising funds. Even amidst the carnage of the war, the Archbishop of Canterbury declared that the massacres in the Ottoman Empire were unparalleled in "scale and horror" and urged generous donations.[162] Throughout the British Empire, the renewed massacres were used as evidence of the justness of the Allied cause and the barbarity of its enemies. Despite limited evidence, British propaganda particularly blamed Germany, charging German authorities with instigating the atrocities and condoning the massacres by not doing enough to restrain their ally. Allied publicists built on longstanding accusations of Germany's malign influence at the Porte, widely circulated during the Hamidian massacres, and further encouraged after construction of the Berlin-Baghdad railway.[163] British imperial officials and journalists sought to demonstrate that only an Allied victory could ensure the security and independence of the Armenians.[164]

These same arguments were employed to convince Americans and their government of the essential righteousness of the Allied war effort.[165] The Allies were increasingly dependent on the United States for munitions, food, shipping, and money. Correspondingly, there was growing American anger at Britain's blockade of neutral ships suspected of carrying goods to the Central Powers and British censorship of cable and mail correspondence, felt not least by Wilson himself. In addition, Russian forces had committed atrocities against Jews when retreating across the Polish-Lithuanian frontier in the spring of 1915; advancing German troops had ensured that American journalists were informed and "lurid" accounts were published in the American press.[166] Therefore, to justify Britain's blockade, ensure continued American economic support, and redirect attention to the crimes of its enemies, the British government publicized the Armenian atrocities in the United States.

As soon as confirmation was received in September 1915 that accounts of Armenian persecution were not exaggerated, the Parliamentary Secretary of Foreign Affairs Lord Robert Cecil wrote to his colleagues: "This should be published—for U.S."[167] Whenever the Foreign Office received pictorial evidence or fresh reports of massacres, it was suggested that "good use might be made of them in America."[168] Foreign Office officials cultivated relations with A. Harvey Bathurst, the European editor of the *Christian Science Monitor*, and provided him with graphic accounts of the massacres.[169] British diplomats in the United States informed London that the massacres were receiving extensive coverage in the American press. When Roosevelt's letter to the Committee on Armenian Atrocities was published in the *New York Times*, his old friend Cecil Spring Rice, British ambassador in Washington, passed it on to the Foreign Office. Spring Rice informed his superiors that US intervention with the Ottomans was unlikely unless its missionaries were seriously endangered. Nevertheless, he suggested that Britain should build on Roosevelt's indignation, and the sympathy for the Armenians represented by the ACASR, to ensure public hostility to the Central Powers continued to grow.[170]

The Viscount and the Missionaries

Spring Rice reported to the Foreign Office in October 1915 that a statement by his predecessor Viscount James Bryce condemning the Armenian atrocities had attracted "very great attention."[171] As the author of *The American Commonwealth*, Bryce was widely respected in the United States. Foreign Secretary Grey recalled that "we used to hear it said, in days when Bryce was ambassador at Washington, that he was the most popular European in America since Lafayette."[172] He had previously appointed Bryce to act as Chairman of a Royal Commission on German conduct in Belgium and its report helped convince many Americans of the occupation's brutality.[173] Grey also knew that the former ambassador had a longstanding interest in the Armenian, and larger Eastern, question. Bryce had championed the cause of Eastern Christians since taking a prominent part in the Bulgarian agitations in 1876.[174] That same year he developed an attachment to the Armenians after a trip to Transcaucasia during which he became the first European to climb Mount Ararat.[175] He subsequently established the Anglo-Armenian Society and became the most internationally renowned supporter of the Armenian cause.[176] When the Hamidian massacres occurred, Bryce had appealed for relief and enforcement of the Berlin Treaty.[177] He denounced Ottoman "maladministration" but suggested the European powers were also morally responsible because they had insisted on treating the Empire as a "civilized state" with which it could engage in diplomatic intercourse to improve Armenian welfare.[178] However, the massacres were proof to Bryce that the Ottoman government "deserves to die." He reflected that the British government protests were ineffectual, as the other European powers, suspecting British motives, provided little support.[179]

Despairing of a united European response, Bryce sought to use his celebrity status to impress on the Americans that they had a "special reason, over and above their quick responsiveness to sentiments of humanity, for feeling a warm interest in the condition of the Armenian Christians." This exceptional rationale was that "nearly everything which has been done for these ancient seats of Christianity by modern Christian nations has been done by American missionaries."[180] Bryce had developed close relations with ABCFM leaders, and when the deportations and massacres began in 1915, he received firsthand reports from the missionaries that he passed to the Foreign Office.[181] Consequently, Grey commissioned Bryce and Oxford historian Arnold Toynbee, an active member of the British Armenian Committee and a wartime intelligence analyst in Whitehall, to produce an edited account of eyewitness reports. It was published in late 1916 and Bryce's authority assured Americans of its authenticity.[182]

Over half the documents in Bryce's book came to American mission boards from Armenian refugees and other witnesses. Nevertheless, Barton remained unwilling to compromise missionary operations in the Ottoman Empire and asked Bryce and Toynbee to avoid publishing "anything that could give any indication of [a document's] source."[183] Barton hoped Bryce's report would encourage greater American support for relief work. He ordered three thousand copies, ensuring that Wilson, House, and every Congressman received one, and a three-page excerpt appeared in the *New York Times*.[184] Barton had another purpose for distributing the report so widely and to so many high officials, one that he shared with Bryce. Both men believed that the wartime massacres provided the final confirmation of Ottoman incapacity to govern non-Muslims. Bryce and Barton shared the hope that Ottoman rule was "forever extinct in the Armenian Provinces." They wanted to spread this idea as widely as possible on both sides of the Atlantic.[185] If the Ottomans were not going to control the Empire's Armenian provinces, then there remained the question of who would. Through his contacts with the Liberal government, Bryce was aware of the secret wartime Sykes-Picot Agreement whereby Britain, France, and Russia agreed to divide up the Ottoman Empire in the event of an Allied victory, with the Armenian provinces split between the French and the Russians. Bryce was satisfied that no part of Armenia would remain under Ottoman rule. He confided to his friends on the British Armenian Committee and contacts in the Armenian diaspora, who had heard rumors of the agreement, that they would be in a better position to insist on greater autonomy for a united Armenia once the war was won and the security of the Armenians ensured.[186]

The missionaries' own solution to the Armenian question was evolving. The Ottoman entry into the conflict and the unprecedented scale of the wartime atrocities had ended any hope of establishing a stable, independent Ottoman state based on a constitutional system of government. As early as June 1915, Barton had written to Bryce that the Armenians should not be subject to Ottoman rule after the war. Following the massacres, Barton declared: "The Turk has demonstrated his lack of capacity to govern even Mohammedans with a fair degree of justice, to say nothing of his absolute inability to rule righteously over any races not Mohammedan." The missionary vision of Armenians and Turks coexisting under the Young Turk regime was well and truly over. Nevertheless, based on his experience as a missionary in the Ottoman Empire and his contacts there, Barton was convinced that the Armenians could not yet become self-governing, "owing to the lack of unity and experience, in the presence of so large a number of alien people." Instead, Barton was convinced that only an outside power could provide the "righteous administration [that] would command the loyal allegiance not only of the Armenians but of nearly if not quite all races ... [who] are heartily sick of the disorder of the last generation and would welcome and support any government that promised them a rule of law and order." With international supervision, Barton was confident that an "autonomous Armenia" could be established within five years.[187] It was not entirely clear from his recommendations who would be responsible for administering this territory. Nor was it evident whether the occupying power's jurisdiction would be confined to the provinces where the Armenians were collected or would extend over the entire Ottoman Empire. As the war continued, Barton's ideas on the nature of that protectorate would continue to develop. What remained constant, however, was the belief that any permanent solution to the Armenian question depended on postwar intervention from an external power.

As Barton and the rest of the Board's leaders gathered for their annual conference in October 1916, the two sides in Europe were still deadlocked and the future control of the Near East hung in the balance. Regardless of how the Ottoman Empire was reorganized after the war, the missionaries were convinced that "in that center of Islam, the American Board has an opportunity which it has not faced in all the century of its history." A number of factors gave them encouragement. The failure of many Muslims in the Ottoman Empire, or indeed elsewhere in the Islamic world, to heed the call for a Holy War was taken as evidence that "the solidarity of Mohammedanism seems to be broken . . . and the two hundred millions of Mohammedans of the world are groping for leadership." The Board's leaders believed that Christianity was primed to assume this role, and the continued high attendance of Muslim pupils in missionary schools was evidence of this. Furthermore, they felt that the "willingness of many American missionaries to remain at their posts in the midst of unparalleled hardships had done more to reveal to Muslims what Christianity stands [for] than a generation of preaching." The ABCFM retained the largest mission field in Asia Minor, having preserved its position despite the challenges posed by the war. The Board's leaders were confident that when the postwar conference met to settle the future

of the Empire, "America will be represented . . . and [its] missionary institutions will be amply safeguarded for all time to come."[188] With its position in the
Near East secured, the missionary leadership was confident that it would also
have the support of the US government and their British friends, like Bryce, for
reconstructing the Ottoman Empire and resolving the Armenian question. The
missionaries' solution, therefore, also involved a close association with Britain,
albeit more pacific and less public in nature than the one that Roosevelt desired.

Toward a Wilsonian Solution

While the Board's leaders were assembled, Wilson was preoccupied with his
bid for re-election. When formally accepting the Democratic nomination in
September, he had reaffirmed neutrality was "the fixed and traditional policy of
the United States to stand aloof from the politics of Europe."[189] Although his
party lauded him as the man who "kept us out of war," Wilson was concerned
German resumption of unrestricted submarine warfare would threaten US neutrality. While embracing the campaign slogan of "Peace with Honor," he sought
to educate the American public in its global responsibilities.[190] At the close of the
campaign Wilson declared, "immediately in front of us, in the years to come—I
hope very soon, indeed, for I mean after the war—we have a distinct part to
play in the world which we never played before." At the same event, aware of
the swell of sympathy for their suffering, Wilson made his first public reference
to the Armenians. He told the audience, "you know the feeling of this nation
towards those unorganized people who have no political standing in Europe,
like the Armenians . . . who seem caught between the forces of this terrible
struggle and seem likely to be crushed almost out of existence." He declared,
"our heart goes out to those helpless people who are being crushed and whom
we would like to save."[191] For Wilson, the Armenian massacres were emblematic
of an immoral Old World order with its balance of power politics and imperial
intrigues. However, he was becoming increasingly convinced that when peace
came, Americans should take the lead in establishing a new international order,
which would protect minorities such as the Armenians.

Following his narrow re-election victory in 1916, Wilson stepped up efforts
to mediate an end to the war before German submarines prompted American
intervention. Early in January 1917, drafting the text of a speech to the Senate,
which would call for a "peace without victory," Wilson discussed the territorial
terms of such a peace with House. They agreed the Ottoman Empire in Europe
should cease to exist but expressed concern that this declaration might lead
to reprisals against missionary and relief activity in the Empire. In the event,
Wilson did not outline any specific territorial terms, which may have provoked

opposition and undermined his appeal for peace.[192] However, by proposing an end to the Ottoman presence in Europe—albeit in private—the president revealed his commitment to the dissolution of the Empire and the future of its subject peoples. For the first time, and no doubt inspired by their suffering, Wilson connected the fate of the Armenians with America's future world role, giving a hint that he might offer his own solution to the Armenian question.

4

The Wilsonian Solution

Woodrow Wilson's relationship with Britain was complex. His ancestors were from Britain and he enjoyed numerous vacations there before assuming the presidency. He admired the British Cabinet system, even recommending its adoption by the United States in his first book, and especially revered the authors and exponents of British Liberalism, notably John Bright, Richard Cobden, and above all William Gladstone, whose picture he hung above his desk at Princeton.[1] Yet while Wilson was a renowned expert on comparative Anglo-American politics, he had not taken as avid an interest as Roosevelt in contemporary British colonial practices. However, after overcoming his initial hesitancy about US overseas expansion, Wilson came to believe that US colonialism was more akin to Britain's than that of any other nation.[2] In 1902, writing in the *Atlantic Monthly*, he urged Americans to teach Filipinos the principles of self-government that the United States itself had derived from the "strenuous processes of English history." With missionary zeal, Wilson had proclaimed: "The East is to be opened and transformed, whether we will or no [*sic*]; the standards of the West are to be imposed upon it. It is our peculiar duty, as it is also England's, to moderate the process in the interests of liberty." While providing tutelage, Americans must remember their promise to give the Philippines eventual independence and self-government.[3] He would officially pledge the United States to Philippine sovereignty in 1916 when he signed the Jones Act, legally ceding Filipino control of both legislative houses and granting Philippine independence "as soon as a stable government is established."[4] This pledge confirmed Wilson's belief that Americans were "chosen and prominently chosen to show the way to the nations of the world how they shall walk in the paths of liberty."[5]

While Wilson was a great admirer of British liberalism, his presidential relations with Asquith's Liberal government got off to a shaky start. He differed vigorously with Britain over how best to respond when General Victoriano Huerta violently seized power in Mexico in the midst of a revolution. While the British government quickly recognized Huerta's regime, hoping it would restore stability, Wilson refused to accept an undemocratic and bloody coup, even though the

Figure 4.1 Portrait of Woodrow Wilson. Library of Congress, LC-USZ62-13028.

US ambassador in Mexico had covertly assisted it.[6] Anglo-American differences over Mexico were soon overshadowed by tensions during World War I. Britain's blockade and its censorship practices angered Wilson. He was also increasingly frustrated by Allied unwillingness to co-operate in his attempts to mediate an end to the war. Relations deteriorated further when Britain responded to the 1916 Easter Rebellion in Ireland by executing its leaders. This provoked widespread American anger and, in particular, intensified anti-British hostility among politically influential Irish Americans. That summer Britain published a blacklist of US and Latin-American firms accused of trading with the Central Powers. This was the "last straw" for Wilson, who had become increasingly antagonistic to British politicians' undisguised irritation at his mediation efforts.[7] He received congressional backing for trade restrictions on countries that discriminated against American firms or interfered with US shipping. Furthermore, Wilson committed the United States to challenging British naval supremacy, declaring to House in September: "Let us build a navy bigger than hers and do what we please."[8] The British government was already concerned that its increasing economic reliance on the United States meant Wilson would soon be in a position, "if he wishes, to dictate his own terms to us."[9] After his re-election victory, Wilson sought to take advantage of this financial dependency to exert fresh pressure on Britain to accept his peace overtures.

An opportunity presented itself when J. P. Morgan & Co., the British government's financial agent in the United States, attempted to alleviate Britain's dire economic condition by selling its short-term debt to American banks. Wilson approved the Federal Reserve Board's cautionary message to its member banks to avoid overexposure to Allied bonds and strengthened the language by extending the warning to private investors. Following the resultant flight from sterling, Asquith's coalition government fell, to be replaced by one led by David Lloyd George. In December 1916, Wilson again attempted to facilitate an end to the war. British officials were incensed by Wilson's peace note, especially his suggestion that the "objects which the statesmen of the belligerents on both sides have in mind in this war are virtually the same."[10] They found Wilson's "peace without victory" address in January 1917 even more exasperating.[11] By the end of the month, however, Britain's gold reserves were practically exhausted and it was down to its last three weeks' supply of wheat, with little hope of raising new loans in the United States for fresh supplies. Wilson was unaware of the extent of Britain's financial crisis. Despite his irritation with the British government, he would have regarded an Allied defeat as an alarming prospect. The United States relied on the transatlantic trade for sustained prosperity and Wilson's own personal desire was for neither side to win outright. Germany was equally unaware of Britain's precipitous position and unwittingly handed its enemy a reprieve by announcing it would resume unrestricted submarine warfare at the end of January.[12] This new German–American crisis averted an Anglo-American one. Nevertheless, Wilson remained suspicious of the British government's war aims, which would help shape US policy toward Germany's ally, the Ottoman Empire, and consequently his solution to the Armenian question.

War with Germany but not the Ottoman Empire

Germany's announcement on unrestricted submarine warfare compelled Wilson to break diplomatic relations in February 1917 but not to issue a war declaration. Noninterventionist sentiment remained strong, particularly in the Midwest, and he feared leading a divided nation to war. However, the interception of the Zimmermann telegram, in which Germany's foreign minister proposed an alliance with Mexico in the event of a German-American conflict, excited anti-German opinion in even the most stridently isolationist areas. This was heightened by the sinking of three American merchant vessels by German U-boats, with the loss of fifteen lives, on March 17, 1917, and convinced Wilson that Germany was preparing for war with the United States. The president believed he had no alternative but to declare war to preserve his own, and the nation's, honor. However, he was mindful that his declaration needed to be phrased to command popular support.[13] Lansing advised presenting the conflict as one of democracy against autocracy, which was more feasible since the March overthrow of the Russian Tsar. House urged him to emphasize war was with Germany's government not its people.[14] His private secretary Joseph Tumulty counseled that the balance of American public opinion, represented by newspaper editorials across the country, felt that if there was to be war with Germany it should be on an issue "exclusively between that Empire and this Republic." He warned that the United States should not be tied to Allied war aims, reminding Wilson that one such objective was the "expulsion of the Turk from Europe but America had no call to fight for it."[15] Although Wilson had confided to House that he wished to see the Ottomans driven from Europe, he was suspicious of Allied war aims to realize long-standing territorial ambitions in the Empire.[16] These were not aims with which he wished Americans to be associated.

Considering the advice that he had received, Wilson drafted his declaration and addressed Congress on April 2, 1917. He claimed Germany's submarine campaign constituted an act of "war against all nations," that peace and justice were threatened by autocratic governments, in particular the Kaiser's, and that Americans would fight "for the ultimate peace of the world and for the liberation of its peoples, the German people included." Wilson's professed American aims were utterly selfless, seeking no material gain. The United States would fight for its ideals, democracy, the right of all people to have a voice in how they are governed, the protection of small nations, and "a universal dominion of right by such a concert of free peoples as shall bring peace and safety to all nations and make the world itself at last free."[17] Even while entering the war, Wilson was determined to keep the United States apart from the intrigues of the Old World. His justification for US intervention and his invocation of its unselfish war aims were intended to demonstrate that it did not share the political ambitions of the Europeans. Wilson stated that as Austria-Hungary had committed no act of war against the United States, he would not yet declare war on it. He made no mention of the Ottoman Empire, nor of Bulgaria, which had recently joined the Central Powers, and asked for a declaration of war on Germany only. Congress overwhelmingly supported his request.

Despite Wilson confining America's war to Germany, Austria-Hungary severed diplomatic relations on April 8, 1917. As for the Ottomans, Lansing had advised Ambassador Elkus in Constantinople that although the Wilson administration did not wish to break relations with the Ottomans, Germany might force it.[18] The US–Ottoman relationship was sensitive. America's long-standing missionary and educational interests in the Empire not only symbolized "the American spirit at its best," as Morgenthau had noted, but also gave it influence in the region.[19] This was now challenged by the German-Ottoman alliance. The ABCFM and ACASR were only able to operate with the acquiescence of the Ottoman authorities. Some ABCFM property had been damaged and seized by Ottoman authorities during the massacres, but war with the Empire could result in missionary expulsion, complete seizure of property, worth over $100 million, and the disruption of nearly a century of work.[20] Barton had already prepared a case against war with the Ottomans in February. Writing to the State Department that the United States, unlike the European nations, had no designs on Ottoman territory, he warned that Germany's influence at the Porte would increase if relations were terminated and advised that the United States could exert a decisive influence in the region after the war if it remained at peace with the Ottomans. Furthermore, Armenian aid would flow if friendly relations were maintained and ACASR relief continued uninterrupted.[21] Dodge supported Barton's arguments. Wilson had written to his old friend, after breaking relations with Germany, of his concern for Dodge's family in the Near East and confided he hoped to "manage things so prudently" that Americans in the region were not endangered.[22] Despite the president's assurances, Dodge remained apprehensive. He visited the White House in the days before Wilson declared war on Germany, urging him not to include the Ottoman Empire in his declaration, and echoing the counsel of Barton, who Dodge claimed knew "more about the situation in the Near East than almost anyone else."[23]

Ultimately it was the Ottomans who broke relations with the United States on April 20, 1917, although they continued to allow American missionaries and relief workers to operate within the Empire as attaches to the Swedish embassy.[24] Barton believed missionary influence had been decisive in the decision to exclude the Ottoman Empire from the war declaration, later asserting, "President Wilson, sympathetically interested in the American institutions and influence in the Near East, withheld a formal declaration of war against Turkey and Turkey simply broke off diplomatic relations."[25] However, Barton's comment does not adequately reflect the rationale behind Wilson's decision. The president was undoubtedly sympathetic to the missionary movement, whose institutions represented America's most significant interest in the Near East. To endanger them risked strengthening German influence. Yet Wilson was also aware an Ottoman war might well be unpopular despite deep American hostility to the Empire. The failure of the Gallipoli campaign had already underlined the difficulties of an invasion.[26] Above all, Tumulty had warned of the limited grounds on which the American public would support war, and Wilson felt a conflict with the Ottomans would identify the United States with Allied self-interest. If the Armenians featured in his thinking at this time, it would have been to ensure the flow of aid, which would certainly have met with public approval. Missionary counsel therefore supported advice Wilson received from within the administration. It also strengthened Wilson's conviction that while Germany was the principal threat to the peace of the world, the United States should disassociate itself from all European ambitions in the Near East.

An Understanding Between the Democracies of Britain and the United States

To emphasize its distinction, Wilson made clear that the United States would not join the Allies but fight alongside them as an "associate power." This detached arrangement demonstrated Wilson's awareness that many Americans were still hostile to any suggestion of a formal alliance, particularly one with its former colonial ruler. It also reflected his continued distrust of Allied intentions.[27] The British government's principal source on both popular American attitudes to Britain and Wilson's own views was Sir William Wiseman. A businessman with prewar commercial experience in North America, Wiseman had been sent to New York in early 1916 to establish Britain's Secret Intelligence Service agency in the United States. Presenting himself as head of the British government's Military Mission, he developed an intimate acquaintance with House and consequently also became a confidant of Wilson. The president had never trusted Britain's ambassador, Cecil Spring Rice, regarding him as being too close to the Republicans. Many of House's contacts with Asquith's government, especially Grey, were no longer in the Cabinet. Wilson and House therefore welcomed Wiseman as a valuable channel of communication with Britain's new government, and he became the most important link between the two wartime associates.[28]

Soon after US intervention in the war, Wiseman confirmed to Whitehall that Americans were strongly opposed to a formal alliance with the Entente powers, noting that they "sub-consciously feel themselves to be arbitrators rather than allies." He reported to London there was little "pro-Ally feeling on the part of the great mass of the American people" and "it would be certainly wrong to assume any pro-British sentiment." Indeed, he suggested that Britain was the least popular of the Allied nations. In addition to the antipathy of Irish Americans, Wiseman believed that mistrust of Britain was "inherited from the days of the War of Independence and kept alive by the ridiculous history books still used in National schools" that taught Americans "to regard the British as a nation of Imperialists, who want to boss the whole world." Hostility to British conduct during the years of neutrality, intensified by German propaganda, had deepened American antagonism. Opponents of American intervention in the conflict claimed that Britain had enticed the United States into the war and planned to use the Americans for their own selfish aims. Even the majority of

Americans who supported involvement in the war were reluctant to participate "under British control or as part of a British campaign." Despite sharing a common German enemy, an Anglo-American alliance clearly remained anathema to most Americans.[29]

Wiseman was more encouraged by the administration's attitude, particularly that of House. The British agent moved into the same building in New York as Wilson's chief adviser and met with him several times a day to discuss all manner of administration business. Wiseman was aware that House had been decidedly pro-Ally during the period of neutrality and a persistent advocate to Wilson of US intervention on the Allied side.[30] He informed his government that House felt "very strongly that England and America ought to work together, because, as he expresses it, 'what is good for the one is good for the other.'"[31] Wiseman also assured his superiors that the president "believes that the security of the world can best be maintained by an understanding between the democracies of Great Britain and the United States."[32] It is unclear whether Wiseman had heard these sentiments via House or directly from Wilson. However, the emphasis on shared Anglo-American democratic ideals no doubt reflected Wilson's separation of Britain's tradition of self-government, which he admired, from its imperial practices, of which he was increasingly distrustful. Wiseman evidently recognized this distinction, repeatedly warning the British government that Wilson was, in British political terms, an "Advanced Radical" and highly suspicious of "Tory Imperialists."[33] He reminded London that the United States had limited its war to Germany and was not bound by any of the inter-Ally treaties. Wilson and the American people believed that the United States was "fighting solely for the cause of human liberty" and saw themselves as the "only disinterested parties in the war."[34]

When Wilson received written evidence of Allied territorial designs in the Near East in the spring of 1917 his belief that the United States was the only power without aggressive war aims was confirmed. During a meeting in Washington to discuss war objectives, British Foreign Minister Arthur Balfour revealed to House that the Allies had negotiated a series of secret agreements to establish the division of spoils after the war. House discovered it was in the Near East that these treaties "come in most prominently." The Ottoman Empire was to be carved into spheres of influence. Britain would receive Mesopotamia, France and Italy would share Anatolia, including French control of the southern Armenian populations, and Russia would take the northern Armenian provinces, Constantinople, and the Straits region. House noted in his diary, "It is all bad and I told Balfour so. They are making it a breeding place for future wars."[35] At House's request, Balfour sent Wilson copies of the secret treaties the following month.[36] Wilson revealed his own disapproval of Allied postwar policy during a private discussion with House in July. Britain was on the "verge of a financial disaster" that summer and the United States had agreed to loan billions of dollars for the purchase of Allied war supplies.[37] Wilson outlined his rationale to House for assuming the financial responsibility for Allied war purchases: "England and France have not the same views with regard to peace that we have by any means. When the war is over we can force them to our way of thinking, because by that time they will, among other things, be financially in our hands."[38]

German Power Inserted into the Heart of the World

Before that could happen, Germany would need to be defeated. During the period of neutrality, Lansing and House had counseled that German domination of Europe threatened American security but the president was not convinced.[39] However, Wilson now expressed growing concern over the extent and nature of Germany's geopolitical ambitions. US diplomats returning from Constantinople confirmed Germany exercised a malign influence at the Porte, echoing Entente propaganda that this extended to complicity in the massacres. Ambassador Henry Morgenthau later reflected that although Germany had not instigated the atrocities, "she is responsible in the sense that she had the power to stop them and did not use it."[40] Lewis Einstein recorded in his diary, published in 1917, that "German officialdom [cannot] easily escape its terrible share of responsibility."[41] While there is no evidence Wilson shared this belief, he had begun to express publicly, and also privately to House, his concern that the Ottomans were, militarily and economically, under German dominance.[42] In his Flag Day address, on June 14, Wilson claimed the Ottoman leaders had "no choice but to take their orders from Berlin" and in a speech to the American Federation of Labor, the president declared Germany had "absolute control of Austria-Hungary, practical control of Turkey, control of Asia Minor, [with] the bulk of German power inserted into the heart of the world."[43] The president ordered George Creel's American Committee on Public Information, responsible for the administration's propaganda, to publicize written evidence of the German threat, hoping to convince those Americans still uncommitted to the war.[44]

Soon after the United States entered the conflict, the Wilson administration explored an initiative to offset German domination of Middle Europe through a separate peace with the Ottomans. The State Department had received information from Henry G. Alsberg, Elkus's private secretary from his time in Constantinople, that the Ottoman leaders were friendly to the United States and had only broken diplomatic relations under German pressure. Alsberg suggested that the Ottomans were fearful of German ambitions to rule the Empire after the war and would welcome a separate peace. Morgenthau confirmed Alsberg's analysis. The former ambassador informed Lansing that the Ottomans were "heartily sick of their German masters." Convinced there was a possibility of detaching the Ottoman Empire from the Central Powers, Morgenthau offered to undertake a secret mediation mission.[45] Lansing was skeptical whether this could be achieved but wrote to Wilson that it was worth considering, as the United States should "leave no stone unturned which will lessen the power of Germany."[46] Wilson was also unconvinced by Morgenthau's proposal but reasoned that if it was successful it could prove decisive in the outcome of the war and if it failed they would be no worse off. Besides weakening Germany, a separate peace appealed to Wilson principally as a means "to prevent the bargain of the Allies with regard to Asia Minor from being carried out at the end of the war."[47]

The British government was willing to explore the proposed peace initiative. Ottoman withdrawal from the war would allow the transfer of Allied troops to the Western Front and enable direct communications with Russia, whose new provisional government was struggling to reinvigorate its war effort.[48] A scheme was devised whereby Morgenthau, accompanied by the prominent American Zionist Felix Frankfurter, traveled to Gibraltar in July to meet the British Zionist leader Chaim Weizmann. Also present at the meeting were the French intelligence agent Colonel Weyl and Arshag K. Schmavonian, an Ottoman Armenian who had previously served as an adviser at the US Embassy in Constantinople. Under the façade of a commission investigating the condition of Jews in Palestine, Morgenthau envisaged traveling to Egypt to establish a meeting with the Young Turk leaders. However, in Gibraltar, it became apparent that Morgenthau had given little thought to how this plan would be enacted. Furthermore, Schmavonian, who had recently been in Constantinople, made clear that indiscreet talk about the peace mission, which had been leaked to the press, had angered the Ottomans. Morgenthau was now persona non grata at the Porte. In any case, Ottoman leaders were unwilling to terminate the alliance with Germany.[49] The mission was abandoned and House privately admitted that it had "turned out to be a fiasco."[50] Arabs, Zionists, and Armenians had protested to the Foreign Office and State Department on hearing of the proposed mission and welcomed its failure on the basis that their national aspirations rested on the destruction of the Ottoman Empire.[51] The British were also relieved that the mission had failed. After initially authorizing the initiative, the government had subsequently decided to press on with the Ottoman war and in May had drawn up plans for a military campaign in Palestine. Unwilling to further consider a separate peace, Britain resolved to fight until the Ottoman Empire was defeated. The Wilson administration, chastened by the experience, also concluded that a separate peace with the Ottomans was "chimerical and of questionable advantage, even if it could be accomplished." The United States would focus on defeating Germany and leave the fate of the Ottoman Empire to a future peace conference.[52]

Morgenthau was not entrusted with any more sensitive wartime diplomatic assignments. However, to galvanize public opinion and overcome lingering American indifference to war, he offered to write a book on German plans for world domination. He informed Wilson that his account would emphasize that "in Turkey, we see the evil spirit of Germany at its worst—culminating at last in the greatest crime of all ages, the horrible massacres of the helpless Armenians." Morgenthau believed the Armenian issue would mobilize "small town" America as no other aspect of the war could.[53] Wilson thought Morgenthau's "plan for a full exposition of German intrigue an excellent one."[54] The president clearly recognized horror at the massacres and the allegation of German complicity could be used to strengthen support for the US war with Germany.

Our People Will Not Fight For Any Selfish Aim

In October 1917, Germany's position was strengthened further. Italy, which had joined the Allies in 1915, was heavily defeated at the Battle of Caporetto. To aid Allied morale, Wilson agreed to declare war on Austria-Hungary, but he was aware this would inevitably raise the question of war with the Ottomans.[55] By this time, the Allied secret agreements had become public after the Bolsheviks seized power in Russia in November 1917 and published copies of the treaties.[56] Wilson confirmed his opposition to Allied postwar plans for the Near East on December 1 when he wrote to House: "Our people and Congress will not fight for any selfish aim on the part of any belligerent . . . least of all the division of territory such as have been contemplated in Asia Minor."[57] Wilson's horror at the Armenian massacres had led him to confide to House his belief that the Ottoman Empire should be "effaced" and arranged into autonomous regions along ethnic lines.[58] However, the secret treaties would merely transfer these lands to Allied control without consideration of the subject peoples. Wilson would not allow the United States to become entangled in the Allies' fight for control of Ottoman territories.

The president planned to reaffirm American war objectives and the administration's position on the Ottoman Empire in his Annual Message to Congress. In December, Dodge wrote to Wilson, expressing fear that a declaration of war on Austria-Hungary would provoke calls for war with all the Central Powers. Dodge warned that "war with Turkey would be a terrible blow," as it would endanger many American lives besides hampering relief efforts to save "hundreds of thousands of natives."[59] Two days later, in his annual message, Wilson asked Congress to declare war on Austria-Hungary only. He asserted the Habsburg Empire had become "simply the vassal of the German government" and that the Central Powers be regarded "as but one." Acknowledging this logic would lead also to declarations against the Ottoman Empire and Bulgaria, Wilson contended, while they "also are the tools of Germany, they are mere tools and do not yet stand in the direct path of our necessary action."[60] Congress voted for war with Austria-Hungary but on the same day, Democratic Senator William H. King introduced a resolution calling for war against all the Central Powers.[61] The next day, Wilson replied to Dodge that he sympathized with his every word about a war with the Ottomans and was "trying to hold Congress back" from including all the allies of Germany in a declaration of war.[62]

When the Foreign Relations Committee considered King's resolution, it asked the administration to explain its position. With Wilson's approval, Lansing prepared a lengthy memorandum for the Committee, echoing Barton's arguments about US interests in the Empire and the need to contain German control. He emphasized that the United States had no military force to deploy in the Eastern Mediterranean and would concentrate all its resources on defeating Germany on the Western Front, drawing attention to the possibility that war would endanger missionary interests, hamper relief efforts, and possibly provoke further atrocities against the Armenians. Bulgaria's involvement in the war was dismissed as a local conflict with Serbia, presenting no threat to the Allies or the United States. Lansing confirmed there was no Allied pressure for war with either and a declaration could always be considered later if necessary.[63] Lansing's analysis was supported by Newton D. Baker, the US Secretary of War. Baker was adamant that the United States should focus its attention on the Western Front, emphasizing the extra shipping and time that was required to transport troops to the Eastern Mediterranean, the absence of land transport if the forces were even able to reach the region, and the speed with which the Germans could move their divisions eastward over their military railroad system to thwart any incursion. The Senate was prepared to defer to the administration at this time and the King resolution was not reported out of Committee.[64]

On hearing this decision Dodge wrote to Wilson again, stating that the president's actions, "coupled with the action of Congress, in not pushing the Turkish question, has made me very happy."[65] As an expert on Near East affairs and Wilson's political confidant and close friend, Dodge was kept informed about all policies regarding the Near East. It has been argued that he decisively influenced the president's decision to withhold a declaration of war on Turkey.[66] However, Dodge's family concerns and missionary interests matched the administration's own geopolitical and ideological war aims. Above all, Wilson's objection to war with the Ottomans reflected his ever-present concern to keep the United States separate from Allied ambitions in the Near East. Therefore, Wilson considered a declaration of war on Austria-Hungary as the only "immediate and practical consideration" at this time.[67]

The Foreign Relations Committee had accepted the administration's position, but calls to extend the US war effort to the Ottoman Empire continued. Republicans were quick to question the administration, using the Armenian massacres as justification. Henry Cabot Lodge, although prepared to follow the president's advice at this time, contended that he and the majority of senators believed the United States must, sooner or later, declare war on the Ottomans, arguing it was impossible to distinguish the Empire from Germany and that the "massacres of which the Turks have been guilty surpass belief."[68] Roosevelt was unrelenting in his criticism. If anything his attacks after the US declaration of war on Germany had grown fiercer, following the administration's refusal to allow him to lead a volunteer division on the Western Front.[69] By autumn 1917, he was attacking the administration weekly in a widely syndicated column for the *Kansas City Star*. Wilson's failure to declare war on the Ottomans appalled him. He wrote it was "hypocritical to shed crocodile tears over Armenia and not to declare war on Turkey" and repeated this message in a series of public addresses in cities across the East Coast. At a Pennsylvania Society Dinner in New York, Roosevelt declared that "neither democracy nor civilization [was] safe" while the Ottoman Empire existed in its current form. It was on America's "part culpable weakness" and a "betrayal of the rights of others, not to fight for the complete independence of the oppressed nationalities."[70] Over two decades of outrage at Ottoman treatment of the Armenians had strengthened hostility across the country. The *Los Angeles Times* maintained that "for 500 years the Turks have been a curse to Christendom, engaged in war after war and massacre after massacre," culminating in the wholesale slaughter of the Armenian people, and there was as much reason to overthrow Ottoman rule as to depose the Kaiser.[71] However, Wilson did not believe it was America's duty to declare war on the Ottomans to avenge the Armenians; there would be a diplomatic opportunity to address the future of the Empire and its subject people in the postwar peace settlement. In any event, the expert advice Wilson had received only confirmed his belief that intervention would endanger both Americans and Armenians.

Wilson's position was endorsed at this time by Miran Sevasly, chairman of the Boston-based Armenian National Union of America. This organization attempted to bridge the theological and social divide between Armenian Orthodox Christians and Protestant Armenian converts in the United States. Sevasly also served as the agent in the United States for Boghos Nubar, the Paris-based leader of the Armenian National Delegation, which represented the Ottoman Armenians and served as their liaison with the Western powers.[72] On December 13, 1917, Sevasly reported to Nubar that he had been granted an interview with Roosevelt, who expressed his belief that "Armenia has greater claims on America than even Belgium and that he considered this country should declare war against Bulgaria and Turkey." However, Sevasly reminded his chief that "President Wilson does not share entirely this view." He advised Nubar that it was "very questionable whether a declaration of war at this juncture by the United States against Turkey can greatly help the sufferers of the Armenian massacres and deportations, while it may hamper the relief work now carried on in that country." This perspective was shared by Morgenthau, who assured Sevasly that sympathy for the Armenians in the United States was "extensive and sincere." However, the former ambassador urged the Armenians to continue promoting "their services to the cause of civilization and human progress and their inalienable rights to self-government and their recognition in the family of nations" so that there would be American public support for the postwar "reconstruction of Armenia."[73] Like Wilson, Morgenthau believed that the United States could render its most effective service to the Armenians through diplomatic rather than military means once the conflict was over.

Fourteen Points and a Possible Diplomatic Solution to the Armenian Question

The publication of the Allied secret treaties convinced Wilson that he must set out a comprehensive vision for the postwar world, redefining the goals for which the conflict was being fought, enhancing public morale, and appealing to the subjects of the Central Powers over the heads of their governments. Wilson had asked House to establish "the Inquiry," a collection of academics, principally historians and geographers, to formulate America's postwar plans. The president now requested a memorandum from this group on the issues to be resolved by a future peace conference.[74] Its principal architect was Walter Lippmann, an editor of the *New Republic* and the Inquiry's secretary. The main theme of the memo was strategic. It examined how the United States could ensure "the disestablishment of a Prussian Middle Europe" and prevent Germany from becoming "the master of the continent." Critical to this was the weakening of German control over the Near East by internationalizing Constantinople and the Dardanelles Straits, and ensuring that "the two military terminals of Berlin-Baghdad remain in the hands of an administration friendly to the western nations." To achieve this, there must be "guaranteed autonomy for the Armenians, not only as a matter of justice and humanity but in order to re-establish the one people of Asia Minor capable of preventing economic monopolization of Turkey by the Germans." However, the memorandum's authors were concerned that the Armenians and other minorities of Asia Minor might not prove strong enough to provide a bulwark against

Germany's thrust to the East through Anatolia. It would therefore be essential to first establish "strong Allied control over the essential parts of Turkey—Armenia, Palestine, and Mesopotamia."[75]

Wilson drafted his own thoughts on America's peace program, condensing these suggestions and removing much of the strategic rationale. This provided the basis for his Fourteen Points Address, which he delivered before Congress on January 8, 1918.[76] Wilson called for open diplomacy rather than entangling alliances and secret treaties. A global pledge should be made to establish "equality of trade conditions among all nations." Arms control and freedom of the seas would help prevent future conflicts. At the heart of Wilson's postwar world would be a league of nations, affording "mutual guarantees of political independence and territorial integrity to great and small states alike."

A number of Wilson's Points dealt with specific territorial issues; of these, Point Twelve referred specifically to the future of the Ottoman Empire. This asserted the Turkish portions would be assured full sovereignty, "but the other nationalities which are now under Turkish rule should be assured an undoubted security of life and an absolutely unmolested opportunity of autonomous development."[77] This was less specific than the Inquiry's recommendation that it was "necessary to free the subject races of the Turkish Empire from oppression and misrule: this implies at the very least autonomy for Armenia."[78] Wilson had considered explicitly mentioning Armenia and other parts of the Empire by name. However, House, who helped draft the address, disagreed, feeling that there was already sufficient indication of this in Point Twelve and Wilson followed his advice.[79] Even without a specific reference to Armenia, the speech represented a fundamental departure from the traditional US policy, that of political noninvolvement in the Near East. Although he had phrased his commitment in broad terms, Wilson had made a unilateral pronouncement on the future of the Ottoman Empire and, by doing so, raised the possibility of a diplomatic solution to the Armenian question.

Renewed Calls for Intervention

The Fourteen Points address was intended, in part, to encourage dissent within Germany and the Habsburg Empire, but the speech's main purpose was to challenge Russian Bolshevik peace propaganda and its impact on war-fatigued liberals in Allied countries. The Russians were negotiating peace terms at Brest-Litovsk, although talks were suspended when Germany refused to yield occupied territory until a general peace was negotiated.[80] The Bolshevik leader, Vladimir Ilyich Lenin, had publicly advocated "the liberation of all colonies; the liberation of all dependent, oppressed and non-sovereign peoples."[81] Wilson recognized the wide appeal of this rhetoric. However, he was cautious in his own embrace of national self-determination, avoiding the concept directly in his Fourteen Points. In any case, the application of this principle was complicated in the Near East by Allied imperial designs and overlapping ethnic populations. This was particularly evident in relation to the Armenians. At the outset of the war the majority were based on the Ottoman-Russian border, and they had been dispersed yet further by the deportations and massacres, with many fleeing to the Russian controlled Caucasus.[82] In his Fourteen Points Address, the president called for evacuation of troops from "all Russian territory," distinguishing American "good will" from German greed. Consequently, he did not demand independence for Russian Armenians, instead calling for preservation of Russia's territorial integrity.[83]

As the war continued, the Wilson administration was urged by American diplomats in the Near East, and by the Allies, to use the Armenians as a bulwark against Germany's bid for hegemony from Berlin to Baghdad. Felix Willoughby Smith, the US consul in Tiflis, was the most persistent advocate, pressing for the promotion of nationalist sentiment in the Caucasus to rally minorities against the Central Powers.[84] Lansing dismissed Smith's suggestions, concerned it would encourage the "disruption of Russia."[85] However, the Armenian plight and the Allied military position in the region deteriorated further when Germany imposed the Treaty of Brest-Litovsk in March 1918, forcing the Bolsheviks to surrender some of Russian Armenia to Turkey.[86] Russia's withdrawal left a vacuum in Transcaucasia. The significance of this region centered on the large oilfields around Baku in Azerbaijan. Oil had become increasingly important as fuel for the new tanks, trucks, and airplanes that generals on both sides regarded as decisive to the outcome on the Western Front. The Allies had sabotaged the Central Power-controlled Galician and Romanian oilfields, and Britain's capture of Baghdad denied the Ottomans access to the abundant, untapped resources of northern Mesopotamia. The oil reserves in the Caucasus were therefore vital to the Central Powers and the Allies were determined to deprive their enemies of these resources. The Armenians in the Caucasus were precariously positioned in the middle of this geostrategic struggle.[87]

America's principal intelligence analyst on events in the region was Samuel Edelman, a former consular official in the Ottoman Empire, serving as US vice consul in Geneva. Edelman reported to the State Department that the Russian collapse had revived Ottoman ambitions to establish itself as "a Mohammedan world power." Its officials planned to acquire the entire Caucasus and unite it with Turkestan to form a pan-Turanian bloc of Turkish speaking peoples, materially benefitting the Central Powers' war effort. Edelman suggested that the "only real obstacle to Turkish aggrandizement is the Armenian element."[88] He urged the United States to provide assistance to them. Due to the paucity of American

intelligence resources on the Near East, Edelman was reliant on his British counterpart in Switzerland, and his twenty-five strong corps of intelligence agents, for
information on current events in the Ottoman Empire.[89] It is therefore unsurprising that Edelman's analysis of Transcaucasian affairs supported Allied arguments that the United States should provide them with financial assistance for
military operations in the region. Wiseman was told to impress on the administration that if the "Turco-Germans get possession of Baku . . . we might easily
have to face a very formidable Moslem movement" that would not only threaten
the British position in Asia, but endanger the "unhappy populations . . . of the
South Caucasus also, including remnants of Armenians."[90] However, Lansing's
constant concern for legality led him to inform the British government that since
the United States was not at war with the Ottoman Empire "it would be wrong
for U.S. Government to advance money for war-like operations against her." The
State Department even blocked the British government's purchase of a fleet of
Ford motorcars, despite Britain's protests that without them its troops in Persia
would be "practically helpless and may even have to withdraw." Ultimately, the
British were forced into the "very unsatisfactory position" of applying again
to the US Treasury Department for the vehicles, "stating merely that the supplies are required for military purposes without specifying where they are to
be used."[91] The incident showed just how determined the Wilson administration was to avoid any American association with the British campaign in the
Near East.

Concern for the Armenians was also used as an Allied argument for intervention elsewhere in Eurasia. Since the Bolshevik Revolution, the Entente powers
had encouraged Wilson to sanction military intervention in Russia to re-establish
an Eastern Front against the Central Powers. These efforts increased after Brest-
Litovsk. Among Britain's arguments for intervention was that in the East, the
Germans planned to overcome the effects of the Allied blockade, upsetting the
security of British India, and extending the war to Afghanistan and Persia, "inci-
dentally giving the Turks a free hand in Armenia." Wilson did not find any of
the arguments for intervention "at all persuasive."[92] He eventually approved limited US involvement in the Allied military intervention in Russia, resulting in
some British troops being deployed in the Caucasus.[93] However, Wilson was not
prepared for a major American military commitment in the Near East. He was
already suspicious of Allied designs in the region and unwilling to undermine
Russia's territorial integrity. When the Russian Armenians proclaimed their own
separate republic in the spring of 1918 the United States did not grant even de
facto diplomatic recognition, although the administration did sanction some
covert financial assistance to the people of Transcaucasia.[94]

Armenians remained imperilled under Ottoman rule, and calls for an
American war with the Ottomans resurfaced in April 1918, when Senator King

introduced a new resolution.[95] He was supported by Republican Senator Frank Brandegee, who hoped to regain congressional initiative in foreign policy from an increasingly dominant executive that kept the Senate in "dense ignorance about our foreign affairs."[96] Called to testify before the Foreign Relations Committee, Lansing informed the Committee there was "everything to lose and nothing to gain from war with Turkey" and re-emphasized the disastrous effects of war on Armenian relief.[97] Despite this, Lansing noted that all the Republicans and many Democrats on the Committee favored war with the Ottomans.[98] This time, the Committee requested that the secretary obtain Allied opinion on whether they considered an American war with the Ottomans necessary. The Allies replied in favor of issuing the additional declaration. The British Foreign Office instructed Wiseman to confirm that it attached "great importance to an immediate declaration of war on Turkey by U.S. Government."[99] Lansing informed Wilson that the Allied consideration was "entirely military" to encourage resistance among Armenians, and other Caucasians, and prevent Ottoman exploitation of Russian withdrawal from the war. However, Lansing believed the Allies had neglected the "humanitarian" aspect: over a million dollars a month was being sent to American missionaries to provide relief for Near Eastern Christians and this would be suspended in the event of war. Lansing had revealed little personal interest in humanitarian concerns when the massacres first occurred, unless American lives were at risk, and the fact that the Ottomans had not committed any hostile act against the United States probably weighed more heavily with him.[100] He emphasized the humanitarian crisis, knowing that this would appeal to Wilson, and the president upheld his decision not to declare war. The British Foreign Office was bewildered by the administration's position. As Principal Private Secretary Eric Drummond informed Wiseman, the "theory that the presence of American missionaries in Turkish territory has, up to now, prevented massacres and atrocities, is quite untenable."[101] Despite its misgivings, the British had no choice but to accept the administration's decision, as did the disgruntled Senate Foreign Relations Committee, and the United States remained at peace with the Ottomans.[102]

Roosevelt versus Wilson and the Missionaries

The missionary lobby remained anxious. Dodge wrote to Barton, "Whenever I begin to hope the agitation for war with Turkey has died out, I get a new shock."[103] The lobby feared it would become the "victim" of its own propaganda and relief campaign, and that the pro-Armenian and anti-Ottoman sentiment it had fomented would force the president to declare war on the Empire against his own better judgment.[104] It aimed to convince Americans that war with the

Ottomans was detrimental to the national interest and to the Armenians. Barton wrote an open letter to Lodge, the most influential Republican Senator favoring war, to outline the case against it, emphasizing the Armenian provinces lay at the crossroads of Germany's drive from Berlin to Baghdad and, in the event of an Ottoman-American war, the Armenians "under German insistence would be savagely maltreated if not generally massacred."[105] In an article for *The Congregationalist*, a widely circulated religious newspaper, the missionary leader claimed that "the large majority of Turks were not friendly to Germany," but a US declaration of war would cement German control over the Ottoman Empire and lead to further atrocities. Furthermore, as the United States did not have sufficient troops to send to the Near East, it could do nothing to protect the Armenians, while missionary property would be confiscated.[106] Barton and other ABCFM leaders argued the same in an editorial in the *Missionary Herald*, claiming that a declaration of war "would be a tactical blunder, an outrage against humanity and a moral crime."[107] The connection between the missionary lobby's opposition to war and its links to the White House did not go unnoticed. The *New York Tribune* noted that the president had quietly rejected calls for a war declaration against the Ottomans despite support for war among "a considerable section of influential opinion." The missionary lobby was described as "the silent, unofficial Cabinet" that dictated US policy on the Near East.[108]

No one was more forceful in condemning this perceived influence than Roosevelt. In a letter to Dodge, who he had known since childhood, the former president denounced the "peculiarly odious form of hypocrisy" that characterized the official US response to the Armenian question. Roosevelt condemned the missionaries for being ineffective bystanders to the tragedy and argued that their lobbying against war with the Ottomans served to "counterbalance the good they have done in the past." He accused Wilson's administration of failing to intervene to prevent the massacres and then alleging, "the fact that we are helping the survivors as a reason why we should not follow the only policy that will permanently put a stop to such massacres." Roosevelt demanded that the United States declare war immediately, as "the Armenian massacre was the greatest crime of the war, and failure to act against Turkey is to condone it." Contrary to Wilson, Roosevelt believed the United States was fighting in a common cause with Britain and France, so not declaring war on the other Central Powers was a show of "bad faith towards our allies." Above all, he claimed if the United States failed to vindicate the Armenians by punishing the Ottomans it would reveal that "all talk of guaranteeing the future peace of the world is mischievous nonsense."[109] For Roosevelt, the US intervention in the war had offered a unique opportunity to realize two of his longest held objectives—intervention in the Ottoman Empire on behalf of the Armenians and consummation of the Anglo-American rapprochement in a more formal alliance. Having invoked Armenian suffering in his 1904 declaration of principles on America's duty to intervene in response to crimes against civilization, he now publicly acknowledged that at that time, the United States had "neither the power nor the right ourselves to begin world war by our going to war with Turkey." However, America's involvement in World War I enabled it to fight alongside the Allies in the "only chance that has ever been offered to us to interfere by force of arms in entirely disinterested fashion for the oppressed nationalities that are ground under the Turkish rule."[110] Instead of fulfilling its duty, Roosevelt accused the Wilson administration of evading its responsibilities to "the lasting disgrace to our nation."

The different approaches of Roosevelt and Wilson to the Armenian question encapsulated their wider clash over the contribution of the United States to the war and its wider global role. Roosevelt believed that the United States was engaged with "all the allies in this great war for liberty and justice."[111] He was convinced that "for America to bear her full share of the common burden" it must declare war on all of Germany's allies.[112] Roosevelt was out of office and was free to advocate policies without any obligation to consider the practicalities. Nevertheless, his position reflected a consistent conviction, expressed in and out of office, that nations must uphold their most cherished values, by force if necessary, when they were challenged. For Roosevelt, the US unwillingness to join with the Allies in making these sacrifices on behalf of the Armenians compromised any claim it had to be the guardian of the highest civilized ideals. Even more hypocritical in Roosevelt's eyes was Wilson's continued lofty pronouncements on behalf of democracy and liberty while refusing to take action against the Ottomans.

Yet Wilson did not conceive of a military solution to the Armenian question, and certainly not during the war. His prime concern was the defeat of Germany, not vindication of the Armenians. Unlike Roosevelt, the president did not believe that the Allied powers shared America's values in foreign affairs. Furthermore, it would seem Wilson was unwilling to pursue a policy that he was advised might worsen an already critical situation and would threaten US interests and influence in the Empire. For Wilson, the United States could only address a solution to the Armenian question, diplomatically, after the war, and the missionaries shared his belief.

Barton was concerned by Roosevelt's capacity to shape public opinion and released a second open letter, addressed to the former president.[113] His argument did not convince Roosevelt. When Roosevelt made a donation to relief for the Armenian survivors, he publicly declared he did not wish this to go to Barton's ACASR, but to a relief campaigner who "has never sought to excuse or justify" what he regarded as America's "inexcusable dereliction of duty in having failed to declare war on Turkey."[114] Despite Roosevelt's efforts, and Barton's fears, the United States would remain at peace with the Ottoman Empire until the end of the war.

The Armenian Question Will Be Disposed of Once and For All

The missionary lobby's campaign to keep the United States out of the conflict also caused tension with Armenian Americans. Although Sevasly had previously dismissed Roosevelt's belief that the United States should declare war on the Ottomans, the deterioration in the Armenian position after Brest-Litosk changed his perspective. He now joined the former president in denouncing the missionaries for their outspoken opposition to a US–Ottoman conflict. In a private discussion, Sevasly urged Barton to stop publicly saying that the United States should avoid war with the Ottoman Empire as, "far from serving the Armenian cause, a great deal of harm was done to it because the Turks, realizing that this country is divided on the question, would get more emboldened against the surviving Armenians." Sevasly suggested that the manner in which the missionaries were conducting their campaign, their willingness to "partially exonerate the Turks" by emphasizing German dominance over Ottoman policy, would convince the Ottomans that they could continue persecuting the Armenians without any fear of US intervention. The Armenian American leader warned Barton that as a result, the missionaries had "injured the feelings of the Armenians throughout the United States." While Barton defended the missionaries by stating this stance was necessary as the United States was not yet in a position to influence events in the Near East, Sevasly remained unconvinced. He reported to Nubar that although Barton always claimed that "he is animated by the sole interest of the Armenians, I am not prepared to say that this is absolutely true, and it is sometimes a puzzle to me."[115]

Nubar acknowledged that it was a "misfortune" for the missionaries to be lobbying so vociferously against a US–Ottoman conflict that they were willing to blame Germany almost exclusively for Ottoman conduct. However, he was prepared to accept Barton's argument that the United States did not currently have sufficient forces to commit to the Mediterranean and that therefore a declaration of war would be futile, although he hoped the situation would "change early enough to render it possible to send some American divisions to the East." He urged Sevasly to avoid directly attacking the missionary lobby as the Armenians would need their assistance "at the time of final settlement." Nubar clearly recognized the influential connections that missionary leaders enjoyed with the White House and realized that the Armenians would need to work with them to ensure American support for their cause. Furthermore, Barton had promised him that the missionaries "will never lend themselves to a solution that would not liberate Armenia from the domination of the Turkish rulers."[116]

Sevasly would soon receive an even more emphatic declaration from Wilson himself of the US commitment to Armenia's ultimate liberation. On the Fourth of July, the president delivered an address at Mount Vernon in which he declared that the war's settlement must not be based on great power interests but on "the settlement of every question . . . upon the basis of the free acceptance of that settlement by the people immediately concerned." All nations had the right to be governed on the "same principles of honour and respect that govern individual citizens of all modern states." Postwar international harmony would rest on "the establishment of an organization of peace" backed by the "combined power of free nations." After the speech, Sevasly and the representatives of a number of other small nations were entertained by the president on board the *Mayflower*. Sevasly thanked Wilson for his address, declaring it "was a new Magna Charta [*sic*] and a new Declaration of Independence for all nations and that the Armenians will consider it as the best safeguard for the realization of their national aspirations." In response, Wilson took the opportunity to explain that he had not declared war on the Ottomans because "the work of reconstruction was being undertaken in Turkey and he was afraid that a declaration of war might jeopardize the program they had in view." Sevasly informed Wilson that the Armenians were concerned that the Ottomans might take advantage of the US decision to withhold a declaration of war "to save her hegemony over Armenia." Wilson reassured him that the Armenians need not be afraid of this as "at the Peace Congress there will be no question left half settled, that all questions will be disposed of, including the Armenian Question, once and for all." In this conversation, Wilson had gone further than ever before in committing the United States to helping resolve the Armenian question. Sevasly excitedly reported to Nubar that the president "will stand by the Armenians at the Peace Conference." Recognizing the significance of Wilson's statement, Nubar responded that this was "much clearer than all the public declarations he had previously made about Armenia" and "allows us for the first time to penetrate his thoughts."[117]

Wilson's comments were soon made public. During an interview with the *Christian Science Monitor*, Sevasly remarked that Armenian Americans had previously expressed concern that the United States had not declared war on the Ottomans, "which they consider the most tyrannical and cruel government in the world." Echoing Roosevelt's rhetoric, Sevasly stressed that his compatriots felt it was "inconsistent" for the United States to assert its commitment to "making the world safe for democracy, and defeating autocracy, [but] not attack the one government which is most flagrant in these respects." As a result, they had been worried that the Ottomans might take advantage of the American position to retain control over their Empire after the war. However, Sevasly declared that "all cause for anxiety on this score has been removed," as the president had stated that the United States would "use the weight of its counsel and influence at the peace conference to settle the Armenian Question once and for all."[118] Wilson's intention to help resolve the Armenian issue, irrespective of whether the United States was at war with the Ottomans, was now clearly on the record.

While the war still raged, the principal American role in the Near East remained the facilitation of relief. By the end of the year, the ACASR had raised and distributed over ten million dollars for Near East relief.[119] *American Review of Reviews* editor Albert Shaw, like his patron W. T. Stead, a supporter of both the Armenians and the missionary movement, later recalled that the relief campaign "transcended anything in the way of a national movement of charity and brotherhood that we have ever known."[120] The extent of the response was due in great part to the efforts of Morgenthau, who had become the leading spokesman for the ACASR. Nationally renowned for his exposition of the massacres, he was the figure Americans most associated with the Armenian cause. With presidential approval, he had conducted speaking tours across the country publicizing the massacres, and Germany's involvement in them, while helping raise money for relief. In October 1918 he published *Ambassador Morgenthau's Story*, an account of his experiences in Constantinople. It appeared, prepublication, in installments in over a dozen of the country's largest newspapers with a combined circulation of almost three million.[121] Morgenthau asked for Wilson's opinion on translating the book into a motion picture to emphasize "the true nature of German aggression" and German responsibility for the massacres.[122] However, the president disapproved of the idea: "There is nothing practical that we can do for the time being in the matter of the Armenian massacres, for example, and the attitude of the country toward Turkey is already fixed."[123] He did, however, approve, Morgenthau's inscription on the flyleaf of the book, which read:

> To Woodrow Wilson
>   The exponent in America of the enlightened public opinion of the
> world, which has decreed that small nations shall be respected and that
> such crimes as are described in this book shall never again darken the
> pages of history.[124]

The dedication in Morgenthau's book epitomized the power of Wilson's rhetoric in defining his vision of a new world order. Furthermore, the weight of American public sympathy for the Armenian cause and the president's own statements on the subject ensured it would be a diplomatic consideration for the US delegation at a future peace conference. As a result, when the war came to a close, both the Armenians and the Allies looked to the Americans, and their president, to safeguard the future of the Armenian people.

Do in the Near East What Was Done for Cuba and the Philippines

The Mudros Armistice, signed on October 31, 1918, ended war in the Near East. The Ottoman government had asked Wilson to take the lead in the peace negotiations, requesting the armistice be based on the president's Fourteen Points. However, as the United States had not been at war with the Ottomans, Washington deferred to the Allies and took no part in the negotiations.[125] The Allied victory was decisive and under the armistice all Ottoman troops would be demobilized except for a small policing force. With Constantinople impotent, the Ottoman Armenians proclaimed their independence, joining Russian Armenians who had already declared a separate republic in spring 1918.[126] American Armenophiles rejoiced at Armenian liberation. The *Los Angeles Times* declared: "When we think of Armenia, safe after more than a thousand years from the incessant butchery of the filthy and unspeakable Turks, we behold miracles not less than any told in holy writ."[127] The *New Republic* looked to the peace conference to confirm Armenia's independence, asserting that the Ottoman Empire must be dissolved "because it has proved itself physically impotent and morally broken." The Armenian massacres "argued against her retention of any shred of authority over non-Turkish people."[128]

The war on the Western Front ended on November 11, 1918, after Germany sued for an armistice on the basis of Wilson's Fourteen Points and his subsequent pronouncements. The war had witnessed the collapse of the German, Russian, Austro-Hungarian and Ottoman Empires. Even among the victors, Britain and France suffered great losses. Only the United States emerged stronger, more powerful economically and militarily, and with greater influence in world affairs. When Wilson announced he would lead the US delegation in Paris, he seemed in a position to shape a new world order; his wartime proclamations captivated colonized, oppressed, and stateless peoples.[129] Subject peoples invested their aspirations in him, as the personal representative of American power, and none more so than the Armenians. American missionaries and relief workers had kept Armenians alive during the war; the Armenian Patriarch of Constantinople remarked to one American relief worker, "We owe everything to the Americans."[130] As the conference approached, the Armenian author A. P. Hacobian summed up his nation's expectations: "When the time for reconstruction comes, American aid moral, material and cultural will be forthcoming on a scale and in a manner worthy of that great country and the lofty aims for which she entered the war."[131]

American missionaries also looked forward to a new era. The ABCFM leaders rejoiced that the "American nation [had] broken from the narrow nationalism of the past and taken her place permanently among those who bear the banner of civilization throughout the world."[132] They believed that America's new internationalist outlook and the favorable balance of power in the postwar world offered them the most advantageous circumstances that they had ever known for spreading the gospel. At the ABCFM's annual meeting in December 1918, its leaders proclaimed: "We come into the new order with an inspiring heritage: We bear the American name and prestige; we incarnate the democratic ideals which are sweeping over the earth; we stand for simplicity, for vitality, for union; we have the confidence of great governments; we have the good will of the people among whom we work." As the United States possessed greater power and influence than it had before, its pre-eminent missionary organization felt uniquely placed to shape global reconstruction in America's Christian image.[133] The ABCFM's position appeared particularly strong in the Near East. Having maintained its presence in the Empire during the war, ABCFM leaders felt confident that the decision to maintain peace with the Ottomans had been justified. Barton wrote to Dodge that the United States could now "take the lead in reorganizing the Near East," which, as he had warned during the war, would not have occurred if it was classified as a belligerent.[134] The missionary leader was convinced that the United States could now ensure the Armenian question "was settled right for time and eternity."[135] Dodge wrote to Wilson that one of America's aims should be establishment of "permanent peace" in the Near East and the "rehabilitation of the Christian races in Asia Minor."[136]

Even before the end of the war, the administration had begun to explore how this could be achieved and Allied imperial ambitions contained. When establishing the Inquiry, Wilson had informed House that its purpose was to "ascertain as fully and precisely as possible just what the several parties to this war on our side of it will be inclined to insist upon as part of the final peace arrangements, in order that we may formulate our own position for or against them."[137] At the president's instigation, House had directed the group to commission studies throughout 1918 on every conceivable issue requiring settlement at the postwar conference.[138] While there is no single listing of all the reports produced by the Inquiry, the most comprehensive inventory of its records lists 220 studies on various aspects of "Western Asia," the term that the Inquiry used to encompass the Ottoman Empire and the Persian Gulf region. This is a greater number than all the documents on Africa, the Far East (including India) and the Pacific region (encompassing Australasia) combined, and a greater number than on any single European territory, including Germany and Austria-Hungary.[139] Considering that the United States was not even at war with the Ottomans and had limited political interaction with the Empire prior to the conflict, the attention devoted to the region was no doubt due to the administration's awareness that this was the region where Allied territorial ambitions were focused.

Despite the quantity of reports produced, the Inquiry's work was hindered by the difficulty of finding qualified American experts on the region. Lippmann confided to Newton Baker that there was a "famine in men" with the requisite expertise on the Ottoman Empire, just as there was on other areas such as Russia, the Balkans and Africa.[140] This lack of knowledge was evident in the composition of the Inquiry's ten-man Western Asia team. None of this group, which operated out of Princeton University, was a specialist on the contemporary history of the region. Its head was a medievalist with an interest in the Crusades; his son, a Latin American specialist, was also a member. A number of the other members were authorities on the ancient, classical civilizations of Western Asia but had little expertise on regional developments in the succeeding millennium. Their reports were reliant on encyclopaedias, foreign trade statistics, and missionary publications for information. Some studies were simply summaries of these reference sources. Others admitted merely copying sections verbatim from official French and British publications. The reports rarely touched upon America's regional interests. Many expounded at length upon subjects such as a nation's literary or architectural heritage, with little attempt to relate their studies to the problems that would confront the peace conference.[141] Struggling to find academics with sufficient expertise, House turned for counsel to the Americans with the greatest knowledge of the region, the missionaries.

House had developed an association with missionary leaders through his work for Wilson. Earlier in 1918, he had met with Barton when the Board leader was lobbying the administration against war with the Ottomans. House confided to his diary that his and Barton's views on the Near East "do not materially differ. I regard him highly."[142] Barton was invited to contribute his thoughts to the Inquiry. Since America's intervention in the war, the ABCFM leader had continued to correspond with James Bryce, who hoped that the United States would assume a temporary protectorate over the Armenian provinces of the Ottoman Empire after the war.[143] With this in mind, Barton established an ACASR sponsored committee, comprised mainly of professors at American missionary colleges in the Near East, to collect materials on the future disposition of the Ottoman Empire. This Committee published a report recommending the Empire, with the exception of Arabia and British-controlled Egypt, be reconstituted as a loose federation under a Western power charged with developing the territory based on America's system in Cuba and the Philippines.[144] The ACASR passed this report on to the Wilson administration and Barton supported its conclusions in his own studies for the Inquiry.[145] He had celebrated the US expansion into the Caribbean and Pacific after the war with Spain for opening the territories to "Christian civilization and enlightenment" and enabling the "direct work of evangelization."[146] The ACBFM leader viewed potential US expansion into the Near East after the war in a similar light. He was convinced that an American protectorate over the region would safeguard the Armenians and ensure the dissemination of Christian values throughout the region.

Other commission reports supported Barton's argument. Inquiry member and Columbia historian James Shotwell argued that "geography, history and economics all point to one and the same solution for the problems of Western Asia . . . an agreement by the liberal powers of the world to do for this country what the United States has done in Cuba and is engaged in doing in the Philippines."[147] Barton also helped arrange for Nubar, with whom both he and Bryce corresponded, to submit a memorandum to the Inquiry. Nubar was adamant that Ottoman control over its Armenian provinces must end after the war and was therefore disinclined to entertain Barton's idea for a federal empire. However, Nubar also invoked the US colonial record as a justification for its protectorate over an independent Armenia. He informed a US State Department agent in Paris that "his hope lies with America and the words of Wilson's Proclamation which he keeps always on his table [and] he would like to see America play the part in Armenia that she played in Cuba and is playing in the Philippines."[148] Nubar had also informed the French government that he hoped for an autonomous Armenia under France's suzerainty. He clearly recognized that Armenia's liberty depended upon great-power sponsorship. Aware that Armenia's territory was less prosperous and sought after than other parts of the Empire, the Armenian leader employed any argument with the Western powers that would help advance his goal of independence. His celebration of America's rule in Cuba and the Philippines was flattering to Americans who felt that their nation's expansion was exceptional. Wilson was susceptible to this argument.[149] At Versailles, he hoped America's example as "trustee of the Filipino people" would serve as a model for reforming other empires.[150] The US colonial record would also encourage British officials, albeit for very different reasons, to urge Americans to extend their trusteeship to the Near East.

Armenia at the Front of the American Mind

At the end of the war, the extent of the Armenian crisis emerged. Deportations had spread the multitude of Armenians across the deserts of Syria and Mesopotamia, where starvation and disease were rife.[151] To meet the desperate need for aid, the ACASR incorporated under Congressional charter, becoming Near East Relief (NER), but its leadership and sponsorship remained principally with the ABCFM.[152] The Ottoman defeat meant the NER could abandon all restraint in vilifying the Empire's dominant group to raise funds. In the *Red Cross Magazine*, Morgenthau described the Turks as "diabolically" uncivilized and the Armenians as "fine, old civilized Christian peoples" caught in the "fangs

Figure 4.2 Campaign poster of the American Committee for Relief in the Near East, "Save the Survivors." Cornell University—PJ Mode Collection of Persuasive Cartography, 2029.01.

of the Turk."[153] The relief campaign appealed to the nation's historic sense of global mission and its traditional concern for Near Eastern Christianity. At the NER's request, Wilson appealed for Americans to raise $30 million in aid for the people of the Near East. The response was an unprecedented expression of private charity. By the end of 1919, nearly $20 million had been raised.[154]

The Armenian cause also enjoyed significant bipartisan support among political elites. Prominent Democrats and Republicans joined the American Committee for the Independence of Armenia (ACIA), established in 1918, and chaired by James Gerard, a former ambassador to Germany. Business and religious leaders were represented, including Barton and Dodge, as were the governors of more than twenty states. This influential lobby group also included presidential candidates William Jennings Bryan and Charles Evans Hughes, former Secretary of State Elihu Root, Senator Henry Cabot Lodge, and Oscar Straus. The former ambassador to Constantinople had worked on behalf of Armenian relief during the war and became an outspoken supporter of Armenian independence as he learned the full horror of the wartime massacres.[155] Selected by Wilson as an unofficial adviser on the rights of European Jewry at the peace conference, Straus remained concerned with the fate of the other persecuted minority with which his career had been intertwined. Writing to an Armenian leader during

Figure 4.3 Campaign poster of the American Committee for Relief in the Near East,
"They Shall Not Perish." Library of Congress, LC-USZC4-3173.

his voyage to Paris, Straus declared, "Armenia should, and must be free, and she
should have her ancient country under the guarantee that all nationalities shall
have equal political and religious rights."[156]

The Armenian American community—some one hundred thousand—was
also active in organizations for Armenian independence. Vahan Cardashian, a
New York attorney, served as the ACIA's conduit to the two Armenian delega-
tions in Paris, one led by Avetis Aharonian representing the Russian Armenian
Republic and the other by Nubar on behalf of the Ottoman Armenians.
Cardashian informed both delegations that while the abstract ideal of Armenian
independence enjoyed widespread American support, the absence of a unified
Armenian delegation was complicating advocacy for Armenian independence.[157]

The lack of a united de facto Armenian government led to neither Armenian delegation securing official recognition at the conference. However, Wilson assured Nubar that this "will not mean the slightest neglect of the interests of Armenia."[158] Wilson confirmed this after a message from Pope Benedict XV urged him to aid persecuted Christians, particularly Armenians, at the forthcoming peace conference. On Christmas Eve 1918, replying from Paris where he was awaiting the start of the Peace Conference, Wilson affirmed that "the sufferings of no other people have appealed to [Americans] more deeply than those of the Armenians," and he wished to secure their "complete deliverance from unjust subjection."[159] No other new nation enjoyed such widespread American support. As Herbert Hoover would recall, in 1919 when the Paris Peace Conference opened, "the name Armenia was at the front of the American mind."

5

The American Solution

In the opening weeks of the Paris Peace Conference, the renowned British Arabist T. E. Lawrence withdrew to his hotel room to be interviewed by the American progressive journalist Lincoln Steffens. Steffens hoped the exchange with this "Imperial pioneer" would offer his readers some insights into the practical politics of the Near East. However, Lawrence had his own agenda. He wanted the United States to "take charge of the Armenians" and cited recent American foreign policy to support his case. Lawrence reminded Steffens that his nation had annexed Hawaii, occupied the Philippines and Puerto Rico, liberated Cuba but kept a mortgage on it, put marines ashore in Central America, and intervened militarily in Mexico. And yet Lawrence stated, "You are still for self-determination for small nations; you are a small empire, and you warned us in your Monroe Doctrine that you are going to be a great empire; and yet you are anti-imperialists; you have just fought a war against German imperialism."

"So did you," Steffens shot back. "Ah, but that is different," Lawrence replied. "We frankly call ourselves an Empire and we fought honestly for our Empire against Germany's. But you—you fought against empire for—self-determination." For Lawrence, though, this American idealism was salutary: "Americans can do whatever and not be doubted either by the world or by themselves; there is something very great about that, something useful to the world."[1] Only later did Steffens realize that Lawrence's purpose had been to "load him up" with propaganda to publicize to Americans that the United States must take a mandate for an independent Armenia through the League of Nations. In his first month at Versailles Lawrence met with ten American journalists and commissioners to push for a US mandate in the Near East. He privately described it as "the campaign in favour of the US co-operating in the East to secure the practice of her ideals."[2] Rudyard Kipling, another advocate of a US mandate, more succinctly termed it "the American scheme."[3]

In addition to Lawrence and Kipling, the scheme's proponents included many prominent British officials. They were aware that overwhelming public sympathy for the Armenian cause, and consequent hostility toward the Ottomans, had not translated into effective action by the US government during the war. However, British lobbyists hoped that humanitarian concerns, economic ambitions, and missionary interests would encourage the United States to accept mandates for Armenia and also an internationalized Constantinople in the war's aftermath. These mandates would satisfy domestic demands for Armenia's protection and serve Britain's strategic interests. The overriding motivation was to establish what Colonial Secretary Lord Milner called "a bond of union between the United States and the British Empire."[4] The vision of an Anglo-American "colonial alliance," advocated by prominent British statesmen in the 1890s and reawakened by US intervention in the war, would finally be achieved.

While the British government viewed these mandates as solid US commitments to an Anglo-American led global order, Wilson continued to distrust Allied imperialism. He had privately noted that the Allies did not share his views on the postwar peace; this was the main reason why the United States had refused to declare war on the Ottomans. After the war, rather than acting in partnership with Britain, Wilson wanted the United States to take the lead in establishing a reformed international system, dismembering the Ottoman Empire and guaranteeing its subject peoples from imperial exploitation. However, the clash over whether the United States would assume a mandate would become entangled in a wider debate over its membership in the League of Nations and its future world role. Central to this debate was the question of whether it should join with the British Empire to construct a new global order.

Uniting the Two Great English-Speaking Commonwealths

When the Peace Conference opened on January 12, 1919, the principal issues to be resolved were the German peace treaty, establishment of a European settlement, and Wilson's priority, the creation of a League of Nations. The Near Eastern settlement was a secondary consideration. However, the area remained of critical significance to the Allies and its interconnection with European affairs ensured its place on the agenda. On January 30 the Allied and American leaders adopted a statement of principles on the mandate system, assigning former German colonies and Ottoman territories to a major power to govern on the League's behalf. The mandate concept emerged from ideas on reforming colonial government that germinated on both sides of the Atlantic during the war.[5] The South African leader Jan Christian Smuts outlined it in detail in a preconference pamphlet, *The League of Nations: A Practical Suggestion*, which caught Wilson's attention.[6] Smuts's proposal served as the basis for a compromise between Wilson's insistence that territories should not be distributed as spoils and a general consensus that these nations were not yet capable of standing alone. In the section relating to the Ottoman Empire the leaders stated, "particularly because of the historical mis-government by the Turks of subject peoples and the terrible massacres of Armenians and others in recent years . . . Armenia, Syria, Mesopotamia, Palestine and Arabia must be completely severed from the Turkish Empire." These lands, along with Germany's former possessions, were made the "sacred trust of civilization" under the League and their "tutelage . . . entrusted to advanced nations."[7]

Deciding where the Armenian state would be and which "advanced nation" should assume the mandate was more difficult. The application of national self-determination in the Near East was complicated by Allied imperial designs and overlapping ethnic populations. At the war's outset, the majority of Armenians were based on the Ottoman-Russian border. The deportations and massacres had dispersed them further afield. The mandatory power would need to carve out an Armenian majority state, combining the Armenian Republic in the Caucasus with the historic Armenian provinces of the Ottoman Empire, and safeguard its security. Russia, the traditional protector of Christians in the region, had been the obvious choice. The Allied secret treaties provided for Russian control over Armenia but the Bolshevik Revolution made Russia an international pariah. In any case, Lenin had renounced any claims to Armenia, and Russia was embroiled in civil war.[8] Prior to the conference, the Allies all expressed support for Armenia. French Prime Minister Georges Clemenceau wrote to an Armenian leader that the Allies would settle Armenia's fate "according to the supreme laws of Humanity and Justice." Vittorio Orlando, Italy's premier, announced, "Say to the Armenians that I make their cause my cause."[9] British Prime Minister David Lloyd George pledged to an Armenian delegation that "Britain will not forget its responsibilities toward your martyred race."[10] Despite their sympathy, Allied priorities lay elsewhere; they therefore hoped the United States would assume responsibility.

British statesmen in particular hoped for an American mandate. The wartime atrocities had heightened British popular concern for the Armenians.[11] The *Manchester Guardian* summarized British sentiments: "Another word remains— Armenia—a word of ghastly horror, carrying the memory of deeds not done in the world since Christ was born—a country swept by the wholesale murder of its people; to Turkey that country must never and under no circumstances go back."[12] Lloyd George publicly declared Armenian independence a British war aim. He later recalled that the "redemption" of Armenia from Turkish misrule was an essential peace term for every leading British politician.[13] However, he looked to establish an independent Armenia without Britain assuming responsibility. An American mandate served British strategic interests, checking France's regional influence and guarding against potential Bolshevist, pan-Turanian, or pan-Islamic threats to the access routes to British India. Lloyd George also hoped Wilson's anti-imperialist credentials would legitimize the Ottoman settlement and counter accusations the mandate system was merely cover for a colonial land-grab.[14]

The prime motive was summarized by Colonial Secretary Lord Milner. "The future of the world," Milner declared, "depended upon a good understanding between us [Britain and the United States]." An American mandate was not "a mere cloak of annexation, but a bond of union." Lloyd George agreed that if Americans assumed their "share of guardianship, it would have a great effect on the peace of the world."[15] Smuts and the Canadian Prime Minister Sir Robert Borden were also determined to see the United States take its share of the burden of international governance through the mandate system. Smuts informed his colleagues that "our line of policy should be, if possible, to work with America." Emphasizing the argument that he would later make in his pamphlet, Smuts stated that the Allies were confronted by the collapse of large-scale Empires in Eurasia. Unwilling to simply divide the territories as "loot," Smuts argued that the only way to conserve global peace and provide effective government for the new states was if the Allies, and especially the United States, assumed a tutelary role through the League for one or more of them. The nation over which Americans assumed a mandate was immaterial to Smuts. His priority was to get the United States into European politics; "it is no use her sitting outside, let her undertake the burden and let her feel the responsibility."[16] This did not extend to offering Americans a mandate in Africa, where Smuts hoped the British Empire would expand its territory. Conversely, Borden made clear that the Canadians did not believe the war was fought for territorial aggrandizement. While reluctantly supporting other Dominion leaders' territorial ambitions, Borden's principal aim was "to unite by the closest possible ties of purpose, of interest and of action, the two great English speaking commonwealths which are of themselves sufficiently powerful to dictate the peace of the world." To further this ideal and dispel accusations, particularly from the United States, that the war was fought to expand Britain's Empire, it was necessary to encourage Americans, however reluctant, to undertake "world-wide responsibilities in respect of undeveloped territories and backward races." Borden dismissed suggestions that Americans were insufficiently experienced in colonial administration, pointing to the Philippines. Regardless, it was time for Americans to learn so they could share such responsibilities with Britain. To colleagues who were sceptical that Americans could be persuaded to assume any responsibilities outside the Western Hemisphere, Borden responded that however unlikely, it was worth the effort: "No such wonderful opportunity has ever presented itself before; it may be that no such opportunity will ever arise in the future."[17] Borden and Smuts were determined to seize this unique opening to realize their ideal of an Anglo-American alliance.

British policymakers debated potential US mandates prior to the conference. Smuts's opposition torpedoed any suggestion of German East Africa,
while Lloyd George ruled out placing an "absolutely new and crude Power" in
Palestine. Ultimately, they settled on Armenia and Constantinople. It was Lord
Milner who proposed Armenia: "The mere fact that we did not want it ourselves
was no reason for not assigning the responsibility to the United States." Lord
Curzon articulated the rationale for a Constantinople mandate: the Turkish
presence there was "an ulcer in the side of Europe" and should be removed.
The case for the United States undertaking these responsibilities did not meet
with unanimous approval. Naval leaders, in particular, had been opposed to
an American mandate in the Near East. Former First Lord of the Admiralty
Winston Churchill echoed their concerns, warning that "if America were introduced in the heart of European politics, in Armenia, or anywhere else in the
Mediterranean region, this would be an incentive to her to make herself the
greatest Naval Power." However, with Britain unwilling to assume these mandates, and France ruled out, opposition to the United States was overruled.
As diplomat Sir Eyre Crowe remarked, there was general agreement that "the
American solution was the best."[18]

At the forefront of the mandate movement was the Round Table, the influential pressure group for imperial federation. A month before the conference, the
editor of its journal, Lionel Curtis, published an article declaring: "The future
of the [international] system depends upon whether America will now assume
her fair share of the burden, especially in the Near East."[19] The most prominent
advocate was Philip Kerr, the journal's former editor and Lloyd George's private
secretary. Kerr wrote for the journal throughout the war, outlining the case for
a reformed international system centered on an Anglo-American alliance.[20] He
argued that defeating Germany was only the first step in securing peace. The
greatest problems confronting the peace conference were in countries "inhab-
ited by peoples who have never yet succeeded in maintaining a stable form of
Government." His central thesis was that "all the backward peoples have some-
how or other to be converted into self-governing nations" in order to make the
world truly "safe for democracy." The victorious nations should each assume "a
share in making the world a fit place for all men to live in."[21] He was aware that
many Americans would regard this as "iniquitous imperialism" but was convinced that they could be persuaded.[22]

In an article outlining "The Practical Organization of Peace," Kerr recalled
that the 1823 announcement of the Monroe Doctrine was accompanied by US
refusal to recognize Greek belligerency against the Ottoman Empire and that this
had led to Americans assuming "America had no responsibilities in Europe." Yet
the United States had subsequently become deeply embroiled in Near Eastern
affairs through the work of its missionaries and educational institutions, which

provided training in political ideas to statesmen throughout the region. Kerr regarded this traditional approach of denying US official interest in regional politics "while applauding the activities of American educationalists and missionaries and boasting of the power of American democratic propaganda" as "one of the most curious phenomena ever presented to the student of social psychology." However, the United States was gaining an appreciation for the interconnection between religious teaching, political education, and great power conflict over "the less developed regions of the world." Kerr credited the establishment of joint boards of Protestant missions in Britain and the United States and the summoning of the World Missionary Conference at Edinburgh for this evolution. Transnational cooperation between transatlantic missionaries provided a model for an international organization that would assume "responsibilities as trustees for less developed peoples." With regard to the Ottoman Empire, the unofficial role played by American missionaries in spreading principles of constitutional government would provide the basis for the US government's assumption of regional mandates, helping to ensure the permanent settlement of the "problem of the Middle East." Not only would this bring order to a troubled region, but it would also ally Britain and the United States in a joint mission to advance their shared "ideas of government and principles of justice."[23]

In an interview with the *Philadelphia Inquirer* during the war, Kerr had already stressed that it was not the oft-invoked rhetoric of "blood brotherhood or common Anglo Saxon descent" that would unite Britain and America but recognition that "common ideals for the future of the world . . . will be realized only when they begin to promote them in co-operation."[24] In the months leading up to the peace conference he attempted to build on the wartime work of his Round Table colleague, the banker Robert H. Brand, who had mounted a subscription drive for the journal while based in Washington, DC. Brand had advertised in the *New Republic* and sent copies of the periodical to leading publicists, libraries, and scholars. Although the journal's circulation was limited to roughly two hundred US subscribers, Kerr and the other editors were heartened that most of its readers were influential journalists and members of the governing elite.[25] Brand's network ensured that Kerr's articles were distributed to delegates of the American Commission to Negotiate Peace.[26]

Kerr traveled to Paris determined to personally lobby American decision-makers to take up the mandates. He was aided by fellow Round Table members who served on the British delegation, including Curtis and Arnold Toynbee, and others sympathetic to the cause, such as Lawrence and Kipling.[27] Personally ill-disposed to Armenians, claiming they had a "passion for martyrdom," Lawrence was nonetheless a zealous advocate for an American mandate.[28] Having acted as a wartime liaison officer between Britain and Prince Feisal, leader of the Arab Revolt against the Ottomans, Lawrence was in Paris as both an advisor to the

British delegation and a member of Feisal's staff. His determination to secure an American presence in the Near East was motivated by a desire to counter France's regional influence and he also hoped to use Wilson's commitment to self-determination to thwart French claims to Syria, which he envisaged Feisal ruling under either British or American protection.[29] Kipling was eager to use a mandate to advance an Anglo-American "entente" that ensured the two nations shared in the reconstruction of the Near East, just as previously he had urged Americans to assume "the White Man's Burden" in the Philippines and join Britain in spreading "civilization."[30] Writing to his American publisher Frank Doubleday, who shared his commitment to an alliance, Kipling expressed concern that the continued strength of Anglophobia in American politics, particularly among Irish Americans, would tarnish the League as a British imperial project and preclude Americans from assuming their global responsibilities. Kipling argued that the "only way of stopping the fuss is for the U.S.A. to come into the game via either Constantinople or Armenia."[31]

As far as Kipling was concerned, the one man capable of furthering Anglo-American relations and bringing the United States "into the game" was Theodore Roosevelt.[32] Immediately after the armistice, Roosevelt was prepared to state publicly that "as regards the British Empire (Great Britain and Ireland and Australia, Canada, South Africa and New Zealand), I would go in for any alliance and agree to arbitrate every question of any kind that comes up." Roosevelt, increasingly spoken of as the next Republican presidential nominee, also continued to promote Armenia's cause. He repeatedly declared in public speeches and articles that at the peace conference "the Turk should be driven from Europe" and "Armenia made free."[33] Some Armenians even suggested that if the United States assumed a protectorate over Armenia, Roosevelt should become its governor.[34] When he died in January 1919, shortly before the peace conference opened, both the British and Armenians mourned him. In Britain, the man that Kipling eulogized as "Great Heart" was given the signal honor of a memorial service at Westminster Abbey.[35] For Armenians, Roosevelt would "be remembered among the first of those who nobly and effectively championed Armenia in her heroic struggle for independence!"[36]

Even without Roosevelt, however, Republican support remained strong. Indeed, as the historian Lloyd Ambrosius illustrates, the support of leading Republicans, such as Henry Cabot Lodge and Elihu Root, for protecting Armenian independence was second only to maintaining French security in the long-term commitments they were prepared to accept in the Old World.[37] Following Roosevelt's death, his close friend Lodge, the Republican Senate Majority Leader and Chairman of the Foreign Relations Committee, became Wilson's staunchest opponent. Like Roosevelt, Lodge was a long-standing advocate of greater American involvement in world affairs and an early supporter of participation in an international organization.[38] However, he too had regarded Wilson's wartime promotion of the League concept as untimely, naïve, and indicative of the president's unwillingness to prosecute the war effectively. Lodge and Wilson disliked each other intensely, but both were committed to protecting Armenian security. Lodge was a leading member of the ACIA and sponsored a Senate resolution in December calling for US recognition of, and assistance to, an independent Armenian republic.[39]

Lodge's championship of the Armenians, and his support for a more assertive US foreign policy, attracted the attention of British proponents of US mandates, who lobbied him to champion the cause in the Senate. Most notable was Lodge's long-time correspondent Moreton Frewen, a former Member of Parliament, vice president of the Imperial Federation League, and uncle to Winston Churchill. His Anglo-Irish gentry background and experience as a cattle-rancher in Wyoming had helped him to establish a network of high-level contacts on both sides of the Atlantic.[40] When Lodge visited Britain in the late 1890s, Frewen had introduced him to W. T. Stead, who had attempted to interest Lodge in his solution to the Armenian, and larger Eastern, question. At the time, although Lodge had informed Frewen that he hoped to "live to see the Turkish Empire go to pieces," he had dismissed Stead's scheme for a US protectorate in the Near East as "perfectly crazy" and "a wild impossibility."[41] However, US intervention in World War I encouraged Frewen, a passionate exponent of an Anglo-American alliance, to take up Stead's proposal again. After Lodge delivered a speech in the Senate in September 1918 calling for the Ottomans to be "put out of Europe," Frewen urged him to help realize "Stead's Vision" by campaigning for a US mandate for Constantinople, the Dardanelles, and the surrounding region. Frewen justified this with a mixture of strategic rationale and an idealistic appeal to the unity of the English-speaking people; he was less concerned than Stead had been with the security of the Armenians. Frewen argued that US control over Constantinople would reinforce Britain's position in Gibraltar, containing the German threat to the Near East and ensuring Anglo-American dominance of the Mediterranean. Above all, Frewen suggested, it would help to establish a "formal alliance" between Britain and the United States. He assured Lodge that if the United States moved into the Eastern Mediterranean then "you could make the world ready for the growth of the United States thirty years after and for Peace forever."[42] Lodge remained skeptical of the plausibility or desirability of "Stead's Vision." While he accepted that the United States was best placed to assume the mandate for Constantinople, as its principal interest in the region was peace, he did not believe it was necessary and was doubtful that the American public would agree to it. Nevertheless, Lodge emphasized his belief that "the war will not be completely won unless the allies take possession of Constantinople and put it under guardians of whom the United States would naturally be one."[43]

Although more limited than Stead's original proposal of an exclusively American protectorate, Lodge did indicate a willingness to see the United States work with Britain and the other Allies to stabilize the region, which would result in the resolution of the Armenian question. Eager to promote a proposition that he believed would advance Anglo-American relations, Frewen passed on Lodge's views to his friends in the press and the British government, including Foreign Secretary Arthur Balfour.[44]

Whitehall's chief source on American mandate supporters was James Bryce. An early advocate of a league of nations, Bryce looked to a postwar international organization to realize two of his most cherished ideals: an Anglo-American alliance and an independent Armenia.[45] When Balfour asked him to ascertain American attitudes toward undertaking the mandates, Bryce took up the task with relish. Having sought the views of his many prominent American correspondents, particularly the missionary lobby, he reported, "the public feeling of the USA would favour such a plan."[46] Throughout the peace conference, Bryce, Kerr, and their fellow schemers urged Americans to resolve the Armenian question and assume their share of responsibility for postwar reconstruction.

A General Indefiniteness of Opinion

Few Americans in Paris were as sympathetic as Bryce's contacts. At a meeting with Kerr, Curtis, and Toynbee, Fredric Howe, the progressive publicist and Wilson confidant, responded wearily to entreaties for an Armenian mandate: "America is to be asked to carry the bag; to police Europe and remove from England and France the burden of protecting imperialistic ventures."[47] Legal advisor David Hunter Miller was also distrustful. "Doubtless [America] will get such of those as Great Britain thinks too difficult for herself," he complained, "and those will lie in the hands of the United States as a bulwark of the British Empire, such as Armenia."[48] Secretary of State Lansing was most suspicious. He believed American strength lay in its lack of selfish interests and that the Allies would seek to undermine the United States by entangling it in imperial intrigue. He feared the Allies would take advantage of Wilson's "altruism and idealism" by imposing unremunerative mandatory burdens on the United States while they secured resource-rich territories.[49]

However, Wilson would not be enticed so easily. When Curzon raised the issue of mandates in London before the conference, Wilson replied, "if the League of Nations were once constituted . . . the United States might possibly be less reluctant to consider the question of mandatory intervention."[50] The League was Wilson's priority and the means by which he would ensure Americans sustained an active involvement in world politics. He was determined that the

League should be integral to any peace treaty, believing this would make it more difficult for the Senate to reject.[51] Conscious of public opinion, Wilson was as yet unprepared to commit to new responsibilities in the Near East while seeking consent for unprecedented participation in world affairs. In Paris, when the Allies suggested American mandates for Armenia and Constantinople, Wilson was guarded. If the United States was expected to assume these responsibilities then the mandate system would need to be postponed until he could educate Americans about the situation.[52]

Wilson evaded a direct commitment but privately contemplated greater regional involvement. In February 1919, he wrote to Secretary of War Newton Baker inquiring whether US troops should be sent to "garrison portions of the Turkish Empire." This would relieve Britain's burden in anticipation of a final peace settlement and the designation of mandates. Wilson wished to know the legality of sending troops, considering the United States had not been at war with the Ottomans, and the wisdom of such a policy, in view of public opinion and American regional interests. Noting the longstanding concern for missionary schools in Constantinople and "the pitiful fortunes of the Armenians," Wilson assumed that Americans would support the occupation and the region's inhabitants would welcome US troops.[53] Baker cautioned against it. While there were no legal impediments, he thought it preferable to assume some of Britain's duties on the Western Front, so more British troops could be deployed in the Near East. If the president was determined to send a US force, it should be restricted to protecting Christians in Armenia, which Baker believed public opinion would approve, although he warned demands for the army to return home were growing in some quarters.[54] Heeding Baker's advice, and preoccupied with drafting the League Covenant, Wilson decided to hold off on sending American troops to the Near East.

The Armenians appealed to Wilson for protection. The Armenian National Delegation leader Boghos Nubar reminded him that they had lost a quarter of their population during the war, a greater percentage than any belligerent nation. He advocated union between Turkish Armenians and the Armenian Republic, in a territory stretching from the Caucasus to the Mediterranean, under a US mandate, claiming this "would be an act worthy of the great American people who joined this War for the sake of their ideals."[55] However, by the time the Armenian delegations officially presented their joint case to the peace conference on February 26, Wilson had left Paris. Having secured agreement on the Covenant and presented it to the conference, he returned home to handle legislation before Congress adjourned. He received a rapturous welcome on his arrival in Boston. Speaking to the crowd, he emphasized the benevolent image of the United States overseas "as the friend of mankind." Reminding the crowd of Armenia's sufferings, he proclaimed: "You poured out your money to help succour Armenians after they suffered; now set up your strength so that they shall never suffer again."[56] Recognizing its extensive public and Congressional support, the president hoped appealing to the Armenian cause would help sell the League to the American people.

Back in Washington, Wilson spoke even more candidly. Addressing the Democratic National Committee, Wilson revealed he was asked in Paris if the United States would accept the mandates; he replied that he was unsure but was prepared to "stump the country" and see. Wilson confided "personally, and just within the limits of this room, I can say very frankly that I think we ought to." The "whole heart of America has been engaged for Armenia" and Americans knew "more about Armenia and its sufferings than about any other European area." Referring to its missionary enterprises in the region, Wilson declared that the Near East was "a part of the world where already American influence extends." The mandates could only be undertaken as a work of "disinterested philanthropy," but he believed this selflessness would appeal to Americans.[57]

Wilson's support was echoed by the missionary lobby, the ACIA, and the press. The *Missionary Herald* argued Americans could no longer hide behind the Monroe Doctrine but must pursue an active role in world affairs, beginning

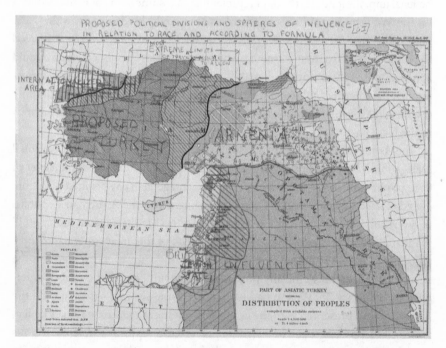

Figure 5.1 Proposal for a large Armenian state, stretching from the Caucasus to the Mediterranean, drawn on an old map of "Asiatic Turkey" in the Woodrow Wilson Papers, Manuscript Division, Library of Congress (171.00.00).

in the Near East.[58] The ACIA concurred in widely distributed pamphlets.[59] The *New York Times* suggested that if Americans accepted a "mandate outside our own neighbourhood, we should probably be as well satisfied to be in Armenia as anywhere."[60] The *New Republic* believed the United States should take the mandates, although there were no material benefits, as "no other people [had] ever given a similar proof of devotion to the principle of self-government."[61] The nation's exceptional history made it the ideal choice.

In Paris, Colonel House represented Wilson in matters requiring attention of the Allied chiefs of staff. During one meeting, when asked whether the United States would accept mandates for Armenia and Constantinople, House replied, "America was not in the least anxious to take these mandates but that she felt she could not shirk her share of the burden." He even suggested that the United States would be prepared to "exercise some sort of general supervision over Anatolia" and outlined a detailed plan for raising capital for the development of Constantinople at a low rate of interest.[62] Kerr excitedly wrote to Lloyd George, who had briefly returned to Britain, informing him of these developments.[63] But House had expressed a far more definite and extensive commitment than Wilson had been prepared to make.

Moreover, Wilson had concluded it was an inopportune time to publicly urge the mandates. In early March, Lodge had publicized the "Round Robin" that denounced the Covenant as unacceptable in its current form and expressed particular opposition to the open-ended "collective security" commitment of its Article X. Signed by thirty-seven senators, it posed a clear threat to Wilson's peace plan. Certain Senators, irreconcilably opposed to League membership, attacked potential American mandates as evidence of the commitments it would impose.[64] William Borah (R-ID) was particularly suspicious of Allied motives and, specifically, the British thirst for oil in the former territories of the Ottoman Empire. "Are there not any undeveloped oil fields in Armenia or Turkey, then?" he inquired in the Senate.[65] Hiram Johnson (R-CA) claimed that the suggestion the United States would be asked to take mandates was the clearest example that the League was designed "to police the world with American boys." If Americans joined the League and accepted a mandate, it would be "the greatest triumph of all history for England's diplomacy."[66] Realizing formal acceptance of mandates could be used to assail the League, Wilson refrained from publicly advocating them, although he continued to express support in private.[67]

Following Wilson's return to Paris in mid-March, Anglo-French disagreement arose over Syria, promised to France under the secret agreements. To resolve the dispute, Wilson proposed sending an inter-Allied commission to the region to ascertain opinion on all potential mandates. The French and British opposed this, fearing it would threaten their territorial claims.[68] The Armenian delegates and Wilson's own advisors were equally hostile, arguing that sufficient information was available and delay to the settlement would outweigh all advantages.[69] However, Wilson was unwilling to allow dismemberment of the Ottoman Empire based on Allied self-interest. A commission would obstruct Allied designs while delaying American mandatory commitments until he prepared public opinion. The Allied decision not to participate failed to deter him. The US representatives, led by theologian Henry King and Charles Crane, a businessman and noted Arabist, set out in May.

While the peacemakers deliberated in Paris, the Armenian situation deteriorated further. Herbert Hoover, head of the American Relief Administration, reported starvation and typhus were widespread, "the dead and dying everywhere in the streets" and "at least 250,000 Armenians were at the absolute point of death."[70] The Armenians pressed the US delegation for immediate assistance. Ray Stannard Baker, the president's press secretary, later wrote: "Scarcely a day passed that mournful Armenians, bearded and black clad, did not besiege the American delegation or, less frequently, the president, setting forth the really terrible conditions of their own ravished land."[71] Direct contact with the delegation was arranged through ancient historian William L. Westermann, the American adviser on Western Asian affairs. Westermann, who was a member of the American Commission to Negotiate Peace, favored an American mandate for Armenia.[72] This angered Lansing, who noted "Westermann's attitude shows [the] folly of having inexperienced men attempting to outline policies of government." Lansing declared he was "not particularly interested" in Armenia and informed Wilson that he opposed a mandate.[73] Lansing's opposition, and his suspicion of Allied designs, was shared by Hoover, who supported sending relief but was against a mandate.[74] In mid-May, when House asked Hoover, on Wilson's behalf, to become governor for the mandate, Hoover was reluctant. He believed at least 150,000 troops would be needed to defend Armenia against threats from the Turks, Azerbaijanis, and Bolsheviks, and argued the mandatory acquiring the riches of Mesopotamia—Britain—should also assume responsibilities for barren Armenia.[75]

However, opposition from his advisers did not sway Wilson from his conviction that the United States should help in the reconstruction of the world by assuming mandates. After the draft treaty was presented to Germany on May 7, Wilson was optimistic of American approval and entrance into the League. Consequently, he was hopeful of securing League membership and winning domestic support for American mandates, as his consideration of Hoover's appointment as governor shows. Lansing bitterly noted that neither his nor Hoover's counsel had any impact on Wilson, who welcomed "the moral duty of the great and enlightened nations to aid the less fortunate" and protect them until they were capable of self-government.[76] Wilson was not as naive to Allied intrigue as Lansing and Hoover assumed. As he informed Westermann, if the

United States assumed a mandate in the Near East, it "would be in a strategic position to control that portion of the world" and check Allied imperialism.[77]

On May 14, in the Council of Four, Wilson agreed to accept mandates for Armenia and Constantinople, "subject to the assent of the Senate."[78] In addition to awarding the US mandates for Constantinople and Armenia, the Council agreed to place the remainder of Turkish Anatolia under French and Italian mandates.[79] However, later that month Lloyd George, fearing opposition from Muslim subjects of the British Empire and concerned by growing French influence in the Near East, argued against Turkey being divided. Instead he suggested that the United States should take a mandate for all of Turkey, as well as one for Armenia. This initiative, besides arousing strong opposition from Clemenceau, was immediately rejected by Wilson. The United States had no direct interests in Anatolia and the mandate would be opposed by the American public. However, he emphasized an Armenian mandate would appeal to Americans for "humanitarian reasons," declaring, "Americans have already sent missionaries, money and relief societies to Armenia. American opinion is interested in Armenia."[80]

By the end of June, the peace treaty with Germany had been agreed and Wilson prepared to return home. With the Turkish settlement still unresolved, the president and the Allied leaders believed it would be unreasonable to maintain a technical state of war with Turkey until the United States decided on a mandate. Wilson proposed that Turkey, while retaining its sovereignty in Anatolia, should be simply informed which parts of the Empire would no longer belong to her; these regions could be immediately detached and placed under Allied occupation until a final settlement was agreed. The president declared he "had studied the question of the Turks in Europe for a long time, and every year confirmed his opinion that they ought to be cleared out." Wilson failed to recognize the implication of his suggestion. As Lloyd George and Clemenceau warned, there were no Allied troops in Turkish Armenia and the withdrawal of Ottoman forces, who were maintaining order in the territories, could result in fresh massacres. Although he wished to have the settlement resolved, Wilson was unwilling to make any commitments until he had assessed American sentiments on the matter. When Lloyd George suggested "a short, sharp peace with Turkey" be established at once, Wilson would give no positive response.[81] Unable to agree on an early settlement, on June 27 the Council declared the Turkish settlement would be suspended until the American people had determined whether they would accept a mandate.[82]

That same day Wilson held his first and only press conference during his time in Paris. At the urging of Ray Stannard Baker, he agreed to meet with reporters but only on the condition that what he said could not be quoted or even attributed to him. Wilson informed the correspondents that he personally favored mandates for Armenia and Constantinople but emphasized that only Congress

Figure 5.2 British cartoon responding to rumors that Woodrow Wilson had rejected a mandate for Constantinople during the Paris peace conference. "The Great Renunciation," *Punch*, May 28, 1919.

could decide whether to assume this duty. He had only promised to present this request but confided: "I am inclined to think that our people would consider it favourably, for they have always shown much interest in Armenia."[83]

The first of Wilson's Fourteen Points had stated that "diplomacy shall proceed always frankly and in the public view." It was therefore ironic that the privacy in which the president conducted his peacemaking left his countrymen perplexed as to the nature of the commitments the country was preparing to undertake. Nevertheless, rumors abounded in the US press that Americans would be asked to assume mandates. Before the advent of scientific public opinion polling, the *Literary Digest*'s survey of newspaper and journal editorial opinion offered the clearest indication of popular sentiments. It reported that commentators were left asking: "What, really, is meant by Armenia?" and "Would our responsibilities be limited to Constantinople and Armenia or extended over Syria as well and perhaps additional regions?" This did not prevent them debating the merits of potential mandates. The editor of the Helena (Mont.) *Independent* wanted the United States to have nothing to do with "two caterwauling neighbors like Turkey and Armenia" and demanded that the Allies "act as the wet-nurses of the incorrigibles: We want none of them." Other publications objected to departing from the traditional policy of "no entangling alliances" and stressed the financial and military burden a mandate would entail. Yet others argued that Americans should take the mandate to showcase their altruism. A number of pundits suggested Americans were best equipped to assume the mandates, considering they already exercised a similar role for numerous nations in the Western Hemisphere and the Philippines. Christian humanitarian ideals animated many responses. The *Chicago Evening Post* claimed it was natural for a "country whose coin bears the legend 'In God We Trust' to play the part of the good Samaritan" by aiding Armenia. Appeals to America's idealism and historic world mission mingled with a desire to limit international responsibilities and refrain from burdensome overseas commitments. Surveying the political scene, the Wheeling, West Virginia *Register* summed up the public mood: "Leaders of thought in all parts of the United States recognize the decision to be taken on this subject is the most difficult [the president] will have to make," but there "is on this side of the water a general indefiniteness of opinion and no confirmed attitude." It was into this confused atmosphere that Wilson sailed home from Paris on June 28.[84]

America First: Executive Authority or Congressional Consent?

On July 10, 1919, Wilson personally delivered the treaty to the Senate. He argued that America's isolation had ended following the Spanish-American War, and there was no question of it ceasing "to be a world power." Americans could only decide whether they would accept the "moral leadership" that was offered to them. Wilson did not delve into the fine details of the settlement. He mentioned the mandate system only in passing, and although he stated that the peoples of the Ottoman Empire would be released "from unspeakable distress" and "given adequate guarantees of friendly protection, guidance and assistance," he made no reference to potential US mandates.[85] Wilson was confident that the League's general concept appealed to Americans and he was determined not to let specific obligations prevent treaty approval.[86] Irreconcilable opponents of the League had already warned that this "supergovernment" would entangle Americans in the world's worst "garbage heaps" and condemned suggestions of a mandate.[87] Although in Paris Wilson had promised to present the mandates to the American people, he now realized the fight he faced to secure ratification. Consequently, he decided to postpone his request. The morning of his Senate address he held a press conference; this time, his comments were on the record. When asked whether he expected the United States to assume any mandates, Wilson responded: "Let us not go too fast. Let's get the treaty first."[88]

The League certainly appeared to have wide public support: thirty-two state legislatures, thirty-three governors, and a clear majority of newspaper editors had endorsed it by the time Wilson returned from Paris.[89] However, many Republicans, the majority party in the Senate, favored more limited international involvement and insisted on certain reservations before support- ing the treaty.[90] Lodge was among the "reservationists," but also remained a firm supporter of the Armenian cause. He continued to serve on the ACIA's executive and up to spring 1919 believed Americans would accept the man- dates. However, by the time the treaty was presented to the Senate, he was fun- damentally opposed.[91] After Frewen had again appealed to him to champion "Stead's Vision" in June, Lodge replied that "the general feeling of the country is against our being a mandatory anywhere; and the League, especially Article 10, has done a great deal to kill the possibility of our doing what I think would very likely have been a great help to the world."[92] As well as his belief that the mandates were unpopular with the American public, Lodge now feared that if accepted, they would lead to an open-ended commitment in the Near East, detrimental to US interests. Furthermore, Republican "irreconcilable" oppo- nents of the League were unalterably opposed to a mandate. If Lodge as their leader supported a mandate, which was dependent on League membership, the Republican position would be weakened. Instead, Lodge hoped Wilson would aid Armenia using executive authority. In late June he put his name to an appeal, which ACIA Chairman Gerard cabled to Wilson. It was also signed by Hughes and Root, Senator John Sharp Williams (D-MS), former Ambassador to Austria-Hungary Frederic Courtland Penfield, New York Governor Alfred Smith, and former Harvard President Charles Eliot. The appeal emphasized that Americans, "without regard to party or creed," were deeply concerned for Armenia's welfare and dismayed that the conference had not dealt with this as "one of its first duties." It proposed the United States should immediately join the Allies in providing the Armenians with supplies to equip an army of 50,000 men and help them occupy their historic territories.[93]

At this time, Wilson was also receiving reports from Hoover on the Armenian situation. Hoover believed that they were the "most appalling" to have emerged from the war.[94] As Turkish Nationalist forces were advancing into the Armenian

Republic, and Britain was planning to withdraw its troops from the Caucasus, Hoover warned that unless military protection was provided "we are faced with a practical extermination of the Armenians."[95] In view of the urgency Assistant Secretary of State Frank Polk, now in charge of the US delegation in Paris, asked Washington whether a decision could be made on American mandates as soon as possible. With Senate opposition to the League growing, Wilson reasoned it would be unwise to ask Congress to accept a mandate or to dispatch American troops to replace the British, "just at this stage of its discussion of the Covenant." However, there was extensive press coverage of the Armenian plight, and Wilson was concerned that American public opinion might not "tolerate our doing, at least our attempting, nothing."[96] The *New York Times* was particularly critical, claiming that safeguarding Armenia's security should have been "one of the first tasks of the Peace Conference" and while there was "debating in Paris, a tragedy has been in the making in Turkey."[97]

Distressed by Hoover's reports, and determined to placate public opinion, Wilson appointed James Harbord, Chief of Staff of American Expeditionary Forces in Europe, to lead a commission to Armenia. Like the King-Crane group, still in the midst of its mission, the Harbord Commission was an investigative team, but with a military perspective. The dispatch of a second commission would inevitably delay the settlement, and the prime minister of the Armenian Republic scornfully remarked that the situation resembled "a physician so pains-taking in diagnosis that the patient died before the treatment could be decided upon."[98] For Wilson, dispatching another commission was a pragmatic move, deferring consideration of the mandate while demonstrating concern.

In Britain, Lloyd George recognized that American inability to decide on the mandates would further delay the settlement. He informed Clemenceau that Britain could no longer afford to maintain over 400,000 troops in the Near East. As British soldiers prepared to withdraw from the Caucasus, Armenian leaders and American relief workers beseeched the British Government to stay, impressing on them that an evacuation would result in renewed massacres. This infuriated Kerr, whose patience with American procrastination was wearing thin. He informed the US commissioners in Paris that Britain was already polic-ing as much of the world as it could manage and it was up to Americans "who professed such high principles and were a nation of a 100,000,000 people and owning almost all the fluid wealth of the world to do something for these peo-ple." Kerr even suggested that it would likely require "massacres of this kind to bring home the sense of their responsibility to the American Senate." Disgusted that Americans expected Britain to maintain conscription so they could "play party politics," he advised Lloyd George to inform Washington that Armenia was solely America's responsibility.[99] While committed to withdrawing troops, British policymakers indicated their intention to wait to conclude a settlement.

Despite increasing exasperation at American deferment, they were reluctant to act while there was still a chance America would undertake the mandates.[100]

Wilson recognized that only military assistance would ensure Armenia's protection. He confided to the Democratic Senator from Mississippi John Sharp Williams his wish that "Congress and the country would assent to our assuming the trusteeship for Armenia and going to the help of those suffering people in an effective way."[101] However, he was unwilling to antagonize his Senate opponents by deploying troops to the Near East while the treaty was under consideration. As Wilson informed Dodge, although he would like to do so, it was "manifestly impossible, at any rate in the present temper of Congress, to send American troops" to Armenia.[102] Seeking an alternative method of aiding the Armenians, on August 16 he issued a strongly worded warning to Constantinople: Unless immediate and effective measures were taken to prevent atrocities, Wilson would remove all support for Ottoman sovereignty over Turkish portions of the Empire, under Point 12 of his Fourteen Points. This would lead to the "absolute dissolution of the Turkish empire and a complete alteration of the conditions of the peace." The Allies were infuriated at this unilateral declaration, particularly as the United States had not even been at war with the Ottomans. The administration was forced to agree there would be no further threats.[103] However, Wilson's protest reveals how Armenia featured in his mind at this time. He was now prepared to remonstrate on Armenia's behalf, something he had not been willing to do during the war, but no US troops would be sent until passage of the treaty was secured. On this occasion, with the Ottomans isolated and powerless, Wilson hoped an official protest would check any aggression without necessitating an American military commitment.

In late August, ACIA Chairman James Gerard wrote to the State Department that leading Republicans, both inside and outside Congress, supported sending US troops to protect Armenia. Hughes and Lodge both informed Gerard that "responsibility" for action lay with Wilson, and "he can order to Armenia if he sees fit."[104] Although Lodge claimed that that he was in favor of the United States aiding Armenia militarily, he wanted the issue kept out of the Senate, where it would undermine cooperation among Republicans on the treaty. Lodge's insistence that the president act on executive authority was challenged by Wilson's assertion that specific congressional sanction was required. When Charles Eliot urged him to immediately send troops, Wilson regretted that he had "no authority in law to do what you suggest, though every consideration justifies it."[105] Considering Wilson had committed US troops in Haiti, the Dominican Republic, Russia, and in Mexico twice without Congressional authorization, it is unlikely he felt constrained by strict legality.[106] His reluctance to take personal responsibility stemmed from concern over the political price. The presence of American soldiers in distant trouble spots would be used to attack the treaty.

Wilson could only avert this if he acted with Congressional consent. He was right to be wary. Lodge's commitment to Armenia had waned as he became increasingly cynical over Allied motives for saddling Americans with the mandate. On August 19 he wrote to Henry White, the Republican commissioner on the American peace delegation, that he felt "badly about Armenia" but there was a limit to what the Allies had "the right to put off on us."[107]

When the Senate Foreign Relations Committee adopted its first treaty amendment, an infuriated Wilson headed west on a cross-country speaking tour to rally public support for the League.[108] Early on, he addressed Armenia. On September 6, in Kansas City, Wilson argued that the peace settlement would protect defenseless nations and pointed to Armenia as the "one pitiful example which is in the hearts of all of us." Appealing to religious sentiment, he claimed the Armenians were a Christian people whom the Ottomans "thought it the service of God to destroy." While Americans debated the treaty's merits, the Armenians were threatened with destruction. Wilson exclaimed: "When I think of words piled upon words, of debate following debate, when these unspeakable things are happening in these pitiful parts of the world, I wonder that men do not wake up to the moral responsibility of what they are doing."[109] Wilson hoped concern for the vulnerable Armenians would encourage popular outrage at Senate intransigence, thus improving his bargaining position and helping to secure immediate treaty ratification and League membership.

Wilson's speech provoked a swift reaction. The Democratic Senate leadership introduced a resolution on September 9 endorsing a free integral Armenia and the dispatch of American soldiers, arms, and money to protect the new state. Republicans were opposed. Republican Senator from Ohio Warren Harding offered the most eloquent explanation: it was appealing to portray "the outrages, the massacres, the awakening hopes of Armenia, and visualize the doubts and distresses and sacrificed lives while the Senate waits." Harding acknowledged Armenian suffering touched "the heart of Christian America." Yet mandate advocates failed to appreciate the costs: more soldiers sent to the Near East than America had ever previously maintained during peacetime and stationed at the "gateway between Orient and Occident," involved in every conflict of the Old World. Americans would be in a state of perpetual war, their "splendid isolation a memory" and their "boasted peace a mockery." Dismissing suggestions that he was insensitive to the atrocities, Harding declared: "I am thinking of America first. Safety, as well as charity, begins at home."[110] Harding's sentiments were echoed by the leading "irreconcilables" Borah and Johnson. They were trailing Wilson across the Midwest, speaking against the treaty before large audiences, and their attacks on Wilson's plans to send American troops to the Near East were greeted with applause.[111] As Wilson feared, his opponents were exploiting his commitment to Armenia to attack the treaty.

Armenian Americans and Armenian Republic representatives called to tes-
tify before the resolution's subcommittee in late September implored America
to send military aid. Writing in the *New York Herald*, Arshak Safrastian, a former
British vice consul in the Ottoman Empire, urged Americans to recognize the
Christian Armenians as "strong guardians of Western ideals in the Middle East."
Pointing to the work performed by American missionaries, Safrastian claimed
that the United States was best placed to reconstruct Armenia and ensure
Western Asian stability. He was vague about the mandate's economic and commercial possibilities; humanitarian justifications were paramount. His principal
argument was that Americans could "redress one of the greatest wrongs recorded
in history" and "also serve the higher interests of humanity."[112] Others joined the
debate. The *New York Sun* was indignant that Americans, "having asked for nothing should be saddled with the plague-spots of the world."[113] The *Los Angeles
Times*, though, an early mandate champion, now wavered, reflecting that the
question was dividing the nation.[114] The *New York Times*, however, remained
steadfast: "Americans who would not favour acceptance of any other responsibilities in the Near East feel that Armenia is in quite a different category."[115] The
Times was pro-League and supported treaty ratification without reservations.
Although the *New Republic* opposed the treaty, it was a passionate advocate of
an Armenian mandate. Its editors argued that Americans should accept responsibility, despite the financial burdens and risk of entanglement in "old diplomacy." If Americans failed "to vindicate Armenia's right to freedom," they would
"never again persuade the world that [their] moral sentiments are anything but
empty rhetoric playing over a gulf of selfishness and sloth."[116] Even former US
ambassadors to Constantinople clashed over the appropriate response. While
Morgenthau argued that "the United States accept a mandate for a large part of
the Ottoman Empire," his predecessor Straus, mindful of the legal and geopolitical consequences of intervention, warned that the United States should restrict
itself to financial aid and avoid a "barb-wire entanglement."[117] The mandate had
stimulated a public debate over America's moral example.

Wilson's allusion to the Armenians in his Kansas speech reveals his awareness that their suffering had emotional appeal. Yet he mentioned them only once
more on his speaking tour; in Salt Lake City on September 23. The Mormon
Church was a strong advocate for Armenia, raising extensive relief funds, and
one of its congregants, Senator King, was a leading Congressional supporter.[118]
Appealing to his audience's sympathy, Wilson recounted the Armenian plight
and castigated the Ottomans for their inability "to restrain the horrible massacres which have made that country a graveyard." But Armenia's suffering was
over, as it would be "under trust of the League." Wilson referred to a "redeemed"
Armenia as a symbol for his new world order and as justification for treaty ratification without reservations. However, he made no mention of a mandate or

the possibility of sending US troops. Popular sympathy for Armenia could win support for the League, but a definite commitment to its future protection might work against it.[119]

Two days later, Wilson collapsed from a stroke. For the remainder of his term an incapacitated president had to fight his campaigns for the treaty, the League, and the Armenian mandate, debilitated by ill health.[120]

Turning to America: Louis E. Browne and the Turkish Nationalist Movement

While Wilson was on his speaking tour, the King-Crane Commission submitted its report to the peace conference.[121] Crane cabled Wilson summarizing its recommendations: in addition to separate mandates for Armenia and an internationalized Constantinople, the United States should also take mandates for the Turkish regions of the Empire and a united Syria, including Palestine and Lebanon. Crane informed Wilson that there was "raw material here for a much more promising state than we had in the Philippines."[122] The report stressed America's Christian responsibility in the Near East and claimed that only Americans could demonstrate the "absolutely honest unselfishness" necessary to administer these territories. Crane argued it would help Wilson's campaign for treaty ratification to have the report published: it was proof of the need for American leadership, as the "only trust" in the Near East was in the United States and its president.[123] Wilson may have welcomed this allusion to American moral force, but it is inconceivable he would have submitted to Congress a program requiring acceptance of substantial military and economic responsibilities over such a vast area and in a region where, traditionally, the United States had limited political involvement. In Paris, he emphasized the difficulty in convincing Americans to take a mandate even for Armenia, in which they had a deep, historic interest. However, Crane's appeal illustrates how the search for a solution to the Armenian question was increasingly drawing Americans into the larger Eastern question, of what should replace the moribund Ottoman Empire.

The full report didn't reach Washington until September 27, after Wilson's collapse. It is doubtful he read it. The commissioners refused to release their recommendations without Wilson's permission but did briefly discuss their findings with the press.[124] Crane suggested that unless Americans took the mandate for all these "stricken nations," whose only faith lay in American aid, global peace would be endangered. If Americans helped the region "develop along democratic lines," then the international benefits were inestimable.[125] The Commission traveled extensively throughout Greater Syria but growing instability prevented them visiting Anatolia. This was the Turkish heartland but also where the Ottoman Armenian provinces lay. It was in Anatolia that the complexities of applying national self-determination to an intermixed Turkish and Armenian population were most evident.[126] Before the commissioners left Constantinople in late August they met with a delegation of Turkish nationalists, opposed to the sultan's government. This delegation informed the commission that if it recommended an American mandate for Turkey, then "we Turks won't name a single condition . . . the country won't require much policing; everyone will be so happy to come under the wing of America."[127] Lewis Heck, American commissioner in Constantinople, had already reported that there was a "fairly overwhelming turning to America by all classes of the Ottoman population." Even members of the sultan's cabinet privately urged Heck to convince America to accept a mandate for the entire Empire, rather than just the Armenian provinces.[128] They wished to curb aggrandizement by avaricious European powers and believed an American mandate offered the means to end Allied occupation, maintain Turkey's territorial integrity, and eventually gain independence. As one mandate supporter, future Turkish President Ismet Inonu, recalled, it was "the golden pill of the moment."[129]

Pushing this most fervently was the Turkish Wilsonian League. Formed in Constantinople by writers, publicists, and lawyers, it was led by journalist and Columbia University PhD Ahmet Emin Yalman, along with renowned novelist and American Girls' College in Constantinople graduate Halide Edib. Yalman and Edib hoped that co-operation with the United States would ensure Turkish sovereignty, as enshrined in Wilson's Twelfth Point. They published a series of articles advocating an American mandate in the Turkish press.[130] In pursuit of this, Edib urged Turkish Nationalist leader Mustafa Kemal to invite Crane to the movement's congress in Sivas.[131] Kemal's position, and that of his cause, was precarious. Having resigned his army commission, he was uncertain what sway he retained over the Turkish public. Ottoman authorities were determined to suppress his nationalist movement. Much of Anatolia was under Allied occupation; Greek forces, sanctioned by the Allies and Wilson at Versailles in May, had occupied Smyrna, resulting in hundreds of deaths.[132] Concerned at the instability, Kemal seized on Edib's proposal. He privately lamented, "Let [America] accept [the mandate] as soon as possible, so that the country may get free of this chaos!"[133] Kemal instructed Edib to invite Crane to the Congress. Preparing to leave for Paris, Crane asked *Chicago Daily News* correspondent Louis E. Browne to go instead. Browne had arrived in Constantinople from Moscow, where he had helped shape American perceptions of the Russian Revolution, and was again thrust into the maelstrom of revolutionary upheaval. He played a crucial role in bringing the Turkish nationalist movement to American attention.

Browne was forced to take precautions on his journey to Sivas to avoid Allied and Ottoman authorities. Edib furnished him with secret permits and introductions to agents. However, after it was discovered that an American was traveling through Anatolia, Browne informed his readers that he received "one tremendous ovation after another." Wherever he spent the night a lamb was slaughtered and Turkish peasants surrounded his cavalcade to ask "whether it were true that the great United States was coming to help Turkey along the road to peace and prosperity."[134] Browne's snapshots echoed Heck's dispatches and press reports from elsewhere in the region. The *New York Herald*'s Damascus correspondent claimed that the King-Crane commission's "presence in the Holyland" had created an extraordinary impression and that both "natives [and] foreigners look wistfully to America as deliverer." One Syrian demanded to know why the United States "taught us the watchwords of liberty, and aroused our hopes by sending a commission" if it refused to take a mandate, and warned that if America did not take regional responsibility then "grave consequences [from this] miscarriage of justice were upon her head."[135] These snippets offered Americans a unique insight into their nation's regional image and revealed that US guardianship was regarded as an alternative to European imperialism in territories other than Armenia and Constantinople.

When Browne arrived at Sivas, he discovered that with the exception of a few relief workers, he was the only American there and the only Allied or US citizen attending the Congress. Sharing quarters with the Nationalist leaders, he sat through most sessions. He informed his readers that the Sivas Congress took no action without first informing him, as they were unwilling to prejudice potential American "assistance." The nature of that assistance was unclear. Browne reported that the Congress discussed the issue as an urgent priority and was "unanimously in favour of an American mandate," with some delegates unconditionally supportive, while others suggested limitations. Kemal and Rouef Bey, the Congress' deputy chairman, privately warned Browne that while all the delegates hoped that the United States would become "Turkey's guardian," many objected to the word "mandate." Claiming that the term was foreign to the Turkish language, Kemal stated that the term "assistance" should be used instead. Kemal left no doubt in Browne's mind of his position: "We want the United States to take a mandate for Turkey." Kemal informed Browne that foreign aid was required for Turkey to develop industrially, build a modern transport system, and reform its government. He suggested that Turkey would "pay double if necessary for any official aid the United States will give." Rather than a burden, Kemal claimed an American mandate for Turkey would "net private exploitations through concessions and industrial development, [ensuring] enormous returns on billions of invested capital." These potential benefits of a

Turkish, rather than solely Armenian, mandate tallied with what Browne was hearing from the American business community in the Near East. He informed an American journalist friend that "mention of a mandate for an independent Armenia causes howls of protests," but Americans in the region favored a mandate over the broader Turkish provinces of the Ottoman Empire.[136] By relaying these arguments for a Turkish mandate's material benefits Browne provided a fresh perspective to Americans, who were used to hearing that an Armenian mandate was a costly burden.

Kemal confided that he was opposed to any European power assuming a protectorate over Turkey, characterizing them as imperialistic and concerned only with their own national self-interest. Conversely, he claimed, "Every Turk has heard" how "Congress voted to haul down the American flag from Cuba and sent warm congratulations to the new republic." Kemal also celebrated the American role in the Pacific, declaring, "We know of your action in the Philippines and what you are doing for Moslems there and we hope that your mandatory for those Isles continues for many years yet." Emphasizing the contrast between American colonialism and British imperialism, he asked Browne: "Can you show me a Cuba in Britain's history? There are many Irelands." Kemal was not the only nationalist leader to invoke the colonial conduct of the United States as justification for an American mandate for his country. Boghos Nubar had made a similar allusion in his memorandum to the Inquiry, while Crane noted that everywhere the mission went in Syria, they were told, "We want America to come here and do for us what she has been doing for the Philippines." Near Eastern nationalist leaders recognized that great-power sponsorship was necessary to advance their goals of independence and considered a protectorate by the United States, whose prior official involvement in the region was limited, to be better than the European alternatives. As president of the Ottoman Senate, Ahmet Riza Bey informed Heck, many members of the Ottoman elite believed Americans had brought "material progress without attempting to suppress [Filipino] national aspirations."[137] In fact, the United States had fought a brutal war with Filipino nationalists after acquiring the archipelago and Sultan Abdul Hamid, responding to Minister Oscar Straus's entreaties, had helped US authorities to pacify the rebellious Moro Muslim population of the Southern Philippines by assuring them their freedom of religion would be secure if they accepted US occupation.[138] It is unclear how widely known this was in Ottoman society. Yet in emphasising the manner in which Americans were preparing the Philippines for self-government, Kemal and Bey were echoing statements by anticolonial nationalists in other parts of the world, who also found it politically useful to argue that US colonialism was more progressive than European rule.[139] These remarks flattered Americans, confirming their conviction of America's exceptional world role and its distinction from European—particularly British—imperialism.

Browne stressed that he could not speak for Washington. Although personally sympathetic, he admitted that it was unlikely Americans would accept a Turkish mandate. Accordingly, Kemal explained that officially admitting Turkey required external assistance risked damaging the Caliphate's prestige and encouraging imperial exploitation. He hoped the United States could nonetheless be convinced to assist Turkey's independence. The Congress sent a telegram to the US Senate, via Browne, requesting that a delegation be dispatched to investigate Near Eastern conditions, "with the clear vision of a disinterested nation." However, Edib was aware that prevailing pro-Armenian and anti-Turkish sentiments among Americans would undermine this impartiality and Turkey's appeals for assistance, whatever the government's inclination. Consequently, Edib drafted a "Letter to the American Public," which she asked Browne to publish. Edib noted that Americans had heard about the Eastern question from "many different sources but never [from] a Turk." Admitting the Armenian massacres had caused justified indignation, she urged Americans to recognize them as facts of a "more vital whole" and that "there is a Turkish tragedy as much as there is an Armenian tragedy." External guidance was required for both peoples but "European methods of approach had failed." Rather than being treated as a possible colony, Edib called for aid to develop Turkey's commercial, industrial, and agricultural potential and to establish a modern, democratic government. This could only be undertaken by a non-European power, aware of Turkish internal conditions and "efficient in methods of teaching the people self-government." Edib declared that the United States was the only power with these attributes.[140] Committed to securing greater freedom, and ultimately political suffrage, for Turkish women, Edib was convinced that this goal could best be served under American tutelage.[141] Browne informed his readers that Kemal, Edib, and Turkey's nationalist leaders represented the moral and intellectual elements of world Islam and "like ripples from a stone dropped in water their opinions will sweep through the Mahomedan world and the U.S. will be the gainer whether we take the mandate or not."[142]

With Washington consumed by the treaty fight and Wilson incapacitated, Turkish appeals received little attention; no official response was ever received. The "Turkish Wilsonian League" died out within two months. It had always been regarded as an elite project, attracting little popular support outside Constantinople and arousing outright hostility in eastern Anatolia due to distrust of pro-Armenian sympathies among American missionaries.[143] Kemal himself quickly retreated from the mandate as his own position improved. Immediately after the Congress, attempts by the Ottoman government to suppress the nascent nationalist movement failed, forcing the resignation of the sultan's cabinet and the withdrawal of British forces from western Anatolia. Presiding over a renewed nationalist movement, Kemal proved less willing to sanction foreign tutelage.[144] Consequently, when a few weeks later he encountered Harbord, in the midst of his military mission, Kemal proposed a "big brother" relationship, accepting American advice but without interference in Turkish internal affairs.[145]

By this point, Browne had already returned to Paris and discovered that there was little enthusiasm for any American mandate among the remaining US peace commissioners. The commissioners suggested there was no chance that Americans would agree to any mandates and that the "question is getting an undeserved black-eye merely because the President wants them."[146] Browne's friend Herbert Corey of The Associated Newspapers wrote to him from New York confirming the public mood. Corey declared that Americans were thoroughly sick of the war and were opposed to "any suggestion of a mandate, be it Armenian, Turkish or what-not." Corey assumed Americans would have accepted a mandate at the beginning of the Peace Conference—when "we were still wide eyed, juvenile and credulous"—but as distrust of Allied intrigue had grown there had been a "swing away from the somewhat ill digested and academic internationalism of the recent past to the most independent sort of nationalism." While Americans were vehemently opposed to taking a mandate at the price of more taxes, Corey suggested it might have been possible for the Allies to involve the United States in the Near East if they had offered a potentially profitable territory. Instead they had "shoved off the deadest horse in the stable on us and linked us forever in an alliance to protect G. B. and France from Germany—no, Louis. We're not having any."[147] Corey's message illustrated that in the United States, the evolving response to the mandate issue reflected the dwindling support for Wilson's brand of internationalism.

Wrecked Hopes and Broken Dreams

As Corey indicated, American opposition to any type of mandate was widespread and entrenched in the Senate by October. Lansing cabled Polk that there was an increasing sentiment against "taking a mandate over any portion of the Turkish Empire," with even many Democrats opposed. While Armenia enjoyed more support than any other possible mandate, Lansing noted that "the demands of humanity are beginning to weaken."[148] These demands were never likely to appeal to Lansing.[149] He had continued to counsel Wilson against a mandate and his opposition was made public during the Senate hearings on the treaty. William Bullitt, who had quit the American peace delegation in protest over the severity of the German treaty, revealed Lansing had expressed grave doubts about the League and was "absolutely opposed to the United States taking a mandate in either Armenia or Constantinople."[150] Despite his own bias, Lansing's assessment of the Senate's attitude was undoubtedly correct. Like Wilson, Lodge recognized the Armenian question had become entangled with the battle for treaty ratification and League membership.[151] For both men, American aid for Armenia was subordinated to this wider struggle.

The British government reached a similar conclusion. Viscount Edward Grey, in Washington as special ambassador, reported that Senate acceptance of an American mandate was rendered "altogether out of the question" by Wilson's illness.[152] In Britain, a dejected Kerr informed Lloyd George that it was clear that Americans would not take a mandate and this would "kill the mandatory theory just as much as other aspects of the League." Kerr reminded Lloyd George that "the fundamental point" underpinning British strategy was the "assumption that the great powers including America were going to stand together and more or less run world affairs." This included shared responsibility for maintaining Near Eastern stability. Believing the whole basis for a new world order had collapsed, Kerr urged the withdrawal of British troops from all its mandates in the region, after establishing indigenous governments and arranging for advisors and the development of resources.[153] Kipling shared Kerr's disillusionment. He wrote to Lawrence that "one can't expect people whose forebears went West to avoid trouble to stand up to responsibility in a far land for no immediate cash return." Summing up the mood of all those involved in "the American scheme," Kipling remarked that "we are all sitting in the middle of wrecked hopes and broken dreams."[154] The cherished ideal of an Anglo-American colonial alliance was receding, along with the possibility of US League membership and any chance that the United States would take a mandate.

The Senate rejection of the Versailles Treaty and the League Covenant on November 19 seemed to end any hopes of an American mandate. Technically the United States could have assumed a mandate "on behalf of the League," even without being a member, and the Allied leaders continued to hope it would do so. However, Americans were becoming increasingly opposed to the assumption of any type of international responsibility. Recognizing this, Lansing informed Polk that "as for assuming a mandate over anything or anybody, the present state of the public mind makes the idea almost out of the question."[155] Armenians grudgingly acknowledged this. The Armenian American newspaper *Hairenik* bitterly observed:

> Why fool ourselves with false hopes? All our big and little allies have abandoned us to our fate. America remains only distant America,

lulling us today with hopes, unfortunately only with hopes. When will those be fulfilled, when will this powerful republic hasten to aid us, that is unknown.[156]

Nevertheless, although Wilson had subordinated any definite commitment to Armenian security to his struggle with the Senate over the treaty, he remained convinced that the United States had a moral duty to protect the Armenians and was determined that it should be fulfilled.

6

Dissolution

In a November 1919 article for the mass-circulation British publication, the *Illustrated Sunday Herald*, Winston Churchill outlined the grave consequences arising from the Senate's rejection of the Versailles Treaty and its repudiation of the League of Nations. If the United States did not ultimately ratify the treaty and join the League, then the Allied victory would be squandered. France would be left vulnerable to the threat of a revanchist Germany. Without the stabilizing influence of the Austro-Hungarian Empire, dismantled and reordered on the basis of national self-determination "due mainly to American initiative," Central Europe would become a disordered vacuum into which German power and Bolshevist propaganda would flow. And then there was the Ottoman Empire. This had "remained in a state of quasi-dissolution all these months waiting an American decision, and now perhaps for many months more all those millions of helpless human beings must remain sinking ever deeper into bankruptcy, famine and anarchy, without being able to make a single plan to save themselves."[1] The long awaited decision to which Churchill alluded concerned American mandates in the Near East. In 1898, Churchill had regarded it as futile to expect the United States to pluck Britain's "chestnuts out of the fire" in Eurasia or Africa. Twenty years later he had argued in the Cabinet prior to the Peace Conference against inviting a rival naval power into the Eastern Mediterranean to take a mandate. But his perspective had shifted after becoming war secretary in January 1919 and assuming responsibility for drawing down Britain's forces in the Near East. He then hoped the United States would share the burden of maintaining stability in Western Asia and in doing so cement an Anglo-American alliance.[2]

Churchill concluded his 1919 article by warning Americans that "to destroy the old organisation without attempting to supply the new, to sweep away the imperial system without setting in place a League of Nations system, would indeed be an act from which America should recoil and which posterity would certainly condemn." He tempered his pessimism with a stirring peroration that "the two great branches of the English-speaking family" had overcome their antagonisms of the past to defeat Germany and could now act together to overcome any future peril. Churchill hoped that the wartime cooperation had established the community of interests and ideals necessary for the two nations to act together in world affairs.[3] Despite his optimistic forecast, the old American antipathy for Britain remained and had again burst into the open during the treaty fight. Anti-British hostility was particularly evident in the ongoing American public debate over assuming a mandate and the reordering of the territories of the Ottoman Empire.

PUNCH, OR THE LONDON CHARIVARI.—November 19, 1919.

WAITING FOR THE U.S.A.

The Turk (*sick with deferred hope*). "WHERE IS THE *MAYFLOWER II*.? THE HUSTLERS TARRY."

[The conclusion of the Peace Treaty with Turkey is being delayed by the United States, which have not yet signified whether they will accept the mandate of the Conference in respect to the administration of Armenia.]

Figure 6.1 Cartoon blaming US indecision over accepting an Armenian mandate for the delay in signing a peace treaty with the Ottoman Empire. It was published on the day that the US Senate rejected the Treaty of Versailles. Waiting for the U.S.A., *Punch*, November 19, 1919.

Leaving Unfinished the Task for Which America
Entered the War

The same month that Churchill published his article, Major General James Harbord delivered his commission's report to the White House. The report reinforced the American stereotype of the Turks, portraying them as "bloodthirsty, unregenerate and vengeful," and declaring that they should never rule over Armenians again. However, immediate separation was complicated by economic considerations and regional ethnography. The report recommended a single mandate for the entire region, from Constantinople to the Caucasus. It suggested that two army divisions, amounting to around 59,000 troops, were required to pacify the territory, repatriate the Armenians, and establish a functioning government. By the end of the third year this number would be halved as responsibility was handed over to a native constabulary. Harbord estimated that the total cost of this larger mandate would amount to $750 million across the first five years. Only an altruistic nation, devoted to maintaining the "peace of the world," could undertake this task. The report outlined fourteen reasons for the United States assuming the mandate and thirteen against. The recommendations in favor were based on America's traditional concern for Christians in the Near East, evidenced by its missionary and relief activity. A mandate would bring peace to a volatile region and an end to Armenian persecution. The task offered the "greatest humanitarian opportunity of the age," which the United States was "morally bound to accept." Furthermore, its traditional isolation from the self-interest of the Old World and record of "developing peoples rather than resources alone" in the Americas and the Philippines made the United States better suited for this duty than any other power. The arguments against focused on the need to adhere to the Monroe Doctrine; the United States should remain in its own sphere of influence, detached from the politics of Europe. This was a European problem, not one of America's making, and the mandate could be efficiently managed by any great power. Above all, a mandate would be costly, both financially and militarily, and Americans might be better advised to concentrate their resources closer to home.[4]

Harbord's fourteenth point in favor, with no corresponding negative, revealed his personal bias. He asserted that this was a "man's job" that the world believed Americans could do better than any other nation. The United States could "afford the money; she had the men; no duty to her own people would suffer; her traditional policy of isolation did not keep her from successful participation in the Great War." If Americans refused the mandate, it could only be assumed that they feared to undertake new and challenging responsibilities. Harbord concluded his report with a warning that America's refusal would betray the hopes

of many millions by leaving "unfinished the task for which she entered the war."
His conclusion attested to the power of Wilson's wartime proclamations and the
expectations that they had aroused among all subject peoples.[5]

Polk had received an advanced copy of Harbord's recommendations when
the General passed through Paris on his return to the United States. He cabled
Lansing with a summary of Harbord's "remarkable report" and urged him to
arrange a meeting between Harbord and Wilson, if the president's health permitted.[6] It did not.[7] The report was neither immediately publicized nor circulated, and, like the King-Crane report, was filed away in the executive archives.
Requests from Congress for its release were ignored.[8] The lack of response was
unsurprising; the First Lady carefully screened which state papers her invalid
husband saw, and the majority of correspondence went unanswered. While the
report remained unpublished, speculation grew that its recommendations were
hostile to a mandate.[9]

The Great Opportunity for Clear Understanding between GB and the United States

Although Harbord's recommendations went largely unreported in the
United States, he had shared his findings with the US High Commissioner in
Constantinople, Admiral Mark Bristol, who endorsed them.[10] As the United
States had yet to resume diplomatic relations with Constantinople after the
1917 rupture, Bristol, commander of American naval forces in the Eastern
Mediterranean, was also serving as the senior US diplomatic representative
in the capital. Like many other American officials, he was distrustful of Allied
motives for saddling the United States with the Armenian mandate, convinced
that it was intended to serve British and French imperial ends by implicating
the United States in the partition of the Ottoman Empire. While the European
powers helped themselves to areas rich in natural resources, America's sympathy
for the Armenians was being used to entice it into taking responsibility for the
least profitable territory.[11] Bristol was particularly suspicious of Britain, which
he accused of carrying out "her old policies of grabbing everything she can
without regard for anyone."[12] His wartime naval experience meant that he had
grasped more quickly than most US officials the crucial importance that oil had
assumed in modern warfare. He was also aware that the Standard Oil Company
of New York ("Socony") had secured prewar concessions in Palestine and Syria,
where it was the principal supplier of petroleum products, and hoped to begin
exploration in Mesopotamia. Other American firms soon joined Socony in seeking concessions in Mesopotamia, well aware of its potentially bountiful, undeveloped reserves. When British officials prevented American geologists from

entering the territory before peace was settled, Bristol was quick to protest.[13] This confirmed his suspicion that Britain intended to monopolize the market for its nationals, leaving the United States with a mandate for a territory with no oil. He urged his superiors in Washington to recognize the "selfish motives of England" in its desire to have the United States as mandatory for Armenia, where it would replace the Ottomans as a buffer against Russia and protect the Suez Canal, the oil fields in Mesopotamia, and Britain's monopoly of Persian oil resources."[14]

Bristol was a strenuous advocate for the interests of American businessmen and was determined to advance his nation's trade interests in the region. He viewed the division of mandates as merely a cover to organize the Ottoman Empire into spheres of influence and shut out American merchants.[15] Furthermore, having served as a member of an international committee of inquiry into the Greek occupation of Smyrna, he had already seen firsthand the consequences of European intervention. He was concerned that further Allied meddling would threaten the stability on which the advancement of American economic interests depended.[16] Nevertheless, Bristol was convinced that none of the different peoples of the Near East were capable of self-government and therefore lobbied for a single mandate over the entire Ottoman Empire.[17] He was delighted when Harbord, with whom he had discussed this idea, recommended a larger mandate. Bristol hoped that Americans could be convinced to accept it and expand their commercial operations in the region.[18]

As Bristol competed vigorously with the Europeans to expand America's regional trade, his belligerent attitude to Britain deepened. He even informed one correspondent that as the United States had "fought to destroy the Prussian power, we may still have to fight to destroy the British power."[19] Paradoxically, Bristol enjoyed good relations with many individual British naval officers. On arriving in Constantinople, he had instinctively felt that "the solution of this Near Eastern question was the great opportunity of bringing about a clear understanding between Great Britain and the United States" and that "the future peace of the world depends upon such an understanding."[20] However, he had become convinced that "so long as the British practice their present political methods it is impossible for us to play the game."[21] Bristol vehemently opposed unchecked Allied economic penetration of the Empire and this led him to sympathize with Kemal's Nationalist Movement. He regarded it as "the best thing that has taken place since I have been out here."[22]

Bristol's outspoken hostility to British actions and championship of the Nationalists did not go unnoticed in London. The new Foreign Secretary Lord Curzon informed the US Ambassador to Britain John W. Davis that Bristol's "anti-British attitude" had been "noted." Curzon objected to Bristol's view that Britain was intriguing in the region. He reminded Davis that the British government was desperate to withdraw from Asia Minor.[23] Davis was acutely aware of this, as British politicians had constantly sought to impress it on him since his arrival in early 1919.[24] In October, he had accompanied Lloyd George on a trip to Sheffield during which the prime minister had publicly declared that "the demobilization of the British Army was awaiting the decision of America on the question of mandates and that he hoped America would realize her duty to share in the responsibilities of world reorganization." If nothing else, Lloyd George hoped that the situation in the Near East would assure Americans that "the British Empire was not a landgrabbing institution but was engaged in the discharge of duties forced upon it."[25] While far more pro-British than Bristol, Davis was equally concerned about Britain's petroleum policy. He devoted considerable energy to challenging British attempts to monopolize access to the resources in its assigned Ottoman mandates. Davis considered Britain's "colonial monopoly," alongside America's "competitive naval building," as "the most serious menaces to good relations between the two countries."[26] The vision of an Anglo-American alliance was threatened by the reality of competing national interests. Ironically, the mandate system, devised as a "bond of union," had become a bone of contention.

From Paris, Polk had also frequently complained to Washington about Allied imperialism. He condemned the Ottoman settlement as a "disgraceful scramble for territory and oil wells."[27] Nevertheless, he was concerned when he received instructions to return home following the Senate's rejection of the treaty. He warned Washington that complete withdrawal from the Ottoman settlement would disappoint the Allies and damage US prestige.[28] Allied statesmen were complaining that the United States was "the last to arrive in the emergency and first to leave."[29] Lloyd George made clear to Polk that an American mandate was the only possible solution to the Armenian question and he hoped that the United States would still play a role in drafting the settlement. However, Wilson's illness had left a power vacuum in Washington and Polk could give no assurances before departing with the rest of the American delegation on December 9.[30]

Lloyd George was under increasing domestic pressure to finally resolve the Ottoman settlement. Supporters of the Armenian cause in Parliament pointed to the government's wartime assurances that the security of the Armenians would be provided for and their independence guaranteed. They demanded to know why peace in the Near East had been delayed and the Armenians left defenseless. Other MPs protested against the cost of continued deployment of British forces in Asia Minor.[31] In a speech to the House of Commons in mid-December, Lloyd George responded to their charges. The government had considered a solution to the "Turkish problem" impossible until it knew America's intentions. European security and British imperial interests required a "gatekeeper" in Constantinople to police the Dardanelles and a "guardian" in Asia Minor was needed to protect the Christian minorities. As the United States, unlike the European powers, had "no extraneous burdens" and "gigantic resources," it had been hoped that it would take its "share in this great task of civilization." American acceptance of these mandates would ensure that a "League of equal nations" was established, without one nation left "absolutely free and untrammelled" in its responsibilities while another had "its hands tied behind its back." He argued that rushing the peace settlement would only have caused tensions. Indeed, the British government considered an entente with the United States so crucial that it held off on establishing an Ottoman peace and was prepared to maintain troops in Anatolia whatever the cost.[32] This speech reflected the increasingly contradictory British postwar strategy in the Near East. Under increasing pressure to draw down its commitments in the region, the government was still anxious to respond to public demands for Armenian protection. The stability of the Eastern Mediterranean and Asia Minor was a vital goal, but Britain was unwilling to shoulder the responsibility itself. An alliance with the United States, underpinned by shared commitments in the Near East, was paramount. Yet in pushing for such a commitment, the government had unwittingly aroused long-held American suspicions of British imperialism and an increasing unwillingness to take any role in global reconstruction.

In the Upper House, the Foreign Secretary Lord Curzon lamented that the once "cherished hope" of an "Armenia stretching from sea to sea," under great power protection, had now faded. Unfortunately Britain did not possess the means, the money, or the men to realize this vision. Only the United States, "with her large ideas and her great resources," could have accomplished this goal. But as this now looked unlikely, Curzon confirmed that the Allies would proceed with the Ottoman settlement without the Americans.[33]

No Propaganda, no Recognition

Clinging to his twin dream of an Anglo-American alliance and an Armenian protectorate, Viscount Bryce thought it was "premature" of the British government to conclude that the United States would not accept the mandate. In December 1919, he informed the House of Lords that after intervening in the war, the United States might feel bound "to do something further to aid the Allies in the establishment of peace, and to give some assistance to these countries which have suffered so much, and for which her sympathy has been in many ways so strong."[34] In the early part of 1920 there remained some grounds for his optimism. The annual meetings of the Methodist and Presbyterian churches adopted resolutions calling on the United States to fulfill its humanitarian duty by accepting a mandate for Armenia.[35] The *New York Times* and the

New Republic remained committed supporters, while sixteen state legislatures passed pro mandate resolutions.[36] The clearest indication of America's continuing concern was the vast amounts still being raised in relief; in 1920 the NER collected twelve million dollars, bringing the total since its founding to over forty million dollars.[37]

At Wilson's request, the missionary lobby had refrained from publicly campaigning for a mandate for fear of hindering ratification of the treaty.[38] Following the treaty's defeat and reports of fresh Armenian massacres, Barton suggested to Morgenthau that they initiate a propaganda drive, educating Americans on their responsibility to end Constantinople's "atrocious misrule" over non-Moslems. He asked Morgenthau to secure presidential approval for the campaign.[39] However, when Morgenthau suggested this to the White House in late February, he was told that Wilson would rather he postponed "speaking on subjects of this kind for the present."[40] The response from the White House was probably influenced by the Senate's decision to resume consideration of the treaty on February 9. Until the final vote on the treaty in mid-March, it was still considered inopportune to agitate for an Armenian mandate, which might prejudice the Senate's decision. Aware of the focus on the treaty, Morgenthau informed Barton that although an American mandate was the only way to "permanently save" the Armenians, nothing could be done "until the President and Senate [got] back on speaking terms."[41]

In any event, divisions over the type of mandate threatened to complicate any propaganda campaign. Some proposed an American protectorate over the entire Near East, as recommended by Bristol, and the King-Crane and Harbord commission reports, arguing that this was the only way to safeguard Armenian security and America's regional interests. President Caleb F. Gates of Robert College in Constantinople was the most vocal advocate of this position. He informed Bristol that he was doing all that he could to convince Americans that the only way to save the situation was for the United States to take a mandate for both Armenia and Turkey.[42] However, those who wanted nothing to do with the "unspeakable Turks" accused Gates of prioritizing missionary and economic interests over Armenian welfare. This group, which included Armenian Americans, opposed any suggestion that Armenians be placed under the same administrative system as the Turks and continued to call for a single mandate for an independent Armenian state. Their position was endorsed by the *New York Times*: "There is much to be said in favour of an American mandate for Armenia [and] something can be said, though not very much, in favour of an American mandate for Constantinople [but] it is hard to see what can be said in favour of an American mandate for the residuary Turkish state in Anatolia; or, worst of all, for an American mandate over the whole Turkish Empire."[43] Those who emphasized the humanitarian and religious justifications for a single Armenian mandate only alienated politicians, businessmen, and military leaders who prioritized commercial benefits and strategic considerations.[44]

While Barton vacillated between the different mandatory schemes, James Gerard and the ACIA had concluded a mandate for Armenia was no longer feasible.[45] Lodge informed Gerard that Congress would never approve any mandate, but suggested that he and other leading Republicans might support direct political, economic, and military assistance.[46] Consequently Gerard came out in opposition to a mandate, instead urging the president to first provide direct assistance and then de facto recognition for the Armenian Republic. He could then work toward the creation of an independent Armenia from the Black Sea to the Mediterranean.[47] However, despite ACIA pressure and Allied recognition of the Armenian Republic in January 1920, the United States still withheld recognition. The Wilson administration continued to oppose radical dismemberment of the Russian Empire, of which the Armenian Republic remained technically a component part. Furthermore, Lansing, with his strict interpretation of international law, refused to recognize Armenia until its final borders were settled. The debilitated president did not overrule him.[48] Without official recognition, the Armenian Republic was unable to secure the American military and economic assistance that Gerard proposed and the fledgling state desperately needed.

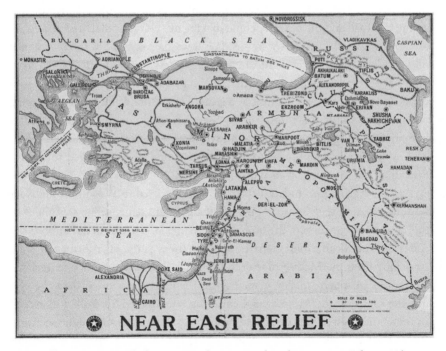

Figure 6.2 Near East Relief map. Beinecke Rare Book and Manuscript Library, Yale University, 53 1923.

An International Police Is Needed

In February and April 1920, Allied representatives—without their American associates, who declined representation—gathered first in London and then San Remo to prepare a final Near Eastern settlement.[49] The Allies soon realized that the Ottoman settlement would prove more difficult than had first appeared in Paris. It was over a year since the peace conference determined Armenia and the other non-Turkish provinces of the Empire should be liberated. The Allies found it convenient to blame this delay on Wilson, claiming he had misled them by promising to provide a quick response on American acceptance of mandates.[50] In fact, Wilson had repeatedly warned of the difficulties he faced in convincing Americans to assume these new duties. If anything, it was Allied eagerness, particularly on the part of the British, for American involvement in the Near East that had encouraged them to wait so long. Anglo-French differences over Syria had also proved a critical stumbling block.[51]

Whatever the reason, the delay had resulted in Mustafa Kemal's Turkish Nationalists increasing their power, and they posed a formidable challenge to both the Ottoman government and the Allies. By this point, as Margaret MacMillan notes, Kemal's army had grown larger while the available Allied forces diminished. From then on it was clear that "two different worlds—one of international conferences, lines on maps, peoples moving obediently into this country or that, and the other a people shaking off their Ottoman past and awakening as a Turkish nation—were heading towards collision."[52] The resurgence of Turkish nationalism also threatened the Armenians. Reports of fresh massacres confirmed the Allied belief that regional stability and Armenian security depended on military occupation by a great power. Britain and France remained unwilling to assume this responsibility themselves. Although the United States had rejected League membership and withdrawn from the peacemaking process, Allied leaders continued to hope that it could be encouraged to resolve their dilemma by taking an Armenian mandate.[53]

Back in Washington in late February, Polk reported to Wilson on the Near Eastern situation and "most important of all, as far as the public sentiment of this country is concerned, the question of Armenia." He claimed that both the Allies and American experts were opposed to the creation of an Armenian state stretching from the Mediterranean to the Black Sea, regarding it as unrealistic and unjust. A much smaller Armenia was therefore envisioned than the one that the ACIA, or the Armenians themselves, had lobbied for. Polk declared an "international police" was needed to protect the Armenians and maintain peace. It was clear to Polk that the British and French were unprepared to commit the troops necessary and he feared there was no chance Americans would feel "this obligation so strongly as to compel Congress to consent to a mandate, and appropriate the necessary money."[54] Polk recognized American popular sympathy for Armenia would not extend to the military commitment required to safeguard its security.

Incapacitated and secluded in the White House, Wilson relied on his aides to interpret the mood in the country and in Congress. Despite their counsel, the president was becoming increasingly divorced from political reality. Although there had been a minor improvement in his condition in February, Wilson never regained his health in any meaningful way. As Arthur Link has noted, the president remained "severely impaired physically and mentally" for the rest of his term. His stroke had rendered him increasingly inflexible and truculent, seeing issues only "in terms of black and white."[55] The psychological effects of his illness were particularly evident in his perspective on the Armenian question. Disregarding Polk's warning, in early March the president reaffirmed his belief that the United States should take the mandate as an example of national selflessness and moral leadership. He believed it was America's "clear duty" to do so and he wished to remain free to urge assumption of this "responsibility at the opportune time." His emphasis on timing indicates Wilson had not completely lost his grasp of political realities. The treaty remained his priority and it was unwise to raise the mandate question while it was under Senate consideration. On March 17, two days before the Senate voted again, Wilson confided to Polk that a mandate request would result in a "long fight with Congress," and he hoped to delay this if possible.[56]

A number of analysts, of different political perspectives, agreed that support for the League had diminished since the summer of 1919.[57] However, Wilson's isolation encouraged his belief that the majority of Americans still favored membership. He was convinced the reaction of the crowds on his Western speaking tour was an indication of the current state of public opinion.[58] As the Senate prepared to vote, many of his closest supporters urged him to accept ratification of the treaty even with the Lodge reservations.[59] Yet Wilson refused to compromise, indicating even if the treaty passed with these reservations, he would refuse to approve it.[60] In the end, he was not put in that position. On March 19, 1920, just over half the Democrats voted with the Republican "irreconcilables" against the treaty with the Lodge reservations. The treaty fell seven votes short of the required two-thirds majority, and the United States did not join the League of Nations.

A Back Door to the League

Rather than seeing this as an indication Americans wished to retreat from major involvement in global affairs, Wilson switched his attention to securing the mandate. Many observers at the time, and particularly his opponents in the Senate, believed the president viewed the mandate as his "back door" to the League.[61] Wilson did not expressly state this was his intention, but it is clear the mandate would have realized an aspect of his new world order. It would be an example of America's benevolent global leadership and ensure peace in an unstable region. A month after defeat of the treaty he confided to Dodge that he had set his "heart on seeing this Government accept the mandate for Armenia" and believed it was "plainly marked out for us as the course of duty." The president now urged Dodge and the missionary-relief lobby to devise some "legitimate propaganda" that would convince the American public to undertake this responsibility and influence Congress, which "at first blush would be shy about accepting any mandate at all."[62]

The president had already attempted to influence public and congressional opinion by sending the Harbord Report to the Senate in early April. In response, Barton wrote to the New York Times, stating the report so evidently confirmed the need for a mandate that if the United States failed to protect the Armenians from "crucifixion at the hands of their murderers, we put ourselves in the same class with Pontius Pilate."[63] Barton's emotive allusion to "the Passion" aside, the prevailing reaction was negative. Herbert Hoover, considered as a presidential candidate by both major parties for the upcoming election, came out publicly against the mandate.[64] He claimed the report was evidence that the United States would become entangled in the "very maelstrom of European politics."[65] Even the New York Times, which still favored a mandate, declared the report had been published too late to have any effect.[66] Sentiments in the country at large, and in the Senate, were moving away from any type of international commitment, particularly one that guaranteed protection of another nation's security and the assumption of responsibilities devoid of material interests.[67] The Republican presidential aspirant, Warren Harding, captured this mood in May when he proclaimed: "America's present need is not heroic, but healing; is not nostrums but normalcy; . . . not submergence in internationality, but sustainment in triumphant nationality."[68] The country's growing aversion to shouldering international responsibilities was reflected in waning sympathy for the Armenians. The author, Clarence Day Jr., writing in the "Editor's Drawer" of Harper's Magazine, expressed frustration at the "everlasting Armenians." Americans were initially horrified by the massacres, Day noted, but as time passed and "the calls of these people for sympathy and friends have continued, a secret annoyance with them has begun to appear." The Armenians had "asked for help so much that they are boring us."[69] This change in mood boded ill for the mandate campaign.

Before his illness, Wilson had always been sensitive to the opinion of the American people and adept at deciphering their demands. Once removed from the political scene, he was out of touch with public attitudes and construed his recollections of previous experiences as an indication of the current state of opinion. In the case of Armenia, he interpreted the generous funds raised for relief and the extensive outpouring of sympathy since 1915 as evidence that the American people were still interested in Armenia and prepared to take responsibility for their security.

Moreover, having forced Lansing's resignation in February, the president no longer had a secretary of state vehemently opposed to a mandate. Wilson's relationship with Lansing had become ever more fractious since their return from the peace conference. When Wilson accused the secretary of insubordination for calling cabinet meetings during his illness, Lansing, still resentful over the way the president had "ignored and openly humiliated" him in Paris, took the opportunity to resign on his own terms.[70] The nature of Lansing's departure and his replacement by Bainbridge Colby, a former Bull Moose Progressive with no previous foreign policy experience, perplexed many political observers, leading some to question the soundness of the president's judgment and the state of his health.[71] However, Colby's relative inexperience made him less concerned about diplomatic precedent and under his secretaryship the State Department was willing to show a firmer commitment to Armenia, finally extending de facto diplomatic recognition on April 23, 1920.[72]

Following the Senate's final defeat of the treaty, Wilson declined renewed Allied requests to participate in the Near Eastern settlement. However, he took the opportunity to contribute his thoughts on the proposed Ottoman treaty. In addition to insisting that the open-door economic principle be maintained in mandated territories, the president proclaimed that the United States was genuinely interested in Armenia's future and was convinced "the civilized world demands and expects the most liberal treatment of that unfortunate country."[73] Wilson's message irritated the Allied leaders. Phillipe Berthelot, the foreign office minister representing France at San Remo, declared that the Allies could not subordinate the treaty to "the whims of the American President." Lloyd George agreed that it was intolerable to conduct correspondence with America on the subject, for at that rate there would be no treaty.[74] He reflected that the Allies had "only received requests from America to protect Armenia, without any offer to assume responsibility."[75] The prime minister convinced the conference to make a direct appeal to the United States to assume a mandate. He suggested that if American assistance was not forthcoming, then the United States could not continue to complain of Allied failure to protect Armenia.[76] By this time, Lloyd George had given up all hope of a tangible American commitment in the Near East. He simply wanted to divert the blame for regional instability, and Armenia's insecurity, onto the Americans: "If the United States refused, let their refusal be definitely placed on the record," he reasoned. It was vital that the Armenian case should be aired publicly.

In late April, the Allies formally requested that the United States take the mandate. Wilson was also asked to arbitrate the nation's western boundaries, effectively deciding the expanse of territory that the United States would protect.[77] The Allies emphasized that they had directed their appeal to the United States as "the only great power qualified alike by its sympathies and material resources to undertake this task on behalf of humanity." Furthermore, a liberated Armenia had been one of the objectives for which the Allied and Associated Powers fought the war, and this goal had "nowhere received more eloquent expression than in the speeches of President Wilson."[78] The Allies could justify passing off responsibility for the Armenians by referring to America's longstanding sympathy for their cause and the potency of Wilson's rhetoric in defining his vision of a new international system.

The Allied appeal coincided with Republican plans to demonstrate continued concern for the Armenians in the US Senate. Harding introduced a resolution deploring their "conditions of insecurity, starvation and misery" and affirming his hope that their "nationalistic aspirations may soon be attained." He also called on the president to dispatch a warship and a force of marines to protect the lives and property of American citizens in the region. Assured that this was "entirely advisory" and responsibility for action still lay with the president, the Senate passed the legislation without debate.[79] This limited expression of support was not an indication that Republicans were willing to accept the extensive military commitment of a mandate and its association with the League. Democratic Senator Henry Ashurst recognized the resolution as no more than "a gesture" and if the Armenians expected the United States to take a mandate, they would call on it "in vain."[80] Lodge had already conveyed this impression to James Bryce, remarking that the protracted League debate "had wrought a great change in public opinion" and there was now a growing feeling against the United States involving herself at all "in the quarrels of Europe." As a result, not only was a mandate "impossible," but Lodge was also doubtful he could secure a loan "for any political or military purpose."[81] For a previously committed Armenophile, this indicated the extent to which the evolution of opinion during the treaty fight had pushed him toward an isolationist position.

While press speculation mounted that Wilson would seek congressional approval for a mandate, Gerard warned the administration that his Senate contacts had assured him there was no chance of this succeeding. This failure would only give the "impression to Turks and Tartars that the United States is not interested and thus ruin Armenia." Instead, he again urged Wilson to use his executive powers to aid the Armenians directly. He reminded the president that Lodge and other leading Republicans had already confirmed that he possessed the authority to send troops without Congressional approval.[82] By this time, however, Wilson was fixated on putting the mandate request to Congress, determined that this should be seen as a decision approved by the American people at large. On May 11, he wrote to Colby: "It has all along been my purpose to urge upon the Congress the acceptance of a mandate over Armenia." Colby advised him to proceed. If the United States refused it might provoke further bloodshed, the ruin of the present Armenian Republic, and "the opening of the way to further Bolshevism, pan-Turanism and pan-Islamism in Turkey and in Asia." Furthermore, he assured Wilson that it was entirely consistent with his previous policy and speeches on the subject, as well as "expedient from every point of view," to urge Congress to accept a mandate.[83] Colby's counsel was ill-advised; political observers agreed general sentiment in Congress was opposed.[84] Herbert Hoover later suggested Wilson's determination to submit the request to Congress was due to the absence of "experienced advice" at this time.[85] Not only had Lansing resigned but Wilson was also estranged from House, believing he had been too accommodating to the Allies in Paris.[86] However, Wilson had ignored Lansing's opposition to the mandate in the past and there is no reason to believe he would have heeded any counsel against it now. Although he had been cautious about making a public commitment during the treaty fight, he had been unwavering in his personal belief that the United States should accept the mandate, and his illness only seemed to increase his resolve.

Observing from the sideline, Lansing informed Davis that Wilson's proposition for a mandate had no chance, as public opinion was opposed to "mixing up in the complex problems of the Near East." The former secretary reiterated his own aversion to "letting our country get into the boiling cauldron of intrigue." America's "British cousins" had "taken the cream and expect us to make butter out of the skimmed milk."[87] Davis agreed. He was utterly unconvinced by Lloyd George's protestations that the Allies, "exhausted by their purely altruistic and unselfish efforts" in assuming more profitable mandates, "could not possibly undertake the heavy burden of a mandate for Armenia [so] turn to America and ask her to accept the most difficult, thankless and impossible task of all. It is bald to the point of indecency."[88] Lansing and Davis's private suspicions of British imperial intrigue would be echoed publicly during the Senate debate.

Arresting the Hopeful Processes of Civilization

On May 24, Wilson asked Congress to assume the mandate. He declared it was "providential" that the Harding resolution had expressed concern for Armenia at the same time as the Allies had asked him to accept a mandate. Echoing the language that he used to rally support for the treaty, the president claimed if America refused this duty it "would do nothing less than arrest the hopeful processes of civilization." Wilson did not expect Congress to shirk this responsibility.

Emphasizing the religious and altruistic principles that had inspired the relief effort, he proclaimed the nation's sympathy for Armenia had "sprung from untainted conscience, pure Christian faith, and an earnest desire to see Christian people everywhere succoured in their time of suffering."[89]

The Senate immediately responded to the president's request. In the Foreign Relations Committee three days later Lodge proposed a substitute motion, respectfully declining to accept a mandate over Armenia. While Lodge believed the Armenians deserved American sympathy, this was wholly different from "taking the mandate and assuming the care of the country for we can not say for how many years to come." The Foreign Relations Committee, with its Republican majority, adopted Lodge's resolution by a vote of 11 to 4.[90] Previous resolutions on the Armenian question had been held up in committee, with only Harding's relatively weak expression of support ever brought to a vote. On this occasion, everything was accelerated; there were no subcommittee hearings or extended discussion of the president's request and, on May 29, debate began on the Senate floor. With an eye to the 1920 election, the Republican leadership wanted the issue resolved before Congress adjourned on June 5 and in time for the Republican National Convention three days later.[91] They planned to humiliate Wilson by crushing the mandate request and embarrass the Democrats by forcing them to either abandon the president or support an unpopular policy with all its political repercussions. No doubt there was an element of partisanship in the Republican's position, but it also reflected their unwillingness to assume the open-ended and onerous commitments a mandate would entail.

In the Senate debate, the Republicans launched a withering assault on the president's proposed mandate. Wilson was accused of demanding Americans undertake undefined responsibilities for a nation with undefined boundaries. They claimed it was unconstitutional to tax Americans for altruistic service to other peoples or to send American troops to this far-flung "plague-spot." While the United States was burdened with the world's "poorhouse," the Allies, particularly Britain, would seize regions rich in natural resources. For Wilson's critics the mandate represented everything they most disliked about his brand of internationalism, and they feared it was being used as a ploy to gain League membership. They cited George Washington's "Farewell Address" and the Monroe Doctrine as evidence the United States should preserve its policy of nonentanglement in the affairs of the Old World. Americans should focus their humanitarianism on domestic problems emerging from the war rather than exhausting their resources overseas. In fact, Wilson's opponents were skillfully manipulating the Harbord Report, ignoring the recommendations for and concentrating on those against. The irreconcilable opponents of the treaty led the attack on the mandate. Senator Frank Brandegee summarized their position, declaring he hoped "the malignant disease of internationalism had not so poisoned the native American common sense" that Americans felt compelled to interfere in the affairs of every other country on the grounds that "their self-determination is a matter of our constitutional concern." It was not for the United States to assume the moral responsibility of the world.[92]

There was even opposition to the mandate among Democrats. James Reed of Missouri joined the Republicans, claiming the mandate was the most "monstrous proposition" ever put to the American people.[93] Reed had been one of the principal opponents of the treaty and the League, so his opposition was expected, but a number of other Democrats joined him, including Gilbert Hitchcock, Wilson's floor leader in the treaty fight, who recognized it was a lost cause.[94] However, there was still some support on humanitarian grounds. John Sharp Williams, one of the president's strongest supporters, offered the most eloquent defense for a mandate from an internationalist perspective. Now that the United States had seen fit to involve itself in world affairs, it could not take all the advantages of this new position while "shirking all the burdens and responsibilities." America should accept the invitation of civilization to protect the Armenians until they "can stand upon their own feet."[95] This argument was not persuasive enough. The Senate rejected Wilson's request for a mandate by a vote of 52 to 23. No Republican supported the mandate, not even Lodge, who had always proclaimed himself a champion of the Armenian people. In addition, thirteen Democrats also opposed it.[96] As far as the Senate was concerned, the mandate issue was over.

The Senate debate was mirrored in the press. Wilson's appeal to humanitarian ideals was denounced by Republican organs, who wanted no part in an imperial carve-up of the Near East.[97] The *Chicago Tribune* suggested that it was "Armenia's crowning misfortune, with a 'mandate' gone begging, that it has no oil wells . . . What a difference oil makes in the white man's burden."[98] The changing stance of the *Los Angeles Times* from a previously pro-mandate position revealed the extent to which public sentiments had shifted. Its editors declared all "thoughtful persons" were opposed to a mandate "excepting perhaps a few idealists who never consider practical questions of public safety and are always advocating sacrifices." They asserted that not only should the United States reject the mandate, it should also refuse to "lend the Armenians any of [its] money." Americans had problems to deal with on their own continent and had no interest in involving themselves in the troubles of the Old World, particularly not in Armenia, which was the "worst card in the deck." Only the previous summer, this publication had seen "the hand of God" in Armenia's liberation, and declared that Americans should "unhesitatingly accept the mandate."[99]

The *New York Times* lamented that "altruism has been denounced as un-American." Charging Republicans with turning the mandate into a partisan issue, *The Times* bemoaned: "Our vehement patriots have managed to attach a

moral stigma to anything that looks like disinterested aid to others, and they control Congress." However, the rejection of the mandate might have one beneficial
result; as Americans were obviously unwilling to live up to their "expressions
of Christian sympathy," their illusion that they were "the most moral, altruistic
and beneficent people on the face of the earth" would hopefully be dispelled.[100]
Walter Lippmann and his fellow editors of the *New Republic* found it incredu-
lous that in all "Christendom" it was not possible to find "fifty thousand men
to volunteer in the best cause ever offered to democracy." It was a poor excuse
for a "people that pretends to democracy and Christianity" to claim that as the
United States had not signed the treaty and was not a League member, it could
not take the mandate.[101] The Armenian question had forced Americans to rede-
fine the ethos of the nation and to measure the extent of their altruism.

A Return to Normalcy

The Republicans continued to attack Wilson on Armenia at their national convention. In his keynote speech, Lodge accused Wilson of focusing on the mandate to the neglect of problems closer to home.[102] The partisanship surrounding
the issue was emphasized in the Republican election platform, which argued
that "no more striking illustration can be found of President Wilson's disregard
for the lives of American boys or American interests" than his request for an
Armenian mandate. The Republicans sympathized with the Armenians but
opposed "now and hereafter the acceptance of a mandate for any country in
Europe or Asia."[103] The author of this plank was Lewis Einstein, foreign policy
consultant to the Republican presidential nominee, Warren Harding.[104] Seeking
to explain his position, Einstein published an article in *The Nation* criticizing
Wilson for his previous record on Armenia. He stated that although the United
States had been the only neutral power at Constantinople during the massacres,
its government confined its "protests to consciously ineffectual remonstrances"
and to its "shame remained apathetic before the most elementary duties of civilization." Following entry into the Great War, the United States had refused to
declare war on the Ottomans and "left one of the greatest moral issues of all
time without so much as the expression of our indignation." Now Wilson was
trying to "dragoon" an unwilling country to atone for his failings by taking the
mandate. Einstein argued that this commitment was divorced from any appreciation of the national interest. The United States should not assume exclusive and
unlimited responsibility for one of the "greatest problems of today," particularly
when Europe had a stronger interest and political involvement in the region. He
urged Americans not to confuse "the humanitarian and material aid we ought
to extend and the political control we ought to avoid."[105] For Einstein and the

[AMERICAN CARTOON]

—*San Francisco Chronicle*

THE CORE

Figure 6.3 Cartoon from the *San Francisco Chronicle* that shows John Bull, representing Great Britain, pocketing lucrative colonies in Mesopotamia, Persia, Egypt, and South Africa, while dispensing the meagre Armenian mandate to Uncle Sam. "The Core," *The New York Times Current History*, Vol. 12, No. 1, April 1920.

Republicans, the failure lay in Wilson's inaction during the war, not in their rejection of the mandate.

By contrast, the Democrats sought to avoid the issue at their New York convention. Their platform committee adopted a vague and ambiguous expression of sympathy for the Armenians and suggested that the United States extend aid "consistent with its Constitution and principles."[106] Wilson had hoped the convention would make a firmer commitment. When Senator Carter Glass, who chaired the convention's Resolutions Committee, had called at the White House before leaving for New York, Wilson had handed him a slip of paper, saying: "I wish you could get this into the platform." This note, typed by Wilson and initialled "W. W.," was a declaration for an Armenian mandate, which the president reaffirmed was America's "Christian duty" to assume.[107] Despite the crushing defeat of the proposal in the Senate, Wilson, undoubtedly affected by the psychological impact of his illness, had convinced himself Americans would still commit to a mandate. Although Glass was successful in his fight for a plank

Get Out! You're Breaking My Heart! By J. H. Cassel

Figure 6.4 Cartoon rebuking Congress for bemoaning the plight of the Armenians but refusing to accept a mandate. "Get Out You're Breaking My Heart," *The Evening World* (New York), May 27, 1920. *Chronicling America: Historic American Newspapers.* Library of Congress.

approving the treaty and the League, he confessed that opposition to the president's policy on Armenia was "overwhelming."[108]

On August 10, 1920, the Treaty of Sevres was signed, finally establishing a peace settlement between the Allies and the Ottomans. The treaty provided for a free and independent Armenia.[109] Although there was now no chance of the United States assuming a mandate for the new state, Wilson had agreed to draw Armenia's western boundaries and delegated the task to a small committee of Near Eastern experts, headed by Professor William Westermann. Wilson submitted these recommendations to the Allies in late November 1920, but by this time Mustafa Kemal's Nationalists had invaded and conquered nearly all of Turkish Armenia.[110] On November 22, the League of Nations Council requested that Wilson mediate an end to hostilities between Armenia and Turkey. Although Wilson responded that he had no authority to send any military assistance, he agreed to use his "good offices" to try and resolve the conflict and appointed Henry Morgenthau as his personal representative. However, by this time the

Turkish Nationalists controlled the western sections of the new state, while the Soviets absorbed the Armenian Republic in the Caucasus.[111] Ultimately, Wilson had arbitrated the boundaries for a state that no longer existed and attempted to mediate a conflict that had already ended.

In the 1920 presidential election, Warren Harding won a crushing victory over his Democratic opponent, Governor James Cox of Ohio, with the promise of a "return to normalcy." During his campaign, Harding accused Wilson and the Democrats of trying to force a mandate on the American people; he had made clear his personal opposition to any political or military commitment to Armenia.[112] Although Near East Relief continued to raise funds, Armenia, as an independent state, had all but disappeared.[113] The following year, during a series of talks in Philadelphia on "What Really Happened" at the Paris Peace Conference, William Westermann reflected on America's rejection of the mandate and the subsequent collapse of Armenian independence. He charged the United States with responsibility for Armenia's plight by "default of service." Westermann believed the initial wrong had been the failure to declare war on the Ottomans. If the United States had done so, it would have been able to protect Armenia with troops during the armistice and been able to make a greater contribution at the peace conference. However, ultimately it was the American people, not Wilson, who were to blame. The Founding Fathers' warning against entangling alliances may have served the new nation well at the turn of the nineteenth century, but it had become "a counsel of cowardice in the twentieth century." The American people could have saved Armenia by accepting the mandate: "The decision was ours and we took it. American safety first."[114]

Harding's new Secretary of Commerce Herbert Hoover saw things differently. During a campaign address in Philadelphia, he admitted that an appeal for an Armenian mandate pulled at America's "heartstrings" and flattered its "sense of greatness." However, the commitment would have forced the United States to assume responsibility for all of Asia Minor and brought it "into direct political entanglement with the whole weight of Russia." By assuming this responsibility, the United States would "exhaust those moral influences and economic resources that we should contribute to the progress of the world generally." Hoover was convinced that Americans could perform "our greatest service to humanity if we keep ourselves free from such political and economic entanglements." He reminded his audience that there were many Americans, like him, who believed that "the intervention of the American Government in European problems must, except in a complete danger to civilization and our democracy, be restrained to the applications of our organized moral strength and to our charity."[115] Ultimately, it was Hoover's more circumscribed vision of America's world role that the American people had endorsed and this shaped the foreign policy outlook of the incoming administration.

Economic But Not Political Interlocking
of Interests

From Britain, Bryce lamented to Barton: "What a cruel fate follows Armenia!" All the Western nations, he felt, were at fault for allowing Armenia to "perish" within six months of the Treaty of Sevres. Bryce's expertise on the American constitution made him particularly scornful of the Allied excuse that Wilson had promised them that the United States would take the mandate, claiming they should have known that the president did not possess the legal power to do so. Despite the bleak outlook, Bryce continued to hope that a combination of American money and British officers could establish a League of Nations sanctioned administration for the Armenians in the Sevres defined territories. Of course, this was completely unrealistic as Kemal's Turkish Nationalists now controlled this region. It was going to take more than the "severe diplomatic pressure" prescribed by Bryce "to get the Turks to clear out."[116] Nevertheless, missionary leaders in the Near East favored a similar solution. The treasurer of the American Board of Commissioners for Foreign Missions (ABCFM) in Constantinople, W. W. Peet, informed Barton that his conversations with British occupation authorities had convinced him that another Anglo-American "rapprochement" was required. This would ensure the "reconstruction of the Near East" and also benefit "commercial matters and all our national relationships with the mother country." Peet reported that prominent British officials in Constantinople shared this view. He quoted one as saying: "The other nations in the Entente group are civilized and are our friends, [but] they do not stand for the ideals which our two nations stand for. If these ideals are to be realized, we must go hand in hand for the accomplishment for them . . . or the high purpose for which the great war was fought will be lost." Despite all that had occurred, the most persistent advocates of an Anglo-American alliance continued to see it as the only viable solution to the problems in the Near East and the only possible basis for global order.[117]

Yet Anglo-American tensions in the region remained. France and Britain had taken advantage of America's absence from the San Remo Conference to conclude a secret agreement, which essentially established an Anglo-French monopoly over all future oil production in the former Ottoman territories. When this became public knowledge in the summer of 1920, the State Department was outraged. The extensive monopoly claimed by its wartime associates was considered an insult to American companies and a threat to the United States national interest. Bristol's dispatches had alerted State Department officials to the growing significance of petroleum. Although the United States controlled 80 percent of the world's then-known oil reserves, the sharp rise in the price of crude oil after the war had raised fears its domestic resources would soon run low. Access to foreign oil was therefore considered essential to power America's merchant marine and navy and also to maintain its standing as the world's pre-eminent oil supplier.[118] Colby protested against the San Remo agreement, demanding that Britain recognize the open door principle and ensure equal commercial opportunity in its mandates. However, Curzon retorted that economic equality was tied to political responsibilities. The United States had refused to share the burden of maintaining the Ottoman settlement by assuming a mandate and was therefore not entitled to enjoy the same commercial privileges.[119]

The British denial of equal American opportunities in its mandated territories fanned smoldering anti-British hostility in the United States. William Wiseman, who had returned to the United States in an attempt to improve Anglo-American relations, reported that "echoes of Senatorial fulminations against unscrupulous acquisitiveness of British diplomacy are heard about the land." Ever alert to an opportunity to advance American economic interests, Hoover insisted that Britain could offset these attacks by offering Americans a share in the financing and output of its Persian and Mesopotamian oil fields. The commerce secretary suggested to Wiseman that "no better means could be found of starting an economic and perhaps subsequently political inter-locking of British and American interests."[120] By the summer of 1922, the British government had decided to invite American companies to participate in the concessionary corporation in Mesopotamia in a bid to smooth relations with the US government, and because the potential prospects were so vast that it lacked the resources to exploit them alone. Correspondingly, American oil executives and officials in Washington concluded that Britain's regional dominance was necessary to ensure the stability on which petroleum exploration, development, and production depended.[121] Earlier that same year, Anglo-American naval rivalry was also cooled by a series of agreements at the Washington Naval Conference.[122] The two issues identified by Davis as most threatening to harmonious Anglo-American relations appeared to be moving toward resolution. Yet an interconnection of Anglo-American political interests remained elusive. British resentment at American unwillingness to share political obligations in the post-Ottoman Near East continued to fester. American mistrust of British strategy in the region persisted.

Who Will Shoulder the Burden?

After it had become apparent that the United States would play no active role in the Near East, Lloyd George invested his hopes, and his government's prestige, in the Greek premier Eleftherios Venizelos and his project for a greater Greece. Greek control of the Dardanelles would serve as a substitute for an American mandate and ensure Britain's maritime interests in the Eastern Mediterranean. The ideal of an Anglo-American alliance in the region was replaced by a British partnership with Greece, an equally romantic vision for the philhellenic prime minister.[123] Other members of the Cabinet, notably Churchill and Curzon, were opposed, fearing the impact of Greek expansion into Asia Minor on Muslims in the British Empire, especially in India. Curzon, in particular, was also alarmed at the prospect of a Turkish backlash that would lead to a complete breakdown of order in the Near East. Lloyd George ignored these concerns. In the summer of 1920 he sanctioned a Greek offensive into Anatolia, convinced by Venizelos's claims that his forces could check Kemal's Nationalists and enforce the Sevres Treaty. Although Venizelos soon fell from power, the Greeks, encouraged by Lloyd George, initially forced Turkish troops back into the interior. By the summer of 1921 they were pushing toward Kemal's capital at Ankara. However, this was the limit of the Greek incursion and their forces were soon in retreat, committing a series of atrocities in their wake.[124] Lansing's nephew, Allen Dulles, an aide to Bristol in Constantinople and soon to be appointed chief of the Division of Near East Affairs, was appalled by the whole episode. He complained to his uncle that "the situation here is worse than ever," and "England is especially to blame for letting the Greeks wage an entirely unjust war in Anatolia to retain possession of lands to which they have no past claim."[125]

Strengthened by his adroit manipulation of a partnership with the Soviet Union and emboldened by the willingness of France and Italy to recognize his government, Kemal launched a counteroffensive and pushed the Greeks back to the Mediterranean.[126] On September 10, 1922, his victorious forces entered Smyrna, where tens of thousands of Armenian refugees had fled from the advancing Turkish troops. The following day the city was in flames. Responsibility for who started the fire is still disputed, but eyewitnesses reported seeing Turkish soldiers going through Armenian and Greek quarters of the city with cans of petrol.[127] The exact number of Greeks and Armenians who died remains unknown, with estimates ranging from 10,000 to 100,000. As the carnage unfolded, European and American ships watched impotently from the harbor. Initially limiting their rescue operation to their own nationals, British and American crews eventually joined their French and Italian counterparts in aiding Greek and Armenian Christians. The powers ultimately succeeded in evacuating masses of civilians but the Armenian and Greek quarters of Smyrna were completely destroyed.[128] The American consul in Smyrna, George Horton, who had witnessed the wartime massacres, deplored "the gradual and systematic extermination of Christians and Christianity" in the Near East and condemned "the political rivalries of the Western world, that have made such a fearful tragedy possible." Nor did his own government escape censure: "No Gladstonian note of horror, protest or revulsion has as yet issued from any official American source."[129]

Horton was not alone in appealing for action from Washington. Barton was horrified by events in Smyrna, not least as over one hundred thousand dollars worth of ABCFM property was damaged in the flames. He had no doubt that the Turks were responsible and, in a letter to President Harding, prophesied with familiar rhetoric that "we are witnessing what promises to be the beginning of another European war, in which barbarism will be arraigned against civilization." Barton urged Harding to join the European powers in issuing an ultimatum to Kemal and requested the dispatch of US troops to the Near East to safeguard the rights of Americans and protect Christian minorities.[130] Several large-scale Protestant church groups also demanded American action, although their appeals were less prescriptive. An agent of the Armenian National Delegation, James A. Malcolm, reported excitedly to the Ottoman Armenian leadership, still residing in Paris, that "a nation wide movement is on foot to induce the United States Government to do 'something' in the Near East." While the church organizations were somewhat vague in their expectations of the Harding administration, Malcolm was more enthused by the definite demands of the Episcopal Churches. Their leaders urged the establishment of an Armenian National Home, along the lines of what the British government had promised the Zionists under the Balfour Declaration, and "would have the United States go as far as to use force" to achieve it.[131] The prominent Methodist Episcopal Bishop James Cannon Jr. personally delivered a resolution from his church to Secretary of State Charles Evans Hughes, appealing to the administration "to take whatever steps may be necessary to stop . . . the complete annihilation of the Christians in the Near East." Cannon suggested that this would be in keeping with the tradition of a nation that had gone to "war with Spain because of the persecution of the Cubans [and] entered a war because of what we held to be German atrocities." Undeterred by America's unwillingness to intervene directly in the Near East during the war or afterward, missionary minded spokesmen pressed for a military solution.[132]

Inundated with petitions from concerned Americans, Hughes decided, with presidential endorsement, to publicly defend the administration's response to events in the Near East and outline its wider foreign policy philosophy.[133] In late October, during an address in Boston, he confessed that "the Christian world has been filled with horror at the atrocities committed [in] Anatolia, especially in connection with the burning of Smyrna, rivalled only by the wholesale massacres and deportations of the Armenians in 1915." While it was not his intention to excuse Turkish actions, Hughes stated that any appraisal of the situation must take into account the Greek army's incursions into Anatolia and the atrocities that they had committed in retreat. Noting that the situation was more complex than the interventionists claimed, he denied that the United States had any responsibility to interfere. The current turmoil was the consequence of an

Allied war with the Ottomans in which the United States had not involved itself, "despite the occurences of 1915." It was the European powers, not the United States, that had turned the Near East into a "checkerboard for diplomatic play." If Europeans, who were closer at hand, refused to intervene to protect Near Eastern Christians then there was little hope that the American people would be "willing to shoulder this burden of armed intervention." The secretary of state was particularly scathing toward those who urged the US government to threaten intervention even if it had no intention of declaring war. In support of his conviction that the United States must only issue threats that it was prepared to execute, Hughes quoted Theodore Roosevelt's maxim, stated in relation to anti-Jewish pogroms in Russia, to "never draw unless you mean to shoot." A leading member of the ACIA, Hughes had urged the Wilson administration to dispatch troops to protect the Armenians in 1919 but the American people, through their Senate representatives, rejected this role. Like Roosevelt earlier, Hughes had concluded from this experience that a statesman must not bluff by advocating a policy that he would or could not carry out because the country would never support it. Hughes therefore informed his audience that the government would limit its actions to the protection of American interests and the provision of humanitarian relief where possible.[134]

Hughes had judged the mood of the country accurately. Most American newspapers endorsed the administration's position. The *Washington Post* expressed relief that the United States had rejected the Versailles settlement and escaped entanglement in the Allied intrigue in the Near East, where its "part in this scheme was to be that of uncompensated burden-bearer." Its editor was grateful that the Harding administration had unequivocally stated America's refusal to become politically embroiled in any of "Europe's political tangles" and, above all, its unwillingness to provide the "solution [to] the Near East question."[135] The *Salt Lake Telegram* agreed: "By keeping out of the league of nations and refusing to accept the offer of a mandate in Armenia, the United States avoided contact with Europe's hot potato, which the Near East has been for centuries and doubtless will continue to be indefinitely."[136] The noninterventionist position taken by a leading publication in Utah, where support for the Armenians was previously so strong, was a clear indication of popular support for the Harding administration's disengaged Near East policy. Famed American humourist Will Rogers, writing in *Life* magazine, captured American attitudes: "You would never get this Country to go to War over the Dardanelles unless they had to cross them going from their offices to their Golf Course."[137]

The defeat and subsequent departure of the Greek army meant only a small Allied occupation force stood between Kemal and Constantinople. Lloyd George and Churchill were adamant that Constantinople and the Dardanelles Straits, due to their strategic significance, must be defended at all costs.[138]

Churchill reminded the Cabinet that the current "misfortunes of the Allies were probably due to the fact that owing to the delay on the part of America in declaring their position, their armies had apparently melted away."[139] He and Lloyd George convinced the Cabinet that they should ask France and the Dominions, who since 1919 could decide for themselves whether to support the metropole in a war, to join the British army at Chanak in defending the Straits. However, French and imperial statesmen, with the exception of the leaders of New Zealand and Newfoundland, informed London that they had no intention of fighting. Despite Britain's isolation, Lloyd George and Churchill remained committed to war, but the British commander at Chanak and Kemal agreed to negotiate an armistice. The Cabinet endorsed the compromise, as did most newspapers, horrified at the thought of fighting to defend remote Constantinople just four years after the armistice on the Western Front.[140] Andrew Bonar Law, retired leader of the Unionist-Conservative party, summed up the national mood in a letter to *The Times* in October. Ensuring the neutrality of the Dardanelles Straits and the prevention of fresh massacres in the Near East was not an exclusively British interest but a global concern, which affected all the victors in the war, including the United States. The British Empire could not "alone act as the policemen of the world. The financial and social conditions of this country make that impossible." Bonar Law maintained that Britain, without French support in the Near East, could not "bear the burden alone" and like the United States would have to focus on its own interests.[141] When Lloyd George's coalition fell the following month, it was Bonar Law, with his less interventionist foreign policy, who replaced him as prime minister.[142]

Later in November, during a meeting in Washington, the British Ambassador Auckland Geddes and Secretary Hughes reviewed the situation in the Near East. Geddes attributed the current crisis to the delay caused by the Allies awaiting an American decision on mandates. Other British statesmen had made a similar criticism, but Geddes took the opportunity to issue it in person to the secretary of state. The ambassador, a Cabinet member during the peace conference, claimed that Britain had only agreed to establish the mandate system to appease American sentiments and to ensure its cooperation in the Near East. He suggested that the "British had taken up their share of the burden in the expectation that America would take its share and now they feared they were being left alone." Hughes completely rejected the premise of Geddes's argument. The secretary argued that anyone who understood American public opinion would have recognized that America's acceptance of a mandate was never likely, although he failed to disclose that he himself had previously advocated dispatching troops to the region. Hughes was on firmer ground when he dismissed Geddes's protestation that the British Empire had not desired to acquire any further territory. He argued that Britain's policy was determined by the desire to maintain its "imperial power, the question of India, the question of Egypt, of the Suez Canal and their relations to the Near East in connection with their vast imperial domain." Hughes had no objection to Britain looking out for its own interests, but resented the United States being blamed for the Near Eastern situation when it "had not sought to parcel out spheres of influence . . . was not responsible for the catastrophe of the Greek armies during the last year and a half . . . diplomacy in Europe was responsible for the late disaster."[143]

This exchange revealed the extent to which the old antagonisms were still very much alive. Attempts to draw the United States into the Near East, through accepting mandates, had only made Americans more suspicious of Britain's motives and the British increasingly frustrated at America's unwillingness to undertake any political commitments. The recriminations over who was at fault for the breakdown of order in the Near East would continue.[144] But the project for an Anglo-American alliance based on shared political commitments, and with it a solution to the Armenian question, had long since disappeared.

That same month, officials from the major Allied nations, Britain, France, Italy, and Japan, met with a Turkish nationalist delegation at Lausanne to resolve the Near Eastern settlement.[145] Delegations from Greece, Romania, Bulgaria, Yugoslavia, and even the Soviet Union were also present. Notable for their attendance as observers, rather than active participants, were the Americans.[146] Months of hard fought negotiations were interrupted by the spectacular departure of the leading British delegate Lord Curzon in a bid to force the hands of the Turks. Negotiations ultimately resumed in late April 1923. The Treaty of Lausanne, finally signed on July 24, substantially revised the Sevres settlement. The new Turkish state renounced its claims to the non-Turkish portions of the former Ottoman Empire lost during the war. However, it regained sovereignty over a territory stretching from eastern Thrace to Syria, and the European powers relinquished their spheres of influence. The capitulations were abolished and, although minorities were promised protection, the treaty contained no mechanism for outside powers to intervene to ensure their rights.[147] Furthermore, there was no provision for an Armenian "national home." During the conference, the American delegation publicized its willingness to support British demands for this but quickly retreated after Turkish representatives absolutely rejected the suggestion. Moreover, the principal US observer, Ambassador to Italy Richard Child, recognized that if the United States insisted on a protectorate for the Armenians, the Allies would naturally expect them to back up their demands with force and accept a mandate. The American retreat convinced Curzon that the proposition was hopeless, and the idea was abandoned.[148]

The Treaty of Lausanne brought an end to a dozen years of war in the Near East, which had begun with the Turkish-Italian War of 1911. It was without doubt a Turkish triumph, acclaimed by Kemal as "a political victory unequalled in the history of the Ottoman era."[149] Lausanne was the first treaty to overturn the settlements devised in Paris and Joseph Grew, an American observer, claimed it was "the greatest blow to the prestige of the Great Powers that has occurred in history." In time, it would come to be regarded as an Allied success for stabilizing the region and ensuring the demilitarization of the Dardanelles Straits.[150] For the Armenians, however, and for all those who had worked to find a permanent political solution to the Armenian question, Lausanne represented a tragic failure. There was no mention of an Armenian homeland and no guarantee of the protection of their rights. Churchill would capture this failure best when he later recalled, "in the Treaty of Lausanne, which registered the final peace between Turkey and the Great Powers, history will search in vain for the word 'Armenia.' "[151]

Conclusion

Without denying that present conditions have, of necessity, modified the old policy of isolation and without minimizing the influence of that fact in the conduct of American foreign affairs, it did not seem essential for the United States to become the guardian of any of the peoples of the Near East, who were aspiring to become independent nationalities, a guardianship which the President held to be a duty that the United States was bound to perform as its share of the burden imposed by the international cooperation which he considered vital to the new world order.
  —Robert Lansing, *The Peace Negotiations: A Personal Narrative* (1921)

President Wilson was inclined to recommend that the United States of America should undertake the mandate for the Armenians. Had he succeeded, what a different story would now have been told! What a different story the generations to come would tell! But his health broke down at the vital moment and America would have none of his humanitarian schemes.
  —David Lloyd George, *Memoirs of the Peace Conference* (1939)

For more than two decades, the Armenians' cause commanded such support, and occupied so prominent a place in the public and political discourses of both Britain and the United States, that their protection came to be seen as an essential component of a reformed international system. As Winston Churchill recalled, the atrocities committed against the Armenians aroused widespread anger around "the English-speaking world" and fervent appeals to see them "righted." Yet after the war, Armenian independence proved fleeting. Since neither the United States nor Britain was able to prevent the wartime atrocities or secure Armenia's national self-determination in the conflict's aftermath, the importance of the Armenian question to the international affairs of the period has been underestimated. Its solution was central to the foreign policy philosophies of both Theodore Roosevelt and Woodrow Wilson. It was pivotal to missionary strategies to spread Christian ideals and constitutional government around the world. For leading British politicians, it would forge a "bond of union" between the United States and the British Empire, first in the Near

East and then beyond. Failing to recognize its significance belies the fierceness of the debate that the issue engendered over America's global role, its relationship with the British Empire, and ideas about world order at the turn of the twentieth century. The proposed American mandate offers a window into an international system that might have been. Resurrecting the debates over the mandate reveals the alternative visions that American and British leaders envisaged for the League of Nations. Despite its ultimate rejection, the two-year debate over a mandate would have a profound impact on American ideas about the League and on attitudes to the British Empire that would continue to reverberate in the years after the Senate's rejection of the Versailles Treaty. Furthermore, the search for a solution to the Armenian question helps explain enduring dilemmas in the politics of humanitarian intervention that continue to resonate today.

The collapse of the Armenian cause in the United States and Britain symbolized the end of an era. Reviewing the Armenian question in 1922, the year of Smyrna's destruction, the British liberal politician and Near Eastern expert Noel Buxton, who had traveled to the United States to publicize the Armenian atrocities six years earlier, observed that "although the plight of Armenia is today more compelling of sympathy than perhaps at any point in history, opinion, wearied with the length of time the problem has lasted, has become apathetic." Atrocities were "too familiar and too frequent to arouse emotion, forming as they have done almost a weekly news item for the last thirty years or more."[1] On both sides of the Atlantic the public had become inured to the suffering and their capacity for compassion, the emotion on which humanitarianism rests, had become exhausted.[2] Yet Buxton detected a more profound reason for this shift in attitudes: "Contemporary progressive opinion now assumes a cynical leer about anything which savours of the idealism of the 'nineties.' Is not Armenia, they say, an irrelevant pre-occupation of Christian politicians? Why bother about these worn-out cries to-day?"[3]

The coalitions that had emerged in both countries in support of the Armenians had been underpinned by a missionary minded culture of moral reform that had attracted the support of leading figures from across the political spectrum.[4] After the shattering toll of the First World War, however, there was little appetite for advocating military action on behalf of strangers in far-flung regions and the attention of politicians shifted to more prosaic concerns. Relief organizations did continue to aid Armenian refugees, the overwhelming majority of whom were now scattered between the Armenian Soviet Republic, Greece, and the French mandate territories of Lebanon and Syria. British groups, such as the Lord Mayor's Fund and the British Armenian Committee, helped support the work of League of Nations officials and Near East Relief (NER), which, in 1923, continued to run 124 orphanages housing 64,000 children—operating outside of Turkey after it became clear that the new regime was unwilling to tolerate a foreign institution infringing its sovereignty.[5] This transnational activism would lead to a more secular, institutionalized humanitarianism, albeit one that built on the missionary-led philanthropy of the past and still informed by the same paternalistic notions of bringing civilization to benighted populations.[6] The NER continued to develop ties with large philanthropic institutions, such as the Rockefeller Foundation, and received support from US diplomats in the region. Nevertheless, the formal involvement of the US government was limited, as it remained opposed to assuming any political or military commitments in the Old World and increasingly prioritized establishing relations with Kemal's new regime over lobbying for the dispossessed Armenians. As contributions dwindled, it became apparent that the NER could not keep supporting refugees for an indeterminate period, with little hope of repatriating them in Turkey, and the organization increasingly scaled back its operations, ultimately ending its relief work in 1929.[7]

For a decade after the war, the NER saw itself as fulfilling some of the functions that a mandate would have served, aiding and protecting a vulnerable population. Yet it never had the political authority or the military resources that the US government would have possessed as a mandatory power. As University of Texas professor and international legal specialist Malbone W. Graham observed in 1924, if the United States had engaged in a "humanitarian intervention" over Armenia "such as it did in Cuba in 1898," then it could have inaugurated a new era in international politics. Graham recognized that "the idea of intervention of states for the purpose of ameliorating conditions which were revolting and which called for redress is not new," and, in US foreign policy, he pointed specifically to the diplomatic interventions on behalf of Romanian and Russian Jews, and to the joint action with Britain to remedy the "injustice" in the Congo. These interventions, like other European examples, however, were carried out on an ad hoc basis and at a time when there was "still lacking a definitely coherent, organized Society of Nations capable of both formulation and enforcement of international law." In the early years of the organization's existence, Graham could still hope that the creation of the League had "fundamentally altered the question of humanitarian intervention" by institutionalizing and giving "sanction of social solidarity, on an objective basis, to the hitherto purely sporadic, isolated acts of altruistic nations acting as enforcers of the law of nations." Ultimately, this vision of the League as a "substantive Law of Nations defining the right of humanitarian intervention in a new light" and acting militarily to prevent "international crimes against humanity" did not come to pass. The League did not become an organization with the capacity to appoint an individual government to serve as "its mandatory, its agent . . . for the purpose of removing unfortunate conditions violative of the most elementary human rights," and then undertake a "policy of state-building." Yet as Graham speculated, it was "almost inescapable" that if the

United States had intervened on behalf of the Armenians then this would have led to the establishment of a mandate of this type.[8]

For a moment, in Paris, it seemed that such an intervention might occur, but it proved ephemeral. The first half of 1919 was the only time that elements of all the different American solutions to the Armenian question coalesced. As Secretary of State Charles Evans Hughes reflected in a speech to the Council on Foreign Relations in 1924: "If there was ever a time when we could have successfully intervened and have backed up our intervention by armed forces, it was early in 1919 when we had a large army abroad and were in a position to prosecute such a policy if deemed advisable. But this opportunity passed."[9] Although the tortured debate over American acceptance of the mandate continued for another year, its final outcome was barely noticed in Britain and France. After the US Senate rejected membership of the League in November 1919, British and French leaders recognized that there would be no American role in Armenia or elsewhere in Asia Minor, and following a set of fractious meetings, the two imperial rivals divided up the region between them on the basis of the wartime secret treaties. More broadly, the mandate system was used by both the British and French governments as a means to resolve their differences and validate their imperial acquisitions.

This was not what either Wilson or the British architects of the mandate system had originally envisioned. This system was designed, in Wilson's words, for a League "with the United States in the lead."[10] For him, an American mandate for Armenia, through the League, was a tangible manifestation of his vision for a new, US-led international order. He viewed the "trusteeship" that the United States had assumed over territories in the Pacific and Caribbean as a more progressive approach to colonialism than that practiced by the European imperial powers. This would provide a model for an American mandate in the Near East that could serve as an example to other colonial powers. Moreover, acceptance of a mandate would ensure the United States abandoned its isolation and assumed its global responsibilities. Wilson was convinced this would also be the wish of the American people, and that their deep and longstanding concern for Armenia would lead to acceptance of the mandate and assumption of a pre-eminent role in the new international organization.

Wilson's faith in America's readiness to accept the "burdens and responsibilities" required for global leadership proved unfounded. As evidence of his own growing allegiance to the Armenian cause, however, one of Wilson's last fights as president was over approval for a mandate. How much this final act was influenced by ill health is difficult to judge, but while a healthy Wilson may have displayed greater political prudence, the illness did not account for his dedication to a mandate, which had been growing throughout this period. Wilson's request for a mandate forced Americans to consider making a commitment, through an international organization, to ensuring the stability of the Near East and to guaranteeing a nation's self-determination in the heart of the Old World for the first time. Ultimately, however, the debate over the definition of the nation, one driven by Wilson's notion of a "community of interest" or by more narrowly defined national interests, assuming limited international responsibilities or the president's more extensive brand of internationalism, was won by his opponents. The Armenian mandate became a touchstone for critics of Wilson's approach to statecraft and his conception of the League. In the Republican 1920 election platform, the Armenian mandate was one of three issues that comprised the party's foreign policy plank (after relations with Mexico and before the League of Nations). Wilson's mandate request was used to condemn him for risking the "lives of American boys," ignoring American interests, and attempting to "throw the United States into the very maelstrom of European quarrels."[11] These themes were revisited during the campaign by Harding, as he invoked his opposition to the mandate to illustrate his commitment to put "America First" (a phrase that he deployed regularly during the campaign) and to demonstrate that he did "not want somebody else, across the sea, to tell us what to do or how to do it."[12] The League fight featured many general, abstract debates over what sort of responsibilities membership would entail but Wilson's mandate request was a specific, concrete commitment and the Republicans seized on it to discredit his entire program. As they declared in their platform, under the heading "No mandate wars for our sons":

> No surrender of rights to a world council or its military alliances, no assumed mandatory, however appealing, ever shall summon the sons of this Republic to war. Their supreme sacrifice shall only be asked for America and its call of honor.[13]

An alliance was exactly what Britain's leaders had hoped to use the League, and an American mandate, in particular, to promote. America's intervention in the war on the Western Front had reawakened British dreams of a formal Anglo-American alliance. America's humanitarian concerns, economic ambitions, and, above all, the influence of its missionary stations in the Near East had encouraged British statesmen to believe that the United States might share the burden of reorganizing the Ottoman Empire after the war by assuming mandates for Armenia and the municipal district of Constantinople. As well as satisfying longstanding British domestic demands for Armenia's just treatment, these mandates would help solve the strategic problems posed by the collapse of the Ottoman Empire, serving as a buffer against any assaults on British interests on the road to India, while countering French influence. Above all, the mandates were intended to serve as the basis for an Anglo-American alliance that would underwrite the new global order. The mandate system was devised as a project that would reconcile the United States and the British Empire, enabling the two powers to co-operate in colonial affairs and establishing a great-power partnership that would police the new international system and provide guardianship for the "backward races" of the former German and Ottoman Empires.[14] British champions of this new system viewed the American assumption of mandates as tangible commitments that would tie the United States to the new international order. However, once the US Senate rejected American membership in the League and assumption of the mandates, British leaders fell back on their uneasy arrangement with France. And the League's mandate system, which French leaders had angrily dismissed as an Anglo-American ruse to deprive them of their spoils of war and which its British architects lost enthusiasm for after the United States retreated, came into being without the one power considered essential by its original designers to its proper functioning.

At a public meeting in 1924, Lord Milner, the principal advocate of an Anglo-American alliance in colonial affairs, told his audience that he had championed the mandate system as a means to ensure the continued co-operation of the victorious powers in the postwar world. The former colonial secretary insisted that if that spirit of partnership had endured, and the mandate system been established immediately after the war, then "some great disasters would have been avoided, such as that which had befallen the Christian population of Armenia." He would recall that "it had been in everybody's mind when the mandatory system was first started, that it should be applied to Armenia and to certain other portions, never quite adequately defined, of the Turkish Empire in Asia," but "those projects had long since passed in the limbo of bygone and forgotten dreams." Although he did not explicitly mention it, it was clear that the primary "project" that Milner had in mind was an Anglo-American colonial alliance and he continued to maintain that it would have been "better for the world and for the unfortunate Christian inhabitants" of the Ottoman Empire if it had succeeded.[15]

Milner was not the only member of the Imperial War Cabinet to publicly lament that the American rejection of a mandate had undermined Britain's plans for the postwar world. In his account of the peace treaties, published on the eve of the Second World War, Lloyd George argued that the failure to resolve the Armenian question was intimately connected to the broader decline of international order. The former prime minister recalled that an "independent Armenian State was a hopeless project from the moment America refused to undertake the responsibility of protecting it." As an alternative bulwark against Turkey, he had unstintingly supported Greek expansion in Asia Minor, but when this led to the Chanak Crisis and his government's downfall, he complained that "with it went first the liberation of Armenia and Asiatic Greece, and in the sequel the League of Nations and all the projects for substituting conciliation for armaments." Lloyd

George's recollections were extremely biased and highly self-serving, designed to vindicate his own record, depict himself as an heir of Gladstonian liberalism, and direct blame for the ultimate breakdown of the Paris settlement elsewhere. His former Conservative colleagues, particularly Lord Curzon, received the lion's share of the responsibility for their role in the Lausanne Treaty, which he called the "first of the humiliating and calamitous capitulations which in the end have destroyed most of what was best in the Treaties of Peace." However, Lloyd George also criticized Wilson, claiming that his "narrow and jealous party bias thwarted his most cherished plans and wrecked schemes which would have contributed materially to the permanent beneficence of the Peace settlement." Lloyd George remained convinced that if Wilson had consulted the leading Republican Senators "before he committed himself at the Peace Council, there is every reason to believe they would have pledged themselves to support the proposed Mandate."[16] While the more internationalist minded Republicans supported League membership with reservations and Wilson might have been able to co-operate with them, if he was not convinced that their amendments nullified the treaty, it is highly unlikely that he would have convinced them to agree to an Armenian mandate regardless of his approach. Like the president, his Senate opponents associated the commitment of a mandate with Wilson's broader conception of American League membership. Whereas the president perceived the mandate as a symbol of American selflessness and moral leadership, his opponents interpreted it as evidence of the unrewarding and open-ended commitments that the League would impose.

Would the outcome have been different if the United States had been presented with a more lucrative mandate? Buxton speculated that if, in addition to Armenia, "the offer of a mandate over Turkey, including territories since allocated to the Allies [such as the oil-fields of Mesopotamia and Mosul] been made to the United States of America, a happier chapter would have begun not only in the history of the peoples of the Near East, but also in the history of the League of Nations."[17] Yet in Paris Wilson had shown little interest in acquiring these territories. Indeed in both his private and public justifications for assuming a mandate, Wilson had consistently stressed idealistic rather than materialistic motives. More broadly, and unlike the other major powers, the great power status of the United States was less dependent on its acquisition of overseas possessions, and its initial enthusiasm for establishing a colonial empire after 1898 had long since waned. As even Milner had come to realize, his initial hopes for securing an American mandate were "not altogether reasonable."[18]

British proponents of using a US mandate as a means to establish an Anglo-American alliance would have been wise to have heeded the advice of Alfred Mahan, who had warned in the 1890s that "when, if ever, an Anglo-American alliance does come, naval or other, may it be rather as a yielding to irresistible popular impulse, than as a scheme, however ingeniously wrought, imposed by the adroitness of statesmen."[19] Indeed, rather than advancing Anglo-American relations and encouraging the United States to assume a new global role, the mandate "scheme," as Kipling christened it, helped exacerbate American hostility to the new international organization and their former wartime associates, especially Britain. Opposition to the mandate revived antipathy for the British empire, unresolved by the prewar rapprochement. Irreconcilable opponents of the League were vehemently opposed to membership of a British dominated international organization, in which Britain's Empire expanded by gobbling up the most desirable territories while the United States was forced to carry the unremunerative burden for Armenia. Moreover, the spectacle of Britain and the other European powers seizing the resource-rich regions of the former Ottoman Empire while offering the United States the barren territory of Armenia antagonized even those who were initially sympathetic to League membership. Herbert Hoover, the man Wilson intended to appoint governor of the mandate, would capture this prevailing sentiment when he declared that "the Allies had taken the bank and offered America the slum."[20] Ironically, the mandate system, intended by its British designers as a way to unite Britain and the United States in a common endeavor of international governance, only succeeded in increasing mutual distrust and intensified American hostility to assuming any commitments outside the Western hemisphere for the postwar world. As Buxton lamented, it was unsurprising that "President Wilson's stock went down in the United States and that his successor decided to ignore the League of Nations," considering its members had "collared the swag and hidden it under the Mandatory cloak."[21]

Memories of the Allies' attempt to take advantage of America's altruism over Armenia, while using the League's mandate system for their own imperial aggrandizement, would linger for some Americans. This was especially true of Hoover, who would help shape US foreign policy during the next dozen years, first as commerce secretary and then as president, and continue to influence debates over America's world role long after he left office. The conduct of the major European powers at Versailles, and particularly their approach to the colonial settlement, confirmed Hoover's belief that their governments were reactionary, intractably opposed to American democratic principles and constantly conniving to exploit American ideals for their own ends.[22] These convictions would inform his diplomatic outlook for the rest of his life and were prominent themes in Hoover's memoirs and his account of Wilson's peacemaking, both of which were published in the 1950s. In these books Hoover was particularly scornful of the "mandates compromise," which enabled the Allied powers, particularly the British Empire, to expand at the expense of self-determination while encouraging the United States to assume mandates for unprofitable Armenia and Constantinople.[23] Hoover recalled that he had urged Wilson to reject the mandates because they were an economic burden and a grave strategic error that would enmesh the United States in an unstable region, while acting as a cover to allow the Allies to acquire the world's resources. Over and above these specific disqualifications, however, was Hoover's more general concern that they "would involve America in the whole power politics of Europe."[24] At the time the books were published, the United States had just entered into the North Atlantic Treaty Organization (NATO) to defend Western Europe from Soviet aggression. A prominent and outspoken opponent of the alliance, Hoover used these books as part of his wider campaign. As he wrote to a friend in 1957, shortly before publishing his study of Wilson, he wanted it to "illustrate some lessons on the old world" to the American public.[25] In recalling the rancor over the Armenian mandate, Hoover was seeking to remind Americans that they must remain alert to European schemes and guard against attempts to take advantage of their idealism to serve selfish purposes.

By this time, however, very few Americans would have had any recollection of the mandate debate. Lloyd George's memoirs may have been prejudiced, but he was correct to predict that Wilson's failure to convince Americans to accept an Armenian mandate would impact the story told by future generations. For many years, the American response to the Armenian question received little attention from either the public or historians of US foreign relations. The issue was subsumed in the historiography by the broader issues surrounding US expansion in the Pacific and Caribbean, its intervention in World War I, and the larger League fight. However, when a series of humanitarian atrocities occurred across the world in the 1990s, a number of scholars were drawn back to studying the international response to the twentieth century's first genocide in an attempt to uncover historical precedents for dealing with humanitarian atrocities.[26] Most notable was Samantha Power's A Problem From Hell: America and the Age of Genocide, which begins with the slaughter of Armenians in the Ottoman Empire. Power argues that the Wilson administration's indifference to the massacre of the Armenians inaugurated a century of US presidents adopting a "consistent policy of noninervention in the face of genocide."[27]

Power is correct that Wilson followed a policy of noninterference during the war, but the emphasis on American inaction fails to acknowledge the genuine attempts that the president made to address the Armenian problem once the conflict had ended. Furthermore, focusing too narrowly on the genocide itself and not considering America's response in relation to Britain's misses the richness of the debate that America's duty to Armenia provoked. Rather than initiating an American diplomatic tradition of turning a blind eye to genocide, the search for a solution to the Armenian question represented the first time that US politicians were forced to seriously grapple, both domestically and internationally, with the moral dilemmas that come when confronting atrocities on this scale.

The period from the mid-1890s to the early 1920s witnessed the emergence of new norms in US foreign policy and humanitarian politics. As American power expanded, so did the sense that the nation could use this strength to aid oppressed minorities and persecuted peoples such as the Armenians. Events that would have been lamentable but unresolvable earlier in the nineteenth century, occurring in regions beyond American reach, now provoked intense debate over whether the United States should respond and, if so, how. The humanitarianism was certainly selective and the subjects of interest were overwhelmingly religiously based, drawing principally on cultural tropes of "civilization" and "barbarism" to justify a responsibility to rescue Christians from the tyranny of the "unspeakable Turk." Nor were these concerns a constant preoccupation of American politicians or the wider public. The Armenians occupied an exceptional place in America's public conscience, as the special wards of its missionaries, but the issue largely gained purchase on policymakers owing to its linkage with other questions. It became intertwined with the issue of American action over Cuba as interventionists justified their cause by comparing Spain's conduct to the persecution of the Ottoman Armenians, the era's emblematic example of inhumanity. It became intimately connected with Anglo-American relations as politicians and publicists attempted to use shared sympathy for the Armenians to advance the rapprochement between the two countries and encourage greater US engagement in global affairs. And it became entangled in the debates over the League, as Wilson sought to leverage sympathy for Armenia to encourage Americans to assume a leadership role in global affairs. Ultimately this concern did not lead to a political commitment. The official US response to the Armenian plight was primarily limited to relief and rhetoric. Yet in attempting to convince their fellow countrymen of their responsibility to the Armenians, both Roosevelt and Wilson extended the parameters of debate on the purpose of American power and the nature of the national interest. Their search for a solution to the Armenian question encapsulated the nation's internal conflict over its world role at the turn of the twentieth century.

The debate over the Armenian question reveals the norms and values that animated American society during a pivotal period in the nation's history. It also demonstrated dilemmas that would continue to bedevil American policymakers in the decades to come. First, there was the problem of ensuring that presidential rhetoric did not become detached from political realities. This was an issue that particularly concerned Roosevelt and, in response, he invoked the dictum: "Never draw unless you mean to shoot." That maxim directly influenced the later conduct of Secretary Charles Evans Hughes in the aftermath of the Smyrna tragedy and offers an abiding lesson for statecraft, if one often ignored. Yet even while pursuing this cautious approach, Roosevelt remained convinced that if the opportunity arose, then the United States should intervene on behalf of the Armenians. This illustrated a competing dilemma of how far a leader should go to reconcile his personal ideals with the electorate's conception of the nation's interests. During his presidency, Roosevelt publicly promoted the Armenian cause as far as he felt possible but accepted that despite their sympathies, few Americans believed that action for the Armenians was compatible with US interests. His rival Wilson faced this predicament even more acutely in his attempts to secure a mandate, with his opponents pointing to it as evidence that the president's internationalism was utterly divorced from the national interest and designed to benefit other nations at America's expense. The backlash against Wilson's idealism, and the subsequent reluctance to assume broader international commitments, reflected a pattern that would repeat itself after other instances where policy seemed to be guided by excessive utopian thinking. Yet in responding to the Armenian crisis, Wilson was forced to wrestle with a dilemma that every would-be intervener faces in the wake of a humanitarian atrocity: "Either to assume the burden of the administration of the territory, or to constrain the unworthy sovereign to mend his ways."[28] Moreover, having decided that the United States should assume the burden, Wilson faced a related dilemma over the legitimate basis for an intervention, whether it required the mandate of an international organization, as he now proposed, or should be pursued either unilaterally or with a coalition of willing partners, as Roosevelt had insisted. Ultimately, however, all those who worked to resolve the Armenian question for over three decades were confronted with the cruellest dilemma of all—that sometimes, it is simply not possible to achieve a good solution.

Wilson made sure that he never forgot the Armenian tragedy. In November 1917, a delegation of Armenians had visited the White House and presented the president with a portrait of a young Armenian girl in traditional dress. The girl's haunted expression symbolized the destruction of her nation. In her hand, however, she clasped a mountain snowdrop, a flower whose appearance Armenians regarded as a sign that winter was over and spring was on its way. The Armenians' faith that better days were ahead was captured by the painting's inscription: *L'Esperance* (Hope). The portrait was displayed in the White House for the remainder of Wilson's term. After leaving office, the former president brought the painting to his new home in Washington, DC, where it hung over the fireplace in his drawing room, a constant reminder of the tragic question that neither he nor any other American was able to resolve.

ACKNOWLEDGMENTS

I have benefited from a great deal of support and guidance in writing this book, and I am glad to have the opportunity acknowledge it here.

I was first prompted to think about the Armenian question and the issues surrounding it when Brendan Simms asked me to help him organize a colloquium on the "History of Humanitarian Intervention." Ever since, Brendan has served as an advisor, a mentor, and a friend, and I am extremely grateful for all of his support. Dror Yuravlivker and David Milne inspired my interest in the history of US foreign policy. At Cambridge, Andrew Preston helped me to focus that interest and develop my ideas for this book. Andrew has read numerous drafts of the manuscript and his advice, encouragement, and friendship have been invaluable. I also benefited immensely from the generosity of John Thompson, whose careful reading of my work and constructive comments have been vital in helping me to shape my ideas. I am extremely grateful to David Reynolds and Margaret MacMillan for their advice on helping to turn the manuscript into a book. Tony Badger and Gary Gerstle welcomed me into the American history community at Cambridge, which provided such a stimulating and intellectually rich environment for studying the United States. I would particularly like to thank Chris Gee, Sascha Morrell, Elisabeth Leake, James Cameron, Charles Cadby, Aaron Bartels-Swindells, Neil Rogachevsky, Jonathan Bronitsky, John Heavens, and Asa McKercher for their friendship and support.

The opportunity to spend two years at Yale University was formative in the development of this book. I am profoundly grateful to the generosity of Joseph and Alison Fox, and the Smith Richardson Foundation, for making that possible. Yale's International Security Studies was the ideal place to explore international history and its director Paul Kennedy encouraged me to broaden my intellectual horizons. He and Cynthia Farrar were always available to help, welcomed me into their home, and made my time in New Haven so special. I was hugely fortunate to have the chance to learn from, and share ideas with, John Gaddis, Jay

Winter, Adam Tooze, Patrick Cohrs, Julia Adams, and Jennifer Van Vleck. I was very lucky to overlap at Yale with Ryan Irwin, Chris Miller, Sulmaan Khan, Chris Dietrich, Nathan Kurz, and Alexander Evans, who helped me test out my ideas and offered sage advice.

The convenors of the National History Center's International Seminar on Decolonization—Wm. Roger Louis, Dane Kennedy, Philippa Levine, Jason Parker, Pillarisetti Sudhir, and Lori Watt—offered valuable feedback as my project developed and provided me with the opportunity to share my ideas with a remarkable group of scholars. I was extremely fortunate to have two fellowships at the John W. Kluge Center at the Library of Congress in the course of writing this book and would particularly like to thank Mary Lou Reker, Jason Steinhauer, Travis Hensley, and my research assistant Becky Barker for their assistance during my time there. The staff in the Manuscript Reading Room and the Geography and Map Division were always ready to provide advice and assistance. I was also lucky to have Emily Baughan, Jon Chandler, Bronwen Colquhoun, Oliver Cox, and Hazel Wilkinson for company and support.

Through a Raphael Lemkin Fellowship, I had a unique opportunity to spend a month researching at the Armenian Genocide Museum Institute, and I am grateful to its Director Hayk Demayan, Suren Manukyan, and particularly Anna Aleksanyan for making my time in Yerevan so productive. I am also extremely grateful to have received research support from the Arts and Humanities Research Council, the Parry Dutton Fund at Sidney Sussex College, the Society of Historians of American Foreign Relations, the Eccles Centre for American Studies at the British Library, the Prince Consort and Thirlwall Prize and Fund, E. J. W. Gibb Memorial Trust, and the Moody Stuart Scholarship in Turkey Studies.

Fellowships at two wonderful institutions were essential to give me the time and space to complete the manuscript. I am grateful to the Fellows of Peterhouse, Cambridge, and particularly to then Master Adrian Dixon for welcoming me into the fellowship and affording me the freedom to concentrate on research and writing. The final stage of writing was completed in Austin, Texas, at the Clements Center for National Security, thanks to the generosity of the Donald D. Harrington Faculty Fellows Program. The Clements Center is the most marvelous place for any scholar interested in history and statecraft to reside and I am particularly grateful to Director William Inboden for the invitation to spend a year in Austin, his wise and insightful comments on my work, and for helping immerse me in Texas culture. Cathy Evans and Del Watson helped make me an honorary Longhorn. I am also profoundly grateful to Paul Miller, Ian Johnson, Ionut Popescu, Cindy Ewing, Jacqueline Chandler, Ashlyn Webb, Jennifer Johnson, Mark Lawrence, and Jeremi Suri for their advice and assistance.

The final edits were made after I began a lectureship at the War Studies Department, King's College, London, and I am very grateful for the support of my new colleagues, particularly John Bew and Maeve Ryan, and the assistance of two excellent graduate students, Andrew Ehrhardt and Hillary Briffa. I was extremely lucky to have had Susan Ferber as my editor at Oxford; her patience, advice, and faith in the project were crucial. An earlier version of chapter 5 was published in the September 2016 issue of *Diplomatic History*. I am grateful to the editors for permission to republish sections of this research.

The debts that I owe to my family are too numerous and too extensive to measure. My grandparents, Helen and Cyril, and my brother Patrick have been unceasing in their support and have probably heard far more about the Armenian question than they ever expected to. My wife Emily has lived with this book for the entirety of our relationship. Not only has she borne my immersion in this subject with such remarkable grace and love, but she also provided incisive analysis and generous advice in the final editing stage. And she did so while we prepare to welcome a new addition to our family. I can't wait for us to test Theodore Roosevelt's maxim that "Books are all very well . . . but children are better."

I hope that my parents would still say that after putting up with a son who has been so preoccupied with this book! Without their love and guidance, I would simply not have been able to write it. More than anyone, my mum has gone above and beyond in her support and encouragement. This book is for her.

NOTES

Introduction

1. Fritz Stern, cited in David Fromkin, *Europe's Last Summer: Who Started the War in 1914?* (New York: Doubleday, 2004), 6.
2. Theodore Roosevelt to Cleveland H. Dodge, May 11, 1918, in *The Letters of Theodore Roosevelt*, ed. Elting Morrison (Cambridge, MA: Harvard University Press, 1954), Vol. 8, 6328.
3. House of Commons, *Hansard* (5th Series), Vol. LXXV, November 16, 1915, cols. 1770–1776.
4. Donald Bloxham, *The Great Game of Genocide: Imperialism, Nationalism and the Destruction of the Ottoman Armenians* (Oxford: Oxford University Press, 2005), 1. Ronald Grigor Suny, *"They Can Live in the Desert but Nowhere Else": A History of the Armenian Genocide* (Princeton, NJ: Princeton University Press, 2015), x.
5. *Congressional Record*, vol. 28, 54th Cong., 1st Sess., 854.
6. Merle Curti, *American Philanthropy Abroad: A History* (New Brunswick, NJ: Rutgers University Press, 1963), 22–64, 120, 131–133.
7. Adams address, July 4, 1821, Walter LaFeber, ed., *John Quincy Adams and American Continental Empire: Letters, Speeches and Papers* (Chicago: Quadrangle, 1965), 44–45.
8. Address to Congress, January 8, 1918, Arthur S. Link, ed., *The Papers of Woodrow Wilson* (hereafter *Wilson Papers*) (Princeton, NJ: Princeton University Press, 1966–1994), vol. 45, 534–537.
9. See Daniel Gorman, *The Emergence of International Society in the 1920s* (Cambridge: Cambridge University Press, 2012); Patrick Cohrs, *The Unfinished Peace after World War I: America, Britain and the Stabilisation of Europe, 1919–1932* (Cambridge: Cambridge University Press, 2006); William Mulligan, *The Great War for Peace* (New Haven, CT: Yale University Press, 2014).
10. Peter Jackson, *Beyond the Balance of Power: France and the Politics of National Security in the Era of the First World War* (Cambridge: Cambridge University Press, 2013); Georges Henri Soutou, "Diplomacy," in *The Cambridge History of the First World War, Volume 2: The State*, ed. Jay Winter (Cambridge: Cambridge University Press, 2014), 495–541.
11. Adam Tooze, *The Deluge: The Great War and the Remaking of Global Order 1916–1931* (London: Allen Lane, 2014), 3–33.
12. Zara Steiner, *The Lights That Failed: European International History, 1919–1933* (Oxford: Oxford University Press, 2005), 26–34.
13. George W. Egerton, *Great Britain and the Creation of the League of Nations: Strategy, Politics and International Organization, 1914–1919* (London: Scolar Press, 1979), 83–85; see also David Reynolds, "Rethinking Anglo-American Relations," *International Affairs* 65, no. 1 (Winter 1988–1989), 95; Tooze, *The Deluge*, 17–30.
14. This is demonstrated in pioneering histories of global governance by Mark Mazower, *No Enchanted Palace: The End of Empire and the Ideological Origins of the United Nations* (Princeton,

NJ: Princeton University Press, 2009), 39–46 and Susan Pedersen, *The Guardians: The League of Nations and the Crisis of Empire* (New York: Oxford University Press, 2015), 19.

15. William Roger Louis identified this neglected project in "Great Britain and International Trusteeship: The Mandates System," in *The Historiography of the British Empire-Commonwealth: Trends, Interpretations and Resources*, ed. Robin W. Winks (Durham, NC: Duke University Press, 1966), 302 and "The United States and the Colonial Settlement of 1919," in *Ends of British Imperialism: The Scramble for Empire, Suez and Decolonization: Collected Essays*, ed. William Roger Louis (London: I. B. Tauris, 2006), 225–251. Louis's study focuses on the Africa specialist for the US peace delegation George Louis Beer's agitation for an American mandate for the Cameroons. It was in the Near East, not Africa, however, that Wilson would agree to accept a mandate.

16. Major works on American foreign policy at the time of World War I that have no index reference to the Armenian question include: N. Gordon Levin, *Woodrow Wilson and World Politics* (New York: Oxford University Press, 1968); Lloyd Gardner, *Safe for Democracy: The Anglo-American Response to Revolution, 1913–1923* (New York: Oxford University Press, 1984); Thomas Knock, *To End All Wars: Woodrow Wilson and the Quest for a New World Order* (Princeton, NJ: Princeton University Press, 1992); Ross Kennedy, *Woodrow Wilson, World War I and America's Strategy for Peace and Security* (Kent, OH: Kent State University Press, 2009).

17. In the American case, contemporary analysts have contrasted Wilson's political failure to intervene effectively during the 1915 Genocide with public humanitarian activism, including appeals for intervention, on the Armenians' behalf. In particular see Samantha Power, *A Problem from Hell: America and the Age of Genocide* (New York: Basic Books, 2002), 1–17 and Gary J. Bass, *Freedom's Battle: The Origins of Humanitarian Intervention* (New York: Knopf, 2008), 315–341. For Wilson's perspective on Armenia in a wider diplomatic context see John Milton Cooper Jr., "A Friend in Power? Woodrow Wilson and Armenia," and Lloyd Ambrosius, "Wilsonian Diplomacy and Armenia: The Limits of Power and Ideology," in *America and the Armenian Genocide of 1915*, ed. Jay Winter (Cambridge: Cambridge University Press, 2003), 103–113 and 113–146. For America's engagement with the Armenian question from the 1890s onwards see Peter Balakian, *The Burning Tigris: the Armenian Genocide and America's Response* (New York: Harper Collins, 2003); Merrill D. Peterson, *Starving Armenians: America and the Armenian Genocide, 1915–1930 and After* (Charlottesville, VA: University of Virginia Press, 2004); Simon Payaslian, *United States Policy Toward the Armenian Question and the Armenian Genocide* (New York: Palgrave Macmillan, 2005). For how the US response relates to the longer history of American cultural and religious interactions with the Islamic world see Karine Walther, *Sacred Interests: The United States and the Islamic World, 1821–1921* (Chapel Hill: University of North Carolina Press, 2015), part IV. On Britain's wartime policy see Akaby Nassibian, *Britain and the Armenian Question, 1915–1923* (London: Croom Helm, 1984). For insights into the social and cultural context that shaped Britain's response from the 1890s onwards see Jo Laycock, *Imagining Armenia: Orientalism, Ambiguity and Intervention* (Manchester: Manchester University Press, 2009). For an appreciation of how Britain's response fits within the broader context of European geopolitics and imperial competition see Bloxham, *The Great Game of Genocide*. For an appreciation of the intricate relationship between humanitarianism and imperialism in Britain's response see Michelle Tusan, *The British Empire and the Armenian Genocide: Humanitarianism and Imperial Politics from Gladstone to Churchill* (London: I. B. Tauris, 2017). One recent, focused study that considers British and American wartime policies to the Armenian question is Nevzat Uyanik, *Dismantling the Ottoman Empire: Britain, America and the Armenian Question* (Abingdon: Routledge, 2016).

18. There is a growing body of literature on the American response to these atrocities, also known as the Hamidian massacres. For a comprehensive, up-to-date account that connects this response to the broader history of American humanitarianism see Anne Marie Wilson, "In the Name of God, Civilization, and Humanity: The United States and the Armenian Massacres of the 1890s," *Le Mouvement Social* 227 (April–June 2009), 27–44. For other recent accounts see also Balakian, *Burning Tigris*, 3–135; Peterson, *Starving Armenians*, 21–27; Arman Dzhonovich Kirakosian, ed., *The Armenian Massacres 1894–1896: US Media Testimony* (Detroit: Wayne State University Press, 2004); Bass, *Freedom's Battle*, 5–8, 316.

19. Theodore Roosevelt, *American Ideals, and Other Essays, Social and Political* (New York: G. P. Putnam & Sons, 1898), 239.

20. By contrast, American Catholic missionaries did not establish their first organization dedicated to overseas missions, the Maryknoll Society, until 1911 and did not enjoy the same contacts with governmental establishment. See Grabill, *Protestant Diplomacy*, 130.

21. Howard Sachar, *The Emergence of the Middle East: 1914–1924* (London: Allen Lane, 1970), 346.

22. An indication of the the extent to which the Armenian question increased in importance to American policymakers as the administration began to plan for the postwar world is provided by the records of The Inquiry, the study group established to prepare American plans for the peace negotiations. The Inquiry papers contain a considerable amount of material on the Ottoman Empire, far more than would be expected for a polity with which the United States was not even at war.

23. The standard work on national self-determination and decolonization in the Wilson era is Erez Manela's landmark study, *The Wilsonian Moment*. Manela illustrates how Wilson inspired dreams of independence among fledgling nationalist movements in Egypt, India, China, and Korea, and how these hopes quickly turned to disillusionment when he failed to realise his promise of a new world order. However, as Manela illustrates, these groups were a largely unintended audience for Wilson's rhetoric. In contrast, this book will show that the Armenians were an intended audience. Erez Manela, *The Wilsonian Moment: Self-Determination and the International Origins of Anti-Colonial Nationalism* (New York: Oxford University Press, 2007), vi–xiii. Wilson's own conception of self-determination prioritized self-government over ethno-nationalism, as shown by Trygve Throntveit, "The Fable of the Fourteen Points: Woodrow Wilson and National Self-Determination," *Diplomatic History* 35, no. 3 (2011), 445–481. For more on this theme and Wilson's broader internationalist philosophy see Trygve Throntveit, *Power Without Victory: Woodrow Wilson and the American Internationalist Experiment* (Chicago: Chicago University Press, 2017).

24. For more on the history of ancient Armenia see Charles Burney and D. M. Lang, *The Peoples of the Hills* (London: Pheonix, 2001).

25. Richard G. Hovannisian, "The Historical Dimensions of the Armenian Question, 1878–1923," in *The Armenian Genocide in Perspective*, ed. Richard G. Hovannisian (New Brunswick, NJ: Transaction Books, 1986), 19–20.

26. This term was famously coined by the British diplomat Stratford Canning.

27. See M. E. Yapp, *The Making of the Modern Near East, 1792–1923* (London: Longman, 1988), 108–114; Roderic H. Davidson, *Reform in the Ottoman Empire, 1856–1876* (Princeton, NJ: Princeton University Press, 1963); Bernard Lewis, *The Emergence of Modern Turkey* (London: Oxford University Press, 1961), chapters II-IV.

28. Hovannisian, "The Historical Dimensions of the Armenian Question, 1878–1923," 21.

29. A. L. Macfie, *The Eastern Question, 1774–1923* (London: Longman, 1989), 34–46.

30. Bloxham, *Great Game of Genocide*, 36–37.

31. Quoted in Christopher J. Walker, *Armenia: The Survival of a Nation*, 2nd ed. (London: St Martin's Press, 1990), 116.

32. Erik Jan Zurcher, *Turkey: A Modern History*, 3rd. ed (London: I. B. Tauris, 2004), 53.

33. Louise Nalbandian, *The Armenian Revolutionary Movement* (Berkeley: University of California Press, 1963), 104–150; Payaslian, *United States Policy toward the Armenian Question and the Armenian Genocide*, 4.

34. Roy Douglas, "Britain and the Armenian Question," *The Historical Journal* 19, no. 1 (March 1976), 115–121.

35. While the degree to which the sultan was personally complicit in the full wave of massacres remains unclear, they were carried out in the climate of anti-Christian, and especially anti-Armenian, hostility that he had helped instil. Furthermore, with the central state intent on demonstrating the repercussions of rebellion, local officials rarely intervened to punish the perpetrators of the atrocities. For more extensive accounts of the 1894–1896 Armenian massacres and the domestic and international context in which they were carried out see Suny, *"They Can Live in the Desert,"* 91–141; Bloxham, *The Great Game of Genocide*, 51–57; Taner Akçam, *A Shameful Act: The Armenian Genocide and the Question of Turkish Responsibility*

(New York: Metropolitan Books, 2006), 35–46; William Langer, *The Diplomacy of Imperialism, 1890–1902* (New York: Knopf, 1956), 153–161; Vahakn Dadrian, *The History of the Armenian Genocide* (New York: Berghahn Books, 2003), 61–97; and "The 1894 Sassoun Massacre: A Juncture in the Escalation of the Turko-Armenian Conflict," *Armenian Review* 47, no. 1–2 (2001), 5–39.

36. Mechanisms for intervening on humanitarian grounds had been enshrined in international treaties, including the 1648 Peace of Westphalia. See Brendan Simms and David Trim, eds., *Humanitarian Intervention: A History* (Cambridge: Cambridge University Press, 2011), especially Simms, "'A False Principle in the Law of Nations': Burke, State Sovereignty, Liberty and Intervention in the Age of Westphalia," 89–110.

37. For that theoretical debate see Simon Chesterman, *Just War or Just Peace? Humanitarian Intervention* (New York: Oxford University Press, 2003) 22–45. It was in the mid-nineteenth century that a more expansive notion of "humanitarian" and "humanitarianism," referring to "humanity as a whole" and concerned with actions that advanced "human welfare" rather than pragmatic interests, emerged and replaced a purely theological concept, focused on the divinity or humanity of Jesus. See Simms and Trim, *Humanitarian Intervention*, 3.

38. Bass, *Freedom's Battle*, 31–38.

39. Davide Rodogno, *Against Massacre: Humanitarian Interventions in the Ottoman Empire, 1815–1914* (Princeton, NJ: Princeton University Press, 2011), 1–18, 185–212. For insights into the cultural and political tropes that informed these "state based efforts at public good," and which offers a more skeptical view of these "so-called humanitarian interventions" see Keith David Watenpaugh, *Bread from Stones: The Middle East and the Making of Modern Humanitarianism* (Berkeley, CA: University of California Press, 2015) 1–30. For more on the nuanced interconnection between the rhetoric of the civilizing mission and European interventions in the Ottoman Empire, and its role in the emergence of human rights, see Eric Weitz, "From the Vienna to the Paris System: International Politics and the Entangled Histories of Human Rights, Forced Deportations, and Civilizing Missions," *American Historical Review* 113, no. 5 (December 2008), 1313–1343. For an influential account that argues for a bifurcation between the humanitarianism rhetoric that underlay European interventions in the Ottoman Empire and modern human rights see Samuel Moyn, *The Last Utopia: Human Rights in History* (Cambridge, MA: Harvard University Press, 2010), 1–43.

40. See Hans-Lukas Keiser, *Nearest East: American Millenialism and the Mission to the Middle East* (Philadelphia: Temple University Press, 2010); Joseph L. Grabill, *Protestant Diplomacy and the Near East: Missionary Influence on American Policy, 1810–1927* (Minneapolis: University of Minnesota Press: 1971); John A. DeNovo, *American Interests and Policies in the Middle East* (Minneapolis: University of Minnesota Press, 1963), 8–16.

Chapter 1

1. Address July 4, 1821 in Walter LaFeber, ed., *John Quincy Adams and American Continental Empire* (Chicago: Quadrangle Books, 1965), 44–45.

2. Paul Kennedy, *The Rise and Fall of the Great Powers: Economic Change and Military Conflict from 1500 to 2000* (New York: Random House, 1987), 242–243.

3. Ernest May, *Imperial Democracy: The Emergence of America as a Great Power* (Chicago: Imprint Publications, 1991), 7.

4. "The Week," *Nation* (January 17, 1867), 43; A. H. Guernsey, "The Eastern Question," *Galaxy* 23 (1877), 36.

5. See Frank Ninkovich, *Global Dawn: The Cultural Foundation of American Internationalism, 1865–1890* (Cambridge, MA: Harvard University Press, 2009) 200–201.

6. Charles Dudley Warner, "At the Gates of the East," *Atlantic Monthly*, (November 1875), 529; Edwin L. Godkin, "Art. VI—The Eastern Question," *North American Review* CXXIV (Boston: James R. Osgood and Company, 1877).

7. Edwin L. Godkin, "The Effect of the Russian Reverses on Western Politics," *Nation* (September 27, 1877), 91.

8. George F. Herrick, "The Site of Constantinople," in *The Galaxy*, Volume 22, July 1876, Vol. 1, 774.

9. "American Opinion on the War in the East," *Nation*, 618, p. 260. See also "The Defeat of the Turk," *Scribner's* 16 (1878), 143.

10. "Editor's Table," *Appletons'* 15 (June 17, 1876), 796.

11. United States, President (1877–1881: Hayes) *Letters and messages of Rutherford B. Hayes, president of the United States* (Washington, DC: US Government Printing Office] 1881), 15.

12. *Twenty-First Annual Report of the American Board of Commissioners for Foreign Missions* (Boston: Crocker & Brewster, 1831), 48.

13. The British Church Missionary Society, facing a financial crisis, withdrew from Anatolia in 1877 and left the field to the Americans, in an early instance of Anglophone evangelical burden sharing. See Church Missionary Society, *Church Missionary Society Archive: A Listing and Guide* (Marlborough, Wiltshire, UK: Adam Matthew Publications, 1997), 26.

14. Edwin Munsell Bliss, Henry Otis Dwight, and H. Allen Tupper, eds., *The Encyclopedia of Missions* (1904; reprint ed., Detroit: Gale Research Company, 1975), 29–31; J. C. Hurewitz, *Middle East Dilemmas: The Background of United States Policy* (New York: Harper, 1953), 59.

15. Karine Walther, *Sacred Interests: The United States and the Islamic World, 1821–1921* (Chapel Hill: University of North Carolina Press, 2015), 68–99.

16. *Sixty-Ninth Annual Report of the American Board of Commissions for Foreign Missions* (Boston: Riverside Press, 1879), 21

17. George Washburn, "American Influence in Bulgaria," *Amherst Graduates' Quarterly*, Vol. 2, (October 1912- June 1913), 203.

18. See Ussama Makdisi, *Artillery of Heaven: American Missionaries and the Failed Conversion of the Middle East* (Ithaca, NY: Cornell University Press, 2008)

19. Peterson, *Starving Armenians*, 19.

20. Edwin Pears, *Forty Years in Constantinople: the recollections of Sir Edwin Pears, 1873–1915* (New York: D. Appleton and Company, 1916), 151.

21. *Seventy-First Annual Report of the American Board of Commissioners for Foreign Missions* (Boston: Riverside Press, 1881), 33.

22. Robert Mirak, *Torn Between Two Lands: Armenians in America 1890 to World War One* (Cambridge, MA: Harvard University Press, 1983), 36–44.

23. Wilson, 'In the Name of God, Civilization and Humanity,' 3

24. "Another Armenian Holocaust," September 10, 1895, *New York Times*; "No Help for Armenians: European Nations Criticized Because of Their Inactivity. Slaughter of Innocents Goes On," December 30, 1895, *New York Times*; see also Thomas C. Leonard, "When News Is Not Enough: American Media and Armenian Deaths," in *America and the Armenian Genocide of 1915*, ed. Winter, 294.

25. Arman J. Kirakossian, *The Armenian Massacres, 1894–1896: U.S. Media Testimony* (Detroit: Wayne State University Press, 2004), 40.

26. R. M. Ryan, "Why We Catholics Sympathize with Armenia," *Catholic World* 62, 368 (November 1895), 181–185.

27. Kirakossian, *Armenian Massacres*, 41.

28. John J. O'Shea, "Unhappy Armenia," *The Catholic World*, vol. 60 (January 1895), 553–561.

29. "Appeal for Armenians," *San Francisco Call*, November 25, 1895, 1.

30. Quoted in Wilson, "In the Name of God, Civilization, and Humanity," 40.

31. Clara Barton, *The Red Cross in Peace and War* (Washington, DC: American Historical Press, 1898), 277. See also Moser Jones, *The American Red Cross: from Clara Barton to the New Deal* (Baltimore: Johns Hopkins University Press, 2013), 69–79.

32. Quoted in Laura E. Richard and Maud Howe Elliott, *Julia Ward Howe 1819–1910* (Boston: Houghton Mifflin, Co., 1916), 190.

33. *Congressional Record*, 53rd Cong, 2nd Session, Volume 27, Part 1, 12.

34. Wilson, "In the Name of God, Civilization, and Humanity," 38–39.

35. *The Journal of the Senate of the State of Ohio for the Regular Session of the Seventy-Second General Assembly* (Norwalk, OH: The Laning Ptg, Co., State Printers, 1896), 120.

36. *Congressional Record*, 54th Cong., 1st Session, Volume 28, Part 1, 959–961.

37. Leland James Gordon, *American Relations with Turkey, 1830–1920: An Economic Interpretation* (Philadelphia: University of Pennsylvania Press, 1932), 24–26.

38. "Armenia in the House," *New York Times*, January 28, 1896, 1.

39. *Congressional Record*, 54th Cong., 1st Sess., Vol. 28, 1007–1014.

40. Merle Curti, *American Philanthropy Abroad*, 133.

41. "Mr. Chamberlain on Armenia," *New York Times*, January 27, 1896, 1.

42. Both quoted in "Cullom Resoution on Armenia Passes the Senate," *Chicago Tribune*, January 25, 1896, 4.

43. Americans on both sides of the Civil War divide resented Britain's actions; Northerners remembered Britain's recognition of Confederate belligerency and its flirtation with recognizing it as a state, while Southerners felt Britain had been insufficiently supportive of their cause. See Kathleen Burk, *Old World, New World: The Story of Britain and America from the Beginning* (New York: Grove Press, 2009) 276.

44. Grover Cleveland, "Third Annual Message," December 2, 1895, in James D. Richardson, *A Compilation of the Messages and Papers of the Presidents* (New York: Bureau of National Literature and Art, 1899), Vol. 9, 636. For more on the Venezuelan Boundary Dispute and Anglo-American Relations see Kori Schake, *Safe Passage: The Transition from British to American Hegemony* (Cambridge, MA: Harvard University Press, 2017), 146–183.

45. "The President's Startling Message on Venezuela," *Literary Digest* XII, no. 9 (December 28, 1895), 4.

46. "The Death-Warrant of Armenia, December 21, 1895, *The Spectator*, Vol. 75, 885.

47. Lord Salisbury to Philip Currie, December 17, 1895, in *The Reluctant Imperialists: British Foreign Policy 1878–1902. Vol. 2, The Documents*, ed. C. J. Lowe (London: Routledge & Kegan Paul, 1967), 104.

48. "The Death-Warrant of Armenia," *The Spectator*, Vol. 75 (December 21, 1895), 885–886.

49. Quoted in Peter T. Marsh, *Joseph Chamberlain: Entrepreneur in Politics* (New Haven, CT: Yale University Press, 1994), 382.

50. Quoted in Marsh, *Joseph Chamberlain*, 382.

51. 'Mr. Chamberlain on Armenia,' *New York Times*, September 29, 1896, p. 4.

52. "At Colchester," October 20, 1896, *Liberal Magazine* (1896), 483.

53. Quoted in Gordon Martel, *Imperial Diplomacy: Roseberry and the Failure of Foreign Policy* (London: McGill-Queen's University Press, 1986), 142–145.

54. Quoted in J. L. Garvin and Julian Amery, *The Life of Joseph Chamberlain* (4 vols.; London: Macmillan, 1932–1951), Vol. III, 96.

55. Richard Olney to Thomas F. Bayard, July 20, 1895, *Papers Relating to the Foreign Relations of the United States (FRUS)* (Washington, DC: Government Printing Office, 1895) Vol. I, 545–562.

56. Olney to Grover Cleveland, November 20, 1895, Cleveland to Olney, April 3, 1893 to March 21, 1906, *Papers of Richard Olney* (hereafter *Olney Papers*), Library of Congress, Manuscript Division, Washington, DC, Reel 59.

57. Cleveland to Olney, September 24, 1896, *Olney Papers*, Reel 59.

58. Olney to Cleveland, March 5, 1896, *Olney Papers*, Reel 59.

59. George Douglas Campbell, Duke of Argyll, *Our Responsibilities for Turkey, Memories of Forty Years* (London: J. Murray, 1896), see especially 71–79 and 147–163.

60. For a similar reading of Argyll's pamphlet see *The Spectator*, June 27, 1896, 23.

61. Quoted in Garvin, *Life of Joseph Chamberlain*, III, 167.

62. May, *Imperial Democracy*, 53–54.

63. "Mr Chamberlain on Armenia," *New York Times*, January 27, 1896, 1.

64. M. M. Mangasarian, "Armenia's Impending Doom: Our Duty," *The Forum* 21 (June 1896), 449–459; W. K. Stride, "The Immediate Future of Armenia: A Suggestion," *The Forum* 22(November 1896), 308–320.

65. James Eldin Reed, "American Foreign Policy, the Politics of Missions and Josiah Strong, 1890–1900," *Church History* 41, no. 2 (June 1972), 230–245.

66. E. L. Godkin, "The Armenian Resolutions," *The Nation* 62 (January 30, 1896), 93.

67. "University Calendar," October 23, "Union Debate" October 24, "University Calendar," October 31, "English 6", November 2 and "University Calendar," November 3, all 1896, *Harvard Crimson*.

68. "Mr Chamberlain on Armenia," *New York Times*, January 27, 1896, 1.

69. Contributions for the Armenians did not reach the levels raised for the Russian famine of 1891, the largest relief donations of the era, partly due to the residual effects of a large-scale economic panic that gripped the US in 1893. See Wilson, "In the Name of God, Civilization and Humanity," 38.

70. "Americans and Armenians," *The Spectator* 76 (February 1, 1896), 156–157.

71. *Papers Relating to the Foreign Relations of the United States, with the Annual Message of the President, transmitted to Congress December 7 1896*, Part I–II (Washington, DC, 1897), xxviii.

72. Stephen B. L. Penrose Jr., *That They May Have Life: The Story of the American University of Beirut, 1866–1941* (New York: The Trustees of the American University of Beirut, 1941), 87, note 4.

73. "Our Rights and Duties in Turkey," *New York Times*, October 9, 1896, 1.

74. Oscar Straus, *Under Four Administrations: From Cleveland to Taft* (New York: Houghton Mifflin Company), 128–129; Oscar Straus Diary, August 11 and 26, 1898, 24–25, 32–34, *Oscar S. Straus Papers* (hereafter *Straus MSS*), Library of Congress, Manuscript Division, Box 22.

75. Henry Ward Beecher to Grover Cleveland, July 12, 1887, *Straus MSS*, Box 17 Letterbook 1873–1889.

76. Straus to unnamed American missionary, December 21, 1888, and Straus to Thomas F. Bayard, December 22, 1888, *Straus MSS*, Box 17.

77. Straus to Charles H. Stout, November 18, 1895, *Straus MSS*, Box 2.

78. Straus to Alexandre A. Gargiulo, October 18, 1895, to Henry Otis Dwight, November 14, 1895, *Straus MSS*, Box 2.

79. Naomi W. Cohen, *A Dual Heritage: The Public Career of Oscar S. Straus* (Philadelphia: The Jewish Publication Society of America, 1969), 74.

80. Straus to Henry Otis Dwight, November 14, 1895, *Straus MSS*, Box 2.

81. Straus to Grand Vizier (prime minister of the sultan) Said Pacha, June 11, 1895, *Straus MSS*, Box 2.

82. Straus to Henry Otis Dwight, March 19, 1895, *Straus MSS*, Box 2.

83. Straus to Wheeler, August 5, 1895, Straus to Charles H. Stout, November 18, 1895, Straus to Edward G. Porter, November 22, 1895, Straus to Charles Elliott, December 10, 1895 all *Straus MSS*, Box 2.

84. Straus to Grover Cleveland, November 18, 1895, *Straus MSS*, Box 2.

85. Curti, *American Philanthropy Abroad*, 133.

86. Straus to Cleveland, December 17, 1895, to Dwight, December 24, 1895, *Straus MSS*, Box 2.

87. Straus to Thomas F. Bayard, March 3, 1896, *Straus MSS*, Box 2.

88. Wilkinson Call, "The Right of Cubans to Recognition as Belligerents and to Independence, in Nathan C. Green, *The War with Spain and Story of Spain and Cuba* (Baltimore: International News and Book Co., 1898), 381.

89. *Congressional Record*, 55th Congress, 2nd Session, vol. 31, p 4, 3887.

90. *New York Journal*, December 7, 1896 and *San Francisco Examiner*, September 20, 1895, both quoted in David Nasaw, *The Chief: The Life of William Randolph Hearst* (Boston: Houghton Mifflin, 2001), 125–126.

91. *New York Times*, March 28, 1898, quoted in Louis A. Perez, *Cuba Between Empires, 1878–1902* (Pittsburgh: University of Pittsburgh Press, 1983) 62.

92. *Minneapolis Journal*, March 21, 1898, quoted in Perez, *Cuba Between Empires*, 65.

93. "Cuban Mass-Meeting in Washington," *Chicago Tribune*, May 17, 1897, 2.

94. *San Francisco Examiner*, September 20, 1895, quoted in Ian Mugridge, *The View from Xanudu* (Montreal: McGill-Queen's University Press, 1995), 8–9.

95. John L. Offner, *An Unwanted War: The Diplomacy of the United States and Spain over Cuba, 1895–1898* (Chapel Hill: University of North Carolina Press, 1992), 145–146.

96. Richardson, *Messages and Papers of the Presidents*, Vol. 10, 157–150.

97. Talcott Williams, "Cuba and Armenia," *The Century Magazine*, n.s. XXXV (February 1899), 634–635.

98. Straus to McKinley, May 12, 1898, *Straus MSS*, Box 2.

99. David F. Trask, *The War with Spain in 1898* (New York: Macmillan, 1981), 441–442.

100. Diary, 1898–1900, 22–25, 31–34, *Straus MSS*, Box 22; Straus, *Under Four Administrations*, 125–129.

101. Pauncefote to Salisbury, April 14, 1898, quoted in Campbell, *Great Britain and the United States, 1895–1903*, 142.

102. May, *Imperial Democracy*, 181–219.

103. For an overview of British policy during the war see Burk, *Old World, New World*, 413–415.

104. Sylvia L. Hilton and Steve J. S. Ickringill, *European Perceptions of the Spanish-American War of 1898* (Bern: Lang, 1999).

105. "Sidney Low Says We Are Patient," June 2, 1898, *Christian Work: Illustrated Family Newspaper*, Vol. 64, 884.

106. "The Magazines," May 7, 1898, *The Spectator*, Vol. 80, 663.

107. "A Forecast of the War," April 23, 1898, *The Spectator*, Vol. 80, 565.

108. For more on "civilization" and US foreign policy in this period see Ninkovich, *Global Dawn*, 7–47. For more on the rhetoric of "civilization" and Anglo-American relations see Paul Kramer, "Empires, Exceptions and Anglo-Saxons: Race and Rule between the British and United States Empires, 1880–1910," *Journal of American History*, 88, no. 4 (March 2002), 1315–1353; Bernard Porter, *Empire and Superempire: Britain, America and the World* (New Haven, CT: Yale University Press, 2006), 24, 52–56.

109. William Mulligan, "Introduction: The Global Reach of Abolitionism in the Nineteenth Century," in *A Global History of Anti-Slavery Politics in the Nineteenth Century*, ed. William Mulligan and Maurice Bric (New York: Palgrave Macmillan, 2013), 1–17.

110. For more on the role of Anglo-Saxonism see Stuart Anderson, *Race and Rapprochement: Anglo-Saxonism and Anglo-American Relations, 1895–1904* (London: Associated University Press, 1981); Kramer, "Empires, Exceptions and Anglo-Saxons," 1315–1353.

111. See Frank Luther Mott, "The Magazine Revolution and Popular Ideas in the Nineties," *Proceedings of the American Antiquarian Society*, 64 (April 1954), 195–214 and *A History of American Magazines, vol. IV: 1885–1905* (Cambridge, MA: Harvard University Press, 1957), 131–134, 225–230; Geoffrey Seed, "British Reactions to American Imperialism Reflected in Journals of Opinion, 1898–1900," *Political Science Quarterly* 73, no. 2 (June 1958), 254–272.

112. Iestyn Adams, *Brothers Across the Ocean: British Foreign Policy and the Origins of the Anglo-American 'Special Relationship' 1900–1905* (London: I. B. Tauris, 2005). For additional background see A. E. Campbell, *Great Britain and the United States, 1898–1905* (London: Longman, 1960).

113. Aaron L. Friedberg, *The Weary Titan: Britain and the Experience of Relative Decline, 1895–1905* (Princeton, NJ: Princeton University Press: 1988), 184–189, 208, 299. See also Max Beloff, *Imperial Sunset: Britain's Liberal Empire 1897–1921* (London: Methuen: 1969), 70–108.

114. Burk, *Old World, New World:*, 400–435; see also Bradford Perkins, *The Great Rapprochement: England and the United States, 1895–1914* London: Victor Gollancz Ltd., 1969).

115. Srdjan Vucetic, *The Anglosphere: A Genealogy of a Racialized Identity in International Relations* (Stanford, CA: Stanford University Press, 2011), 22–54. Anglo-Saxonism was also invoked to thwart imperialism. For examples see Eric Tyrone Love, *Race Over Empire: Racism and U.S. Imperialism, 1865–1900* (Chapel Hill: University of North Carolina Press, 2004), 106 and Robert E. Hannigan, *The New World Power: American Foreign Policy, 1898–1917* (Philadelphia: University of Pennsylvania Press, 2002), 276–277.

116. *Nineteenth Century*, XLIV (1898), 501.

117. Quoted in *Edinburgh Review*, CLXXXIX (1899), 258.

118. Geoffrey Seed, "British Reactions to American Imperialism Reflected in Journals of Opinion, 1898–1900," *Political Science Quarterly* 73, no. 2 (June 1958), 254–272.

119. *Nineteen Century*, XLIV (1898), 501.

120. "Topics of the Day: America After the War," *The Spectator*, August 20, 1898), 4.

121. *Fortnightly Review*, LXVIII [New Series] (1900), 789.

122. "The Anglo-Saxon Alliance," *The Spectator*, May 21, 1898, 6.

123. For examples see Anna Maria Martellone, "In the Name of Anglo-Saxondom, For Empire and for Democracy: The Anglo-American Discourse, 1880–1920," in *Reflections on American Exceptionalism*, ed. D. K. Adams and Cornelis A. Van Minnen (Keele: Ryburn, 1994), 83–97; Julian Go, "Global Perspectives on the U.S. Colonial State in the Philippines," in *The American Colonial State in the Global Philippines*, ed. Julian Go and Anne L. Foster (Durham, NC: Duke University Press, 2003), 1–42.

124. First quotation from Albert Beveridge, *For the Greater Republic Not for Imperialism, An Address at Union League of Philadelphia, February 15, 1899* ([Philadelphia], 1899), 5; second quotation from Beveridge speech of September 17, 1898 titled "The March of the Flag," in his *The Meaning of the Times and Other Speeches* (Indianapolis: The Bobbs-Merrill Company, 1908), 47.

125. Kramer, "Empires, Exceptions and Anglo-Saxons," 1338–1341.

126. For commercial rivalry and Anglophobia see Edward P. Crapol, *America for Americans: Economic Nationalism and Anglophobia in the Late Nineteenth Century* (Westport, CT: Greenwood Press, 1973) and Marc William Palen, *The 'Conspiracy' of Free Trade: The Anglo-American Struggle Over Empire and Economic Globalisation, 1894–6* (New York: Cambridge University Press, 2016). For crucial role of Ireland see Alan J. Ward, *Ireland and Anglo-American Relations 1899–1921* (London: Weidenfeld and Nicolson, 1969).

127. Carl Schurz, "The Anglo-American Friendship," *Atlantic Monthly*, 82 (October 1898), 437–438.

128. Richard Olney, "The International Isolation of the United States?" *The Atlantic Monthly*, LXXXI (May 1898), 577–588.

129. Perkins, *The Great Rapprochement*, 55–58; Tyler Dennett, *John Hay: From Poetry to Politics* (New York: Dodd, Mead and Company, 1934), 18; John Taliaferro, *All the Great Prizes: The Life of John Hay, from Lincoln to Roosevelt* (New York: Simon & Schuster, 2013), 294–334.

130. John Hay to Henry White, September 24, 1899, quoted in William Roscoe Thayer, *John Hay, Vol. II* (Boston and New York: Houghton, Mifflin, 1915), 159.

131. Quoted in Garvin and Amery, *The Life of Joseph Chamberlain*, Vol. III, 301–302.

132. Joseph Chamberlain, "Recent Developments of Policy in the United States and Their Relation to an Anglo-American Alliance," *Scribner's* 24 (December 1898), 674–682.

133. Quotes in Winston S. Churchill to Lady Randolph Churchill, May 22, June 1898 in Randolph S. Churchill, *Youth: Winston S. Churchill, 1874–1900* (London: Minerva, 1967), Companion Volume 1, Part 2, 937, 947.

134. W. T. Stead, *The Maiden Tribute of Modern Babylon: The Report of the Secret Commission* (London: Pall Mall Gazette, 1885).

135. W. T. Stead, *If Christ Came to Chicago: A Plea for the Union of All Who Love in the Service of All Who Suffer* (London: The Review of Reviews Office, 1894); J. O. Baylen, "A Victorian's 'Crusade' in Chicago, 1893–94," *Journal of American History* 51, no. 3 (1964), 418–434.

136. "To All English-Speaking Folk," *The Review of Reviews* (Vol. I, January 1890), 15–20.

137. For Stead's thinking on imperial federation see Simon Potter, "W. T. Stead, Imperial Federation and the South African War," in *W. T. Stead: Newspaper Revolutionary*, ed. Laurel Blake, Ed King, Roger Luckhurst, and James Mussell (London: The British Library, 2012), 115–132. For the larger intellectual debate on imperial federation see Duncan Bell, *The Idea of Greater Britain: Empire and the Future of World Order, 1860–1900* (Princeton, NJ: Princeton University Press, 2007), particularly 92–120.

138. W. T. Stead to Albert Shaw, November 24, 1897, *The Papers of W. T. Stead*, Churchill Archives, University of Cambridge, Box 1 Correspondence, Folder 64 Correspondence S, Part 2.

139. Robert P. Frankel, *Observing America: The Commentary of British Visitors to the United States, 1890–1950* (Madison: University of Wisconsin Press, 2007), 69–71.

140. Andrew Carnegie, *The Gospel of Wealth and Other Timely Essays* (New York: Century, 1900), 14–49. See also David Nasaw, *Andrew Carnegie* (New York: Penguin Press, 2006), 346.

141. Andrew Carnegie to Stead, July 22, 1893, *Stead Papers*, Box 1, Folder 16 Correspondence C Part 4.

142. Carnegie to Stead, May 30, 1903, *Stead Papers*, Box 1 Folder 16.

143. "To All English-Speaking Folk," *The Review of Reviews* (Vol. I, January 1890), 15–20.

144. Carnegie to Stead, August 11, 1893, *Stead Papers*, Box 1 Folder 16.

145. W. T. Stead, *The United States of Europe on the Eve of the Parliament of Peace* (London: Review of Reviews Office, 1899), quotes on 66.

146. Stephanie Provost, "W. T. Stead and the Eastern Question (1875–1911)," *19: Interdisciplinary Studies in the Long Nineteenth Century* No. 16 (2013), 1–27, DOI: http://doi.org/10.16995/ntn.654

147. Many in the English-speaking world received this impression from the anonymously published sensual best-selling book, *The Lustful Turk; or, Lascivious Scenes from a Harem* (1828).

148. Richard T. Shannon described Stead as a "fugleman of atrocity-mongers" in his *Gladstone and the Bulgarian Agitation 1876* (London: Nelson, 1963), 28. See also Rebecca Gill, *Calculating Compassion: Humanity and Relief in War, Britain 1870–1918* (Manchester: Manchester University Press, 2013), 66, 78.

149. "The North Country and Turkish Atrocities," August 23, 1876, *Northern Echo*.

150. W. T. Stead, *The Haunting Horrors of Armenia, Political Papers for the People* (London: "Review of Reviews" Office, 1896).

151. Provost, "W. T. Stead and the Eastern Question (1875–1911)," 4.

152. Quoted in John Robertson-Scott, *The Life and Death of a Newspaper* (London: Methuen, 1952).

153. Provost, "W. T. Stead and the Eastern Question (1875–1911)," 15–20.

154. Stead, *The United States of Europe*, 178. For original reference see Richard Cobden, *Political Writings* (London: William Ridgway, 1867), Vol. 1, 23.

155. "The Swoop of the Eagle" *Review of Reviews* (April 1895), Vol. 11, 339.

156. "America and Armenia," *Review of Reviews* (January 1895), Vol. 11, 51.

157. "Will the Americans Intervene in Cuba," *Review of Reviews* (June 1897), Vol. 15, 566.

158. "The Progress of the World," *Review of Reviews* (November 1898), Vol. 18, 431–443.

159. Stead, *United States of Europe*, 176–178.

160. Stead, *United States of Europe*, 178–185.

161. Straus to Angell, January 31, 1899, *Straus MSS*, Box 3.

162. Straus, *Under Four Administrations*, 155.

163. Straus to Hay, September 23, 1899, *Straus MSS*, Box 3.

164. Straus to Bayard Dodge, May 1, 1900, Straus to Gargiulo. May 25, 1900, June 4, 1900 *Straus MSS*, Box 3.

165. Straus to Griscom, June 4, 1900. *Straus MSS*, Box 3.

166. Straus to Nicholas Roderick O'Conor, June 13, 1900, *Straus MSS*, Box 3.

167. April 11–16, 1900 entry with attached clippings from New York *Tribune* and New York *Herald* (both April 19), Straus Diary, *Straus MSS*, Box 22.

168. Straus to Griscom, September 27, 1900, *Straus MSS*, Box 3.

169. "Conclusion," Straus Diary, *Straus MSS*, Box 3.

170. Quoted in George Washburn, *Fifty Years in Constantinople* (Boston: Houghton, Mifflin, 1909), 246–249.

171. "The Progress of the World," *American Review of Reviews* (January 1901), Vol. 23, 9–10.

172. W. T. Stead, *The Americanization of the World, the Trend of the Twentieth Century* (New York, 1902), 1–8, 183–199.

Chapter 2

1. The most in-depth study of Roosevelt's relationship with Britain is William Tilchin, *Theodore Roosevelt and the British Empire: A Study in Presidential Statecraft* (New York: St. Martin's Press, 1997).

2. Tilchin, *Theodore Roosevelt and the British Empire*.

3. William Widenor, *Henry Cabot Lodge and the Search for an American Foreign Policy* (Berkeley: University of California Press, 1980), 121–171.

4. The image of Roosevelt as a president determined to harness the tools of power, and manipulate the global balance, in order to serve the US national interest was cemented by Howard K. Beale, *Theodore Roosevelt and the American Rise to World Power* (Baltimore: Johns Hopkins University Press, 1956), 47, 449, 224. See also G. Wallace Chessman, *Theodore Roosevelt and the Politics of Power* (Boston, Little, Brown, 1969); Raymond A. Esthus, *Theodore Roosevelt and the International Rivalries* (Waltham, MA: Ginn-Blaisdell, 1970), 39, 65, 134; Henry

Kissinger, *Diplomacy* (New York: Simon & Schuster, 1994), 29–55; H. W. Brands, "Theodore Roosevelt: America's First Strategic Thinker," in *Artists of Power: Theodore Roosevelt, Woodrow Wilson and their Enduring Impact on US Foreign Policy*, ed. William N. Tilchin and Charles E. Neu (Westport, CT: Praeger, 2006), 33–44; Fareed Zakaria, "Roosevelt Is the Father of American Internationalism," in *Presidents and their Decisions: Theodore Roosevelt*, ed. Tom Lansford and Robert P. Watson (Detroit: Greenhaven Press, 2002), 112–118.

5. John Morton Blum, *The Republican Roosevelt* (Cambridge, MA: Harvard University Press, 1954), 6, 133–35, 141.

6. The three-time Democratic presidential candidate William Jennings Bryan labeled Roosevelt "a man who loves war," while the author and anti-imperialist Mark Twain judged Roosevelt to be "clearly insane . . . and insanest upon war and its supreme glories." Both quoted in Kathleen M. Dalton, *Theodore Roosevelt: A Strenuous Life* (New York: Knopf, 2002), 9.

7. See William H. Harbaugh, *Power and Responsibility: The Life and Times of Theodore Roosevelt* (New York: Farrar, Straus and Cudahy, 1961); Widenor, *Henry Cabot Lodge and the Search for an American Foreign Policy*, 132, 162. John Milton Cooper Jr., *The Warrior and the Priest: Theodore Roosevelt and Woodrow Wilson* (Cambridge, MA: Harvard University Press, 1983), xii–xiii.

8. Frederick W. Marks III, *Velvet on Iron: The Diplomacy of Theodore Roosevelt* (Lincoln: University of Nebraska Press, 1979). See also Serge Ricard, "Theodore Roosevelt and the Diplomacy of Righteousness," *Theodore Roosevelt Association Journal* 12 (Winter 1986), 3–4; Joshua David Hawley, *Theodore Roosevelt: Preacher of Righteousness* (New Haven, CT: Yale University Press, 2008).

9. Frank Ninkovich, "Theodore Roosevelt: Civilization As Ideology," *Diplomatic History* 10 (Summer 1986), 223. For other scholars who relate Roosevelt's conception of civilization to his strategic position see Anders Stephanson, *Manifest Destiny: American Expansionism and the Empire of Right* (New York: Hill and Wang, 1996), 106–111; Greg Russell, "Theodore Roosevelt, Geopolitics, and Cosmopolitan Ideals," *Review of International Studies* 32, no. (2006), 541–559; James R. Holmes, *Theodore Roosevelt and World Order* (Washington, DC: Potomac Books, Inc., 2007), 2, 4, 84. For Roosevelt's Lamarckian thought see Thomas Dyer, *Theodore Roosevelt and the Idea of Race* (Baton Rouge: Louisiana State University Press, 1980).

10. Roosevelt to Osborne Howes, May 5, 1892 in *Roosevelt Letters*, I, ed. Morison, 279.

11. Quoted in John Morton Blum, "Theodore Roosevelt: Years of Decision," in *Roosevelt Letters*, II, ed. Morison, 1489.

12. Roosevelt to James Brander Matthews, December 6, 1895, in *Roosevelt Letters*, I, ed. Morison, 499.

13. Theodore Roosevelt, *American Ideals and Other Essays, Social and Political* (New York: AMS Press, 1969), 252.

14. Theodore Roosevelt, *The Naval War of 1812; or, The History of the United States Navy during the Last War with Great Britain* (New York: G. P. Putnam's sons, 1882).

15. The most in depth analysis of Roosevelt's relationship with Mahan is Richard W. Turk, *The Ambiguous Relationship: Theodore Roosevelt and Alfred Thayer Mahan* (Westport, CT: Greenwood Press, 1987).

16. Roosevelt to James S. Clarckson, April 22, 1893 in Morison, *Roosevelt Letters*, I, 400.

17. Roosevelt to Lodge, December 20, 1895 and Roosevelt to William Sheffield Cowles, December 22, 1895, in Morison, *Roosevelt Letters*, I, 500–501.

18. Roosevelt to Harvard Crimson, January 2, 1896, in Morison, *Roosevelt Letters*, I, 506.

19. In particular see Brooks Adams, *The Law of Civilization and Decay: an Essay on History* (New York: Macmillan, 1895) and Henry Adams, *The Education of Henry Adams: An Autobiography* (Boston: Houghton Mifflin, 1918).

20. John Morton Blum, "Roosevelt Years of Decision," in Morison, *Roosevelt Letters*, II, 1486.

21. Roosevelt to Lodge, 27th December 1895 in Morison, *Roosevelt Letters*, I, 503–504.

22. Roosevelt to Brooks Adams, March 21, 1898, in Morison, *Roosevelt Letters*, I, 797.

23. Roosevelt to John D. Long, September 30, 1897, in Morison, *Roosevelt Letters*, I, 695.

24. Roosevelt to William Astor Chanler, December 23, 1897, in Morison, *Roosevelt Letters*, I, 746–747.

25. William Widenor makes a similar point in relation to Roosevelt's close friend and collabora-
tor, Henry Cabot Lodge. Widenor, *Henry Cabot Lodge and the Search for an American Foreign
Policy*, 54–55.

26. Roosevelt to Root, April 5, 1898, Elihu Root Papers, Library of Congress Manuscript
Division, Box 162.

27. Quoted in Edmund Morris, *The Rise of Theodore Roosevelt* (New York: Random House,
2001), 638.

28. Roosevelt to William Sheffield Cowles, March 30, 1898 in Morison, *Roosevelt Letters*, II, 804.

29. Roosevelt to James Bryce, March 31, 1898, in Morison, *Roosevelt Letters*, II, 807.

30. Roosevelt, *American Ideals*, 257. The article was first published in *The Bachelor of Arts*,
March 1896.

31. Roosevelt to Long, April 26, 1897, in Morison, *Roosevelt Letters*, I, 602, 604.

32. Roosevelt to William Wingate Sewell, May 4, 1898, in Morison, *Roosevelt Letters*, 823.

33. My thinking on this subject has been influenced by Widenor, *Henry Cabot Lodge and the
Search for an American Foreign Policy*, 66–121.

34. Beale, *Roosevelt and the Rise of America*, 62; Dalton, *Theodore Roosevelt*, 177.

35. David H. Burton, *Theodore Roosevelt: Confident Imperialist* (Philadelphia: University of
Pennsylvania Press, 1968), 34.

36. Richard W. Leopold, "The Emergence of America as a World Power: Some Second Thoughts,"
in John Braeman, Robert Bremner and Everett Walters, *Change and Continuity din Twentieth-
Century America* (Columbus: Ohio State University Press, 1965), 13.

37. Roosevelt to Charles John Bonaparte, March 20, 1901, Morison, *Roosevelt Letters*, III, 36–
37; Roosevelt to Edward Oliver Wolcott—Printed in the Official Proceedings of the Twelfth
Republican National Convention, Philadelphia, June 19–21, 1900 (Philadelphia, 1900),
180–188.

38. Theodore Roosevelt, *Works of Theodore Roosevelt*, ed. Hermann Hagedorn (New York: Charles
Scribner's Sons, 1924), Vol. 9, 321.

39. Roosevelt to Lodge, January 12, 1899, in Morison, *Roosevelt Letters*, 909.

40. Roosevelt to Frederic Rene Coudert, July 3, 1901, in Morison, *Roosevelt Letters*, III, 105.

41. Roosevelt to Ramon Reyes Lala, June 27, 1900, June 27, 1900 in Morison, *Roosevelt Letters*,
II, 1343.

42. Roosevelt to Charles William Eliot, November 14, 1900, in Morison, *Roosevelt Letters*,
II, 1415.

43. For more on this debate see Robert Endicott Osgood, *Ideals and Self-Interests in America's
Foreign Relations: The Great Transformation of the Twentieth Century* (Chicago: University of
Chicago Press: 1953), 19, 47, 87.

44. Originally quoted in Alfred Thayer Mahan, *Some Neglected aspects of war. Together with The
power that makes for peace by Henry S. Pritchett and The capture of private property at sea, by
Julian S. Corbett* (London: Sampson Low, Marston & Company, 1908), 51.

45. Theodore Roosevelt, *The Strenuous Life: Essays and Addresses* (London: Grant Richards,
1902), 11–19. "Expansion and Peace" originally published in *Independent*, December
21, 1899.

46. Moorfield Storey, *The Moro Massacre: Letter* (Boston: Anti-Imperialist League, 1906).

47. Roosevelt to William Bayard Cutting, April 18, 1899, in Morison, *Roosevelt Letters*, II,
990–991.

48. Roosevelt to Arthur Hamilton Lee, July 25, 1900, in Morison, *Roosevelt Letters*, II, 1362. For
another example of this shift in sentiment see Roosevelt to Frederick Courteney Selous,
February 7, 1900, in Morison, *Roosevelt Letters*, II, 1233.

49. Roosevelt to Lee, January 30, 1900, in Morison, *Roosevelt Letters*, II, 1151–1152.

50. Roosevelt to A. J. Sage, March 9, 1900 and Roosevelt to John St. Loe Strachey, November 19,
1900, in Morison, *Roosevelt Letters*, II, 1214, 1424–1426.

51. Roosevelt to Selous, February 7, 1900, in Morison, *Roosevelt Letters*, II, 1233.

52. For Anglo-American relations over the Boer War see Stuart E. Knee, "Anglo-American
Understanding and the Boer War," *American Journal of Politics and History*, 30, 2 (1984),
196–208 and Michael Cullinane, *Liberty and American Anti-Imperialism, 1898–1909*
(Basingstoke: Palgrave Macmillan, 2012) 75–93.

53. Roosevelt to Spring Rice, August 11, 1899, in Morison, *Roosevelt Letters*, II, 1049.
54. Roosevelt to Strachey, January 27, 1900, in Morison, *Roosevelt Letters*, II, 1143.
55. Stone was seized along with Katerina Tsilka, the heavily pregnant Bulgarian born wife of another missionary. See Michael Oren, *Power, Faith and Fantasy: America in the Middle East 1776 to the Present* (New York: Norton, 2008), 311.
56. Leishman to Hay, September 5, 1901, Leishman to Hay, September 24, 1901, Eddy to Hay, October 2, 1901, US Department of State, *FRUS 1902* (US Government Printing Office, 1902), 997, 1000, 1004.
57. Alfred L. P. Dennis, *Adventures in American Diplomacy, 1896–1906* (New York: E. P. Dutton & Company, 1928), 453. For greater background on the hostage crisis see Tessa Carpenter, *The Miss Stone Affair: America's First Modern Hostage Crisis* (New York: Simon & Schuster, 2003) and Russell D. Buhite, *Lives at Risk: Hostages and Victims in American Foreign Policy* (Wilmington, DE: Scholarly Resources Inc., 1995), 57–72.
58. Roosevelt to Frederic Rene Coudert, July 3, 1901, in Morison, *Roosevelt Letters*, III, 105.
59. Roosevelt to Alvey Adee, October 2, 1901, in Morison, *Roosevelt Letters*, III, 156.
60. Adeee to Eddy, October 11, 1901, *FRUS, 1901* (US Government Printing Office, 1901), 1010.
61. Carpenter, *The Miss Stone Affair*, 94–96, 140–142.
62. Eddy to Hay, October 7, 1901, December 13, 1901, *FRUS 1901*, 1009, 1013; Dennis, *Adventures in American Diplomacy*, 454.
63. Ellen Stone, "Six Months among Brigands," *McClure's Magazine* 19, no. 5 (September 1902): 464–471; Buhite, *Lives at Risk*, 69.
64. By the end of the nineteenth century, Jews comprised 90 percent of Romanian immigrants. See Andrew Preston, *Sword of the Spirit, Shield of Faith: Religion in American War and Diplomacy* (New York: Random House, 2012), 203.
65. NA 1198/7/871.4016/51, minute by Adee, December 17, 1913, *US National Archives*, College Park, MD; Tyler Dennett, *John Hay: From Poetry to Politics* (New York: Dodd, Mead and Company, 1934), 395–397; Kenneth J. Clymer, "Anti-Semitism in the Late Nineteenth Century: The Case of John Hay," *American Jewish Historical Quarterly* LX, no. 4 (June 1971), 349–350; Robert L. Beisner, *From the Old Diplomacy to the New, 1865–1900*, 2nd ed. (Arlington Heights, IL: Wiley Blackwell, 1986), 74.
66. Naomi W. Cohen, *Jacob Schiff, A Study in American Jewish Leadership* (Hannover, NH: Brandeis University Press, 1999), 106–107.
67. Straus to Frederick David Mocatta, June 6, 1902, *Straus Papers*, General Correspondence Box 3.
68. Straus to Roosevelt, May 15, 1902, *Straus Papers*, General Correspondence Box 3.
69. Hay to McCormick, August 11, 1902, *FRUS, 1902*, 43–45.
70. Mocatta to Straus, March 31, 1902, *Straus Papers*, Scrapbook—Rumania and Russia, 1902–1903, A–J, Box 27.
71. September 23, 1902, *Daily Telegraph*; September 27, 1902, *The Spectator*.
72. September 24, 1902, *Los Angeles Herald*; Howard Sachar, *The Course of Modern Jewish History* (New York: Vintage Books, 1990), 250. The most detailed discussion of the international protection of Rumanian Jews is Satu Matikainen, "Great Britain, British Jews, and the International Protection of Romanian Jews, 1900–1914: A Study of Jewish Diplomacy and Minority Rights" (Jyvaskyla Studies in Humanities: University of Jyvasklya, 2006), 100–124.
73. Straus to Roosevelt, October 1, 1902, *Straus Papers*, General Correspondence Box 3.
74. Cathal J. Nolan, "The United States and Tsarist Anti-Semitism, 1865–1914," *Diplomacy and Statecraft* 3 (November 1992), 438–467; Stuart E. Knee, "The Diplomacy of Neutrality: Theodore Roosevelt and the Russian Pogroms of 1903–1906," *Presidential Studies Quarterly* 19 (Winter 1989), 71–78; Simon Kuznets, "Immigration of Russian Jews to the United States: Background and Structure," *Perspectives in American History* 9 (1975): 35–124.
75. Roosevelt to Spring Rice, August 5, 1896, in Morison, *Roosevelt Letters*, I, 555.
76. Roosevelt to Spring Rice, August 11, 1899, in Morison, *Roosevelt Letters*, II, 1049.
77. Theodore Roosevelt to G. F. Becker, July 8, 1901, *Roosevelt Papers*; see Brooks Adams, *America's Economic Supremacy* (New York: Macmillan, 1900) and Alfred Thayer Mahan, *The Problem of Asia and Its Effect Upon International Policies* (Boston: Little, Brown & Co., 1900).
78. Hay to Roosevelt, April 25, 1903, *John Hay Papers*, Library of Congress, Box 12 Roosevelt to Hay, May 22, 1903, Morison, *Roosevelt Letters*, III, 478.

79. See Gary Dean Best, *To Free a People* (Westport, CT: Greenwood Press, 1982), 65.

80. Quoted in Edmund Morris, *Theodore Rex* (New York: The Modern Library, 2001), 243.

81. Hay to Schiff, May 20, 1903, *Hay Papers*, Box 4.

82. Straus, [1903 after July 14], Typewritten Account of "The President and the Kishineff Petition," *Straus Papers*, Scrapbook—Roumania and Russia 1902–3, p. 39, A–J, Box 27; Roosevelt to Hay, July 16, 1903, in Morison, *Roosevelt Letters*, III, 509.

83. "Gives the Lie to Russia," *New York Sun*, July 3, 1903, 1.

84. Straus to Roosevelt, March 31, 1904, *Straus Papers*, Box 3.

85. Roosevelt to Littauer, July 22, 1903, in Morison, *Roosevelt Letters*, III, 424.

86. Kennan to Abbott, January 4, 1904 and Kennan to Roosevelt, January 7, 1904, George *Kennan Papers*, Library of Congress, Box 2.

87. Jonathan Frankel, *Prophecy and Politics: Socialism, Nationalism, and the Russian Jews, 1862–1917* (Cambridge: Cambridge University Press, 1984), 474

88. "Christians Protest in Behalf of Jews," *New York Times*, May 28, 1903, 1.

89. "Shall We Send a Protest to Russia?," *Literary Digest* XXVI, no. 22 (May 30, 1903), 775.

90. Frederick Travis, *George Kennan and the American-Russian Relationship 1865–1924* (Athens: Ohio University Press, 1990), 271.

91. Speech delivered at Cooper Union Hall, New York City, Alton B. Parker Campaign, October 14, 1904, *Olney Papers*, Box 158.

92. Robert Zangrando, *The NAACP Crusade against Lynching, 1909–1950* (Philadelphia: Temple University Press, 1980), 6.

93. Mark Twain, "To the Person Sitting in Darkness" and "The United States of Lyncherdom," in *Collected Tales, Sketches, Speeches, and Essays, 1891–1910* (New York: Library of America, 1992), 471, 484–486.

94. "Shall We Send a Protest to Russia?," 775.

95. Quoted in John Taliafero, *All the Great Prizes: The Life of John Hay, from Lincoln to Roosevelt* (New York: Simon & Schuster, 2013), 463.

96. "The Jewish Petition to the Tsar," *Literary Digest* (July 4, 1903), 4–5.

97. Norman E. Saul, *Concord and Conflict: the United States and Russia, 1867–1914* (Kansas: University of Kansas Press, 1996), 476.

98. "Unspeakable Turk to be Called Upon to Settle for the Murder of American Vice-Consul," *Los Angeles Times*, August 28, 1903; Leishman to Hay, August 27 and 28, 1903, *FRUS 1903* (US Government Printing Office, 1903), 770–771; Oren, *Power, Faith and Fantasy*, 312–313.

99. "Turkish Minister to Confer with Hay," August 30, 1904, *New York Times*.

100. William N. Still, *American Sea Power in the Old World: The United States Navy in European and Near Eastern Waters, 1865–1917* (Westport, CT: Greenwood Press, 1980), 159.

101. Roosevelt to Littauer, July 22, 1903, in Morison, *Roosevelt Letters*, III, 424.

102. Like the majority of his generation, Roosevelt accepted the biological basis for Darwinism. He incorporated ideas on evolution-as-struggle into his personal philosophy of "The Strenuous Life." Yet as a competent naturalist himself, Roosevelt understood the shortcomings of Darwinism when transposed to mankind. Human societies had "curious features" that argued against a deterministic application of the law of natural selection. Instead, Roosevelt emphasized that progress in humanity was dependent on "the transmission of acquired characters." Roosevelt did not think that all races were equally endowed with these characteristics. He was unequivocal in his belief that black Americans, like America's colonial dependents, were, as a group, inferior to white Americans. Yet what separated Roosevelt from many other contemporary racial thinkers was his conviction that all races had the potential to acquire the necessary traits and rise up through the ranks of his racial hierarchy. For quotes see Blum, "Theodore Roosevelt: Years of Decision," in *Roosevelt Letters*, II, ed. Morison, 1486–1494. For more on Roosevelt's ideas on race see Thomas G. Dyer, *Theodore Roosevelt and the Idea of Race*, 21–24.

103. Roosevelt to Albion W. Tourgee, November 8, 1901, Morison in *Roosevelt Letters*, III, 190.

104. Gary Gerstle, "Theodore Roosevelt and the Divided Character of American Nationalism," *Journal of American History* 86 (December 1999), 1280–1307; Dalton, *Theodore Roosevelt*, 215, 275–277.

105. Theodore Roosevelt, *Address of President Roosevelt at Arlington Memorial Day, May 30, 1902* (Washington, 1902), 38pp; Roosevelt to W. T. Durbin, August 6, 1903, in Morison, *Roosevelt Letters*, III, 540; Theodore Roosevelt, "Sixth Annual Message to Congress," in *A Compilation of the Messages and Papers of the Presidents*, ed. James D. Richardson (Washington, DC: Bureau of National Literature & Art, 1908), vol. 11, 1202.

106. Roosevelt to James Ford Rhodes, November 29, 1904 and Henry Smith Pratchett, December 14, 1904, in Morison, *Roosevelt Letters*, 1049, 1065.

107. Typewritten memorandum of "A night at the White House as Guest of the President, November 16th 1904" *Straus Papers*, Box 4.

108. July 4, 1903, *The Spectator*, 2.

109. Roosevelt to Joseph Gurney Cannon, September 12, 1904, in Morison, *Roosevelt Letters*, IV, 929–930.

110. Straus to Roosevelt, November 18, 1904, *Straus Papers*, Box 4.

111. Typewritten memorandum of "A night at the White House as Guest of the President, November 16th 1904," *Straus Papers*, Box 4. For the number of lynchings see Ed Ayers, *The Promise of the New South: Life After Reconstruction* (New York: Oxford University Press, 2007) 502–503.

112. Of course, what Roosevelt conveniently overlooked was the extent to which lynchings were carried out with the tacit consent, and even involvement, of local authorities in certain regions of the South. See Ayers, *The Promise of the New South*, 153–159.

113. Theodore Roosevelt, "Fourth Annual Message to Congress," in *Works of Theodore Roosevelt*, Vol. 15, 256–257.

114. Theodore Roosevelt, "Fourth Annual Message to Congress," in *Works of Theodore Roosevelt*, Vol. 15, 256–257.

115. There is a vast and varied literature on this corollary but see especially Jay Sexton, *The Monroe Doctrine: Empire and Nation in Nineteenth Century America* (New York: Hill & Wang, 2011), 199–241; Cyrus Veeser, *A World Safe for Capitalism: Dollar, Diplomacy and America's Rise to Global Power* (New York: Columbia University Press, 2002); Serge Ricard, "The Roosevelt Corollary," *Presidential Studies Quarterly* 36, no. 1 (2006), 17–26 and Mark T. Gilderhus, "The Monroe Doctrine: Meanings and Implications," *Presidential Studies Quarterly* 36, no. 1 (March 2006), 5–16. For broader assessments of Roosevelt's diplomacy in the Caribbean and Central America see the contrasting interpretations: Richard H. Collin, *Theodore Roosevelt's Caribbean: The Panama Canal, the Monroe Doctrine and the Latin American Context* (Baton Rouge: Louisiana State University Press, 1990) and Thomas Schoonover, *The United States in Central America, 1860–1911: Episodes in Social Imperialism and International Rivalry in the World System* (Durham, NC: Duke University Press, 1991). For a detailed critique of the significance of the perceived German threat in Roosevelt's thought see Nancy Mitchell, *The Danger of Dreams: German and American Imperialism in Latin America* (Chapel Hill: University of North Carolina Press, 1999).

116. James Monroe, "Seventh Annual Message," December 2, 1823 in *The Writings of James Monroe*, Volume 4, 1817–1823, ed. Stanislaus Murray Hamilton (New York: G. P. Putnam's Sons, 1902), 325–342.

117. "How the Message is Regarded," *Literary Digest* XXIX, no. 25 (1904), 829.

118. "Police Constable Roosevelt," December 7, 1904, *New York Times*.

119. Comment on the President's Message, *The Outlook*, New York, December 17, 1904, 947. The *Outlook* was one of Roosevelt's favorite weekly journals, and one of which he became editor after his presidency, so it is likely he would have seen this analysis.

120. "New Monroe Doctrine," December 31, 1904, *New York Times*.

121. All quotes in "President Roosevelt as Europe Sees Him," *American Review of Reviews* 30, no. 303 (June 27, 1904); "Jewish Influence on Russo-American Relations," *Literary Digest*, Vol. 26 (June 27, 1903), 930.

122. Sean McMeekin, *The Berlin-Baghdad Express: The Ottoman Empire and Germany's Bid for World Power, 1898–1918* (London: Allen Lane, 2010), 10–11.

123. "Anti-American Policy of the Ottoman Sultan," *Literary Digest* XXIX, no. 10 (September 3, 1904), 297–298.

124. "A European Flurry Over Mr. Roosevelt's World-Politics," *Literary Digest* 29, no. 11 (September 10, 1904), 329.
125. "President Roosevelt as Europe Sees Him," *American Review of Reviews*, Vol. 30, 302.
126. "Europe's Verdict on Mr. Roosevelt's Alleged Militarism," *Literary Digest* 29, no. 16 (October 15, 1904), 497.
127. "A European Flurry Over Mr. Roosevelt's World-Politics," *Literary Digest* 29, no. 11 (September 10, 1904), 329.
128. Henri Hauser, *L'Imperialsme Americaine* (Paris: Pages Libres, 1905), 96–98, 108.
129. Sexton, *Monroe Doctrine*, 47–85, 237–238.
130. December 10, 1904, *The Economist.*
131. December 7, 1904, *Daily Telegraph;* December 7, 1904, *Daily Chronicle.*
132. December 7, 1904, *The Times* (London).
133. "Theodore the First," *Review of Reviews*, 1905, Volume 31, 48.
134. Some examples are "Turk's Sword Red With Blood," May 14, 1904, *Atlanta Constitution;* "Sassoun Armenians Practically Exterminated by the Turks," May 14, 1904, *Washington Post.* For background on Sasun uprising see Gerard J. Libaridan, "What Was Revolutionary About Armenian Revolutionary Parties in the Ottoman Empire?" in *A Question of Genocide,* ed. Ronald Grigor Suny, Fatma Muge Gocek, and Norman M. Naimark (New York: Oxford University Press, 2011), 91; Bloxham, *The Great Game of Genocide,* 57
135. Roosevelt to Straus, September 28, 1904, in Morison, *Roosevelt Letters,* IV, 958 footnote 1.
136. "Call on America to Aid Armenians, Turkish Policy is Cruelty. Extermination of His Christian Subjects the Sultan's Deliberately Chosen Way of Settling Troubles," May 9, 1904, *St. Louis Republic.*
137. Roosevelt to Schiff, December 14, 1904, Roosevelt to Straus, April 10, 1906, Both in *Straus Papers,* Box 4. Roosevelt to Abbott, Morison, January 3, 1907, *Roosevelt Letters,* Vol. V, 536–538.
138. Roosevelt to Trevelyan, May 13, 1905, in Morison, *Roosevelt Letters,* IV, 1173.
139. Roosevelt to Carl Schurz, September 8, 1905, in Theodore Roosevelt, *Theodore Roosevelt: Letters and Speeches,* ed. Louis Auchincloss (New York: Library of America: 2004).
140. Carl Schurz to Roosevelt, September 14, 1904, *Theodore Roosevelt Papers,* Library of Congress Manuscript Division, Letters and Related Material, Reel 59.
141. Roosevelt to Trevelyan, September 12, 1905 and Roosevelt to Spring Rice, November 1, 1905, Morison, *Roosevelt Letters,* V, 23, 61.
142. Luncheon with President, January 6, 1906 and Roosevelt to Straus, September 6, 1906, Both in *Straus Papers,* Box 4
143. Roosevelt to Schiff, December 14, 1905, *Theodore Roosevelt: Letters and Speeches,* 438–439.
144. Roosevelt to Straus, April 10, 1906, in Morison, *Roosevelt Letters,* V, 207.
145. Leopold's regime was regarded at its inception as a sort of international protectorate, open to traders of all nations and an agent for the abolition of the slave trade and advance of civilization. For background see Jan Stengers, "Leopold II and the Association Internationale du Congo," in Stig Forster, Wolfgang J. Mommsen, and John Robinson, eds., *Bismarck, Europe and Africa: the Berlin Africa Conference 1884–1885 and the onset of partition* (Oxford: Oxford University Press for the German Historical Institute, 1988), 229–244; Martti Koskenniemi, *The Gentle Civilizer of Nations: The Rise and Fall of International Law 1870–1960* (Cambridge: Cambridge University Press, 2002), 155–159.
146. See Charles Laderman, "The Invasion of the United States by an Englishman: E. D. Morel and the Anglo-American Intervention in the Congo," in *A Global History of Anti-Slavery Politics in the Nineteenth Century,* ed. William Mulligan and Maurice Bric (New York: Palgrave Macmillan, 2013), 171–194.
147. *Boston Globe,* October 7, 1904.
148. Report of the Honorary Secretary of the CRA, on his visit to the United States, *E. D. Morel Papers* (hereafter *Morel Papers*), London School of Economics Archive, F4/15.
149. Roosevelt to Maria Longworth Storer, December 8, 1902, in Morison, *Roosevelt Letters,* 391.
150. Beecham Storer to Roosevelt, October 22, 1903, *Theodore Roosevelt Papers,* Letters and Related Material, Reel 38.

151. Report of the Honorary Secretary of the CRA, on his visit to the United States, *Morel Papers*, F4/15.
152. Morel to Fitzmaurice, December 21, 1905, *Morel Papers.*, F4/18.
153. John Hay to J. W. Foster, June 23, 1900, in William Roscoe Thayer, *The Life and Letters of John Hay*, 2 vols. (Boston: Houghton Mifflin, 1915), II, 234–235.
154. Theodore Roosevelt to Eugene A. Philbin, September 28, 1904, in Elting E. Morison, ed., *The Letters of Theodore Roosevelt* (Cambridge, MA: Harvard University Press, 1951–1954), IV, 958.
155. A. Mclean to Morel, April 27, 1904, *Morel Papers*, F4/16; Adam Hochschild, *King Leopold's Ghost: A Story of Greed, Terror and Heroism in Colonial Africa* (Boston: Houghton Mifflin, 1998), 134, 244; Robert Benedetto, ed., *Presbyterian Reformers in Central Africa* (Leiden: E.J. Brill, 1996), 221, fn 12.
156. Report on visit to US, *Morel Papers*, F4/15.
157. Kevin Grant, *A Civilized Savagery: Britain and the New Slaveries in Africa, 1884–1926* (New York: Routledge, 2005).
158. Report on visit to US, *Morel Papers*, F4/15.
159. Thomas Pakenham, *The Scramble for Africa: white man's conquest of the dark continent from 1876 to 1912* (New York: Avon Books, 1991), 656–657.
160. For a detailed examination of how Morel did this see Laderman, The Invasion of America by an Englishman, 177–185.
161. Laderman, "The Invasion of America by an Englishman," 183–185. For more on Twain's role see Hunt Hawkins, "Mark Twain's involvement with the Congo Reform Movement: "A Fury of Generous Indignation," *New England Quarterly*, 51, no. 2 (1978), 147–175; For more on Washington's role see Andrew Zimmerman, *Alabama in Africa: Booker T. Washington, the German Empire and the Globalization of the New South* (Princeton, NJ: Princeton University Press, 2010), 219–220; *Outlook*, 78 (October 8, 1904), 375–377.
162. Barbour to Morel, January 17, 1906, *Morel Papers*, F4/19.
163. Harris to Morel, Document 19, *Morel Papers*, F4/18.
164. Phillip C. Jessup, "The Defense of Oppressed People," *American Journal of International Law* 31, no. 1 (1938), 116–119.
165. Root to Barbour, March 8, 1906, *Morel Papers*, F4/18.
166. Harris to Morel, Document 19, *Morel Papers*, F4/18.
167. Roosevelt to Carnegie, August 6, 1906, *Theodore Roosevelt: Letters and Speeches*, 489–491.
168. Quoted in Edmund Morris, *Colonel Roosevelt* (New York: Random House, 2010), 139.
169. Elliott P. Skinner, *African Americans and U.S. Policy Toward Africa, 1850–1924* (Washington, DC: Howard University Press, 1992), 236–237; Pakenham, *Scramble*, 658–659; Peter Duignan and L. H. Gann, *The United States and Africa: A History* (Cambridge: Cambridge University Press, 1984), 194–195.
170. Roosevelt to Straus, April 10, 1906 *Roosevelt Letters*, V, 207. When activists tried to pressure the Republican state convention in Massachusetts to adopt Congo reform, Roosevelt privately remarked to the state's Senator, and his closest political confidant, Henry Cabot Lodge, that "the only tomfoolery that anyone seems bent on is that about the Congo Free State outrages, and that is imbecile rather than noxious." Roosevelt to Lodge, October 2, 1906, in Morison, *Roosevelt Letters*, V, 439.
171. *Morning Post*, November 3, 1906. The story was published under the name of Maurice Low, the paper's US correspondent who was a known confidant of the president.
172. Morel, Louis, Stengers, *History*, 189.
173. Morel to Fitzmaurice, December 21, 1905, *Morel Papers*, F4/18.
174. Acting Secretary of State Robert Bacon to E. D. Morel, November 19, 1906, *Morel Papers*, F4/18.
175. Hochschild, *Leopold's Ghost*, 246–249.
176. Quoted in S. J. S. Cookey, *Britain and the Congo Question, 1885–1913* (London: Longmans, Green & Co. Ltd., 1968), 177.
177. Laderman, "The Invasion of America by an Englishman," 190–194.
178. Morel to Daniels, April 15 and 21, 1909, *Morel Papers*, F4/21.
179. "Tributes to E.D. Morel," *New York Times*, June 17, 1913.

180. An example is Roosevelt to Sydney Brooks, November 20, 1908, in Morison, *Roosevelt Letters*, VI, 1370.
181. Roosevelt to Hay, July 26, 1904, Morison, *Roosevelt Letters*, IV, 865.
182. Roosevelt to Hay, January 28, 1905, *Theodore Roosevelt Papers*, Letters and Related Material, Reel 52. See also Harbaugh, *Theodore Roosevelt*, 265–266.
183. Richard H. Collin, *Theodore Roosevelt, Culture, Diplomacy and Expansion* (Baton Rouge: Louisiana State University Press, 1985), 52. See Rotem Kowner, "Between a Colonial Clash and World War Zero," in *The Impact of the Russo-Japanese War* (New York: Routledge, 2007), 19.
184. Roosevelt to Spring Rice, March 19, 1904, June 13, 1904, in Morison, *Roosevelt Letters*, Volume 4, 759, 829.
185. Roosevelt to David Bowman Schneder, June 19, 1905, in Morison, *Roosevelt Letters*, IV, 1240.
186. Roosevelt to Spring Rice, June 13, 1904, in Morison, *Roosevelt Letters*, IV, 829.
187. Theodore Roosevelt, "Expansion and Peace," *Independent*, December 21, 1899; Roosevelt to Morley, December 1, 1908, in Morison, *Roosevelt Letters*, VI, 1401.
188. Roosevelt to Whitelaw Reid, September 11, 1905, in Morison, *Roosevelt Letters*, V, 20.
189. Roosevelt to Lodge, April 30, 1906, in Morison, *Roosevelt Letters*, V, 252–257. The article in question was Charles Francis Adams, "Reflex Light from Africa," *Century*, 72:101–111 (May 1906).
190. Roosevelt to Henry Waters Taft, September 28, 1904, in Morison, *Roosevelt Letters*, IV, 957.
191. Roosevelt to William Howard Taft, January 22, 1907, in Morison, *Roosevelt Letters*, VI, 560.
192. Roosevelt to Lodge, April 30, 1906, in Morison, *Roosevelt Letters*, V, 252–257.
193. Roosevelt to Taft, August 21, 1907, in Morison, *Roosevelt Letters*, VI, 761; for a succinct discussion of the evolution of Roosevelt's thought on imperialism see Widenor, *Henry Cabot Lodge and the Search for an American Foreign Policy*, 152–153.
194. Roosevelt to Joseph Bucklin Bishop, February 23, 1904, in Morison, *Roosevelt Letters*, IV, 734.
195. Even *The Spectator*, under the editorship of Roosevelt's friend Strachey, cautioned that "schemes for securing social order which work admirably in Massachusetts ... will produce nothing but wild disorder" in the Philippines. *The Spectator*, 1898, Vol. 81, 821.
196. While Britons were more wedded to principles of free trade than Americans, who continued to espouse protectionist positions, differences in economic practice or concern about commercial interests were not the prime grounds for widespread British disgust. See Seed, "British Views of American Policy in the Philippines," 60.
197. They did, however, share the president's positive opinions of Taft and Wood. See Seed "British Views of American Policy in the Philippines," 64. The decline in the popular, evangelical zeal for imperialism that marked the late nineteenth century also inevitably resulted in less attention to the Philippines. See Bernard Porter, *Critics of Empire: British Radicals and the Imperial Challenge* (London: I.B. Tauris, 2008), 221.
198. Herring, *From Colony to Superpower*, 337.
199. Widenor, *Henry Cabot Lodge and the search for an American Foreign Policy*, 162.
200. David H. Burton, *Theodore Roosevelt and His English Correspondents: A Special Relationship of Friends* (Transactions of the American Philosophical Society, New Series 63, no. 2 (1973), 1–70.
201. William N. Tilchin, "Anglo-American Partnership: The Foundation of Theodore Roosevelt's Foreign Policy," in Serge Ricard, *A Companion to Theodore Roosevelt* (Malden, MA: Wiley Blackwell, 2011), 314–321.
202. Roosevelt to Kennan, May 6, 1905, in Morison, *Roosevelt Letters*, Vol. 4, 1168.
203. Quoted in Cooper, *The Warrior and the Priest*, 75. See also Henry Cabot Lodge, "The Monroe Doctrine and Morocco," *Harper's Weekly*, 50 (March 10, 1906), 332–333 and 352.
204. Roosevelt to Lee, October 17, 1908, in Morison, *Roosevelt Letters*, VI, 1292.
205. Roosevelt to Lee, June 6, 1905, in Morison, *Roosevelt Letters*, V, 1206.
206. Selections from the Correspondence of Lodge and Roosevelt (New York: C. Scribener's & Sons, 1925), II, 404–405, 409 (June 12, September 12, 1911); Widenor, *Henry Cabot Lodge and the Search for an American Foreign Policy*, 138.

207. Roosevelt, "The Peace of Righteousness," *The Outlook* 99 (September 9, 1911); and "The Russian Treaty, Arbitration and Hypocrisy," *The Outlook* 99 (Dec 30, 1911), 1047.

208. Roosevelt to Carnegie, February 18, 1910 and Roosevelt to Lee, September 25, 1911, in Morison, *Roosevelt Letters*, Vol. 7, 48, 345–347.

Chapter 3

1. Tilchin, *Theodore Roosevelt and the British Empire*, 222–225.

2. "The Results of Expansion," *Boston Evening Transcript*, January 19, 1909 in *Theodore Roosevelt Collection*, Harvard College Library, Folder Clippings—TR: Africa-Europe, 1909–1910; Theodore Roosevelt, "National Duties," Address at Minnesota State Fair, September 2, 1901, *The Works of Theodore Roosevelt: National Edition*, Vol. 13 (New York: Charles Scribner's Sons, 1926), 476.

3. "The Results of Expansion," *Boston Evening Transcript*, January 19, 1909.

4. Theodore Roosevelt, from an address in the Metropolitan Memorial Methodist Episcopal Church, Washington, DC, in *Missionary Herald*, March 1909, 130.

5. Preston, *Sword of the Spirit, Shield of Faith*, 191.

6. Michael H. Hunt, *Ideology and U.S. Foreign Policy* (New Haven, CT: Yale University Press, 1987), 106–108; Keiser, *Nearest East*, 63–74.

7. Quoted in Colby M. Chester, "The Young Turkey," in *National Geographic Magazine*, Vol. 23, 1912, 47.

8. "The Results of Expansion," *Boston Evening Transcript*, January 19, 1909.

9. Ian Tyrell, *Reforming the World: The Creation of America's Moral Empire* (Princeton, NJ: Princeton University Press, 2010), 69–79.

10. F. T. Gates to John D. Rockefeller, January 31, 1905, copy in *James L. Barton Papers* (hereafter Barton Papers), 3.17, *American Board of Commissioners for Foreign Missions Archives* (hereafter ABCFM) Houghton Library, Harvard University; March 29, 1905, *New York Times*.

11. Annual Message of the President, December 10, 1909, Department of State, *FRUS, 1909* (US Government Printing Office, 1909), xiii–xiv.

12. Leland J. Gordon, *American Relations with Turkey, 1890–1930: An Economic Interpretation* (Philadelphia: University of Pennsylvania Press, 1932), 224.

13. Thomas A. Bryson, *Tars, Turks, and Tankers: The Role of the United States Navy in the Middle East, 1800–1979* (Metuchen, NJ: Scarecrow Press, 1980), 50–51.

14. Grabill, *Protestant Diplomacy*, 38.

15. Straus, "My Third Mission to Turkey, 1909–1910," 74–75, 98–99, 104–105 133–141, *Straus MSS*, Boxes IV and XI; Straus, *Under Four Administrations*, 296–298; DeNovo, 63–79.

16. Gordon, *American Relations*, 262–265.

17. Quoted in Christopher McKnight Nichols, *Promise and Peril: America at the Dawn of a Global Age* (Cambridge, MA: Harvard University Press, 2011), 94.

18. John R. Mott, *The Evangelization of the World in This Generation* (New York: Student Volunteer Movement for Foreign Missions, 1900), 1–2.

19. Tyrell, *Reforming the World*, 49–67.

20. Stead, *The Americanization of the World*, 77–78.

21. Joseph Oldham to the Rt. Rev. Bishop of Southwark, February 23, 1909, *John R. Mott Papers*, Yale University, Special Collections, Divinity School Library, folder 3374, box 214. The remaining delegates were mainly from continental Europe (169). There were 27 representatives from the white colonies of South Africa and Australasia and 19 from the "non-western world" (18 from Asia and 1 from Africa). See Brian Stanley, *The World Missionary Conference, Edinburgh 1910* (Grand Rapids, Michigan: Eerdmans, 2009), 1–12.

22. William R. Hogg, *Ecumenical Foundations: A History of the International Missionary Council and its Nineteenth Century Background* (New York: Harper, 1952), 144–156.

23. William R. Hutchison, *Errand to the World: American Protestant Thought and Foreign Missions* (Chicago: University of Chicago Press, 1987), 135–138.

24. For more on the growing skepticism among British missionaries regarding colonialism and commercialism see Andrew Porter, *Religion versus Empire? British Protestant Missionaries*

and Overseas Expansion, 1700–1914 (Manchester: Manchester University Press, 2004), 282–316.

25. World Missionary Conference, *Report of Commission I: Carrying the Gospel to all the Non-Christian World; with Supplement: Presentation and discussion of the report in the Conference on 15 June 1910* (Edinburgh: Fleming H. Revell, 1910); see also Stanley, *World Missionary Conference*, 14–15; W. H. T. Gardiner, *"Edinburgh, 1910": An Account and Interpretation of the World Missionary Conference* (London: O. Anderssen & Ferrier, 1910), 59, 63.

26. World Missionary Conference, *Report of Commission I*, 27–28.

27. "A Nation's Sudden Conversion," *Missionary Herald*, October 1908, 455–458.

28. Gerard J. Libaridian, "What Was Revolutionary About Armenian Revolutionary Parties in the Ottoman Empire?" in *A Question of Genocide: Armenians and Turks at the End of the Ottoman Empire*, ed. Ronald Grigor Suny, Fatma Muge Gocek, and Norman M. Naimark (New York: Oxford University Press, 2011), 109–111.

29. Both quoted in Raymond Kevorkian, *The Armenian Genocide: A Complete History* (London: I. B. Tauris, 2011), 51–53.

30. Ahmed Emin Yalman, *Turkey In My Time* (Norman: University of Oklahoma Press, 1956), 23–24.

31. Halide Edib Adivar, *Memoirs* (London, J. Murray, 1926), 259.

32. Keiser, *Nearest East*, 63–70.

33. Preston, *Sword of the Spirit, Shield of Faith*, 176–177.

34. James L. Barton, "Missionary Preparations for New Turkey," Graves Lectures 1909, Barton Papers, 7.11, *ABCFM Archives*.

35. World Missionary Conference, *Report of Commission III: Education in Relation to The Christianisation of National Life* (Edinburgh: Fleming H. Revell, 1910), 223.

36. Preston, *Sword of the Spirit, Shield of Faith*, 178–179.

37. James L. Barton, "What the Changes Mean to us," *Missionary Herald* (1908), 467–469; see also James L. Barton, *Daybreak in Turkey* (New York: The Pilgrim Press, 1908).

38. Bloxham, *The Great Game of Genocide*, 60–62.

39. Bloxham, *Great Game of Genocide*, 62–65; Margaret Macmillan, *The War That Ended Peace: How Europe Abandoned Peace for the First World War* (London: Profile Books, 2013), 436–469.

40. James L. Barton, "The Balkan War, Mohammedanism and Christianity," *Missionary Review of the World*, Vol. 36, 87–94.

41. Peet to Barton, June 8, 1914, Volume 48, Western Turkey Mission, 1910–1919, Vol. 10 Peet: 1913–1919, *ABCFM Archives*.

42. James L. Barton, "What the Defeat of Turkey May Mean to American Missions," *The Biblical World*, Vol. 41, 3–8.

43. Keiser, *Nearest East*, 70.

44. James L. Barton, "What the Defeat of Turkey May Mean to American Missions," *The Biblical World*, Vol. 41, 5.

45. Howard S. Bliss, "The Balkan War and Christian Work Among Moslems," in *International Review of Mission* 3 (London: Oxford University Press, 1913), 652–655.

46. "Turkey Revisited: Three Years of Revolution, and After," *Review of Reviews*, August 1911, 133–143; "The Sultan a nd his Policy: Why I Am Hopeful about the Future of Turkey," *Review of Reviews*, September 1911, 234–326.

47. J. L. Garvin, quoted in Frederic Whyte, *The Life of William T. Stead* (London: J. Cape Ltd., 1925), Vol. II, 325.

48. "Story Mr. Stead Could Have Told," *Daily Mirror*, April 18, 1912.

49. DeNovo, *American Interests*, 51–52; see also William C. Askew and J. Fred Rippy, "The United States and Europe's Strife, 1908–1913," *Journal of Politics* 4 (February 1942), 69–75.

50. Ernst Christian Helmreich, *Diplomacy of the Balkan Wars, 1912–1913* (Cambridge, MA: Harvard University Press, 1938), 200–201.

51. Annual Message of the President, December 3, 1912, *FRUS, 1912* (US Government Printing Office, 1912), xx.

52. Woodrow Wilson, "The Ideals of America," *Atlantic Monthly* XC (December 1902).

53. Constitutional Government in the United States, March 24, 1908, Vol. 18, *Wilson Papers*, 120; "The Ideals of America," December 26, 1901, *Wilson Papers*, Vol. 12, 226.

54. Acceptance speech August 7, 1912, *Wilson Papers*, Vol. 25, 16–17.

55. Speech accepting the New Jersey gubernatorial nomination, September 15, 1910, *Wilson Papers*, Vol. 21, 91–4.

56. John A. Thompson, *Woodrow Wilson* (London: Longman, 2002), 78.

57. Quoted in Arthur Link, *Woodrow Wilson: Revolution, War and Peace* (Arlington Heights, IL: AHM Publishing Corporation, 1979), 22.

58. Tyrell, *Reforming the World*, 198–205.

59. Robert L. Daniel, "The Friendship of Woodrow Wilson and Cleveland H. Dodge," *Mid-America*, 43 (July 1961), 182–196; Joseph L. Grabill, "Cleveland H. Dodge, Woodrow Wilson, and the Near East," *Journal on Presbyterian History*, 48 (Winter, 1970), 249–264.

60. House diary, January 8, 1913, *Wilson Papers*, Vol. 27, 23.

61. Quoted in Arthur Link, *Wilson the Diplomatist: A Look at His Major Foreign Policies* (Baltimore: Johns Hopkins University Press, 1957), 24–25.

62. David Mayers, *Dissenting Voices in America's Rise to Power* (Cambridge: Cambridge University Press, 2007), 225.

63. Charles Seymour, ed., *The Intimate Papers of Colonel House* (Boston: Houghton Mifflin Co.), I, 96.

64. Morgenthau Diaries, May 18, 1915, *Papers of Henry Morgenthau Sr.* (hereafter *Morgenthau Papers*), Library of Congress, Division of Manuscripts.

65. Morgenthau Diaries, November 1, 2, 27, 1913, *Morgenthau Papers*, Reel 6.

66. Henry Morgenthau, *All in a Life-Time* (Garden City, NY: Doubleday, 1922), 35–36.

67. Peet to Barton, May 29, 1914, Volume 48, Western Turkey Mission, 1910–1919, Vol. 10 Peet 1913–1919, *ABCFM Archives*.

68. Peet to Barton, March 20, 1914, *ABCFM Archives* Volume 48, Western Turkey Mission, 1910–1919, Vol. 10 Peet 1913–1919.

69. Bloxham, *Great Game of Genocide*, 64–65.

70. Peet to Barton, March 11, 1914, Volume 48, Western Turkey Mission, 1910–1919, Vol. 10 Peet 1913–1919, *ABCFM Archives*.

71. John R. Mott, *The Present World Situation: With Special Reference to the Demands Made Upon the Christian Church in Relation to Non-Christian Lands* (New York: Student Volunteer for Foreign Missions, 1914), 5.

72. Thompson, *Woodrow Wilson*, 102.

73. Address to the Daughters of the American Revolution, Continental Hall, Washington, October 11, 1915, James Brown Scott, *President Wilson's Foreign Policy: Messages, Addresses and Papers* (New York: Oxford University Press, 1918) 110

74. "An Appeal to the American People," August 18, 1914, *Wilson Papers*, Vol. 30, 393–394.

75. Richard Roberts, *Saving the City: The Great Financial Crisis of 1914* (Oxford: Oxford University Press, 2013), 3–6.

76. American Board of Commissioners for Foreign Missions, *Annual Report of the American Board of Commissioners for Foreign Missions*, 1915 (Boston, 1915), Volume 105, 76; Peet to Barton, August 4, 1914, Peet to Getchell, August 11, 1914, Peet to White August 11, 1914; Peet to Barton, August 24, 1914 Volume 48, Western Turkey Mission, 1910–1919, Vol. 10 Peet 1913–1919, *ABCFM Archives*.

77. Peet to Barton, August 11, 1914,Volume 48, Western Turkey Mission, 1910–1919, Vol. 10 Peet 1913–1919, *ABCFM*.

78. Mustafa Aksakal, "The Ottoman Empire," in *The Cambridge History of the First World War, Volume 2: The State*, ed. Jay Winter (Cambridge: Cambridge University Press, 2014), 459–478. For a more in-depth analysis see Mustafa Aksakal, *The Ottoman Road to War in 1914: The Ottoman Empire and the First World* (Cambridge: Cambridge University Press, 2008), especially 93–119.

79. Henry Morgenthau, *Ambassador Morgenthau's Story* (New York: Doubleday and Page, 1918), 105–108.

80. Telegram 38 from Constantinople, November 15, 1914, State Department Record Group 59, 763.72/1238, *US National Archives*.

81. Telegram 64 to Constantinople, November 24, 1914, State Department Record Group 59, 763.72/1238, *US National Archives.*

82. Ahmed Rustem to William Jennings Bryan, September 12, 1914, *FRUS: The Lansing Papers, 1914–1920* (US Government Printing Office, 1914–1920), I, 68–69.

83. DeNovo, *American Interests,* 92.

84. "How Turkish Empire Should be Made Over After the War," *New York Times,* January 24, 1915, VII, 1.

85. Bloxham, *Great Game of Genocide,* 67.

86. Morgenthau, *Morgenthau's Story,* 112–117; *FRUS 1914* (US Government Printing Office: 1914), 1090–1094.

87. Gordon, *American Relations with Turkey,* 64–68.

88. *FRUS 1914,* Morgenthau to Bryan, November 7, 1914, 781.

89. Ralph Harlow to Hon. George Horton, January 23, 1915, Correspondence of W. W. Peet on the Armenian Situation, 1914, 16.10: Near East Mission: archives from mission stations, *ABCFM.*

90. DeNovo, *American Interests,* 97.

91. Annual Report of the American Board of Commissioners for Foreign Missions, v. 105 (Boston: Board Congregational House, *1915)* 77–86.

92. Niall Ferguson, *The Pity of War* (London: Penguin Books, 1998), 290–291; David Fromkin, *A Peace to End All Peace: The Fall of the Ottoman Empire and the Creation of the Modern Middle East* (New York: Henry Holt and Company, 1989), 124–137.

93. Morgenthau, *Ambassador Morgenthau's Story,* 190.

94. Suny, *"They Can Live in the Desert,"* xix.

95. Morgenthau to Bryan, April 27, 1915, *FRUS: 1915 Supplement: The World War* (US Government Printing Office, 1915), 980.

96. Bryan to Morgenthau, Constantinople, April 27, 1915, sent on April 29; *Morgenthau Papers,* General Correspondence, Container 7.

97. May 24, 1915 Allied declaration, Sharp to Bryan, May 28, 1915, *FRUS 1915 Supplement,* 981.

98. "Allies to Punish Turks Who Murder," *New York Times,* May 24, 1915.

99. Mayers, *Dissenting Voices,* 231–235.

100. Morgenthau to Lansing, July 10, 1915, *FRUS: 1915 Supplement,* 982–984.

101. Library of Congress, Division of Manuscripts, *Papers of Robert Lansing,* Lansing Diary, Blue Boxes, Box 2, Confidential Memoranda and Notes, May 25, 1915.

102. The Diary of Colonel Edward M. House, Yale University Library, July 24, 1915, quoted in James F. Willis, *Prologue to Nuremberg: The Politics and Diplomacy of Punishing War Criminals of the First World War* (Westport, CT: Greenwood Press, 1982), 41.

103. Lansing to Morgenthau, July 16, 1915, *FRUS: 1915 Supplement,* 984.

104. Barton to Lansing, received July 14, 1915, Lansing to Barton, July 19, 1915; *FRUS: 1915 Supplement,* 984.

105. Morgenthau to Lansing, August 11, 1915, *FRUS: 1915 Supplement,* 985–986.

106. Morgenthau, *Ambassador Morgenthau's Story,* 261.

107. Morgenthau to Secretary of State, July 16, 1915, State Department Record Group, 59. 867.4016/76, *National Archives;* Morgenthau, *Ambassador Morgenthau's Story,* xxx.

108. Dr. M. Simbad Gabriel, President of Armenian General Progressive Association to Mabel T. Boardman, September 1, 1915, and Boardman to Gabriel, September 15, 1915, "Correspondence Armenie Amerique, 1915–1917," *Records of the Délégation Nationale Arménienne (RDNA),* Bibliotheque Nubar (BN), Paris.

109. Morgenthau to Lansing, September 3, 1915, *FRUS: 1915 Supplement,* 988.

110. Alvey Adee to Reverend Papgen Guleserian, September 15, 1915, "Correspondence Armenie Amerique, 1915–1917," *Records of the Délégation Nationale Arménienne BN.* For more on Morgenthau's emigration proposal see Keith Pomakoy, *Helping Humanity: American Policy and Genocide Rescue* (Lanham, MD: Lexington Books, 2011), 85.

111. Daniel, *American Philanthropy in the Near East,* 150.

112. Morgenthau to State Department, September 25, 1915, *Morgenthau Papers.*

113. This was a sizeable sum considering the number of funds to which Americans were being asked to donate, including Liberty Loans, the Red Cross, French and Belgian Relief. The

amount raised by the ACASR during the period of American neutrality was dwarfed by the $34,500,000 raised for Belgium. The major campaign led by the Commission on Belgian Relief was halted by the US intervention in the war, however, while the ACASR effort continued to expand. See Curti, *American Philanthropy*, 224–258.

114. James L. Barton, "The Near East Relief: A Moral Force," *International Review of Missions*, 18 (1929), 501–502.

115. James L. Barton, *Story of Near East Relief (1915–1930): An Interpretation* (New York: Macmillan, 1930), 409–410.

116. Dodge to Barton, October 11, 1915, ABC Personal, *James L. Barton Papers*, 3:17, *ABCFM*.

117. Barton, *Story of Near East Relief*, 14–15.

118. Power, *A Problem from Hell*, 9.

119. "Tell of Horrors Done in Armenia: A Policy of Extermination Put in Effect Against a Helpless People," *New York Times*, October 4, 1915.

120. Lou Ann Matossian, "Minnesota Newspapers Reportage About the Armenian Genocide, 1915–1922," www.chgs.umn.edu, accessed April 20, 2013.

121. April 29, 1915, *Los Angeles Times*; October 18, 1915, *The Independent*, both quoted in Leonard, "When News is Not Enough," 304.

122. DeNovo, *American Interests*, 98–104.

123. M. Varton Malcom, *The Armenians in America* (Boston: Pilgrim Press, 1919), 65–77.

124. Quoted in Payaslian, *United States Policy Toward the Armenian Question*, 97.

125. House to Wilson, October 1, 1915, in *Wilson Papers*, Vol. 35, 3.

126. Wilson to Morgenthau, October 28, 1915, *Wilson Papers*, Vol. 35, 337.

127. Haigazoun Hohannes Topakyan to Wilson, October 22, 1915; Wilson to Topakyan, October 28, 1915, both in *Wilson Papers*, Vol. 35, 104, 119.

128. William Nesbitt Chambers to Wilson, December 10, 1915, Wilson to Chambers, December 13, 1915, both in *Wilson Papers*, Vol. 35, 337, 349.

129. Wilson to Assistant Secretary of State William Phillips, July 29, 1916, *Woodrow Wilson Papers*, Manuscript Division, Library of Congress (hereafter *Wilson MSS*), General Correspondence, Reel 82; Ray Stannard Baker, *Woodrow Wilson: Life and Letters* (Garden City, NY: Doubleday Page, 1937), 341.

130. Lansing to Morgenthau, October 4, 1915, *FRUS: 1915 Supplement*, 988.

131. Lansing to Tumulty, October 26, 1915, with enclosed form letter in *Wilson MSS*, General Correspondence, Reel 74.

132. Lansing to Phillip, February 12, 1916, *FRUS: 1916 Supplement*, 847.

133. Lansing to Bernstorff, February 16, 1916, *FRUS: 1916 Supplement* (US Government Printing Office, 1916), 847–848.

134. Lansing to Morgenthau, February 17, 1916, *Morgenthau Papers*, General Correspondence, Container 7.

135. Lansing to Wilson, November 21, 1916, *FRUS: The Lansing Papers 1914–1920*, I, 42.

136. Theodore Roosevelt, "An International Posse Comitatus," *New York Times*, November 8, 1914 in *The Works of Theodore Roosevelt*, ed. Hermann Hagedorn (New York, 1925), XVIII, 74, 79.

137. Quoted in Edmund Morris, *Colonel Roosevelt* (New York: Random House, 2010), 388.

138. Roosevelt to Arthur Hamilton Lee, June 17, 1915, *Roosevelt Letters*, Vol. 8, 937–938.

139. Cooper, *The Warrior and the Priest*, 288–290.

140. Roosevelt to Samuel Dutton, November 24, 1915, in Theodore Roosevelt, *Fear God and Take Your Own Part* (New York: George H. Doran, 1916), 196.

141. Theodore Roosevelt letter, *New York Times*, December 1, 1915.

142. Roosevelt to Sir Edward Grey, June 22, 1915, *Roosevelt Papers*, Library of Congress, Washington, DC, Reel 211.

143. *Congressional Record*, 54th Cong., 1st Sess., 959–965; Widenor, *Henry Cabot Lodge and the Search for an American Foreign Policy*, 74, 95, 106, 154.

144. Roosevelt to Harry V. Osborne, November 1, 1915, *Letters of Roosevelt*, Vol. 8, 976.

145. Roosevelt, *Fear God and Take Your Own Part*, 21–23.

146. Morgenthau, *Ambassador Morgenthau's Story*, 225, 385.

147. February 23, 1916, Morgenthau Diary, *Morgenthau Papers*, Reel 6.

148. Morgenthau to Wilson, May 4, 1916, *Morgenthau Papers*, General Correspondence, Container 8; Grabill, *Protestant Diplomacy*, 74.
149. Phillip to Lansing, February 15, 1916; Phillip to Lansing, October 1, 1916, *FRUS: 1916 Supplement*, 848–849, 856–857.
150. Quoted in Payaslian, *United States Policy Toward the Armenian Question*, 113.
151. *National Review* (January 1913), Vol. LX, 736–750; see also George Kennan, *American Diplomacy* (Chicago: University of Chicago Press, 1951), 70.
152. Lewis Einstein, *Inside Constantinople: A Diplomatist's Diary During the Dardanelles Expedition, April–September 1915* (London: John Murray, 1917), 2.
153. Lewis Einstein, *A Diplomat Looks Back* (New Haven, CT: Yale University Press, 1968), 135–137.
154. Roosevelt to Grey, January 22, 1915, *Roosevelt Letters*, Vol. 8, 879.
155. Einstein, *A Diplomat Looks Back*, 136.
156. Michelle Tusan, "Crimes Against Humanity:" Human Rights, the British Empire and the Origins of the Response to the Armenian Genocide," *American Historical Review* (February 2014), Vol. 119, Issue 1, 52–56.
157. Grey to A. Nicolson, October 14, 1908 in Grey of Fallodon, *Twenty-Five Years, 1892–1916* (London: Hodder & Stoughton, 1925), Vol. I, 185; Nassibian, *Britain and the Armenian Question*, 52–53, 67.
158. Bodleian Library, University of Oxford, *Papers of Herbert Henry Asquith*, 7, f. 206, Cabinet Meeting, September 23, 1914; ff. 210–211, Cabinet Meeting, October 2, 1914.
159. "Ministers on the War," *The Times*, November 10, 1914, 9; "The Need for Recruits," November 11, 1914, 10.
160. As Tusan notes, Britain's Protestant-based "imperial vision of itself as a civilizing force... gave weight to its humanitarian claim on behalf of Ottoman Christians" as it cast itself "as an instrument for protecting civilians during the war." Tusan, "Crimes Against Humanity," 51.
161. "Armenian Massacres," *The Times*, October 14, 1915, 11; Official Statement, The Arm. Refugees (Lord Mayor's) Fund, Papers Relating to Armenia, 1876–1922, Box 204, *Papers of Viscount James Bryce*.
162. *The Times*, December 15, 1916, 7.
163. Donald Bloxham has emphasized, "the idea of a German role in the formation of the genocidal policy, however, has no basis in the available documentation." See Bloxham, *Great Game of Genocide*, 115–133. However, other studies have stressed German complicity. For studies of the wartime German–Ottoman relationship and its bearing on the Armenian question see Ulrich Trumpener, *Germany and the Ottoman Empire, 1914–1918* (Princeton, NJ: Princeton University Press, 1968), 204–205, 221, 232, 266, 370; Frank Weber, *Eagles on the Crescent: Germany, Austria and the Diplomacy of the Turkish Alliance, 1914–1918* (Ithaca, NY: Cornell University Press, 1970), 144–159; Vahakn N. Dadrian, *The History of the Armenian Genocide: Ethnic Conflict from the Balkans to Anatolia to the Caucasus* (Providence, RI: Berghahn Books, 1995), 248–300 and *German Responsibility in the Armenian Genocide: A Review of the Historical Evidence of German Complicity* (Watertown, MA: Blue Crane, 1996); Christoph Dinkel, "German Officers and the Armenian Genocide," *Armenian Review*, 44/1 (1991), 77–133.
164. *Hansard*, 5th Ser. 1915, Vol. 19, cols. 994–1000; For articles in the Canadian and Australian press see Armenian National Committee, *The Armenian Genocide: As Reported in the Australian Press* (Sydney: Armenian National Committee, 1983); Armenian Youth Federation of Canada, *The Armenian Genocide in the Canadian Press*, Vol. 1: 1915–1916 (Montreal: Armenian National Committee of Canada, 1985); see also Vahe G. Kateb, "Australian Press Coverage of the Armenian Genocide, 1915–1923," MA thesis, Graduate School of Journalism, University of Wollogong, 2003 (http://ro.uow.edu.au/theses/215).
165. Nassibian, *Britain and the Armenian Question*, 69–73.
166. Arnold Toynbee, *Acquaintances* (London: Oxford University Press, 1967), 149–152; *New York American*, February 2, 1916.
167. Minutes by H. Nicholson and R. Cecil, September 6 and 9, 1915, *The National Archives*, FO 371 [Foreign Office: General Correspondence from 1906–1966] 2488 [Turkey (War)] File 51009/12595.

168. FO to Buchanan, October 11, 1915. FO 371/2488/51009/148680.

169. Nassibian, *Britain and the Armenian Question*, 74–75.

170. Cutting from the *New York Times*, December 1, 1915; Spring Rice to Grey, October 8, 1915, FO 371/2488/51009/153862.

171. Spring Rice to Grey, October 8, 1915, FO 371/2488/51009/153862.

172. Grey, *Twenty Five Years*, II, 107.

173. In fact, the work of this committee remains controversial and many accounts of the atrocities, provided by lawyers in England without corroboration, were later shown to have been false (although Bryce only learned of the misrepresentations and inaccuracies after the war.) See Phillip Knightley, *The First Casualty: The War Correspondent as Hero, Propagandist and Myth Maker from the Crimea to Vietnam* (New York: Harcourt Brace Jovanovich, 1975), 84.

174. R. W. Seton Watson, *Disraeli, Gladstone and the Eastern Question: A Study in Diplomacy and Party Politics* (London: Macmillan, 1935), 111, 381, 525–526; Shannon, *Gladstone*, Vol. II, 192.

175. For the account of Bryce's ascent see James Bryce, *Transcaucasia and Ararat: Being notes of a vacation in the autumn of 1876, 4th edn* (London: Macmillan & Co. 1896); John Seaman, *A Citizen of the World: the life of James Bryce* (London: I. B. Tauris, 2006), 80–82, 93–94.

176. Davide Rodogno, *Against Massacre*, 205.

177. Nassibian, *Britain and the Armenian Question*, 36–38.

178. James Bryce, "The Armenian Question," *The Century Magazine* 51 (November 1895), 150–154.

179. Bryce, *Transcaucasia and Ararat*, 428, 446, 523–525.

180. Bryce, "The Armenian Question," 150–154.

181. H. A. L. Fisher, *James Bryce: Viscount Bryce of Dechmont, O. M.* (London: Macmillan, 1927), 143.

182. James Bryce (with Arnold J. Toynbee), ed., *The Treatment of Armenians in the Ottoman Empire, 1915–1916: Documents Presented by Viscount Grey of Fallodon, Secretary of State for Foreign Affairs* (London: Joseph Causton, 1916).

183. Bryce to Barton, September 11, 1916, , *Barton Papers*, ABC 76, 3.11, *ABCFM*.

184. Grabill, *Protestant Diplomacy*, 75.

185. Bryce to Barton, May 25, 1916, Barton Papers, Barton to Bryce, June 15, 1915, July 22, 1915,all in Barton Papers, ABC 76, 3.11 Box 2, *ABCFM*.

186. Nassibian, *Britain and the Armenian Question*, 55–56.

187. Barton to Bryce, June 15, 1915 and July 22, 1915, *Barton Papers*, ABC, 3.11, *ABCFM*.

188. American Board of Commissioners for Foreign Missions, *Annual Report of the American Board of Commissioners for Foreign Missions* (Boston: 1916), 73–113.

189. "A Speech in Long Branch, New Jersey, Accepting the Presidential Nomination," September 2, 1916, *in Wilson Papers*, Vol. 38, 126–139.

190. Thompson, *Woodrow Wilson*, 128–130.

191. Wilson speech at Cincinatti, October 26, 1916, in *Wilson Papers*, Vol. 38, 539.

192. Seymour, *Intimate Papers of Colonel House*, I, 414–415 (Diary, January 3, 1917).

Chapter 4

1. Cooper, *Warrior and the Priest*, 22; W. Elliot Brownlee, "The New Freedom and its Evolution," in *A Companion to Woodrow Wilson*, ed. Ross Kennedy (Malden, MA: Wiley Blackwell, 2013), 110. For Wilson's admiration of Gladstone see "Mr Gladstone, a character sketch," *Wilson Papers*, Vol. 1, 624–642.

2. John Milton Cooper Jr., *Woodrow Wilson: A Biography* (New York: Knopf, 2009), 75–76. Cooper also mentions that Wilson and his wife added Kipling to their short list of favorite poets, and that Wilson carried Kipling's poem "If" in his wallet for years.

3. Woodrow Wilson, "The Ideals of America," *Atlantic Monthly* XC (December 1902).

4. Philippine Autonomy Act, August 29, 1916, Public Law 240, 64th Cong.

5. May 25, 1912, *Wilson Papers*, Vol. 24, 443.

6. Arthur Link, *Wilson: The New Freedom* (Princeton, NJ: Princeton University Press, 1956), 347–391; Gardner, *Safe for Democracy*, 45–69; Benjamin T. Harrison, "Wilson and Mexico," in *A Companion to Woodrow Wilson*, ed. Ross Kennedy, 193–206.

7. Quoted in Kathleen Burk, *Britain, America and the Sinews of War, 1914–1918* (London: Unwin Hyman, 1985), 80.

8. September 24, 1916 in Colonel Edward M. House Diary, Volume 4 in *Papers of Colonel Edward M. House* (hereafter *House Papers*), Yale University Sterling Memorial Library, Box 300.

9. Quoted in Arthur Link, *Wilson: Campaigns for Progressivism and Peace, 1916–1917* (Princeton, NJ: Princeton University Press, 1965), 184.

10. Note to Belligerent Governments, December 18, 1916, *FRUS, 1916, Supplement*, 98–99.

11. Address to the Senate, January 22, 1917, *Wilson Papers*, Vol. 40, 536.

12. For overviews of Anglo-American relations in the period leading up to intervention see Burk, *Old World, New World*, 436–446, John Milton Cooper Jr., "The Command of Gold Reversed: American Loans to Britain, 1915–17," *Pacific Historical Review*, 45 (May 1976), 209–230.

13. Thompson, *Woodrow Wilson*, 141–151.

14. Lansing Memorandum, March 20, 1917; House diary, March 28, 1917, *Wilson Papers*, Vol. 41, 440–441, 497–498.

15. Tumulty to Wilson, March 24, 1917, *Wilson Papers*, Vol. 41, 462–464.

16. Diary, January 3, 1917, Seymour, *Intimate Papers of Colonel House*, 414–415.

17. Address to Congress, April 2, 1917, *Wilson Papers*, Vol. 41, 519–527.

18. Lansing to Elkus, February 5, 1917, Lansing to Elkus, March 31, 1917, Elkus to Lansing, February 11, 1917, all in *FRUS: 1917 Supplement 1: The World War* (US Government Printing Office, 1917), 113, 191–192, 134–135.

19. Morgenthau, *All in a Lifetime*, 36.

20. Balakian, *Burning Tigris*, 305–306.

21. Grabill, *Protestant Diplomacy*, 90.

22. Wilson to Dodge, February 6, 1917, *Wilson MSS*, Reel 86.

23. Penrose, *That They May Have Life*, 162–163; Daniel, *American Philanthropy*, 154; Grabill, *Protestant Diplomacy*, 97.

24. DeNovo, *American Interests*, 106.

25. Barton, *Story of Near East Relief*, 55, 64. Many historians echo Barton's interpretation and argue that Wilson's concern for missionary interests dictated his decision not to declare war on the Ottomans. See Joseph L. Grabill, *Protestant Diplomacy and the Near East: Missionary Influence on American Policy, 1810–1927* (Minneapolis: University of Minnesota Press: 1971), 80–105; Merill D. Peterson, *Starving Armenians: America and the Armenian Genocide, 1915–1930 and After* (Charlottesville: University of Virginia Press, 2004), 50; Robert L. Daniel, *American Philanthropy in the Near East: 1820–1960* (Athens: Ohio University Press, 1970), 154; Simon Payslian, "The United States Response to the Armenian Genocide," in Richard G. Hovannisinan, *Looking Back, Moving Forward: Confronting the Armenian Genocide* (New Brunswick, NJ: Transaction Publishers, 2003), 80.

26. Cooper, "A Friend in Power?," 111.

27. Thompson, *Woodrow Wilson*, 152–153.

28. For more background on Wiseman and Anglo-American Relations see W. B. Fowler, *British-American Relations, 1917–1918: The Role of Sir William Wiseman* (Princeton, NJ: Princeton University Press, 1969). For more on British intelligence operations in the US during the war see Christopher Andrew, *Secret Service: The Making of the British Intelligence Community* (London: Heinemann, 1985), 208–209.

29. Quotes in "Memorandum by Wiseman for Chiefs of British Empire," March 8, 1917, "Wiseman advice to Balfour Mission," April 13, 1917, Memorandum on Anglo-American Relations, August 1917, *Papers of Sir William Wiseman* (hereafter *Wiseman Papers*), Yale University, Sterling Memorial Library, Box 4 Folder 110.

30. For more on House's attitude during the period of American neutrality see Charles E. Neu, *Colonel House: A Biography of Woodrow Wilson's Silent Partner* (New York: Oxford University Press, 2015), 139–295.

31. Wiseman to Sir Eric Drummond, October 4, 1917, *Wiseman Papers*, Box 1 Folder 21.

32. Memorandum on Anglo-American Relations, August 1917, *Wiseman Papers*, Box 4 Folder 110.

33. Wiseman to Reading, August 20, 1917, Wiseman to Arthur Murray, August 30, 1918, *Wiseman Papers*, Box 3 Folder 70, Box 2, Folder 36. For an illuminating account with rich insights into the role played by American and British radicals in informing Wilson's "progressive internationalism" see Knock, *To End All Wars*, especially 31-70.

34. Memorandum on Anglo-American Relations, August 1917, *Wiseman Papers*, Box 4 Folder 110.

35. From the diary of Colonel House, April 28, 1917, *Wilson Papers*, Vol. 42, 155-158.

36. Arthur Balfour to Wilson, with enclosure, May 18, 1917, *Wilson Papers*, Vol. 42, 327-342.

37. Sir Eric Drummond to Wiseman, to be passed on to House, June 28, 1917, *Wiseman Papers*, Box 1, Folder 20. For more background on the dire state of British finances see Kathleen Burk, "J. M. Keynes and the Exchange Rate Crisis of July 1917," *Economic History Review* 32, no. 3, 2nd Series (August 1979), 405-416.

38. Wilson to House, July 21, 1917, *Wilson Papers*, Vol. 43, 237-238.

39. Thompson, *Woodrow Wilson*, 142-143; Daniel M. Smith, "Robert Lansing and the Formulation of American Neutrality Policies, 1914-1915" in *The Mississippi Valley Historical Review* 43, no. 1 (June 1956), 59-81.

40. Morgenthau, *Ambassador Morgenthau's Story*, 261.

41. Einstein, *Inside Constantinople*, xxiv.

42. Seymour, *The Intimate Papers of Colonel House*, Vol. 3, 323.

43. Flag Day address, June 14, 1917, *Wilson Papers*, Vol. 42, 501-503; Address to the American Federation of Labour, November 12, 1917, *Wilson Papers*, Vol. 45, 12-14. For an insightful account that emphasizes Wilson's commitment to containing German power to his conception of international peace and security see Kennedy, *The Will to Believe*, especially 128-63.

44. Lawrence Evans, *United States Policy and the Partition of Turkey, 1914-1924* (Baltimore: Johns Hopkins University Press, 1965), 34.

45. June 7, 1917, Desk Diary, *Lansing Papers*, Box 28.

46. Lansing to Wilson, May 17, 1917, *Wilson Papers*, Vol. 42, 316-317.

47. Wilson to State Department, November 23, 1917, *Wilson Papers*, Vol. 42, 162.

48. Richard Ned Lebow, "The Morgenthau Peace Mission," in *Jewish Social Studies* 32, no. 4 (October 1970), 267-285. At this time, British resources were under severe strain due to the German U-Boat campaign and the US had yet to make its July offer of direct financial support. This may also have had an impact on British willingness to attempt to detach the Ottomans. See David Reynolds, *Britannia Overruled: British Policy and World Power In the 20th Century* (London: Longman, 1991), 98.

49. For overview accounts of the aborted mission see F. W. Brecher, "Revisiting Ambassador Morgenthau's Turkish Peace Mission of 1917," *Middle Eastern Studies* 24, no. 3 (July 1988), 357-363; Lebow, "The Morgenthau Peace Mission," 281-285; William Yale, "Henry Morgenthau's Special Mission of 1917," *World Politics* 1, no. 3 (April 1949), 308-320. For Weizmann's account see Chaim Weizmann, *Trial and Error: The Autobiography of Chaim Weizmann* (Philadelphia: Jewish Publication Society of America, 1949), 196-198.

50. July 14, 1917, Colonel Edward M. House Diary, Volume 5 in *House Papers*, Box 301.

51. Oren, *Power, Faith and Fantasy*, 348.

52. Lebow, "The Morgenthau Peace Mission," 267-285, quote on 270.

53. Morgenthau to Wilson, November 26, 1917, Morgenthau Papers, General Correspondence, Container 8.

54. Wilson to Morgenthau, November 27, 1917, *Wilson MSS*, Reel 93.

55. Wilson to House December 3, 1917, *Wilson Papers*, Vol. 45, 187.

56. Fromkin, *A Peace to End All Peace*, 257.

57. Wilson to House, December 1, 1917, *Wilson Papers*, Vol. 45, 177.

58. Seymour, *The Intimate Papers of Colonel House*, Vol. 3, 323.

59. Dodge to Wilson, December 2, 1917, *Wilson MSS*, Reel 93.

60. Woodrow Wilson, *The Public Papers of Woodrow Wilson* (hereafter PPWW), ed. Ray Stannard Baker and William E. Dodd, Vol. V (New York: Harper & Brothers Publishers, 1927), 135-136.

61. S. J. Resolution 109, *Cong. Record*, 65 Cong, 2nd Sess., LVI, part 1, 17.

62. Quoted in DeNovo, *American Interests*, 108.

63. Secretary of State to Chairman of the Committee on Foreign Relations of the Senate, December 6, 1917, *FRUS 1917, Supplement 2: The World War* (Washington, DC: US Government Printing Office, 1917), 448–454.

64. DeNovo, *American Interests*, 108.

65. Dodge to Wilson, December 8, 1917, *Wilson MSS*, Reel 93.

66. Grabill, *Protestant Diplomacy*, 92–93, Daniel, *American Philanthropy in the Near East*, 154; Henry Morgenthau III, "Epilogue: The Rest of the Story," in Henry Morgenthau, *Ambassador Morgenthau's Story*, edited by Peter Balakian (Detroit: Wayne State University Press, 2003), 290; Oren, *Power, Faith and Fantasy*, 344–346.

67. Annual Message on the State of the Union, December 4, 1917, *Wilson Papers*, 194–200.

68. *Congressional Record*, 65th Congress, 2nd Session, Vol. 56, Part 1, Vol. 56, 64.

69. Cooper, *The Warrior and the Priest*, 326–327.

70. Theodore Roosevelt, *Theodore Roosevelt in the Kansas City Star: Wartime Editorials* (Charleston, SC: Bibliolife Books, 2008), 73; Roosevelt speech in Portland, Maine, March 28, 1918, in Morison, *The Letters of Theodore Roosevelt, VIII*, 1294.

71. "The End of Turkey," December 18, 1917, *Los Angeles Times*.

72. See Grabill, *Protestant Diplomacy*, 108–109.

73. Mihran Sevasly to Boghos Nubar, December 13, 1917, "Correspondence Armenia Amerique 1917–1918" Folder, *Records of the Délégation Nationale Arménienne BN*.

74. House diary, December 18, 1917, *Wilson Papers*, Vol. 45, 323–324; Ronald Steel, *Walter Lippmann and the American Century* (New York: Vintage Books, 1981), 133.

75. Memorandum by S. E. Mezes, D. H. Miller, and W. Lippmann, "The Present Situation: The War Aims and Peace Terms it Suggests," December 22, 1917, *Wilson Papers*, Vol. 45, 459–475.

76. Kendrick Clements, *Woodrow Wilson: World Statesmen* (Lawrence: University Press of Kansas, 1992), 188–190.

77. Address to Congress, January 8, 1918, *Wilson Papers*, Vol. 45, 534–539.

78. Memorandum by S. E. Mezes, D. H. Miller and W. Lippmann, "The Present Situation: The War Aims and Peace Terms it Suggests," December 22, 1917, *Wilson Papers*, Vol. 45, 459–475.

79. House diary, January 9, 1918, *Wilson Papers*, Vol. 54, 550–559.

80. Thompson, *Woodrow Wilson*, 165–166.

81. Arno J. Mayer, *Wilson vs Lenin: Political Origins of the New Diplomacy, 1917–1918* (Cleveland, OH: World, 1964), 248, 298–303.

82. Nick Baron and Peter Gatrell, eds., *Homelands: War, Population and Statehood in Eastern Europe and Russia* (London: Anthem Press, 2004), 13.

83. Address to Congress, January 8, 1918, *Wilson Papers*, Vol. 45, 534–539.

84. Smith to Lansing, October 19, 1917 and November 23, 1917, US Department of State, *FRUS, 1918: Russia* (US Government Printing Office, 1918), Vol. II, 578–580, 582; Hovannisian, *Republic of Armenia*, Vol. 1, 179.

85. Lansing to Smith, November 23, 1917, in *FRUS, 1918: Russia*, Vol. II, 582.

86. Summers to Lansing, April 22, 1918, in *FRUS: Russia* (US Government Printing Office, 1918), Vol. I, 471–475.

87. McMeekin, *The Berlin-Baghdad Express*, 318–324.

88. "Summary of Turkish Reports for March 1918," Geneva, April 5, 1918, Intelligence Reports Serial No. 1324–1325, Volume 815, RG 84, *US National Archives*.

89. No. 1 G1, Geneva October 12, 1917, Intelligence Reports Serial No. 1324–1325, Volume 815, RG84, *US National Archives*.

90. Wiseman to Drummond, August 31, 1918, *Wiseman Papers*, Box 1, Folder 24.

91. Wiseman to Drummond, September 8, 1918, *Wiseman Papers*, Box 1, Folder 24.

92. Wilson to Lansing, April 4, 1918, in *Wilson Papers*, Vol. 47, 241–246.

93. Donald Bloxham, *Great Game of Genocide*, 144–145.

94. Garegin Pasdermadjian to Lansing, May 10, 1918, "Correspondence Armenia Amerique 1918–1919" Folder, *Records of the Délégation Nationale Arménienne BN*. See also Lloyd E. Ambrosius, "Wilsonian Diplomacy and Armenia: the limits of power and ideology," 121.

95. Senate Joint Resolution 145, *Congressional Record*, 65th Cong., 2nd Sess., LVI, part 5, 4427 (April 2, 1918).

96. *Congressional Record*, 65th Cong., 2nd Sess., Vol. 66, part 6, 5472–5473 (April 23, 1918).

97. *Lansing Papers*, Memoranda and Notes, May 2, 1918, Diary, Blue Boxes, Box 2, Confidential Memoranda and Notes, April 15, 1915–Dec 30, 1918.

98. Lansing to Wilson, May 2, 1918, *FRUS: Lansing Papers, 1914–1920*, Vol. II, 121.

99. Drummond to Wiseman, July 27, 1918, *Wiseman Papers*, Box 1, Folder 23.

100. Lansing to Wilson, May 8, 1918, *FRUS: Lansing Papers, 1914–1920*, Vol. II, 125–126.

101. Drummond to Wiseman, September 12, 1918, *Wiseman Papers*, Box 1, Folder 24.

102. Evans, *United States Policy and the Partition of Turkey, 1914–1924*, 40–42.

103. Dodge to Barton, June 12, 1918 quoted in Grabill, *Protestant Diplomacy*, 97.

104. "Why the Democrats Defeated the Turkish Treaty," *Literary Digest v.* 92 (Jan. 29, 1927), 10.

105. Barton to Lodge, December 10, 1917, *Morgenthau Papers*, General Correspondence, Container 8.

106. "The Dark Cloud over Armenia," *The Congregationalist and Advance*, March 14, 1918, 326.

107. Editorial, "Leave Turkey and Bulgaria Out," *Missionary Herald*, Volume 114, Number 1, January 1918, 3.

108. H. K. Moderwell, "America's Dilemma on War with Turkey," *New York Tribune*, June 23, 1918, 5.

109. Roosevelt to Dodge, May 11, 1918, *Letters of Theodore Roosevelt*, Vol. 8, 1316–1318

110. Roosevelt to Paul S. Shimmon, July 10, 1918, *Theodore Roosevelt Collection* (hereafter *TR Collection*), Houghton Library, Harvard University, Box 49.

111. Theodore Roosevelt, "Speech at the Chic Society Dinner," January 12, 1918 in *TR Collection*, Speeches 1918.

112. Theodore Roosevelt, "Speech at Sarratoga Springs, N.Y. Convention Hall," July 18, 1918, *TR Collection*, Speeches 1918.

113. Barton to Roosevelt, May 9, 1918, quoted in Grabill, *Protestant Diplomacy*, 96–97.

114. Roosevelt to Gallivan, August 22, 1918, *Letters of Theodore Roosevelt*, Vol. 8, 1365.

115. Sevasly to Nubar, April 27, 1918, "Correspondence Armenia Amerique 1917–1918" Folder, *Records of the Délégation Nationale Arménienne BN*.

116. Nubar to Sevasly, June 26, 1918, Barton to Nubar, March 13, 1918, Nubar to Herbert Adams Gibbons, July 7, 1918, all in "Correspondence Armenia Amerique 1917–1918" Folder, *Records of the Délégation Nationale Arménienne BN*.

117. Sevasly to Nubar, July 16, 1918; Nubar to Sevasly, August 16, 1918, Both in Correspondence Armenia Amerique 1918–1919 Folder, *Records of the Délégation Nationale Arménienne BN*.

118. "United States and Future of Armenia," *Christian Science Monitor*, July 12, 1918 in Correspondence Armenia Amerique 1918–1919 Folder, *Records of the Délégation Nationale Arménienne BN*.

119. Barton, *Story of Near East Relief*, 410.

120. Shaw to James Barton, February 12, 1930, Barton, ABC 6.2 Personal, *ABCFM*.

121. Frank Doubleday to Henry Morgenthau Sr., October 17, 1918, *Morgenthau Papers*, Reel 8.

122. Morgenthau to Wilson, June 11, 1918, *Wilson Papers*, Vol. 67, 284.

123. Wilson to Morgenthau, June 14, 1918, in *Wilson Papers*, Vol. 67, 311.

124. Morgenthau, *Ambassador Morgenthau's Story*, i.

125. Secretary of State to Spanish Ambassador, *FRUS 1918: Supplement 1, The World War* (Washington, DC: US Government Printing Office, 1918), 428.

126. James Gidney, *A Mandate for Armenia* (Kent, OH: State University Press, 1967), 76–77.

127. "The Hand of God," *Los Angeles Times*, November 10, 1918.

128. "Turkey's Approaching End," *New Republic*, November 2, 1918.

129. Manela, *The Wilsonian Moment*, 4. Despite its losses, Britain would emerge from the postwar settlement relatively stronger than its continental rivals. See Reynolds, "Rethinking Anglo-American Relations," 104.

130. Quoted in Moranian, "The Armenian Genocide and American missionary relief efforts," 212.

131. A. P. Hacobian, *Armenia and the War: An Armenian's Point of View with an Appeal to Britain and the Coming Peace Conference* (London: Hodder and Stoughton, 1917), 186.

132. American Board of Commissioners for Foreign Missions, *Annual Report of the American Board of Commissioners for Foreign Missions* (Boston: 1917), 20-21.

133. American Board of Commissioners for Foreign Missions, *Annual Report of the American Board of Commissioners for Foreign Missions* (Boston: 1918), 4.

134. James L. Barton to Cleveland Dodge, October 1, 1918, ABC 3.2. Foreign Department, General Letter Books, v.338, *ABCFM*.

135. Barton to Dodge, October 15, 1918, ABC 3.2, Foreign Department, General Letter Books, v. 338, *ABCFM*.

136. Dodge to Wilson, September 28, 1918, November 19, 1918, *Wilson MSS* Reels 100 and 102.

137. Wilson to House, September 2, 1917, *Wilson Papers*, Vol. 44, 120-121.

138. For background on Inquiry plans for the Near East see House to William Hepburn Buckler, June 10, 1917 and Buckler to House, April 27, October 26, 1917, *William Hepburn Buckler Papers*, Sterling Memorial Library, Yale University, Box 1 Folder 3, 5, 7.

139. Lawrence E. Gelfand, *The Inquiry: American Preparations for Peace, 1917-1919* (New Haven, CT: Yale University Press, 1963), 227-228.

140. Quoted in Steel, Walter Lippmann, 129.

141. Gelfand, *The Inquiry*, 60-62, 240-252.

142. Colonel House Diary, Volume 5, June 15, 1918, *House Papers*, Box 301.

143. Bryce to Barton, July 21, 1917, November 23, 1917, December 17, 1917 in Barton Papers, ABC 76, 3.11, *ABCFM*.

144. The ACASR published this 243-page report in its entirety and as a seven page pamphlet. See William H. Hall, ed., *Reconstruction in Turkey: A Series of Reports Compiled for the American Committee of Armenian and Syrian Relief* (New York: [American Committee for Armenia 1918); William H. Hall and Harold A. Hatch, *Recommendations for Political Reconstruction in the Turkish Empire* (for private distribution, November 1918).

145. James L. Barton, "Suggested Possible Form of Government for the Area Covered by the Ottoman Empire at the Outbreak of the War, Exclusive of Arabia but Inclusive of the Transc-Caucasus," May 21, 1918, Barton, "The Turkish Government: of its Inherent Evils," n.d., both in *U.S. American Commission to Negotiate Peace Records*, Manuscript Division, Library of Congress, Washington, DC, Box 38.

146. Barton to Albert Shaw, May 13, 1898, *Albert Shaw* (hereafter *Shaw Papers*), New York Public Library, Foreign Missions Box 51.

147. James T. Shotwell, "Solutions to Problems in Asiatic Turkey," *Inquiry Papers*, Box 24, Folder 359. Yale University Library.

148. Diary Notes, *William Yale Papers*, Sterling Memorial Library, Yale University, Library, Box 2, Folder 2.

149. Margaret Macmillan, *Paris 1919: Six Months that Changed the World* (New York: Random House, 2001), 17-18.

150. Quincy Wright, *Mandates Under the League of Nations* (Chicago: University of Chicago Press, 1930) 14.

151. Walker, *Armenia: The Survival of a Nation*, 263.

152. Barton, *Story of Near East Relief*, 432-437.

153. Henry Morgenthau, "The Greatest Horror in History," *Red Cross Magazine*, March 13, 1918, 7-15.

154. Dodge to Wilson, November 19, 1918; Proclamation, November 29, 1918, *Wilson MSS*, Reel 102.

155. Undated pamphlet, "More Material for your Sermon on Bible Lands [today A.D. 1918]," enclosed in Charles T. Vickrey to Albert Shaw, March 11, 1918, *Shaw Papers*, NYPL, Box 46—Armenia.

156. Quoted in Armenian National Union of America, *The Case of Armenia* (New York: Armenian National Union of America, 1919), 17. Also quoted in Armen Garo Pasdermadjian, *Armenia: A Leading Factor in the Winning of the War* (New York: American Committee for the Independence of Armenia, 1919).

157. Cardashian to Nubar in *Armenian National Delegation Papers* (hereafter *AND*), Folder 1003, Armenian National Archives (hereafter ANA), Yerevan.

158. Wilson to Nubar, January 23, 1919, *Wilson Papers*, Vol. 53, 226.

159. Wilson to Benedict XV, December 24, 1918, *Wilson Papers*, Vol. 53, 489.

Chapter 5

1. Lincoln Steffens, "Armenians Are Impossible," *Outlook and Independent*, October 14, 1931, 203–223.
2. Lawrence to His Mother, January 30, 1919, "Transcripts of Papers Relating to the Paris Peace Conference, 1919," *T. E. Lawrence Papers*, Bodleian Library, University of Oxford, MS. Eng. d. 3348, folder 64.
3. David Gilmour, *The Long Recessional: The Imperial Life of Rudyard Kipling* (New York: FSG, 2002), 274.
4. Imperial War Cabinet Minutes, December 20, 1918, IWC 44 CAB 23/42, TNA.
5. Louis, *Ends of British Imperialism*, 225–228. See also Pitman B. Potter, "Origin of the System of Mandates under the League of Nations," *American Political Science Review* 16 (November 1922), 563–583.
6. Jan Christian Smuts, *The League of Nations: A Practical Suggestion* (London: Hodder and Stoughton: 1918). See also George Curry, "Woodrow Wilson, Jan Christian Smuts and the Versailles Settlement," *American Historical Review* 66, no. 4, July 1961, 968–986.
7. Allied resolutions, January 30, 1919, *FRUS: The Paris Peace Conference 1919*, Vol. XII (Washington, DC: US Government Printing Office, 1946), 745–746.
8. Gidney, *A Mandate for Armenia*, 77.
9. Both quoted in Macmillan, *Paris 1919*, 389.
10. David Lloyd George, *Memoirs of the Peace Conference* (New Haven, CT: Yale University Press, 1939), Vol. 2, 2811–2812.
11. Nassibian, *Britain and the Armenian Question, 1915–1923*, 267.
12. "Editorial," *Manchester Guardian*, December 29, 1916, 6.
13. David Lloyd George, *Memoirs of the Peace Conference*, Vol. 2, 2811–2812.
14. E. L. Woodward and Rohan Butler, eds., *Documents on British Foreign Policy, 1919–1939* (hereafter *BDFP*), (1st Series, 1952) XII, 557, 563, 565, 577–580, 590–591. See also Thomas A. Bryson, "An American Mandate for Armenia: A Link in British Near Eastern Policy," *Armenian Review* XXI (1968), 23–41.
15. Both quoted in Imperial War Cabinet Minutes, Secret, December 20, 1918, IWC 44 CAB 23/42, TNA.
16. Eastern Committee Minutes, December 2, 1918, *TNA*, CAB 27/24. (These can also be found in *Viscount Alfred Milner Papers*, Bodleian Library, University of Oxford, MS. Milner dep. 137.) These ideas are also developed in a letter to Smuts from Leo Amery, a member of Milner's staff. See Amery to Smuts, April 13, 1918, *Jan Christian Smuts: Correspondence*, Cambridge University Library, Department of Manuscripts and University Archives, Reel 684.
17. Borden to Leo Amery, August 22, 1917, *Kerr Papers*, National Archives of Scotland (hereafter NAS), GD40/17/1064/1. For further discussion of Borden's ideas on relations between the US and British Empire see R. S. Bothwell, "Canadian Representation at Washington: A Study in Colonial Responsibility," *Canadian Historical Review*, 53, no. 2, (1972), 125–148.
18. Imperial War Cabinet Minutes, Secret, December 20, 1918, IWC 44 CAB 23/42 TNA.
19. "Windows of Freedom," *Round Table*, 9 (December 1918), 1–47.
20. For the development of Kerr's ideas on the centrality of an Anglo-American alliance to Britain's postwar strategy see David P. Billington Jr., *Phillip Kerr and the Quest for World Order* (Westport, CT: Praeger, 2006), 39–75.
21. Philip Kerr, "Making the World Safe for Democracy," undated, *Kerr Papers*, GD 40/17/1088, NAS.
22. Quoted in Priscilla Roberts, "World War I and Anglo-American relations: The role of Philip Kerr and the Round Table," *Round Table* 95, no. 383 (2006), 113–139.
23. "The Practical Organisation of Peace," *The Round Table: The Commonwealth Journal of International Affairs* 9, no. 34 (1919), 217–248.
24. "Anglo-American Alliance Urged as World's Hope," *Philadelphia Inquirer*, July 9, 1916. Kerr's words echoed Roosevelt's vision of an Anglo-American alliance. Kerr had earlier written to Roosevelt in 1909 in preparation for the ex-president's visit to Britain, as part of his world tour, advocating an alliance on this basis. See Beloff, *Imperial Sunset*, 168, fn 3.
25. Priscilla Roberts, "World War I and Anglo-American relations: The role of Philip Kerr and the Round Table," *Round Table* 95, no 383 (2006), 113–139.

26. There is a copy of Kerr's "The Practical Organisation of Peace," in the papers of William C. Bullitt, an attaché to the American Commission to Negotiate Peace and chief of the Division of Current Intelligence, alongside drafts of the League of Nations Covenant. See Folder 302—Public and diplomatic papers—World War I and Paris Peace Conf—Original Deposit—Peace Conference—League of Nations (3 of 4) 1918-1919, Box 106, William C. Bullitt Papers, Sterling Memorial Library, Yale University.

27. For an overview of Toynbee's involvement with the Armenian cause during the war and his role in postwar planning for the Ottoman Empire see William H. McNeil, *Arnold Toynbee: A Life* (Oxford: Oxford University Press, 1989), 64–92.

28. Quoted in Gidney, *A Mandate for Armenia*, 52.

29. For more on Lawrence's role in Paris see John E. Mack, *A Prince of Our Disorder: The Life of T. E. Lawrence* (Cambridge, MA: Harvard University Press, 1998), 263–273.

30. Kipling's friend Lewis Freeman, an American journalist, published an article invoking his poem as a call for an American mandate in the Near East. See Lewis R. Freeman, "Take Up the White Man's Burden!" Rudyard Kipling and His Poems of Prophecy," *World's Work*, July 1919, 303–307.

31. Kipling to Frank Doubleday, August 27, 1919, in *The Letters of Rudyard Kipling: 1911–1919*, ed. Thomas Pinney (Basingstoke: Macmillan, 1999), Vol. 4, 567.

32. Kipling passed a letter from Roosevelt, expressing his support for closer Anglo-American relations, to Milner shortly before the peace conference. Kipling to Milner, December 24, 1918, in Pinney, *Letters of Rudyard Kipling*, Vol. 4, 527.

33. First quote in Roosevelt to Bryce, August 7, 1918, in Morison, ed., *The Letters of Theodore Roosevelt*, VIII, 1358–1359. Second quote in "Spirit of Victory Marks Marne Day," *New York Times*, September 7, 1918.

34. American Commissioner in Constantinople Lewis Heck to Secretary of State, January 14, 1919, Volume 407, Turkey General Correspondence 1919, RG 84 350-10-10-3, *US National Archives*.

35. Morris, *Colonel Roosevelt*, 559; For Kipling's poem see Rudyard Kipling, *Rudyard Kipling's Verse* (Garden City: Doubleday Page & Co., 1922), 414.

36. "Theodore Roosevelt and Armenia," *The New Armenia*, March 1919, Volume 11.

37. Lloyd E. Ambrosius, "Wilson, Republicans, and French Security after World War I," *Journal of American History* 59 (September 1972), 341–352.

38. Stephen Wertheim, "The League That Wasn't: American Designs for a Leaglist-Sanctionalist League of Nations and the Intellectual Origins of International Organization," *Diplomatic History* 35, no. 5 (2011) 797–836. See especially 819–821.

39. *Congressional Record*, 65th Cong., 3rd Sess., 237.

40. David Cannadine, "Churchill and the Pitfalls of Family Piety," in *Churchill: A Major New Assessment of his Life in Peace and War*, ed. Robert Blake and William Roger Louis (Oxford: Oxford University Press, 1993), 17.

41. Henry Cabot Lodge to Moreton Frewen, May 10, 1897, Box 10, September 26, 1918 and November 16, 1918, Box 34, *Moreton Frewen Papers* (hereafter *Frewen Papers*), Manuscript Division, Library of Congress (hereafter LOC).

42. Frewen to Lodge, October 14, 1918, Box 34, *Frewen Papers*, LOC. Frewen develops these ideas further in Frewen to Arthur Balfour, October 2, 1918, Box 34, *Frewen Papers*, LOC and Frewen to Lodge, May 26, 1919 and October 9, 1919, Reel 58, *Henry Cabot Lodge Papers* (hereafter *Lodge Papers*), Massachusetts Historical Society Society (hereafter MHS), Boston.

43. Lodge to Frewen, September 26, 1918 and November 16, 1918, Box 34, *Frewen Papers*, LOC.

44. E. J. Dillon to Frewen, September 18, 1918, Balfour to Frewen, September 30, 1918, Valentine Chirol to Frewen, December 3, 1918, Lord Landsdowne to Frewen, December 9, 1918, Box 34, *Frewen Papers*, LOC.

45. For Bryce's advocacy of a League of Nations see Egerton, *Great Britain and the Creation of the League of Nations*, 18–23, 180.

46. Bryce to Balfour, January 15, 1919, in *Kerr Papers*, GD 40/17/107 NAS.

47. Frederic Howe, *The Confessions of a Reformer* (New York: Charles Scribner's Sons, 1925), 295–298. For a similar exchange between Curtis and General Tasker H. Bliss, a US Peace

Commissioner, who was also highly reluctant to take on the mandate see "Diary from Peace Conference," December 22, 1918, *Tasker H. Bliss Papers*, Manuscript Division, Library of Congress, Box 244, Folder—December 1918–January 1919.

48. David Hunter Miller, *The Drafting of the Covenant* (New York: G. P. Putnam's Sons, 1928), Vol. I, 47.

49. Secretary of State to General T. H. Bliss, December 16, 1918, *FRUS*, Paris Peace Conference, Vol. I, 296–297; Robert Lansing, *The Peace Negotiations: a Personal Narrative* (Boston, Mass, 1921), 99–101.

50. Secret Memo, Imperial War Cabinet, December 30, 1918, in *Wilson Papers*, Vol. 53, 558–569.

51. Thompson, *Woodrow Wilson*, 194–196.

52. Meeting of Council of Ten, January 30, 1919, *Wilson Papers*, Vol. 53, 369–371.

53. Wilson to Baker, February 8, 1919, *Wilson Papers*, Vol. 55, 27–28.

54. Baker to Wilson, February 11, 1919, in *Wilson Papers*, Vol. 55, 81–82.

55. Nubar to Wilson, January 29 and February 6, 1919, in *Wilson Papers*, Vol. 54, 346, 516–518.

56. Address in Boston, February 24, 1919, in *Wilson Papers*, Vol. 55, 238–245.

57. Remarks to Democratic National Committee, February 28, 1919, *Wilson Papers*, Vol. 55, 309–324.

58. "Editorial," *Missionary Herald* (March 1919), Vol. 115, 91–96.

59. Vahan Cardashian, ed., *Should America Accept Mandate for Armenia?* (New York, 1919).

60. "Armenia," *New York Times*, February 16, 1919, 1.

61. "America and Armenia," *New Republic*, March 8, 1919, 167–169.

62. Seymour, *Intimate Papers of Colonel House*, 358–359.

63. Kerr to Lloyd George, February 26, 1919, 'Copy notes of interview between M. Clemenceau, Colonel House and "Myself" at the Ministry of War, rue Dominicque,' March 7, 1919, both in *Kerr Papers*, GD 40/17/ 1173 and 1233.

64. *Congressional Record*, 66th Cong., 1st Sess., 7051–7054.

65. *Congressional Record*, 66th Cong., 1st Sess., 7051–7054. See also Borah to O. L. Roberts, December 5, 1919, *Papers of William Borah*, Library of Congress, Manuscript Division, Washington DC, Box 76.

66. Hiram Johnson to Charles K. Mclatchey, March 22, 1919, *Papers of Hiram Johnson*, Bancroft Library, University of Berkeley, California, Part III, Senatorial Papers, Box 2.

67. Wilson to W. J. Bryan, March 19, 1919, *Wilson Papers*, Vol. 56, 95–96.

68. Diary of Dr Grayson, March 20, 1919, Meeting of council of Four, March 20, 1919, Diary of Vance McCormick, March 22, 1919, Memorandum of Arthur James Balfour, March 23, 1919, Memorandum, March 25, 1919, in *Wilson Papers*, Vol. 56, 102–103, 116–118, 180, 203–204, 272–275.

69. Harry N. Howard, *The Partition of Turkey, 1913–1923* (Norman: University of Oklahoma Press, 1931), 47–48.

70. Herbert Hoover, *The Memoirs of Herbert Hoover: Years of Adventure, 1874–1920* (New York: Macmillan, 1951–1952), 386–387.

71. Baker, *Woodrow Wilson and the World Settlement*, Vol. 2, 24.

72. Hovannisian, *Republic of Armenia*, Vol. 1, 282.

73. Commissioners' meeting, March 13, 1919, *FRUS, The Paris Peace Conference 1919*, Vol. II (Washington, DC: US Government Printing Office, 1919), 116; Lansing, *The Peace Negotiations*, 100–101.

74. Hovannisian, *Republic of Armenia*, Vol. 2, 49–50.

75. Herbert Hoover, *The Ordeal of Woodrow Wilson* (New York: McGraw Hill, 1958), 225–229.

76. Lansing, *The Peace Negotiations*, 100–101.

77. "Interview of Magie and Westermann with President Wilson on 22 May 1919," in *Wilson Papers*, Vol. 59, 374–376.

78. Minutes of Council of Four, May 14, 1919, *FRUS, Paris Peace Conference*, Vol. V, 614–623. Wilson's emphasis on obtaining congressional consent should be noted. The record made by official interpreter, Paul Mantoux, states Clemenceau asked if it was possible to predict whether the Senate would approve the mandate and Wilson responded: "I believe it will accept the responsibility." This contrasts with the official minutes, prepared by Sir Maurice Hankey of the British delegation, in which Wilson merely warns he will need American

approval. (Hankey's and Mantoux's Notes, May 14, 1919, in *Wilson Papers*, Vol. 59, 136–147). It is not readily apparent why the French interpretation portrays a president more confident of gaining Senate approval, although the nuances of language probably played a part. However, a statement on the likelihood of Senate consent would have been inconsistent with Wilson's repeated warnings to the Allies that he could not promise American approval. As Westermann later recalled, although Wilson strongly favored the mandate, he never heard anyone claim the president "made any promise which would tend to pre-empt the constitutional right of the American people to answer this question through their representatives in Congress." See William Linn Westermann, "The Armenian Problem and the Disruption of Turkey," in *What Really Happened at Paris: The Story of the Peace Conference, 1918–1919*, ed. Edward Mandell House and Charles Seymour (New York: Charles Scribner's Sons, 1921) 187–188.

79. Minutes of Council of Four, May 14, 1919, in *FRUS, The Paris Peace Conference, 1919*, Vol. V (Washington, DC: US Government Printing Office, 1919), 614–623.

80. Mantoux's Notes, May 21, 1919, in *Wilson Papers*, Vol. 59, 345; Mantoux, *Deliberations*, Vol. II, 137; Macmillan, *Paris, 1919*, 446–448.

81. Meeting of Council of Four, June 25, 1919, *in Wilson Papers*, Vol. 59, 156–157.

82. June 27, 1919, *FRUS, Paris Peace Conference*, Vol. VI, 729.

83. Diary of Dr Grayson, June 27, 1919, Notes of Walter Weyl, June 27, 1919, Report by Charles Thompson, June 27, 1919, Diary of Ray Stannard Baker, June 27, 1919, in *Wilson Papers*, Vol. 59, 238, 240, 246, 253.

84. "Uncle Sam as a Receiver for the Bankrupt Turk," *Literary Digest, Vol.* 61 (June 7, 1919), 10.

85. Wilson speech, July 10, 1919, *Wilson Papers*, Vol. 61, 426–436.

86. Joseph P. Tumulty, *Woodrow Wilson As I Know Him* (London: Heinemann, 1922), 354–380.

87. *Congressional Record*, 66th Cong, 1st Session, Vol. 58, part 1, 128–77.

88. Report of a Press Conference, July 10, 1919, *Wilson Papers*, Vol. 61, 424.

89. Lloyd E. Ambrosius, *Woodrow Wilson and the American Diplomatic Tradition: The Treaty Fight in Perspective* (Cambridge: Cambridge University Press, 1987), 151–152.

90. John Milton Cooper Jr., *Breaking the Heart of the World* (Cambridge: Cambridge University Press, 2001), 73–83.

91. White to Lodge, February 10, April 12, May 25, 1919, *Papers of Elihu Root* (hereafter *Root Papers*), Library of Congress, Washington DC, Box 161.

92. Lodge to Frewen, June 23, 1919, *Lodge Papers*, MHS.

93. The Acting Secretary of State to the Commission to Negotiate Peace, June 28, 1919, *FRUS, 1919*, Vol. II, 824.

94. Hoover, *Ordeal of Woodrow Wilson*, 142–143.

95. Memorandum by the Director General of Relief, [Hoover], July 16 1919, *FRUS*, Paris Peace Conference, Vol. X, 482; Gidney, *Mandate for Armenia*, 170.

96. Wilson to Lansing, August 4, 1919, *Wilson Papers*, Vol. 62, 149.

97. "Turkish Army Moves to Destroy the Armenians," *New York Times*, July 31, 1919.

98. "Armenia Demands Action," *New York Times*, September 24, 1919.

99. Kerr to Lloyd George, July 29, 1919, *Kerr Papers*, GD40/17/791.

100. Lloyd George, *Memoirs*, II, 817–818.

101. Williams, to Wilson, Wilson to Williams, August 9, August 12, 1919, in *John Sharp Williams Papers*, Manuscript Division, Library of Congress, Box 2, Special Correspondence between John Sharp Williams and Wilson.

102. Wilson to Dodge, August 14, 1919, *Wilson Papers*, Vol. 62, 259–260, 285–286.

103. Notes of a Meeting of the Heads of Delegation, August 25, 1919, *FRUS: Paris Peace Conference, 1919*, Vol. VII, 839–840.

104. Gerard to Lansing, August 14, 1919, Internal Affairs of Armenia (Microfilm Publication T1192), file 860J.01/70, RG59, NARA.

105. Eliot to Morgenthau, November 8, 1919, *Morgenthau Papers*, General Correspondence, Containers 9/10, LOC.

106. Frederick S. Calhoun, *Power and Principle: Armed Intervention in Wilsonian Foreign Policy* (Kent, OH: Kent State University Press, 1986), 191; Robert Schulzinger, ed., *A Companion to American Foreign Relations* (Malden, MA: Wiley Blackwell, 2003), 155.

107. Lodge to White, August 19, 1919, *Root Papers*, Box 161.
108. This amendment reversed award of the Shantung Peninsula to Japan and restored it to China.
109. Address in Kansas City, September 6, 1919, *Wilson Papers*, Vol. 63, 71.
110. *Congressional Record*, 66th Congress, 1st Session, Senate Proceedings, Vol. 58, part 5, 5219–5225.
111. Michael A Wetherson and Hal Bochin, *Hiram Johnson: Political Revivalist* (Lanham, MD: University Press of America, 1995), 100.
112. "Why United States Should Accept Armenian Mandate,"*New York Herald*, September 5, 1919, contained in *Armenian National Delegation Papers*, Folder 545.
113. "A Mandate for Armenia," *New York Sun*, August 27, 1919, 197.
114. "The Same Old Turk," *Los Angeles Times*," September 11, 1919.
115. "Washing Our Hands of Armenia," *New York Times*, August 28, 1919.
116. "*Our Duty to Armenia*," *New Republic*, September 10, 1919.
117. "Untitled," *The Commercial & Financial Chronicle*, May 31, 1919, 2169.
118. Mormon missionaries had also been active in the Ottoman Empire since the nineteenth century. Like Protestant missionaries, they had struck up close relations with the Armenians. See Seçil Karal Akgun, "Some Abstracts from the Mormon Missionaries about the Turks and Armenians," *Review of Armenian Studies* 1, no. 1 (2002), 65–79.
119. Address in Salt Lake City, September 23, 1919, *Wilson Papers*, Vol. 63, 449–463.
120. The full extent of the president's condition was concealed from the public, with his doctor Cary T. Grayson informing the press he was suffering from "nervous exhaustion." *Washington Post*, October 4, 1919, in *Wilson Papers*, 634–635.
121. Report by Crane and King, August 28, 1919, in *FRUS: The Paris Peace Conference, 1919*, Vol. XII, 751–863. The most comprehensive account of the King-Crane Commission is Andrew Patrick, *America's Forgotten Middle East Initiative: The King-Crane Commission of 1919* (London: I. B. Tauris, 2015). See also Harry N. Howard, *The King-Crane Commission: an American inquiry in the Middle East* (Beirut: Khayat, 1963).
122. Crane to Wilson, July 10, 1919, in *Donald M. Brodie Papers* (hereafter *Brodie Papers*), Hoover Institution Archives, Stanford University Box 1.
123. Crane to Wilson, August 31, 1919, *Wilson Papers*, Vol. 62, 607–609.
124. *New York Herald*, August 30, 1919; *New York Tribune*, August 30, 1919; Howard, *The King-Crane Commission*, 258.
125. US Naval Radio Press 1919, folder 3d, Box 1, *Louis E. Browne Papers*, Hoover Institution Library, Stanford University.
126. The regional ethnography was further complicated by the large Kurdish presence in the same region. The US commission in Paris had shown little concern for their independence struggle. The British government took greater interest and briefly flirted with the idea of establishing an independent Kurdish state, principally for strategic reasons. See Macmillan, *Paris 1919*, 444–446.
127. Papers concerning Sivas Congress, folder 3b, box 1, *Browne Papers*.
128. Heck to Lansing, February 7, 1919, Volume 405, Turkey General Correspondence 1919, RG 84, US National Archives.
129. Quoted in Lord Kinross, *Ataturk: The Rebirth of a Nation* (London: Weidenfeld & Nicolson, 1971), 217.
130. "Speech at the Annual Luncheon of the American-Turkish Society by Dr. Ahmed Emin Yalman," undated, *Ahmed Emin Yalman Papers*, Hoover Institution Archives, Stanford University, Box 16. See also Adivar, *Memoirs*, 12; Yalman, *Turkey in My Time*, 71–73.
131. Andrew Mango, *Ataturk* (London: John Murray, 1999), 246–248.
132. For more on the background to this see Macmillan, *Paris, 1919*, 438–445.
133. Quoted in Kinross, *Ataturk*, 191.
134. "New Turkey Forced as Sultan Fails to Yield to Ultimatum," *Chicago Daily News*, October 13, 1919, 1–2.
135. International Commission on Mandates, Related Materials, *Donald M. Brodie Papers*, Box 1, HIA.
136. Telegraphic dispatches in draft form from Sivas, September 1919, *Browne Papers*, Box 1, Folder 3e.

137. Heck to Lansing, April 28, 1919, Vol. 405, Turkey General Correspondence 1919, RG 84, NARA.
138. Straus, *Under Four Administrations*, 142–147. See also Isa Blumi, *Ottoman Refugees, 1789–1939: Migration in a Post-Imperial World* (London: Bloomsbury Academic, 2013), 112–114.
139. See Manela, *Wilsonian Moment*, 92.
140. Halide Edib, "Letters to the American Public," Istanbul, August 17, 1919, Folder 3j, Box 1, *Browne Papers*, HIA.
141. Edib to Charles Crane, August 20, 1919, *Crane Family Papers*, Box 6, Butler Library, Columbia University; Adivar, *Memoirs*, xiii.
142. "Kemal Pasha Gives Aims of New Turkey," *Chicago Daily News*, October 16, 1919, 2.
143. Edib, *Turkish Ordeal*, 12.
144. Kinross, *Ataturk*, 219–226.
145. James G. Harbord, "Mustafa Kemal Pasha and his Party," *World's Work* XL (June 1920), 188.
146. Louis E. Browne to Admiral Mark L. Bristol, October 24, 1919, Folder 6, Box 1, *Browne Papers*, HIA.
147. Herbert Corey to Browne, October (1919), Folder 5, Box 1, *Browne Papers*, HIA.
148. Quoted in Hovannisian, *Republic of Armenia*, Vol. 2, 369.
149. Desk Diary of Robert Lansing, August 21, 1919, in *Wilson Papers*, Vol. 62, 453–454.
150. Senate Document 106, Hearings before the Committee on Foreign Relations, United States Senate, on the Treaty of Peace with Germany (Washington, DC, 1919).
151. See Lodge to Root, November 3, *Root Papers*, Box 161.
152. Woodward and Butler, eds., *BDFP*, IV, 1st ser., 797.
153. Memorandum titled Prime Minister–Syria, November 15, 1919, *Kerr Papers*, GD 40/17/56/1348. Kerr would recover from his disillusionment and, as British ambassador to Washington, play a significant role in helping to establish an Anglo-American alliance prior to US entry in World War II. See David Reynolds, *Lord Lothian and Anglo-American Relations, 1939–1940* (Philadelphia: American Philosophical Society, 1983).
154. Gilmour, *The Long Recessional*, 274.
155. Lansing to Polk, November 17, 1919, *Wilson Papers*, Vol. 64, 54–57.
156. November 29, 1919, *Hairenik*, quoted in Hovannisian, *Republic of Armenia*, Vol. 2, 397.

Chapter 6

1. Winston S. Churchill, "Will America Fail Us?," *Illustrated Sunday Herald*, November 30, 1919.
2. For Churchill's perspective on the US in the immediate postwar period see Martin Gilbert, *Churchill and America* (London: Free Press, 2005), 86–96.
3. Churchill, "Will America Fail Us?"
4. Major Gen. James G. Harbord, "Conditions in the Near East: Report of the American Military Mission to Armenia," 66th Cong., 2nd Sess., Document no. 266, oriented April 13, 1920.
5. Major Gen. James G. Harbord, "Report of the American Military Mission to Armenia."
6. Quoted in Gidney, *A Mandate for Armenia*, 189.
7. Harbord to Morgenthau, November 28, 1919, *Morgenthau Papers*, General Correspondence, Containers 9/10; Hovannisian, "The Armenian Genocide and US Post-War Commissions," in Winter, *America and the Armenian Genocide of 1915*, 271–274.
8. *Congressional Record*, 66th Cong., 1st Sess., Vol. 58, pt. 9 (Washington, 1919), 8718.
9. Hovannisian, "The Armenian Genocide and US Post-War Commissions," 271–274.
10. Mark L. Bristol to Polk, October 1, 1919, *Admiral Mark L. Bristol Papers* (hereafter *Bristol Papers*), Box 31, Manuscript Collection, Library of Congress, Washington DC.
11. Examples include Constantinople to Paris, July 25, December 13, 1919, March 30, April 22, 1920, *Bristol Papers*, Box 31.
12. Memorandum, December 14, 1919, *Bristol Papers*, Box 31.
13. William Stivers, *Supremacy and Oil: Iraq, Turkey and the Anglo-American World Order, 1918–1930* (Ithaca, NY: Cornell University Press), 111; Fromkin, *A Peace to End All Peace*, 533–535; DeNovo, *American Interests and Policies*, 169–176.

14. Constantinople to Paris, July 25, 1919, *Bristol Papers*, Box 31.
15. Thomas A. Bryson, "Admiral Mark L. Bristol, an Open-Door Diplomat in Turkey," *International Journal of Middle East Studies*, Vol. 5, No.4, (1974), 450–467; Roger R. Trask, *The United States Response to Turkish Nationalism and Reform, 1914–1939* (Minneapolis: University of Minnesota Press, 1971), 246.
16. Bristol to Knapp, December 19, 1919, Bristol submission for "Who's Who in America," January 20, 1919, *Bristol Papers*, Box 31.
17. Bristol memorandum, May 18, 1919, *Bristol Papers*, Box 31.
18. Mark L. Bristol to Vice Admiral H. S. Knapp, October 11, 1919, *Bristol Papers*, Box 31.
19. Bristol to Caleb F. Gates, December 13, 1919, *Bristol Papers*, Box 31.
20. The US High Commissioner to Turkey to Secretary of State, December 5, 1919, Volume 407, Turkey General Correspondence 1919, RG 84 350-10-10-3, *US National Archives*.
21. Bristol to Polk, August 7, 1920, *Bristol Papers*, Box 31.
22. Bristol to Unnamed Standard Oil representative, December 14, 1919, *Mark Bristol Papers*, Box 31.
23. Quoted in John W. Davis Diary, October 30, 1919, *John W. Davis Papers* (hereafter *Davis Papers*), Sterling Memorial Library, Yale University, Box 13.
24. John W. Davis Diary, August 18, August 26, September 26, October 25, 1919, *Davis Papers*, Box 13.
25. John W. Davis Diary, October 17, 1919, *Davis Papers*, Box 13.
26. Davis to Lansing, April 5, 1920, *Davis Papers*, Box 9.
27. Polk to Davis, November 15, 1919, *John W. Davis Papers*, Box 9.
28. Commission to Negotiate Peace to Secretary of State, November 30, 1919, *FRUS*, Vol. IX, 25.
29. Polk to Davis, December 8, 1919, *John W. Davis Papers*, Box 9.
30. The Commission to Negotiate Peace to the Secretary of State, November 29, 1919, *FRUS*, Vol. IX, 675–676.
31. Nassibian, *Britain and the Armenian Question*, 170–172.
32. "International Situation," House of Commons Debate, December 18, 1919, *Hansard*, 5th Ser. 1919, Vol. 38, cc. 719–729.
33. "Turkish Rule in Armenia" House of Lords Debate, December 17, 1919, *Hansard*, 5th Ser., 1919, Vol. 38, cols. 279–300.
34. "Turkish Rule in Armenia" House of Lords Debate, December 17, 1919, *Hansard*, 5th Ser., 1919, Vol. 38, col. 299. See also Fisher, *James Bryce*, 233–234, 238–239, 242–247.
35. Hovannisian, *Republic of Armenia*, 10–11.
36. Sachar, *The Emergence of the Middle East, 1914–1924*, 357–360.
37. Barton, *Story of Near East Relief*, 124–127.
38. Barton to Bryce, November 29, 1919, Barton Papers, ABC 3.2, *ABCFM*.
39. Barton to Morgenthau, February 26, 1920, March 8, 1920, *Morgenthau Papers*, General Correspondence, Containers 9/10.
40. Grayson to Morgenthau, February 27, 1920, *Morgenthau Papers*, General Correspondence, Containers 9/10.
41. Morgenthau to Barton, March 16, 1920, *Morgenthau Papers*, General Correspondence, Containers 9/10.
42. Gates to Bristol, February 14, 1920, *Bristol Papers*, Box 31
43. "Why Take the Turk?" *New York Times*, November 4, 1919.
44. Hovannisian, *Republic of Armenia*, Vol. 4, 2–3.
45. Hovannisian, *Republic of Armenia*, Vol. 4, 2–4.
46. Lodge to Gerard, November 17, 1919, quoted in Grabill, *Protestant Diplomacy*, 224.
47. "Armenian Mandate Assailed by Gerard," *New York Times*, December 8 1919.
48. Hovannisian, *Republic of Armenia*, Vol. 3, 388.
49. Gidney, *A Mandate for Armenia*, 192–221.
50. *BDFP*, 1st ser., IV, 1085–1087.
51. DeNovo, *American Interests in the Middle East*, 124.
52. Macmillan, *Paris 1919*, 445–446.
53. Hovannisian, *The Republic of Armenia*, Vol 3, 20–112.
54. Polk to Wilson, February 21, 1920, in *Wilson Papers*, Vol. 64, 448–450.

55. Arthur Link, "Woodrow Wilson and the Constitutional Crisis," in *Papers on Presidential Disability and the 25th Amendment by Medical, Historical and Political Authorities*, ed. Kenneth Thompson (Lanham, MD, University Press of America, 1996), 54–71.

56. Polk to Wilson, 6, 10 and March 22, 1920 and Wilson to Polk, 8 and March 17, 1920, in *Wilson Papers*, Vol. 65, 64–65, 72–77, 91, 111–115.

57. Thompson, *Woodrow Wilson*, 236.

58. Jackson Day message, January 8, 1920, *Wilson Papers*, Vol. 64, 257–259.

59. Thompson, *Woodrow Wilson*, 238.

60. Wilson to Hitchcock, March 8, 1920, *Wilson Papers*, Vol. 65, 67–72.

61. Phillip M. Brown, "The Mandate over Armenia," *American Journal of International Law* 14, no. 3, (January 1920): 396–406.

62. Wilson to Dodge, April 19, 1920, in *Wilson Papers*, Vol. 62, 202.

63. "Harbord Report Asks Expulsion of Turk From Europe," *New York Times*, April 4, 1920.

64. Steel, *Walter Lippmann and the American Century*, 168.

65. "Fears Armenian Mandate," *New York Times*, April 10, 1920.

66. "The Harbord Report," *New York Times*, April 6, 1920.

67. Thompson, *Woodrow Wilson*, 241.

68. Quoted in Wesley N. Bagby, *The Road to Normalcy: The Presidential Campaign of 1920* (Baltimore: Johns Hopkins University Press, 1962), 23.

69. Clarence Day Jr., "The Everlasting Armenians," *Harper's Magazine*, January 1920, 281–284.

70. Lansing Diary, January 7, 1920, in *Lansing Papers*, Blue Boxes, Box 2, Confidential Memoranda and Notes, January 1, 1920–May 23. 1922; Cooper, *Breaking the Heart of the World*, 322–324.

71. "Washington Astonished by Nomination of Bainbridge Colby to Succeed Lansing," *New York Times*, February 26, 1920; "President Wilson 'Comes Back,'" *Literary Digest*, February 28, 192; *Wilson Papers*, Vol. 65, 5–7.

72. Colby to Wilson, April 23, 1920, *Wilson Papers*, Vol. 65, 222; Colby to Pastermadijan, April 23, 1920, *FRUS: 1920*, Vol. III, 778.

73. Woodrow Wilson, *The Messages and Papers of Woodrow Wilson*, ed. Albert Shaw, II (New York, 1924), 1183–1187.

74. *BDFP*, 1st ser., VIII, 20–21.

75. Quoted in *Salt Lake Telegram*, March 26, 1920.

76. *BDFP*, 1st ser., VIII, 63.

77. Ambrosius, "Wilsonian Diplomacy and Armenia," 140.

78. US Ambassador to Italy (Robert Underwood Johnson) to Secretary of State, April 27, 1920, *FRUS: 1920*, Vol. III, 779–781.

79. *Congressional Record*, 66th Cong., 2nd Sess. (May 13, 1920), 6973–6979.

80. Henry Fountain Ashurst, Diary, May 24, 1920, *Wilson Papers*, Vol. 65, 323–324.

81. Lodge to Bryce, April 20, 1920, *Lodge Papers*, MSH, Reel 67.

82. Gerard to Wilson, May 14 and 18, 1920, in *Wilson Papers*, Vol. 65, 287–288, 298. Gerard informed Wilson that his perspective was shared by the Armenian Republic's ambassador to Washington, Karekin Pasdermadjian. See Sevasly to Nubar, May 30, 1920, folder 590, AND, ANA.

83. Wilson to Bainbridge Colby, May 11, 1920, and Colby to Wilson, May 20, 1920, *Wilson Papers*, Vol. 65, 202.

84. Hovannisian, *Republic of Armenia*, Vol. 4, 12.

85. Hoover, *Ordeal of Woodrow Wilson*, 228.

86. Clements, *Woodrow Wilson*, 216.

87. Lansing to Davis, May 31, 1920, *Davis Papers*, Box 9

88. John W. Davis Diary, April 29, 1920, *Davis Papers*, Box 9

89. Wilson message to Congress, May 24, 1920, in *Wilson Papers*, Vol. 65, 320–323.

90. *Congressional Record*, 66th. Cong., 2nd Sess. Vol. 69, 6978–6979.

91. *Congressional Record*, 66th Cong, 2nd Sess, Vol. 69, 7714, 7875.

92. *Congressional Record*, 66th Cong, 2nd Sess, Vol. 69, 8051–8074.

93. *Congressional Record*, 66th Cong, 2nd Sess, Vol. 69, 7964–7970.

94. *Congressional Record*, 66th Cong, 2nd Sess, Vol. 69, 7533–7534, 7875–7876; see also Rayford W. Logan, *The Senate and the Versailles Mandate System* (Westport, CT: Greenwood Press, 1975), 97–102.

95. *Congressional Record*, 66th Cong, 2nd Sess, Vol. 69, 7877–7883.

96. *Congressional Record*, 66th Cong, 2nd Sess, Vol. 69, 8072–8073.

97. Thomas A. Bryson III, "Woodrow Wilson, the Senate, Public Opinion and the Armenian Mandate Question, 1919–1920," PhD diss., University of Georgia (1965), 76–97.

98. *Chicago Tribune*, May 26 and 29, 1920, quoted in Grabill, *Protestant Diplomacy*, 243.

99. "For a Free Armenia," May 8, "Armenia Not For Us," May 25, "That Armenian 'Touch,'" 30, 1920, *Los Angeles Times*.

100. "Testing Our Altruism," *New York Times*, May 26, 1920.

101. "The Armenian Swindle," *New Republic*, May 12, 1920.

102. "Full Text of Lodge's Speech Sounding Republican Convention Keynote," *New York Times*, June 9, 1920.

103. "Republican Platform 1920," in Republican National Committee, Speeches of Warren G. Harding of Ohio, Republican candidate for president, from his acceptance of the nomination to October 1, 1920 (New York, 1920), 3.

104. Einstein, *A Diplomat Looks Back*, xxviii

105. Lewis Einstein, "The Armenian Mandate," *The Nation* 110, no. 2866 (June 5, 1920), 762.

106. "Long Fight Over Platform," *New York Times*, July 3, 1920.

107. Note of June 19, 1920, by Carter Glass, cited in Rixey Smith and Norman Beasley, *Carter Glass: A Biography* (New York: Longmans Green & Co., 1939).

108. Stephen Bonsal, *Suitors and Supplicants: The Little Nations at Versailles* (New York: Prentice Hall, 1946), 197.

109. Fred Israel, ed., *Major Peace Treaties of Modern History, 1648–1967* (New York: McGraw-Hill, 1967), 2084–2088;.

110. Wilson to Davis, July 4, 1920 and Colby to Wilson, July 20, 1920, in *Wilson Papers*, Vol. 65, 496–497, 532; Colby to Wilson, August 26 and November 11, 1920, Wilson to Colby, September 10 and November 13, 1920, in *Wilson Papers*, Vol. 66, 65, 110, 349–350, 357. See also Ambrosius, "Wilsonian Diplomacy and Armenia," 142.

111. Colby to Wilson, November 26, 27, 28 and 29, 1920, Davis to Wilson, December 6, 1920, Davis to Hymans, December 15, 1920, in *Wilson Papers*, Vol. 66, 421–423, 426–428, 436–437, 443–444, 480, 517–518; see also Morgenthau III, "Epilogue: The Rest of the Story," 302, Gidney, *A Mandate for Armenia*, 240–245.

112. "Harding Decries 'Meddling Abroad,'" *New York Times*, September 19, 1920.

113. By the time that Near East Relief ceased its work in 1930, it had helped to distribute over a hundred million dollars in aid, operating on a scale that was only surpassed by the American Red Cross and Hoover's American Relief Administration during this period. See Daniel, *American Philanthropy in the Near East*, 169.

114. Westermann, "Armenian Problem," 176–224, 465–469.

115. Herbert Hoover, "Armenian Speech, Philadelphia 10 April 1920," *Herbert Hoover Papers*, Hoover Institution Archives, Stanford University, Box 94. For more on Hoover's foreign policy outlook in this period see David Burner, *Herbert Hoover: A Public Life* (New York: Knopf, 1979), 72–120.

116. Bryce to Barton, January 5, 1921, Barton Papers, ABC 3:11, *ABCFM*.

117. Peet to Barton, June 15, 1920, copy in *Montgomery Family Papers*, Library of Congress, Manuscript Division, Washington DC, Folder, Box 21, Armenia-America Society, Folder 1919–1920.

118. Stivers, *Supremacy and Oil*, 195–199; Evans, *United States Policy and the Partition of Turkey*, 300–303; Fromkin, *A Peace to End All* Peace, 533–536, John A. DeNovo, "The Movement for an Aggressive American Oil Policy Abroad, 1918–1920," *American Historical Review* 61, no. 4 (July 1956), 854–876.

119. "Memorandum on Mesopotamia and the Oil Question," September 22, 1920, *Davis* Papers, Box 9. For more these discussions over oil and the mandates see DeNovo, *American Interests*, 167–184.

120. Quotes in "Memorandum on Anglo-American Relations," (May 1921), *Wiseman Papers*, Folder 110.

121. Stivers, *Supremacy and Oil*, 89–90.

122. See Cohrs, *The Unfinished Peace After World War I*, 85 and Tooze, *The Deluge*, 400–408.

123. Lloyd George, *Memoirs of the Peace Conference*, Vol. 2, 866.

124. Macmillan, *Paris 1919*, 459–461; Mango, *Ataturk*, 306–324; Alan Sharp, *David Lloyd George: Great Britain* (London: Haus, 2008), 161–164.
125. Dulles to Lansing, February 13, 1922, *Lansing Papers*, Letterbook 56.
126. Mango, *Ataturk*, 325–343.
127. Marjorie Housepian, *Smyrna 1922: The Destruction of a City* (London: Faber, 1972), 166; Macmillan, *Paris, 1919*, 461–462. For scholars who dispute Turkish culpability for the fire see Kinross, *Ataturk*, 270; Stanford J. Shaw and Ezel Kural Shaw, *History of the Ottoman Empire and Modern Turkey, Vol. 2: Reform, Evolution and Republic: The Rise of Modern Turkey, 1808–1975* (Cambridge: Cambridge University Press, 1977), 363.
128. Fromkin, *A Peace to End All Peace*, 545–546.
129. George Horton, *The Blight of Asia: An Account of the Systematic Extermination of Christian Populations by Mohammedans and of the Culpability of Certain Great Powers; with a True Story of the Burning of Smyrna* (Indianapolis: The Bobbs-Merrill Company, 1926), 2, 112.
130. Barton to Hughes and Harding, September 18, 1922, Barton Papers, 3.2, *ABCFM*.
131. James A. Malcolm to Gabriel Noradounghian, October 20, 1922, Folder 255, *AND*, ANA.
132. First quote in Secretary of State to President Harding, *FRUS 1922*, July 24 1922, Vol. II, 931–932; Second quote in Richard L. Watson Jr., ed., *Bishop Cannon's Own Story: Life as I Have Seen It* (Durham, NC: Duke University Press, 1955), 225–228.
133. DeNovo, *American Interests*, 133–134; Evans, *United States Policy and the Partition of Turkey*, 374–375.
134. Outline of speech contained in Acting Secretary of State to the Ambassador in France (Herrick), November 1, 1922, *FRUS 1922*, Vol. I, 947–949.
135. "Trouble That America Avoided," September 26, 1922, *Washington Post*.
136. "Europe's Hot Potato," November 3, 1922, *Salt Lake Telegram*.
137. Will Rogers, Arthur Frank Wertheim, and Frank Blair, eds., *The Papers of Will Rogers, Volume 4, From Broadway to the National Stage, September 1915—July 1928* (Norman: University of Oklahoma Press, c1996–c2006), 255.
138. Sharp, *David Lloyd George*, 194–195.
139. Martin Gilbert, *Winston S. Churchill: Companion Volume, Vol. 4, Part 3: April 1921—November 1922* (Boston: Houghton Mifflin, 1978), 1988.
140. Fromkin, *A Peace to End All Peace*, 548–553.
141. "Letter," *The Times*, October 7, 1922.
142. Reynolds, *Britannia Overruled*, 111.
143. Memorandum by the Secretary of State of a Conversation with the British Ambassador (Geddes), November 10, 1922, *FRUS, 1922*, II, 952.
144. For examples see Lloyd George, *Memoirs*, 807–881; Hoover, *The Ordeal of Woodrow Wilson*, 225–229.
145. Kemal had abolished the Caliphate, preventing the Ottoman government in occupied Constantinople from being invited. See Mango, *Ataturk*, 361–377.
146. Bristol was a member of the American group, which also included the US ambassador to Italy Richard Child and America's minister to Switzerland Joseph Grew.
147. Turkey and Greece also agreed to a compulsory population transfer, resulting in roughly 345,000 Muslims in Macedonia being "exchanged" for around 150,000 Greek Christians in Anatolia and eastern Thrace. For more on this and the terms of the treaty see Macmillan, *Paris, 1919*, 464–465; David Gilmour, *Curzon* (London: John Murray, 1994), 555–567.
148. Richard Washburn Child, *A Diplomat Looks at Europe* (New York: Duffield, 1925), 103–124; see also Nassibian, *Britain and the Armenian Question*, 235.
149. Quoted in Mango, *Ataturk*, 388.
150. Gilmour, *Curzon*, 566; Reynolds, *Britannia Overruled*, 110; John Darwin, *The Empire Project: The Rise and Fall of the British World System* (Cambridge: Cambridge University Press, 2009), 364.
151. Winston S. Churchill, *The World Crisis: The Aftermath* (London: Thornton Butterworth, 1929), 409.

Conclusion

1. Noel Buxton and T. P. Conwil-Evans, *Oppressed Peoples and the League of Nations* (New York: E. P. Dutton & Co., 1922), 150.

2. See Michael Barnett, *Empire of Humanity: A History of Humanitarianism* (Ithaca, NY: Cornell University Press, 2011), 49.

3. Buxton and Evans, *Oppressed Peoples*, 150.

4. This was in keeping with the religious dimensions of humanitarianism in this period discussed in Abigail Green, "Humanitarianism in Nineteenth-Century Context: Religious, Gendered, National," *The Historical Journal*, 57, no. 4 (December 2014), 1157–1175.

5. Peterson, *Starving Armenians*, 138.

6. See Watenpaugh, *Bread from Stones* and also "'A pious wish devoid of all practicability': Interwar Humanitarianism, The League of Nations and the Rescue of Trafficked Women and Children in the Eastern Mediterranean, 1920–1927," *American Historical Review* 115, no. 4 (October 2010), 1315–1339; Davide Rodogno, "Non-State Actors" Humanitarian Operations in the Aftermath of the First World War," in Fabien Klose, *The Emergence of Humanitarian Intervention: Ideas and Practice from the Nineteenth Century to the Present* (Cambridge: Cambridge University Press, 2015), 185–207; Bruno Cabanes, *The Great War and the Origins of Humanitarianism, 1918–1924* (Cambridge: Cambridge University Press, 2014), 1–18, 170–173, 300–314. While Cabanes argues that transnational activism for Armenians after World War One contributed to the growth of what he calls "humanitarian rights" (6), Watenpaugh disputes the "gradual linear evolution connecting modern humanitarianism to the legal and cultural formulation of modern individual human rights" (21). Both, however, see the humanitarianism on behalf of the Armenians as a critical step in the transition from pre-war humanitarianism to a more modern conception of the term.

7. That same year, the NER transformed itself into the Near East Foundation, and continues to provide technical assistance and fund economic projects, principally in rural regions of the Near East, to this day.

8. Malbone W. Graham, "Humanitarian Intervention in International Law as Related to the Practice of the United States," *Michigan Law Review* 22, no. 4 (February 1924), 312–328.

9. Summary of Secretary of State Charles Evans Hughes's speech, January 23, 1924, in *FRUS, 1924*, Vol. 2, 409–415.

10. Council of Ten: minutes of meeting, January 27, 1919, *FRUS, The Paris Peace Conference, 1919*, Vol. 3, 742.

11. "Republican Platform 1920," *Speeches of Warren G. Harding of Ohio*, 3.

12. "A Speech by Senator Warren G. Harding to Knights of Pythias, Marion, Ohio, September 18, 1920," *Speeches of Warren G. Harding*, 175

13. "Republican Platform 1920," in *Speeches of Warren G. Harding*, 23.

14. Lloyd George, *The Truth About the Peace Treaties*, 1265.

15. Quoted in Frederick Lugard, "The Mandate System and the British Mandates," *Journal of the Royal Society of Arts* 72, no. 3736 (June 27, 1924), 548–549.

16. Lloyd George, *Memoirs of the Peace Conference*, 1264, 1342, 1351.

17. Buxton and Conwil-Evans, *Oppressed Peoples*, 138.

18. Quoted in Lugard, "The Mandate System," 548.

19. Alfred T. Mahan and Charles T. Beresford, "Possibilities of an Anglo-American Reunion," *The North American Review* 159, no. 456 (November 1894) 560.

20. Quoted in Buxton and Conwil-Evans, *Oppressed Peoples*, 140.

21. Buxton and Conwil-Evans, *Oppressed Peoples*, 140.

22. See Charlie Laderman, "The Ordeal of Paris," in *Historian in Chief: How Presidents Interpret the Past to Shape the Future*, ed. Seth Cotlar and Richard Ellis (Charlottesville: University of Virginia Press, 2019), Chapter 7.

23. Hoover, *The Ordeal of Woodrow Wilson*, 222.

24. Hoover, *Years of Adventure*, 455.

25. Quoted in Gary Dean Best, *Herbert Hoover: The Post-Presidential Years, 1933–1964, Vol. 2, 1946–1964* (Stanford, CA: Hoover Institution Press, 1983), 404.

26. Examples include Gary J. Bass, *Stay the Hand of Vengeance: The Politics of War Crimes Tribunals* (Princeton, NJ: Princeton University Press, 2000) and *Freedom's Battle*, 315–340; Robert Gellately and Ben Kiernan, eds., *The Specter of Genocide: Mass Murder in Historical Perspective* (Cambridge: Cambridge University Press, 2003); Robert Skloot, ed., *The Theatre of Genocide: Four Plays about Mass Murder in Rwanda, Bosnia, Cambodia and Armenia* (Madison: University of Wisconsin Press, 2008); Alan S. Rosenbaum, ed., *Is the Holocaust Unique? Perspectives on Comparative Genocide* (Boulder, CO: Westview Press, 1996). As Susan Pedersen has demonstrated, the end of the Cold War provoked similar questions, of how to reconcile international stability with new claims of sovereignty, to those that confronted statesmen after World War I, prompting scholars to return to studying attempts to establish global order during the interwar years. See Susan Pedersen, "Back to the League of Nations: Review Essay," *American Historical Review* 112, no. 4 (October 2007), 1091–1117. For the role of the Armenian tragedy in inspiring the pioneering studies of Raphael Lemkin, the lawyer who coined the term "genocide," see Philippe Sands, *East West Street: On the Origins of Genocide and Crimes Against Humanity* (London: Weidenfeld & Nicolson, 2016) 143.

27. Power, *A Problem From Hell*, xxi.

28. Ellery C. Stowell, *International Law: A Restatement of Principles in Conformity with Actual Practice* (New York: Henry Holt, 1931), 349.

BIBLIOGRAPHY

Unpublished Manuscripts and Archives

Bibliotheque Nubar, Paris
Records of the Délégation Nationale Arménienne
Columbia University, Butler Library
Crane Family Papers
James T. Shotwell Papers
Harvard University, Houghton Library
American Board of Commissioners for Foreign Missions Archives
James L. Barton Papers
Theodore Roosevelt Collection
Library of Congress, Manuscripts Division
Tasker H. Bliss Papers
William Borah Papers
Admiral Mark L. Bristol Papers
William Jennings Bryan Papers
John Hay Papers
George Kennan Papers
Robert Lansing Papers
Montgomery Family Papers
Henry Morgenthau, Sr. Papers
Richard Olney Papers
Theodore Roosevelt Papers
Elihu Root Papers
Oscar S. Straus Papers
Henry White Papers
John Sharp Williams Papers
Woodrow Wilson Papers
U.S. American Commission to Negotiate Peace Records
London School of Economics, Archives Division
E. D. Morel Papers
Massachusetts History Society
Henry Cabot Lodge Papers
National Archives of Armenia, Yerevan
Armenian National Delegation Papers, 1912–1924
National Archives of Scotland
Lothian (Philip Kerr). Papers

New York Public Library
Albert Shaw Papers
Stanford University, Hoover Institution Archives
Donald M. Brodie Papers
Louis Edgar Browne Papers
Herbert Hoover Papers
Ahmed Emin Yalman Papers
University of Berkeley, California, Bancroft Library
Hiram Johnson Papers
*University of Cambridge, Cambridge University Library, Department of Manuscripts and University
     Archives*
Jan Christian Smuts: Correspondence
Churchill Archives Centre
Cecil Spring Rice Papers
W. T. Stead Papers
University of Oxford, Bodleian Library
Herbert Henry Asquith Papers
Viscount James Bryce Papers
T. E. Lawrence Papers
Viscount Alfred Milner Papers
UK National Archives
Cabinet Papers, CAB 23/Imperial War Cabinet Minutes
Cabinet Papers, CAB 27/ War Cabinet, Eastern Committee. 1919–1919
U.S. National Archives
Record Group 59: General Records of the Department of State
Record Group 84: Records of the Foreign Service Posts of the Department of State
Yale University, Sterling Memorial Library
William Hepburn Buckler Papers
William C. Bullitt Papers
John W. Davis Papers
Colonel Edward M. House Papers
Inquiry Papers
Walter Lippmann Papers
Sir William Wiseman Papers
William Yale Papers
Yale University, Special Collections, Divinity School Library
John R. Mott Papers

Published Documents

American Board of Commissioners for Foreign Missions, *Annual Report of the American Board of
     Commissioners for Foreign Missions* (Boston, 1810–).
Congressional Record (Washington, DC: Government Printing Office, 1831–).
Hansard 5th Series, 1913–1923, vols. 19–38.
Papers Relating to the Foreign Relations of the United States (Washington, DC: US Government
     Printing Office).
Republican National Committee, *Speeches of Warren G. Harding of Ohio, Republican candidate for
     president, from his acceptance of the nomination to October 1, 1920* (New York, 1920).
US Department of State, *Records of the Department of State Relating to Internal Affairs of Armenia,
     1910–1929* (Washington DC: National Archives Microfilm Publications, 1975)., Microfilm
     8 reels.
US Department of State, *Records of Department of State Relating to Political Relations Between
     Armenia and Other States, 1910–1929* (Washington DC: National Archives Microfilm
     Publications, 1975)., Microfilm 2 reels.

Anthologies, Letters, and Personal Papers

Adams, John Quincy, *Memoirs of John Quincy Adams, Comprising Portions of His Diary from 1795 to 1848*, ed. Charles Francis Adams (Philadelphia: J. B. Lippincott, 1875).

Armenian National Committee, *The Armenian Genocide: As Reported in the Australian Press* (Sydney: Armenian National Committee, 1983).

Armenian Youth Federation of Canada, *The Armenian Genocide in the Canadian Press*, vol. 1: 1915–1916 (Montreal: Armenian National Committee of Canada, 1985).

Baker, Ray Stannard. *Woodrow Wilson, Life and Letters, 8 vols.* (New York: Doubleday, Doran and Co., Inc., 1937).

Barton, James L., comp. *"Turkish Atrocities": Statements of American Missionaries on the Destruction of Christian Communities in Ottoman Turkey, 1915-1917* (Ann Arbor, MI: Gomidas Institute, 1998).

Beveridge, Albert, *The Meaning of the Times and Other Speeches* (Indianapolis: The Bobbs-Merrill Company, 1908).

Bryce, Viscount, preface, Arnold Toynbee, editor. *The Treatment of Armenians in the Ottoman Empire 1915-1916: Documents presented to Viscount Grey of Falladon, Secretary of State for Foreign Affairs* (London: Sir Joseph Causton and Sons, Limited, 1916).

Cobden, Richard, *Political Writings* (London: William Ridgway, 1867).

Garnett, David, ed. *The Letters of T. E. Lawrence* (London, 1938).

Gilbert, Martin, *Winston S. Churchill: Companion Volume, Vol. 4, Part 3: April 1921—November 1922* (Boston: Houghton Mifflin, 1978).

Hamilton, Stanislaus Murray, ed., *The Writings of James Monroe*, Volume 4, 1817–1823 (New York: G. P. Putnam's Sons, 1902).

Holmes, Oliver Wendell, and Lewis Einstein, edited by James Bishop Peabody, *The Holmes-Einstein Letters: Correspondence of Mr Justice Holmes and Lewis Einstein 1903-1935* (London: Macmillan, 1964).

Israel, Fred, ed., *Major Peace Treaties of Modern History, 1648-1967* (New York: McGraw-Hill, 1967).

Kipling, Rudyard, *Rudyard Kipling's Verse* (Garden City, NY: Doubleday Page & Co., 1922).

LaFeber, Walter, ed., *John Quincy Adams and American Continental Empire: Letters, Speeches and Papers* (Chicago: Quadrangle, 1965).

Link, Arthur S., *The Papers of Woodrow Wilson*, 69 vols. (Princeton, NJ: Princeton University Press, 1966–1994).

Lodge, Henry Cabot, *Selections from the Correspondence of Theodore Roosevelt and Henry Cabot Lodge, 1884, 1918*, 2 vols. (New York: Charles Scribner's Sons, 1925).

Morison, Elting E., ed., *The Letters of Theodore Roosevelt*, 8 vols. (Cambridge, MA: Harvard University Press, 1951–1954).

Pinney Thomas, ed., *The letters of Rudyard Kipling: 1911-1919* (Basingstoke: Macmillan, 1999)

Richardson, James D., ed., *A Compilation of the Messages and Papers of the Presidents* (Washington, DC: Bureau of National Literature & Art, 1908).

Roosevelt, Theodore, *American Ideals and Other Essays, Social and Political* (New York: AMS Press, 1969).

Roosevelt, Theodore, *Presidential Addresses and State Papers and European Addresses* 8 vols. (New York: The Review of Reviews Company, 1910).

Roosevelt, Theodore, *Theodore Roosevelt in the Kansas City Star: Wartime Editorials* (Charleston, SC: Bibliolife Books, 2008).

Roosevelt, Theodore, and Louis Auchincloss, ed., *Theodore Roosevelt: Letters and Speeches* (New York: Library of America: 2004).

Roosevelt, Theodore, and Hermann Hagedorn, ed., *Works of Theodore Roosevelt* (New York: Charles Scribner's Sons, 1924).

Root, Elihu, collected and edited by Robert Bacon and James Brown Scott, *Addresses on International Subjects* (Cambridge, MA: Harvard University Press, 1916).

Root, Elihu, collected and edited by Robert Bacon and James Brown Scott, *Latin America and the United States* (Cambridge, MA: Harvard University Press, 1917).

Root, Elihu, collected and edited by Robert Bacon and James Brown Scott, *Military and colonial policy of the United States: addresses and reports* (Cambridge, MA: Harvard Univeristy Press, 1916).

Sarafian, Ara, ed., *United States Official Documents on the Armenian Genocide* (Waretown, MA: Armenian Review, 1995).

Sarafian, Ara, ed., *United States Official Records on the Armenian Genocide* (Princeton, NJ: Gomidas Institute, 2004).

Scott, James Brown, *President Wilson's Foreign Policy: Messages, Addresses and Papers* (New York: Oxford University Press, 1918).

Seymour, Charles, ed., *The Intimate Papers of Colonel House* (Boston: Houghton Mifflin Co, 1926).

Twain, Mark, *Mark Twain: Collected Tales, Sketches, Speeches, and Essays, 1891–1910* (New York: Library of America, 1992).

United States, President (1877–1881: Hayes), *Letters and messages of Rutherford B. Hayes, president of the United States*, (Washington, DC: US Government Printing Office] 1881)

US Department of State, *Papers Relating to the Foreign Relations of the United States: The Lansing Papers, 1914–1920. 2 vols.* (Washington, DC: Government Printing Office, 1939–1940).

Washington, Booker T., *The Booker T. Washington Papers*, 14 vols. (Urbana: University of Illinois Press, 1972–).

Wertheim, Arthur Frank, and Frank Blair, eds. *The Papers of Will Rogers, Volume 4, From Broadway to the National Stage, September 1915—July 1928* (Norman: University of Oklahoma Press, c1996–c2006).

Wilson, Woodrow, *The Public Papers of Woodrow Wilson*, ed. Ray Stannard Baker and William E. Dodd, vol. V (New York: Harper & Brothers Publishers, 1927).

Wilson, Woodrow, *The Messages and Papers of Woodrow Wilson*, ed. Albert Shaw II (New York: Harper & Brothers, 1924).

Woodward, E. L., and Rohan Butler, eds., *Documents on British Foreign Policy, 1919–1939*, 1st Series (London: Her Majesty's Stationary Office, 1952).

World Missionary Conference, *Report of Commission I: Carrying the Gospel to all the Non-Christian World; with Supplement: Presentation and Discussion of the Report in the Conference on 15 June 1910* (Edinburgh: Fleming H. Revell, 1910).

Memoirs and Autobiographies

Adams, Henry, *The Education of Henry Adams: An Autobiography* (Boston: Houghton Mifflin, 1918).

Adivar, Halide Edib, *Memoirs* (London, J. Murray, 1926).

Child, Richard Washburn, *A Diplomat Looks at Europe* (New York: Duffield, 1925).

Einstein, Lewis, *A Diplomat Looks Back* (New Haven, CT: Yale University Press, 1968).

Einstein, Lewis, *Inside Constantinople: A Diplomatist's Diary during the Dardanelles Expedition* (London: J. Murray, 1917).

Grey of Fallodon, *Twenty-Five Years, 1892–1916* (London: Hodder & Stoughton, 1925).

Hoover, Hoover, *The Memoirs of Herbert Hoover: Years of Adventure, 1874–1920* (New York: Macmillan, 1951–1952).

Howe, Frederic, *The Confessions of a Reformer* (New York: Charles Scribner's Sons, 1925).

Lansing, Robert, *The Peace Negotiations: A Personal Narrative* (Boston: Houghton Mifflin Company, 1921).

Lansing, Robert, *War Memoirs of Robert Lansing, Secretary of State* (New York: BobbsMerill Co., 1935).

Morgenthau, Henry, *All in a Life-Time* (Garden City, NY: Doubleday, 1922).

Morgenthau, Henry, *Ambassador Morgenthau's Story* (New York: Doubleday and Page, 1918).

Roosevelt, Theodore, *Theodore Roosevelt: An Autobiography* (New York: Charles Scribner's Sons, 1929).

Straus, Oscar, *Under Four Administrations: From Cleveland to Taft* (New York: Houghton Mifflin Company, 1923).

Ussher, Clarence D., *An American Physician in Turkey: A Narrative of Adventures in Peace and War* (Boston: Houghton Mifflin, 1917).

Washburn, George, *Fifty Years in Constantinople* (Boston: Houghton, Mifflin, 1909).

Watson, Richard L. Jr., ed., *Bishop Cannon's Own Story: Life as I Have Seen It* (Durham, NC: Duke University Press, 1955).

Yalman, Ahmed Emin. *Turkey in My Time* (Norman: University of Oklahoma Press, 1956).

Periodicals

American Review of Reviews
Amherst Graduates' Quarterly
Appletons' Journal
Atlanta Constitution
Atlantic Monthly
The Biblical World
Boston Evening Transcript
Catholic World
Chicago Daily News
The Century Magazine
Contemporary Review
Daily Chronicle
Daily Mirror
Daily Telegraph
The Economist
Edinburgh Review
The Fortnightly Review
Galaxy
Harvard Crimson
The Independent (NY)
Illustrated Sunday Herald
Liberal Magazine
The Literary Digest
Los Angeles Herald
Los Angeles Times
Macmillan's Magazine
Manchester Guardian
Mclure's Magazine
The Missionary Herald
Missionary Review of the World
The Nation
National Geographic Magazine
National Review
The New Armenia
New York American
New York Herald
The New Republic
New York Sun
New York Times
New York World
The Nineteenth Century
North American Review
Northern Echo
The Outlook
The Outlook and Independent

Philadelphia Inquirer
Quarterly Review
Red Cross Magazine
The Review of Reviews
Round Table
Salt Lake Telegram
Scribner's
The Spectator
The St. Louis Republic
The Times
Washington Post
World's Work

Books

Adams, Brooks, *America's Economic Supremacy* (New York: Macmillan, 1900).

Adams, Brooks, *The Law of Civilization and Decay: an Essay on History* (New York: Macmillan, 1895).

Adams, D. K., and Cornelius A. Van Minnen, eds. *Reflections on American Exceptionalism* (Keele: Ryburn, 1994).

Adams, Iestyn, *Brothers Across the Ocean: British Foreign Policy and the Origins of the Anglo-American "Special Relationship" 1900–1905* (London: I. B. Tauris, 2005).

Adeleke, Tunde, *Unafrican Americans: Nineteenth Century Black Nationalists and the Civilizing Mission* (Lexington: University Press of Kentucky, 1998).

Adler, Cyrus, *Jacob H. Schiff: His Life and Letters*, 2 vols. (Garden City, NY: Doubleday, Doran, 1928).

Aksakal, Mustafa, *The Ottoman Road to War in 1914: The Ottoman Empire and the First World* (Cambridge: Cambridge University Press, 2008).

Akçam, Taner, *A Shameful Act: The Armenian Genocide and the Question of Turkish Responsibility* (New York: Metropolitan Books, 2006).

Alfonso, Oscar M., *Theodore Roosevelt and the Philippines, 1897–1909* (Quezon City: University of Philippines Press, 1970).

Ambrosius, Lloyd E., *Wilsonianism: Woodrow Wilson and his Legacy in American Foreign Relations* (New York: Palgrave Macmillan, 2002).

Ambrosius, Lloyd E., *Wilsonian Statecraft: Theory and Practice of Liberal Internationalism during World War I* (Wilmington, DE: Scholarly Resource Books, 1991).

Ambrosius, Lloyd E., *Woodrow Wilson and the American Diplomatic Tradition: The Treaty Fight in Perspective* (Cambridge: Cambridge University Press, 1987).

Andrew, Christopher, *Secret Service: The Making of the British Intelligence Community* (London: Heinemann, 1985).

Anderson, M. S., *The Eastern Question, 1774–1923: A Study in International Relations* (London: Macmillan, 1966).

Anderson, Stuart, *Race and Rapprochement: Anglo-Saxonism and Anglo-American Relations, 1895–1904* (London: Associated University Press, 1981).

Anonymous, *The Lustful Turk; or, Lascivious Scenes from a Harem* (London: John Benjamin Brookes[1828]).

Argyll, George Campbell Douglas, Duke of, *Our Responsibilities for Turkey, Memories of Forty Years* (London: J. Murray, 1896).

Ayers, Ed, *The Promise of the New South: Life After Reconstruction* (New York: Oxford University Press, 2007).

Bagby, Wesley N., *The Road to Normalcy: The Presidential Campaign of 1920* (Baltimore: Johns Hopkins University Press, 1962).

Bailey, Thomas A., *A Diplomatic History of the American People* (New York: F. S. Crofts, 1944).

Baker, Ray Stannard, *Woodrow Wilson and the World Settlement* vol. 3 (Garden City, NY: Doubleday Page, 1922).

Balakian, Peter, *The Burning Tigris: The Armenian Genocide and America's Response* (New York: Harper Collins, 2003).

Barnett, Michael, *Empire of Humanity: A History of Humanitarianism* (Ithaca, NY: Cornell University Press, 2011).

Baron, Nick, and Peter Gatrell, eds., *Homelands: War, Population and Statehood in Eastern Europe and Russia* (London: Anthem Press, 2004).

Barton, Clara, *The Red Cross in Peace and War* (Washington, DC: American Historical Press, 1898).

Barton, James. L., *Daybreak in Turkey* (New York: The Pilgrim Press, 1908).

Barton, James L., *Story of Near East Relief, 1915–1930: An Interpretation* (New York: Macmillan, 1930).

Bass, Gary J., *Freedom's Battle: The Origins of Humanitarian Intervention* (New York: Knopf, 2008).

Bass, Gary J., *Stay the Hand of Vengeance: The Politics of War Crimes Tribunals* (Princeton, NJ: Princeton University Press, 2000).

Beach, Harlan, and Burton St. John, eds. *World Statistics of Christian Missions* (New York: Foreign Missions Conference of North America, 1916).

Beale, Howard K. *Theodore Roosevelt and the Rise of America to World Power* (Baltimore: Johns Hopkins University Press, 1956).

Bederman, Gail, *Manliness and Civilization: A Cultural History of Gender and Race in the United States, 1880–1917* (Chicago: University of Chicago Press, 1995).

Beisner, Robert L., *From the Old Diplomacy to the New, 1865–1900*, 2nd ed. (Arlington Heights, IL: Wiley Blackwell, 1986).

Beisner, Robert L., *Twelve Against Empire: The Anti-Imperialists, 1898–1900* (New York: McGraw-Hill, 1968).

Bell, Duncan, *The Idea of Greater Britain: Empire and the Future of World Order, 1860–1900* (Princeton, NJ: Princeton University Press, 2007).

Beloff, Max, *Imperial Sunset: Britain's Liberal Empire 1897–1921* (London: Methuen, 1969).

Bemis, Samuel Flagg, *A Diplomatic History of the United States* (New York: H. Holt and Company, 1936).

Benedetto, Robert, ed., *Presbyterian Reformers in Central Africa* (Leiden: Brill, 1996).

Best, Gary Dean, *Herbert Hoover: The Post-Presidential Years, 1933–1964, vol. 2, 1946–1964* (Stanford, CA: Hoover Institution Press, 1983).

Best, Gary Dean, *To Free A People: American Jewish Leaders and the Jewish Problem in Eastern Europe, 1890–1914* (Westport, CT: Greenwood Press, 1982).

Beveridge, Albert, *For the Greater Republic Not for Imperialism, An Address at Union League of Philadelphia, February 15, 1899* (Philadelphia, 1899).

Biagini, Eugenio F., *British Democracy and Irish Nationalism, 1876–1906* (Cambridge: Cambridge University Press, 2007).

Billington Jr., David P., *Phillip Kerr and the Quest for World Order* (Westport, CT: Praeger, 2006).

Bliss, Edwin M., Henry O. Dwight, and Allen H. Tupper, eds. *The Encyclopedia of Missions*, reprint ed. (Detroit: Gale Research Company, 1975).

Bliss, E. M., *Turkey and the Armenian Atrocities* (London: Unwin, 1896).

Bloxham, Donald, *The Great Game of Genocide: Imperialism, Nationalism and the Destruction of the Ottoman Armenians* (Oxford: Oxford University Press, 2005).

Blum, John Morton, *The Republican Roosevelt* (Cambridge, MA: Harvard University Press, 1954).

Blum, John Morton, *Woodrow Wilson and the Politics of Morality* (Boston: Little, Brown, 1956).

Blumi, Isa, *Ottoman Refugees, 1789–1939: Migration in a Post-Imperial World* (London: Bloomsbury Academic, 2013).

Bonsal, Stephen, *Suitors and Supplicants: The Little Nations at Versailles* (New York: Prentice Hall, 1946).

Bothwell, Robert, and Daudelin, Jean, eds. *Canada Among Nations, 2008: 100 Years of Canadian Foreign Policy* (Montreal: McGill-Queen's University Press, 2009).

Bowden, Brett, *The Empire of Civilization: the evolution of an imperial idea* (Chicago: University of Chicago Press, 2009).

Braeman, John, Robert Bremner and Everett Walters, *Change and Continuity in Twnetieth-Century America* (Columbus: Ohio State University Press, 1965).

Brake, Laurel, Ed King, Roger Luckhurst, and James Mussell, eds. *W. T. Stead: Newspaper Revolutionary* (London: The British Library, 2012).

Brands, H. W., *TR: The Last Romantic* (New York: Basic Books, 1997).

Brands, H. W., *What America Owes the World: The Struggle for the Soul of Foreign Policy* (Cambridge: Cambridge University Press, 1998).

Brands, H. W., *Woodrow Wilson* (New York: Times Books, 2003).

Bryce, James, *Transcaucasia and Ararat: Being notes of a vacation in the autumn of 1876*, 4th ed. (London: Macmillan & Co. 1896).

Buhite, Russell D., *Lives at Risk: Hostages and Victims in American Foreign Policy* (Wilmington, DE: Scholarly Resources Inc., 1995).

Burk, Kathleen, *Old World, New World: The Story of Britain and America from the Beginning* (New York: Grove Press, 2009).

Burney, Charles, and D. M. Lang, *The Peoples of the Hills* (London: Pheonix, 2001).

Burman, John, *Britain's Relations with the Ottoman Empire During the Embassy of Sir Nicholas O'Conor to the Porte, 1898–1908* (Istanbul: The Isis Press, 2010).

Burton, David H. *Theodore Roosevelt: Confident Imperialist* (Philadelphia: University of Pennsylvania Press, 1968).

Burton, David H., *Theodore Roosevelt and His English Correspondents: A Special Relationship of Friends* (Transactions of the American Philosophical Society, New Series), Vol. 63, No. 2 (Philadelphia: American Philosophical Society, 1973).

Bryson, Thomas A., *American Diplomatic Relations with the Middle East, 1784–1975* (Metuchen, NJ: Scarecrow Press, 1977).

Bryson, Thomas A., *Tars, Turks, and Tankers: The Role of the United States Navy in the Middle East, 1800–1979* (Metuchen, NJ: Scarecrow Press, 1980).

Burk, Kathleen, *Britain, America and the Sinews of War, 1914–1918* (London: Unwin Hyman, 1985).

Burk, Kathleen, *Old World, New World: The Story of Britain and America from the Beginning* (New York: Grove Press, 2009).

Burner, David, *Herbert Hoover: A Public Life* (New York: Knopf, 1979).

Burton, David H., *Theodore Roosevelt: Confident Imperialist* (Philadelphia: University of Pennsylvania Press, 1968).

Buxton, Noel, and T. P. Conwil-Evans, *Oppressed Peoples and the League of Nations* (New York: E. P. Dutton & Co., 1922).

Cabanes, Bruno, *The Great War and the Origins of Humanitarianism, 1918–1924* (Cambridge: Cambridge University Press, 2014).

Calhoun, Frederick S., *Power and Principle: Armed Intervention in Wilsonian Foreign Policy* (Kent, OH: Kent State University Press, 1986).

Callwell, C. E., *Field Marshall Sir Henry Wilson Bart, G.C.B., D.S.C: His Life and Diaries* (London: Cassell, 1927).

Campbell, A. E., *Great Britain and the United States, 1898–1905* (London: Longman,1960).

Carnegie, Andrew, *The Gospel of Wealth and Other Timely Essays* (New York: Century, 1900).

Carpenter, Tessa, *The Miss Stone Affair: America's First Modern Hostage Crisis* (New York: Simon & Schuster, 2003).

Cardashian, Vahan, ed., *Should America Accept Mandate for Armenia?* (New York: American Committee for the Independence of Armenia and Armenian National Union, 1919).

Chessman, G. Wallace, *Theodore Roosevelt and the Politics of Power* (Boston: Little, Brown, 1969).

Churchill, Randolph, *Youth: Winston S. Churchill, 1874–1900* (London: Minerva, 1967).

Churchill, Winston S., *The World Crisis: The Aftermath* (London: Thornton Butterworth, 1929).

Clarke, James Freeman, *Ten Great Religions: An Essay in Comparative Theology* (Boston: James R. Osgood and Company, 1871).

Clements, Kendrick A., *The Presidency of Woodrow Wilson* (Lawrence: University Press of Kansas, 1992).

Clements, Kendrick A., *Woodrow Wilson: World Statesman*, rev. ed. (Chicago: Ivan R. Dee, 1999).

Cohen, Naomi W., *A Dual Heritage: The Public Career of Oscar S. Straus* (Philadelphia: The Jewish Publication Society of America, 1969).

Cohen, Naomi W., *Jacob Schiff: A Study in American Jewish Leadership* (Hannover, NH: Brandeis University Press, 1999).

Collin, Richard H., *Theodore Roosevelt, Culture, Diplomacy, and Expansion* (Baton Rouge: Louisiana State University Press, 1985).

Cohrs, Patrick, *The Unfinished Peace after World War I: America, Britain and the Stabilisation of Europe, 1919–1932* (Cambridge: Cambridge University Press, 2006).

Collin, Richard H., *Theodore Roosevelt's Caribbean: The Panama Canal, The Monroe Doctrine and the Latin American Context* (Baton Rouge: Louisana State University Press, 1990).

Cookey, S. J. S., *Britain and the Congo Question, 1885–1913* (London: Longmans, Green & Co. Ltd., 1968).

Cooper. John Milton Jr., *Breaking the Heart of the World: Woodrow Wilson and the Fight for the League of Nations* (Cambridge: Cambridge University Press, 2001).

Cooper, John Milton Jr., *The Warrior and the Priest* (Cambridge, MA: Harvard University Press, 1983).

Cooper Jr., John Milton, *Woodrow Wilson: A Biography* (New York: Knopf, 2009).

Cooper, John Milton Jr., and Charles E. Neu, eds. *The Wilson Era: Essays in Honour of Arthur S. Link* (Arlington Heights, IL: Harlan Davidson, 1991).

Cotlar, Seth, and Richard Ellis, eds. *Historian in Chief: How Presidents Interpret the Past to Shape the Future* (Charlottesville: University of Virginia Press, 2019).

Crapol, Edward P., *America for Americans: Economic Nationalism and Anglophobia in the Late Nineteenth Century* (Westport, CT: Greenwood Press, 1973).

Cullinane, Michael Patrick. *Liberty and American Anti-Imperialism, 1898–1909* (Basingstoke: Palgrave Macmillan, 2012).

Curti, Merle, *American Philanthropy Abroad: A History* (New Brunswick, NJ: Rutgers University Press, 1963).

Dadrian, Vahakn, *German Responsibility in the Armenian Genocide: A Review of the Historical Evidence of German Complicity* (Watertown, MA: Blue Crane, 1996).

Dadrian, Vahakn, *The History of the Armenian Genocide* (New York: Bergahn Books, 2003).

Dalton, Kathleen, *Theodore Roosevelt: A Strenuous Life* (New York: Random House, 2002).

Daniel, Robert L., *American Philanthropy in the Near East, 1820–1960* (Athens: Ohio University Press, 1970).

Daniels, Josephus, *The Life of Woodrow Wilson* (London: Allen & Unwin, 1924).

Darwin, John, *The Empire Project: The Rise and Fall of the British World System* (Cambridge: Cambridge University Press, 2009).

Davidson, Roderic H., *Reform in the Ottoman Empire, 1856–1876* (Princeton, NJ: Princeton University Press, 1963).

Dennett, Tyler, *John Hay: From Poetry to Politics* (New York: Dodd, Mead and Company, 1934).

Dennett, Tyler, *Roosevelt and the Russo-Japanese War* (New York: Doubleday Page, 1928).

Dennis, Alfred L. P., *Adventures in American Diplomacy, 1896–1906* (New York: E. P. Dutton & Company, 1928).

DeNovo, John A., *American Interests and Policies in the Middle East 1900–1939* (Minneapolis: University of Minnesota Press, 1963).

Dimbleby, David, and David Reynolds, *An Ocean Apart: The Relationship Between Britain and America in the Twentieth Century* (London: Hodder & Stoughton: BBC Books, 1988).

Duignan, Peter, and L. H. Gann, *The United States and Africa: A History* (Cambridge: Cambridge University Press, 1984).

Dyer, Thomas G., *Theodore Roosevelt and the Idea of Race* (Baton Rouge: Louisiana State University Press, 1980).

Egerton, George W., *Great Britain and the Creation of the League of Nations: Strategy, Politics and International Organization, 1914–1919* (London: Scolar Press, 1979).

Einstein, Lewis, *Roosevelt: His Mind in Action* (Boston: Houghton & Mifflin Co., 1930).

Esthus, Raymond A., *Theodore Roosevelt and the International Rivalries* (Waltham MA, Ginn Blaisdell, 1970).

Evans, Laurence, *United States Policy and the Partition of Turkey, 1914–1924* (Baltimore: Johns Hopkins University Press, 1965).

Ferguson, Niall, *The Pity of War 1914–1918* (London: Penguin Books, 1998).

Ferguson, Niall, *The War of the World* (London: Penguin Books, 2006).

Ferrell, Robert H., *Woodrow Wilson and World War I, 1917–1921* (New York: Harper and Row, 1985).

Fisher, H. A. L., *James Bryce: Viscount Bryce of Dechmont, O.M.* (London: Macmillan, 1927).

Foglesong, David S., *America's Secret War against Bolshevism: U.S. Intervention in the Russian Civil War, 1917–1920* (Chapel Hill: University of North Carolina Press, 1995).

Foner, Phillip S., *Mark Twain: Social Critic* (New York: International Publishers, 1958).

Forster, Stig, Wolfgang J. Mommsen, and John Robinson, eds. *Bismarck, Europe and Africa: the Berlin Africa Conference 1884–1885 and the Onset of Partition* (Oxford: Oxford University Press for the German Historical Institute, 1988).

Fowler, W. B., *British–American Relations, 1917–1918: The Role of Sir William Wiseman* (Princeton: NJ: Princeton University Press, 1969).

Frankel, Jonathan, *Prophecy and Politics: Socialism, Nationalism, and the Russian Jews, 1862–1917* (Cambridge: Cambridge University Press, 1984).

Frankel, Robert P., *Observing America: The Commentary of British Visitors to the United States, 1890–1950* (Madison: University of Wisconsin Press, 2007).

Friedberg, Aaron L., *The Weary Titan: Britain and the Experience of Relative Decline, 1895–1905* (Princeton, NJ: Princeton University Press: 1988).

Fromkin, David, *A Peace to End All Peace: The Fall of the Ottoman Empire and the Creation of the Modern Middle East* (New York: Henry Holt and Company, 1989).

Fromkin, David, *Europe's Last Summer: Who Started the War in 1914?* (New York: Doubleday, 2004).

Gardiner, W. H. T., *"Edinburgh, 1910": An Account and Interpretation of the World Missionary Conference* (London: O. Anderssen & Ferrier, 1910).

Gardner, Lloyd, *Safe for Democracy: the Anglo-American Response to Revolution, 1913–1923* (New York: Oxford University Press, 1984).

Garvin, J. L., and Julian Amery, *The Life of Joseph Chamberlain*, 4 vols. (London: Macmillan, 1932–1951).

Gelfand, Lawrence, *The Inquiry: American Preparations for Peace, 1917–1919* (New Haven, CT: Yale University Press, 1963).

Gellately, Robert, and Ben Kiernan, eds. *The Specter of Genocide: Mass Murder in Historical Perspective* (Cambridge: Cambridge University Press, 2003).

Gilmour, David, *The Long Recessional: the Imperial Life of Rudyard Kipling* (New York: FSG, 2002).

Lloyd George, David, *Memoirs of the Peace Conference*, vol. 2 (New Haven, CT: Yale University Press, 1939).

Gill, Rebecca, *Calculating Compassion: Humanity and Relief in War, Britain 1870–1918* (Manchester: Manchester University Press, 2013).

Gidney, James B., *A Mandate for Armenia* (Kent, OH: Kent State University Press, 1967).

Gilbert, Martin, *Churchill and America* (London: Free Press, 2005).

Gilbert, Martin, *The First World War: A Complete History* (New York: Henry Holt, 1994).

Gilmour, David, *Curzon* (London: John Murray, 1994).

Go, Julian, and Anne L. Foster, eds. *The American Colonial State in the Philippines: Global Perspectives* (Durham, NC: Duke University Press, 2003).

Godkin, Edwin L., "Art. VI—The Eastern Question," *North American Review* CXXIV (Boston: James R. Osgood and Company, 1877).

[Godkin, Edwin L.,] "The Effect of the Russian Reverses on Western Politics," *Nation* (September 27, 1877).

Gorman, Daniel, *The Emergence of International Society in the 1920s* (Cambridge: Cambridge University Press, 2012).

Gordon, Leland James, *American Relations with Turkey, 1830–1930: An Economic Interpretation* (Philadelphia: University of Pennsylvania Press, 1932).

Grabill, Joseph L., *Protestant Diplomacy and the Near East: Missionary Influence on American Policy, 1810–1927* (Minneapolis: University of Minnesota Press, 1971).

Grant, Kevin, *A Civilized Savagery: Britain and the New Slaveries in Africa, 1884–1926* (New York: Routledge, 2005).

Graubard, Stephen, *The Presidents* (London: Penguin 2006).

Grayson, Cary T., *Woodrow Wilson: An Intimate Memoir* (New York: Holt, Rinehart and Winston, 1960).

Green, Nathan C., *The War with Spain and Story of Spain and Cuba* (Baltimore: International News and Book Co., 1898).

Greene, F. D., *The Armenian Crisis in Turkey: The Massacre of 1894, its antecedents and significance; with a consideration of some of the factors which enter into the solution of this phase of the eastern question* (New York: G. P. Putnam's Sons, 1895).

Gulick, Sidney Lewis, *The White Peril in the Far East: An Interpretation of the Significance of the Russo-Japanese War* (New York: F. H. Revell Company, 1905).

Gywnn, Stephen, ed., *The Letters and Friendships of Cecil Spring Rice: A Record* (London: Constable, 1929).

Hacobian, A. P., *Armenia and the War: An Armenian's Point of View with an Appeal to Britain and the Coming Peace Conference* (London: Hodder and Stoughton, 1917).

Hall William H., and Harold A. Hatch, *Recommendations for Political Reconstruction in the Turkish Empire* (for private distribution, November 1918).

Hall, William H., ed., *Reconstruction in Turkey: A Series of Reports Compiled for the American Committee of Armenian and Syrian Relief* (New York: American Committee of Armenian and Syrian Relief, 1918).

Hannigan, Robert E., *The New World Power: American Foreign Policy, 1898–1917* (Philadelphia: University of Pennsylvania Press, 2002).

Harbaugh, William Henry, *Power and Responsibility: The Life and Times of Theodore Roosevelt* (New York: Farrar, Straus and Cudahy, 1961).

Hartz, Louis, *The Liberal Tradition in America* (New York: Harcourt, Brace & World, 1955).

Harris, J. R., and Harris, H. B., *Letters from the Scenes of the Recent Massacres in Armenia* (New York: Fleming H. Revell Company, 1897).

Hauser, Henri, *L'Impérialsme Américaine* (Paris: Pages Libres, 1905).

Hawley, Joshua David, *Theodore Roosevelt: Preacher of Righteousness* (New Haven, CT: Yale University Press, 2008).

Healy, David, *U.S. Expansionism: The Imperialist Urge in the 1890s* (Madison, WI: University of Wisconsin Press, 1970).

Heater, Derek, *National Self-Determination: Woodrow Wilson and his Legacy* (Basingstoke: Macmillan, 1994).

Helmreich, Ernst Christian, *Diplomacy of the Balkan Wars, 1912–1913* (Cambridge, MA: Harvard University Press, 1938).

Herring, George C., *From Colony to Superpower: US Foreign Relations since 1776* (Oxford: Oxford University Press, 2009).

Hilton, Sylvia L., and Steve J. S. Ickringill, *European Perceptions of the Spanish-American War of 1898* (Bern: Lang, 1999).

Hochschild, Adam, *King Leopold's Ghost: A Story of Greed, Terror and Heroism in Colonial Africa* (Boston: Houghton Mifflin, 1998).

Hodgson, Godfrey, *Woodrow Wilson's Right Hand: The Life of Colonel Edward M. House* (New Haven, CT: Yale University Press, 2006).

Hogan, Michael J., ed., *Paths to Power: The Historiography of American Foreign Relations to 1941* (Cambridge: Cambridge University Press, 2000).

Hogg, William R., *Ecumenical Foundations: A History of the International Missionary Council and its Nineteenth Century Background* (New York: Harper, 1952).

Holmes James R., *Theodore Roosevelt and World Order* (Washington, DC: Potomac Books, Inc., 2006).

Horton, George, *The Blight of Asia: An Account of the Systematic Extermination of Christian Populations by Mohammedans and of the Culpability of Certain Great Powers; with a True Story of the Burning of Smyrna* (Indianapolis: The Bobbs-Merrill Company, 1926).

Hoover, Herbert, *The Ordeal of Woodrow Wilson* (New York: McGraw-Hill, 1958).

House, Edward M., and Charles Seymour, *What Really Happened in Paris: The Story of the Paris Peace Conference* (New York: Charles Scribner's Sons, 1921).

Housepian, Marjorie, *Smyrna 1922: The Destruction of a City* (London: Faber, 1972).

Hovannisan, Richard G., *Armenia on the Road to Independence, 1918* (Berkeley: University of California Press, 1967).

Hovannisian, Richard G., *The Armenian Genocide: History, Politics, Ethics* (New York: St Martin's Press, 1992).

Hovannisian Richard G., ed., *The Armenian Genocide in Perspective* (New Brunswick, NJ: Transaction Books, 1986).

Hovannisian, Richard G., *Looking Back, Moving Forward: Confronting the Armenian Genocide* (New Brunswick, NJ: Transaction Publishers, 2003).

Hovannisian, Richard G., *The Republic of Armenia*, 4 vols (Berkeley: University of California Press, 1971–1996).

Howard, Harry N., *The King-Crane Commission: An American Inquiry in the Middle East* (Beirut: Khayat, 1963).

Howard, Harry N., *The Partition of Turkey, 1913–1923* (Norman: University of Oklahoma Press, 1931).

Hunt, Michael H., *Ideology and U.S. Foreign Policy* (New Haven, CT: Yale University Press, 1987).

Hunter Miller, David, *The Drafting of the Covenant*, 2 vols. (New York: G. P. Putnam's Sons, 1928).

Hurewitz, J. C., *Middle East Dilemmas: The Background of United States Policy* (New York: Harper, 1953).

Hutchison, William R., *Errand to the World: American Protestant Thought and Foreign Missions* (Chicago: University of Chicago Press, 1987).

Ikenberry, G. John, *After Victory: Institutions, Strategic Restraint, and the Rebuilding of Order After Major Wars* (Princeton, NJ: Princeton University Press, 2001).

Iriye, Akira, *The Globalizing of America, 1913–1945* (Cambridge: Cambridge University Press, 1993).

Jackson, Peter, *Beyond the Balance of Power: France and the Politics of National Security in the Era of the First World War* (Cambridge: Cambridge University Press, 2013).

Jessup, Philip C., *Elihu Root*, 2 vols. (New York: Dodd, Mead, 1938).

Jones, Moser, *The American Red Cross: from Clara Barton to the New Deal* (Baltimore: Johns Hopkins University Press, 2013).

Karnow, Stanley, *In Our Image: America's Empire in the Philippines* (London: Century, 1990).

Keiser, Hans-Lukas, *Nearest East: American Millenialism and the Mission to the Middle East* (Philadelphia: Temple University Press: 2010).

Kennan, George, *Siberia and the Exile System* (London: J. R. Osgood, McIlvaine, 1891).

Kennan, George F., *American Diplomacy 1900–1950* (Chicago: University of Chicago Press, 1951).

Kennedy, Paul, *The Rise and Fall of the Great Powers: Economic Change and Military Conflict from 1500 to 2000* (New York: Random House, 1987).

Kennedy, Paul, and Anthony Nicholls, eds. *Nationalist and Racialist Movements in Britain and Germany before 1914* (London: Macmillan, 1981).

Kennedy, Ross, ed., *A Companion to Woodrow Wilson* (Malden, MA: Wiley Blackwell, 2013).

Kennedy, Ross, *Woodrow Wilson, World War I and America's Strategy for Peace and Security* (Kent, OH: Kent State University Press, 2009).

Kevorkian, Raymond, *The Armenian Genocide: A Complete History* (London: I. B. Tauris, 2011).

Kinross, Lord, *Ataturk: The Rebirth of a Nation* (London: Weidenfeld & Nicolson, 1971).

Kirakossian, Arman Dzhonovich, *The Armenian Massacres 1894–1896: US Media Testimony* (Detroit: Wayne State University Press, 2004).

Kissinger, Henry, *Diplomacy* (New York: Simon & Schuster, 1994).

Klose, Fabien, *The Emergence of Humanitarian Intervention: Ideas and Practice from the Nineteenth Century to the Present* (Cambridge: Cambridge University Press, 2015).

Knightley, Phillip, *The First Casualty: The War Correspondent as Hero, Propagandist and Myth Maker from the Crimea to Vietnam* (New York: Harcourt Brace Jovanovich, 1975).

Knock, Thomas, *To End All Wars: Woodrow Wilson and the Quest for a New World Order* (Princeton, NJ: Princeton University Press, 1992).

Koskenniemi, Martti, *The Gentle Civilizer of Nations: The Rise and Fall of International Law 1870–1960* (Cambridge: Cambridge University Press, 2002).

Kowner, Rotem, ed., *The Impact of the Russo-Japanese War* (New York: Routledge, 2007).

Kraig, Robert A., *Woodrow Wilson and the Lost World of the Oratorical Statesman* (College Station: Texas A&M University Press, 2004).

LaFeber, Walter, *The Cambridge History of American Foreign Relations, Volume II, The American Search for Opportunity, 1865–1913* (Cambridge: Cambridge University Press, 1993).

LaFeber, Walter, *The New Empire: An Interpretation of American Expansion, 1866–1898* (Ithaca, NY: Cornell University Press, 1967).

Langer, William, *The Diplomacy of Imperialism, 1890–1902* (New York: Knopf, 1956).

Lansford, Tom, and Robert P. Watson, ed., *Presidents and their Decisions: Theodore Roosevelt* (Detroit: Greenhaven Press, 2002).

Laycock, Jo, *Imagining Armenia: Orientalism, Ambiguity and Intervention* (Manchester: Manchester University Press, 2009).

Leventhal, Fred M., and Roland Quinault, eds. *Anglo-American Attitudes: From Revolution to Partnership* (Aldershot: Ashgate, 2000).

Levin Jr., N. Gordon, *Woodrow Wilson and World Politics: America's Response to War and Revolution* (Oxford: Oxford University Press, 1968).

Lewis, Bernard, *The Emergence of Modern Turkey* (London: Oxford University Press, 1961).

Link, Arthur S., *The Higher Realism of Woodrow Wilson* (Nashville, TN: Vanderbilt University Press, 1971).

Link, Arthur, *Wilson: Campaigns for Progressivism and Peace, 1916–1917* (Princeton, NJ: Princeton University Press, 1965).

Link, Arthur, *Wilson: The New Freedom* (Princeton, NJ: Princeton University Press, 1956).

Link, Arthur S., *Wilson the Diplomatist: A Look at His Major Foreign Policies* (Baltimore: Johns Hopkins University Press, 1957).

Link, Arthur S., ed., *Woodrow Wilson and a Revolutionary World 1913–1921* (Chapel Hill: University of North Carolina Press, 1982).

Link, Arthur S., *Woodrow Wilson: Revolution, War and Peace* (Arlington Heights, IL: AHM Publishing Corporation, 1979).

Logan, Rayford W., *The Senate and the Versailles Mandate System* (Westport, CT: Greenwood Press, 1975).

Louis, William Roger, *Ends of British Imperialism: The Scramble for Empire, Suez and Decolonization: Collected Essays* (London: I. B. Tauris, 2006).

Love, Eric Tyrone, *Race Over Empire: Racism and U.S. Imperialism, 1865–1900* (Chapel Hill: University of North Carolina Press, 2004).

Macfie, A. L., *The Eastern Question, 1774–1923* (London: Longman, 1989).

Mack, John E., *A Prince of Our Disorder: The Life of T. E. Lawrence* (Cambridge, MA: Harvard University Press, 1998).

MacMillan, Margaret, *Paris 1919: Six Months That Changed The World* (New York: Random House, 2001).

MacMillan, Margaret, *The War That Ended Peace: How Europe Abandoned Peace for the First World War* (London: Profile Books, 2013).

Mahan, Alfred Thayer, *The Problem of Asia and Its Effect Upon International Policies* (Boston: Little, Brown & Co., 1900).

Mahan, Alfred Thayer, *Some Neglected aspects of war. Together with The power that makes for peace by Henry S. Pritchett and The capture of private property at sea, by Julian S. Corbett* (London: Sampson Low, Marston & Company, 1908).

Makdisi, Ussama, *Artillery of Heaven: American Missionaries and the Failed Conversion of the Middle East* (Ithaca, NY: Cornell University Press, 2008).

Malcolm, Vartan M., *The Armenians in America* (Boston: Pilgrim Press, 1919).

Manela, Erez, *The Wilsonian Moment: Self-Determination and the International Origins of Anticolonial Nationalism* (New York: Oxford University Press, 2007).

Mango, Andrew, *Ataturk* (London: John Murray, 1999).

Marks, Frederick W., *Velvet on Iron: The Diplomacy of Theodore Roosevelt* (Lincoln: University of Nebraska Press, 1979).

Marsh, Peter T., *Joseph Chamberlain: Entrepreneur in Politics* (New Haven, CT: Yale University Press, 1994).

Martel, Gordon, *Imperial Diplomacy: Roseberry and the Failure of Foreign Policy* (London: McGill-Queen's University Press, 1986).

May, Ernest R., *The World War and American Isolation, 1914–1917* (Cambridge, MA: Harvard University Press, 1966).

Mayer, Arno J., *Wilson vs Lenin: Political Origins of the New Diplomacy, 1917–1918* (Cleveland, OH: World, 1964).

Mayers, David, *Dissenting Voices in America's Rise to Power* (Cambridge: Cambridge University Press, 2007).

Mazower, Mark, *No Enchanted Palace: The End of Empire and the Ideological Origins of the United Nations* (Princeton, NJ: Princeton University Press, 2009).

McDermott, Rose. *Presidential Leadership, Illness and Decision Making* (Cambridge: Cambridge University Press, 2008).

McDougall, Walter A., *Promised Land, Crusader State: The American Encounter with the World since 1776* (Boston: Houghton Mifflin, 1997).

McKenna, Marian C., *Borah* (Ann Arbor: University of Michigan Press, 1961).

McMeekin, Sean, *The Berlin-Baghdad Express: The Ottoman Empire and Germany's Bid for World Power 1898–1918* (London: Allen Lane, 2010).

McNeill, William H., *Arnold Toynbee: A Life* (Oxford: Oxford University Press, 1989).

Mesrobian, Arpena S., *"Like One Family": The Armenians of Syrcacuse* (Ann Arbor, MI: Gomidas Institute Press, 2000).

Mirak, Robert, *Torn Between Two Lands: Armenians in America 1890 to World War One* (Cambridge, MA: Harvard University Press, 1983).

Mitchell, Nancy, *The Danger of Dreams: German and American Imperialism in Latin America* (Chapel Hill: University of North Carolina Press, 1999).

Morgenthau, Henry, *The Tragedy of Armenia* (London: Spottiswoode, Ballantyne & Co. 1918).

Morris, Edmund, *Colonel Roosevelt* (New York: Random House, 2010).

Morris, Edmund, *The Rise of Theodore Roosevelt* (New York: Random House, 2001).

Morris, Edmund, *Theodore Rex* (New York: The Modern Library, 2001).

Mott, Frank Luther, *A History of American Magazines, vol. IV: 1885–1905* (Cambridge, MA: Harvard University Press, 1957).

Mott, John R., *The Evangelization of the World in This Generation* (New York: Student Volunteer Movement for Foreign Missions, 1900).

Mott, John R., *The Present World Situation: With Special Reference to the Demands Made Upon the Christian Church in Relation to Non-Christian Lands* (New York: Student Volunteer for Foreign Missions, 1914).

Moyn, Samuel, *The Last Utopia: Human Rights in History* (Cambridge, MA: Harvard University Press, 2010).

Mugridge, Ian, *The View from Xanudu* (Montreal: McGill-Queen's University Press, 1995).

Mulligan, William, *The Great War for Peace* (New Haven, CT: Yale University Press, 2014).

Mulligan, William, and Maurice Bric, eds. *A Global History of Anti-Slavery Politics in the Nineteenth Century* (New York: Palgrave Macmillan, 2013).

Nalbandian, Louise, *The Armenian Revolutionary Movement* (Berkeley: University of California Press, 1963).

Nasaw, David, *The Chief: The Life of William Randolph Hearst* (Boston: Houghton Mifflin, 2001).

Nassibian, Akaby, *Britain and the Armenian Question, 1915–1923* (London: Croom Helm, 1984).

Neu, Charles, *Colonel House: A Biography of Woodrow Wilson's Silent Partner* (New York: Oxford University Press, 2015).

Nevins, Allen, *Henry White: Thirty Years of American Diplomacy* (New York: Harper & Brothers, 1930).

Nichols, Christopher McKnight, *Promise and Peril: America at the Dawn of a Global Age* (Cambridge, MA: Harvard University Press, 2011).

Ninkovich, Frank, *Global Dawn: The Cultural Foundation of American Internationalism, 1865–1890* (Cambridge, MA: Harvard University Press, 2009).

Offner, John L., *An Unwanted War: The Diplomacy of the United States and Spain over Cuba, 1895–1898* (Chapel Hill: University of North Carolina Press, 1992).

Oren, Michael, *Power, Faith and Fantasy: America in the Middle East 1776 to the Present* (New York: Norton, 2008).

Osgood, Robert Endicott, *Ideals and Self-Interest in America's Foreign Relations: The Great Transformation of the Twentieth Century* (Chicago: University of Chicago Press, 1953).

Osmanczyk, Jan Edmund, and Anthony Mango, eds., *Encyclopedia of the United Nations and International Agreements* (New York, London: Routledge, 2002).

Pakenham, Thomas, *The Scramble for Africa: White Man's Conquest of the Dark Continent from 1876 to 1912* (New York: Avon Books, 1991).

Pasdermadjian, Armen Garo, *Armenia: A Leading Factor in the Winning of the War* (New York: American Committee for the Independence of Armenia, 1919).

Patrick, Andrew, *America's Forgotten Middle East Initiative: The King-Crane Commission of 1919* (London: I. B. Tauris, 2015).

Payaslian, Simon, *United States Policy Toward the Armenian Genocide* (New York: Palgrave Macmillan, 2005).

Pears, Edwin, *Forty Years in Constantinople: the recollections of Sir Edwin Pears, 1873–1915* (New York: D. Appleton and Company, 1916).

Pedersen, Susan, *The Guardians: The League of Nations and the Crisis of Empire* (Oxford: Oxford University Press, 2015).

Penrose Jr., Stephen B. L., *That They May Have Life: The Story of the American University of Beirut, 1866–1941* (New York: Trustees of the AUB, 1941).

Perez Jr., Louis A., *Cuba Between Empires, 1878–1902* (Pittsburgh: University of Pittsburgh Press, 1983).

Perkins, Bradford, *The Great Rapprochement: England and the United States, 1895–1914* (London: Victor Gollancz Ltd., 1969).

Peterson, Merrill D., *Starving Armenians: America and the Armenian Genocide, 1915–1930 and After* (Charlottesville: University of Virginia Press, 2004).

Pomakoy, Keith, *Helping Humanity: American Policy and Genocide Rescue* (Lanham, MD: Lexington Books, 2011).

Porter, Andrew, *Religion versus Empire? British Protestant Missionaries and Overseas Expansion, 1700–1914* (Manchester: Manchester University Press, 2004).

Porter, Bernard, *Critics of Empire: British Radicals and the Imperial Challenge* (London: I. B. Tauris, 2008).

Porter, Bernard, *Empire and Superempire: Britain, America and the World* (New Haven, CT: Yale University Press, 2006).

Power, Samantha, *A Problem From Hell: America and the Age of Genocide* (New York: Basic Books, 2002).

Preston, Andrew, *Sword of the Spirit, Shield of Faith: Religion in American War and Diplomacy* (New York: Random House, 2012).

Pringle, Henry F., *Theodore Roosevelt* (New York: Harcourt, Brace, 1931).

Reynolds, David, *Britannia Overruled: British Policy and World Power In the 20th Century* (London: Longman, 1991).

Reynolds, David, *Lord Lothian and Anglo-American Relations, 1939–1940* (Philadelphia: American Philosophical Society, 1983).

Ricard, Serge, *A Companion to Theodore Roosevelt* (Malden, MA: Wiley Blackwell, 2011).

Ricard, Serge, *Theodore Roosevelt: Principes et Pratique d'une Politique etrangere* (Aix-en-Provence: Publications de l'Universite de Provence, 1991).

Ricard, Serge, and Helene Christol, eds., *Anglo-Saxonism in US Foreign Policy: the diplomacy of imperialism, 1899–1919* (Aix-en-Provence: Publications de l'Universite de Provence, 1991).

Richard, Laura E., and Maud Howe Elliott, *Julia Ward Howe 1819–1910* (Boston: Houghton Mifflin, Co., 1916).

Rickover, Hyman G., *How the Battleship Maine Was Destroyed* (Washington, DC: Department of Defense, Department of the Navy, Naval History Division: US Government Printing Office, 1976).

Roberts, Richard, *Saving the City: The Great Financial Crisis of 1914* (Oxford: Oxford University Press, 2013).

Robertson-Scott, John, *The Life and Death of a Newspaper* (London: Methuen, 1952).

Robinson, William S., *Muckraker: The Scandalous Life and Times of W. T. Stead, Britain's First Investigative Journalist* (London: Robson Press, 2012).

Rodogno, Davide, *Against Massacre: Humanitarian Intervention in the Ottoman Empire, 1815–1914* (Princeton, NJ: Princeton University Press, 2011).

Roosevelt, Theodore, *America and the World War* (New York: Charles Scribner's Sons, 1915).

Roosevelt, Theodore, *Fear God and Take Your Own Part* (New York: George H. Doran, 1916).

Roosevelt, Theodore, *The Naval War of 1812; or, The History of the United States Navy during the Last War with Great Britain* (New York: G. P. Putnam's Sons, 1882).

Roosevelt, Theodore, *The Strenuous Life: Essays and Addresses* (London: Grant Richards, 1902).

Rosenbaum, Alan S., ed., *Is the Holocaust Unique? Perspectives on Comparative Genocide* (Boulder, CO: Westview Press, 1996).

Rosenberg, Emily, *Financial Missionaries to the World: The Politics and Culture of Dollar Diplomacy, 1900–1930* (Cambridge, MA: Harvard University Press, 1999).

Sachar, Howard, *The Course of Modern Jewish History* (New York: Vintage Books, 1990).

Sachar, Howard, *The Emergence of the Middle East: 1914–1924* (London: Allen Lane, 1970).

Salt, Jeremy, *Imperialism, Evangelism and the Ottoman Armenians 1878–1896* (London: Frank Cass, 1993).

Sands, Philippe, *East West Street: On the Origins of Genocide and Crimes Against Humanity* (London: Weidenfeld & Nicolson, 2016)

Saul, Norman E., *Concord and Conflict: The United States and Russia, 1867–1914* (Kansas: University Press of Kansas, 1996).

Schake, Kori, *Safe Passage: The Transition from British to American Hegemony* (Cambridge, MA: Harvard University Press, 2017).

Schoonover, Thomas, *The United States in Central America, 1860–1911: Episodes in Social Imperialism and International Rivalry in the World System* (Durham, NC: Duke University Press, 1991).

Schulzinger, Robert, ed., *A Companion to American Foreign Relations* (Malden, MA: Wiley Blackwell, 2003).

Seaman, John. *A Citizen of the World: The Life of James Bryce* (London: I. B. Tauris, 2006).

Seeley, J. R., *The Expansion of England: Two Courses of Lectures* (London: Macmillan, 1883).

Seton Watson, R. W., *Disraeli, Gladstone and the Eastern Question: A Study in Diplomacy and Party Politics* (London: Macmillan, 1935).

Sexton, Jay, *The Monroe Doctrine: Empire and Nation in Nineteenth Century America* (New York: Hill & Wang, 2011).

Shannon, Richard T., *Gladstone and the Bulgarian Agitation 1876* (London: Nelson, 1963).

Sharp, Alan, *David Lloyd George: Great Britain* (London: Haus, 2008).

Shaw, Stanford J., and Ezel Kural Shaw, *History of the Ottoman Empire and Modern Turkey, Vol. 2: Reform, Evolution and Republic: The Rise of Modern Turkey, 1808–1975* (Cambridge: Cambridge University Press, 1977).

Shults, R. L., *Crusader in Babylon: W. T. Stead and the Pall Mall Gazette* (Lincoln: University of Nebraska Press, 1972).

Simms, Brendan, *Europe: The Struggle for Supremacy* (New York: Basic Books, 2013).

Simms, Brendan, and David Trim, eds. *Humanitarian Intervention: A History* (Cambridge: Cambridge University Press, 2011).

Skinner, Elliott P., *African Americans and U.S. Policy Toward Africa, 1850–1924* (Washington DC: Howard University Press, 1992).

Skloot, Robert, ed., *The Theatre of Genocide: Four Plays about Mass Murder in Rwanda, Bosnia, Cambodia and Armenia* (Madison: University of Wisconsin Press, 2008).

Smith, Rixley, and Norman Beasley, *Carter Glass: A Biography* (New York and Toronto: Longmans, Green & Co., 1939).

Smuts, Jan Christian, *The League of Nations: A Practical Suggestion* (London: Hodder and Stoughton, 1918).

Sprout, Harold, and Margaret Sprout, *The Rise of American Naval Power, 1776–1918* (Princeton, NJ: Princeton University Press, 1939).

Stanley, Brian, *The World Missionary Conference, Edinburgh 1910* (Grand Rapids, MI: Eerdmans, 2009).

Stead, W. T., *The Americanization of the World, the Trend of the Twentieth Century* (New York 1902).

Stead, W. T., *The Haunting Horrors of Armenia, Political Papers for the People* (London: The Review of Reviews Office, 1896).

Stead, W. T., *If Christ Came to Chicago: A Plea for the Union of All Who Love in the Service of All Who Suffer* (London: The Review of Reviews Office, 1894).

Stead, W. T., *The Maiden Tribute of Modern Babylon: The Report of the Secret Commission* (London: Pall Mall Gazette, 1885).

Stead, W. T., *The United States of Europe on the eve of the Parliament of Peace* (London: The Review of Reviews Office, 1899).

Steel, Ronald, *Walter Lippmann and the American Century* (New York: Vintage Books, 1981).

Steiner, Zara, *The Lights That Failed: European International History, 1919–1933* (Oxford: Oxford University Press, 2005).

Stephanson, Anders, *Manifest Destiny: American Expansionism and the empire of right* (New York: Hill and Wang, 1996).

Still, William N., *American Sea Power in the Old World: The United States Navy in European and Near Eastern Waters, 1865–1917* (Westport, CT: Greenwood, 1980).

Stivers, William, *Supremacy and Oil: Iraq, Turkey and the Anglo-American World Order, 1918–1930* (Ithaca, NY: Cornell University Press, 1982).

Storey, Moorfield, *The Moro Massacre: Letter* (Boston: Anti-Imperialist League, 1906).

Stowell, Ellery C., *International Law: A Restatement of Principles in Conformity with Actual Practice* (New York: Henry Holt, 1931).

Straus, Oscar S., *The American Spirit* (New York: The Century Company, 1913).

Suny, Ronald Grigor, *"They Can Live in the Desert but Nowhere Else": A History of the Armenian Genocide* (Princeton, NJ: Princeton University Press, 2015).

Suny, Ronald Grigor, Fatma Muge Gocek, and Norman M. Naimark, eds. *A Question of Genocide* (New York: Oxford University Press, 2011).

Taliafero, John, *All the Great Prizes: The Life of John Hay, from Lincoln to Roosevelt* (New York: Simon & Schuster, 2013).

Taylor, A. J. P., *The Troublemakers: Dissent over Foreign Policy, 1792–1939* (London: Pimlico, 1993).

Thayer, William Roscoe, ed., *The Life and Letters of John Hay* (Boston: Houghton Mifflin Co., 1915).

Thompson, Arthur William, and Robert Allan Hart, *The Uncertain Crusade: America and the Russian Revolution of 1905* (Amherst, MA: University of Massachusetts Press, 1970).

Thompson, John A., *Woodrow Wilson* (London: Longman, 2002).

Thompson, Kenneth, ed., *Papers on Presidential Disability and the 25th Amendment by Medical, Historical and Political Authorities* (Lanham, MD, University Press of America, 1996).

Throntveit, Trygve, *Power Without Victory: Woodrow Wilson and the American Internationalist Experiment* (Chicago: Chicago University Press, 2017).

Tibawi, L., *American Interests in Syria: 1800–1901, A Study of Educational Literary and Religious Work* (London: Oxford University Press, 1966).

Tilchin, William N., *Theodore Roosevelt and the British Empire: A Study in Presidential Statecraft* (New York: St. Martin's Press, 1997).

Tilchin, William N., and Charles E. Neu, *Artists of Power: Theodore Roosevelt, Woodrow Wilson and their Enduring Impact on US Foreign Policy* (Westport, CT: Praeger, 2006).

Tillman, Seth B., *Anglo-American Relations at the Peace Conference of 1919* (Princeton, NJ: Princeton University Press, 1961).

Tooze, Adam, *The Deluge: The Great War and the Remaking of Global Order, 1916–1931* (London: Allen Lane, 2014).

Toynbee, Arnold, *Acquiaintances* (London: Oxford University Press, 1967).

Trask, David F., *The War with Spain in 1898* (New York: Macmillan, 1981).

Trask, Roger R., *The United States Response to Turkish Nationalism and Reform, 1914–1939* (Minneapolis: University of Minnesota Press, 1971).

Travis, Frederick F., *George Kennan and the American–Russian Relationship, 1865–1924* (Athens: Ohio University Press, 1990).

Trumpener, Ulrich, *Germany and the Ottoman Empire, 1914–1918* (Princeton, NJ: Princeton University Press, 1968).

Tumulty, Joseph P., *Woodrow Wilson As I Know Him* (London: Heinemann, 1922).

Turk, Richard W., *The Ambiguous Relationship: Theodore Roosevelt and Alfred Thayer Mahan* (Westport, CT: Greenwood Press, 1987).

Turner, Frederick Jackson, *The Significance of the Frontier in American History* (Washington, DC: US Government Printing Office, 1894).

Tusan, Michelle, *The British Empire and the Armenian Genocide: Humanitarianism and Imperial Politics from Gladstone to Churchill* (London: I. B. Tauris, 2017).

Tyrell, Ian, *Reforming the World: The Creation of America's Moral Empire* (Princeton, NJ: Princeton University Press, 2010).

Uyanik, Nevzat, *Dismantling the Ottoman Empire: Britain, America and the Armenian Question* (Abingdon: Routledge, 2016).

Veeser, Cyrus, *A World Safe for Capitalism: Dollar, Diplomacy and America's Rise to Global Power* (New York: Columbia University Press, 2002).

Vucetic, Srdjan, *The Anglosphere: A Genealogy of a Racialized Identity in International Relations* (Stanford, CA: Stanford University Press, 2011).

Walker, Christopher J., *Armenia: The Survival of a Nation*, 2nd ed. (London: St Martin's Press 1990).

Walther, Karine, *Sacred Interests: The United States and the Islamic World, 1821–1921* (Chapel Hill: University of North Carolina Press, 2015).

Ward, Adolphus W., and. George P. Gooch, *Cambridge History of British Foreign Policy* (Cambridge: Cambridge University Press, 1922).

Ward, Alan J., *Ireland and Anglo-American Relations 1899–1921* (London: Weidenfeld and Nicolson, 1969).

Watenpaugh, Keith David, *Bread from Stones: The Middle East and the Making of Modern Humanitarianism* (Berkeley, CA: University of California Press, 2015).

Weber, Frank, *Eagles on the Crescent: Germany, Austria and the Diplomacy of the Turkish Alliance, 1914–1918* (Ithaca, NY: Cornell University Press, 1970).

Weizmann, Chaim, *Trial and Error: The Autobiography of Chaim Weizmann* (Philadelphia: Jewish Publication Society of America, 1949).

Wetherson, Michael A., and Hal Bochin, *Hiram Johnson: Political Revivalist* (Lanham, MD: University Press of America).

Whyte, Frederic, *The Life of William T. Stead* (London: J. Cape Ltd., 1925).

Widenor, William C., *Henry Cabot Lodge and the Search for an American Foreign Policy* (Berkeley: University of California Press, 1980).

Williams, William Appleman, *The Roots of the Modern American Empire: A Study of the Growth and Shaping of Social Consciousness in a Marketplace Society* (New York: Random House, 1969).

Williams, William Appleman, *The Tragedy of American Diplomacy* (New York: Dell Publishing Co., 1962).

Willis, James F., *Prologue to Nuremberg: The Politics and Diplomacy of Punishing War Criminals of the First World War* (Westport, CT: Greenwood Press 1982).

Winks, Robin W., ed., *The Historiography of the British Empire-Commonwealth: Trends, Interpretations and Resources* (Durham, NC: Duke University Press, 1996).

Winter, Jay, ed., *America and the Armenian Genocide of 1915* (Cambridge: Cambridge University Press, 2003).

Wikkopf, Eugene R., and James M. McCormick, eds., *The Domestic Sources of American Foreign Policy* (Oxford: Oxford University Press, 2004).

Winter, Jay, ed. *The Cambridge History of the First World War, Volume 2: The State* (Cambridge: Cambridge University Press, 2014).

Wright, Quincy, *Mandates Under the League of Nations* (Chicago: University of Chicago Press, 1930).

Yapp, M. E., *The Making of the Modern Near East, 1792–1923* (London: Longman, 1988).

Zangrando, Robert, *The NAACP Crusade against Lynching, 1909–1950* (Philadelphia: Temple University Press, 1980).

Zimmerman, Andrew, *Alabama in Africa: Booker T. Washington, the German Empire and the Globalization of the New South* (Princeton, NJ: Princeton University Press, 2010).

Zimmerman, Warren, *First Great Triumph* (New York: FSG, 2002).

Zurcher, Erik Jan, *Turkey: A Modern History*, 3rd. ed (London: I. B. Tauris, 2004).

Articles

Akgun, Seçil Karal, "Some Abstracts from the Mormon Missionaries about the Turks and Armenians," *Review of Armenian Studies* 1, no. 1 (2002), 65–79.

Ambrosius, Lloyd E., "Wilson, Republicans, and French Security after World War I," *Journal of American History* 59 (September 1972), 341–352.

Askew, William C., and J. Fred Rippy, "The United States and Europe's Strife, 1908–1913," *Journal of Politics* 4 (February 1942), 68–79.

Barton, James L., "What America Has Done for Armenia." *Armenia* 1, no. 3 (December 1904), 3–10.

Baylen, J. O., "A Victorian's 'Crusade' in Chicago, 1893–94," *Journal of American History, Vol.* 51, No. 3, (1964), 418–434.

Baylen, J. O., "W. T. Stead: A Christ in Chicago," *British Journalism Review* 3 (1992), 57–61.

Bothwell, R. S., "Canadian Representation at Washington: A Study in Colonial Responsibility," *Canadian Historical Review* 53, no. 2, (1972), 125–148.

Brecher, F. W., "Revisiting Ambassador Morgenthau's Turkish Peace Mission of 1917," *Middle Eastern Studies* 24, no. 3 (July 1988), 357–363.

Brown, Phillip M., "The Mandate over Armenia," *American Journal of International Law* 14, no. 3 (January 1920), 396–406.

Bryson, Thomas A., "Admiral Mark L. Bristol, an Open-Door Diplomat in Turkey," *International Journal of Middle East Studies* 5, no. 4 (1974), 450–467.

Bryson, Thomas A., "An American Mandate for Armenia: A Link in British Near Eastern Policy," *Armenian Review* 21, no. 2 (1968), 23–41.

Burk, Kathleen, "J. M. Keynes and the Exchange Rate Crisis of July 1917," *Economic History Review* 32, no. 3 (August 1979), 405–416.

Bryson, Thomas A., "John Sharp Williams, An advocate for the Armenian Mandate." *Armenian Review* 26 (Fall 1973), 10–25.

Bryson, Thomas A., "Woodrow Wilson and the Armenian Mandate: A Reassessment," *Armenian Review* 21 (Autumn 1968), 10–29.

Cooper Jr., John Milton, "The Command of Gold Reversed: American Loans to Britain, 1915–17," *Pacific Historical Review* 45 (May 1976), 209–230.

Clymer, Kenneth J., "Anti-Semitism in the Late Nineteenth Century: The Case of John Hay," *American Jewish Historical Quarterly* LX, no. 4 (June 1971), 349–350.

Curry, George, "Woodrow Wilson, Jan Christian Smuts and the Versailles Settlement," *American Historical Review* 66, no. 4 (July 1961), 968–986.

Dadrian, Vahakn, "The 1894 Sassoun Massacre: A Juncture in the Escalation of the Turko-Armenian Conflict," *Armenian Review* 47, no. 1–2 (2001), 5–39.

Daniel, Robert L., "The Armenian Question and American-Turkish Relations, 1914–1927," *Mississippi Valley Historical Review* 46 (September 1959), 252–275.

Daniel, Robert L., "The Friendship of Woodrow Wilson and Cleveland H. Dodge," *Mid-America* 43 (July 1961), 182–196.

DeNovo, John A., "The Movement for an Aggressive American Oil Policy Abroad, 1918–1920," *American Historical Review* 61, no. 4 (July 1956), 854–876.

Dinkel, Christoph, "German Officers and the Armenian Genocide," *Armenian Review* 44, no. 1 (1991), 77–133.

Douglas, Roy, "Britain and the Armenian Question," *The Historical Journal* 19, no. 1 (March 1976), 115–121.

Fry, Joseph A., "William McKinley and the Coming of the Spanish-American War: A Study of the Besmirching and Redemption of an Historical Image," *Diplomatic History* 3 (Winter 1979), 77–97.

Gaddis, John Lewis, "New Conceptual Approaches to the Study of American Foreign Relations; Interdisciplinary Perspectives," *Diplomatic History* 14 (Summer 1990), 405–424.

Gardner, Lloyd C., "Lost Empires," *Diplomatic History* 13 (Winter 1989), 1–14.

Gerstle, Gary, "Theodore Roosevelt and the Divided Character of American Nationalism," *Journal of American History* 86 (December 1999), 1280–1307.

Gilderhus, Mark T., "The Monroe Doctrine: Meanings and Implications," *Presidential Studies Quarterly* 36, no. 1 (March, 2006), 5–16.

Graham, Malbone W., "Humanitarian Intervention in International Law as Related to the Practice of the United States," *Michigan Law Review* 22, no. 4 (February 1924), 312–328.

Grabill, Joseph L., "Cleveland H. Dodge, Woodrow Wilson, and the Near East," *Journal on Presbyterian History* 48 (Winter 1970), 249–264.

Green, Abigail, "Humanitarianism in Nineteenth-Century Context: Religious, Gendered, National," *The Historical Journal* 57, no. 4 (December 2014), 1157–1175.

Hawkins, Hunt, "Mark Twain's involvement with the Congo Reform Movement: "A Fury of Generous Indignation," *New England Quarterly* 51, no. 2 (1978), 147–175.

Jessup, Phillip C., "The Defense of Oppressed People," *American Journal of International Law* 31, no. 1 (1938), 116–119.

Kernek, Sterling J., "Woodrow Wilson and National Self-Determination Along Italy's Frontier," *Proceedings of the American Philosophical Society* 126 (1982), 242–300.

Knee, Stuart E., "Anglo-American Understanding and the Boer War," *Australian Journal of Politics and History* 30, no. 2 (1984), 196–208.

Knee, Stuart E., "The Diplomacy of Neutrality: Theodore Roosevelt and the Russian Pogroms of 1903–1906," *Presidential Studies Quarterly* 19 (Winter 1989), 71–78.

Kramer, Paul, "Empires, Exceptions and Anglo-Saxons: Race and Rule between the British and United States Empires, 1880–1910," in *Journal of American History* 88, no. 4 (March 2002), 1315–1353.

Kuznets, Simon, "Immigration of Russian Jews to the United States: Background and Structure," *Perspectives in American History, Vol. 9 (1975)*, 35–124.

Lebow, Richard Ned, "The Morgenthau Peace Mission," *Jewish Social Studies* 32, no. 4 (October 1970), 267–285.

Lugard, Frederick, "The Mandate System and the British Mandates," *Journal of the Royal Society of Arts* 72, no. 3736 (June 27, 1924), 535–550.

Mahan, Alfred Thayer, and Charles T. Beresford, "Possibilities of an Anglo-American Reunion," *North American Review* (November 1894), 551–573.

Matossian, LouAnn, "Minnesota Newspapers Reportage About the Armenian Genocide, 1915–1922," Holocaust and Genocide Studies, University of Minnesota, http://chgs.elevator.umn.edu/asset/viewAsset/57c5982b7d58ae601417ab95#57c598a47d58ae9f4717abd4.

Merguerian, Barbara J., "The American Response to the 1895 Massacres," *Genocide and Human Rights: Lessons from the Armenian Experience*. Special Issue, *Journal of Armenian Studies* 4, no. 1–2 (1992), 53–83.

Morris, Edmund, "A Few Pregnant Days: Theodore Roosevelt and the Venezuelan Crisis of 1902," *Theodore Roosevelt Association Journal* 15 (Winter 1989), 2–13.

Mott, Frank Luther, "The Magazine Revolution and Popular Ideas in the Nineties," *Proceedings of the American Antiquarian Society* 64 (April 1954), 195–214.

Ninkovich, Frank, "Theodore Roosevelt: Civilization As Ideology," *Diplomatic History* 10 (Summer 1986), 221–245.

Nolan, Cathal J., "The United States and Tsarist Anti-Semitism," *Diplomacy and Statecraft* 3, no. 3 (1992), 439–467.

Pedersen, Susan, "Back to the League of Nations: Review Essay," *American Historical Review* 112, no. 4 (October 2007), 1091–1117.

Pletcher, David M., "Rhetoric and Results: A Pragmatic View of American Economic Expansion, 1865–1898," *Diplomatic History* 5 (Spring 1981), 93–106.

Potter, Pitman B., "Origin of the System of Mandates under the League of Nations," *American Political Science Review* 16 (November 1922), 563–583.

Prévost, Stephanie, "W. T. Stead and the Eastern Question (1875–1911)." 19: *Interdisciplinary Studies in the Long Nineteenth Century* 16 (2013), 1–27, DOI: http://doi.org/10.16995/ntn.654

Reed, James Eldin, "American Foreign Policy, the Politics of Missions and Josiah Strong, 1890–1900," *Church History* 41, no. 2 (June 1972), 230–245.

Reynolds, David. "Rethinking Anglo-American Relations," *International Affairs* 65, no. 1 (Winter 1988–1989), 89–111.

Ricard, Serge, "The Roosevelt Corollary," *Presidential Studies Quarterly* 36, no. 1 (2006), 17–26.

Ricard, Serge, "Theodore Roosevelt and the Diplomacy of Righteousness," *Theodore Roosevelt Association Journal* 12 (Winter 1986), 14–17.

Roberts, Priscilla, "World War I and Anglo-American Relations: The Role of Philip Kerr and the Round Table," *Round Table* 95, no. 383 (2006), 113–139.

Rosenberg, Emily, "The Empire Strikes Back," *Reviews in American History* 16 (December 1988), 585–590.

Russell, Greg, "Theodore Roosevelt, Geopolitics, and Cosmopolitan Ideals," *Review of International Studies* 32, no. 3 (2006), 541–559.

Seed, Geoffrey, "British Reactions to American Imperialism Reflected in Journals of Opinion, 1898–1900," *Political Science Quarterly* 73, no. 2 (June 1958), 254–272.

Smith, Daniel, "National Interest and American Intervention, 1917: An Historiographical Appraisal," *Journal of American History* 52, no. 1 (June 1965), 5–24.

Smith, Daniel, "Robert Lansing and the Formulation of American Neutrality Policies, 1914–1915," *Mississippi Valley Historical Review* 43, no. 1 (June 1956), 59–81.

Thompson, John A., "The Exaggeration of American Vulnerability: The Anatomy of a Tradition," *Diplomatic History* 15, no. 1 (Winter 1992), 23–43.

Thompson, John A., "William Appleman Williams and the 'American Empire,'" *Journal of American Studies* 7, no. 1 (April 1973), 91–104.

Throntveit, Tryvge. "The Fable of the Fourteen Points: Woodrow Wilson and National Self-Determination," *Diplomatic History* 35, no. 3 (2011), 445–481.

Tusan, Michelle, "Crimes Against Humanity: Human Rights, the British Empire, and the Origins of the Response to the Armenian Genocide," *American Historical Review* (February 2014), 47–77.

Watenpaugh, Keith David, "'A pious wish devoid of all practicability': Interwar Humanitarianism, The League of Nations and the Rescue of Trafficked Women and Children in the Eastern Mediterranean, 1920–1927," *American Historical Review* 115, no. 4 (October 2010), 1315–1339.

Weitz, Eric, "From the Vienna to the Paris System: International Politics and the Entangled Histories of Human Rights, Forced Deportations, and Civilizing Missions," *American Historical Review* 113, no. 5 (December 2008), 1313–1343.

Wertheim, Stephen, "The League That Wasn't: American Designs for a Leaglist-Sanctionalist League of Nations and the Intellectual Origins of International Organization," *Diplomatic History* 35, no. 5 (2011), 797–836.

Wilson, Anne Marie, "In the Name of God, Civilization, and Humanity: The United States and the Armenian Massacres of the 1890s," *Le Mouvement Social* 227 (April–June 2009), 27–44.

Yale, William, "Ambassador Henry Morgenthau's Special Mission of 1917," *World Politics* 1 (April 1949), 308–320.

Zeidner, Robert F. "Britain and the Launching of the Armenian Question," *International Journal of Middle Eastern Studies* 7, no. 4 (October 1976), 465–483.

PhD Dissertations

Bryson, Thomas A., "Woodrow Wilson, the Senate, Public Opinion, and the Armenian Mandate Question, 1919–1920" (PhD diss., University of Georgia, 1965).

Cook, Ralph Elliott, "The United States and the Armenian Question, 1884–1924" (PhD diss., Fletcher School of Law and Diplomacy, Tufts University, 1957).

Matikainen, Satu, "Great Britain, British Jews, and the International Protection of Romanian Jews, 1900–1914: A Study of Jewish Diplomacy and Minority Rights" (PhD diss,Jyvaskyla Studies in Humanities: University of Jyvasklya, 2006).

McStallworth, Paul, "The United States and the Congo Question, 1884–1914" (PhD diss., Ohio State University, 1954).

INDEX

For the benefit of digital users, indexed terms that span two pages (e.g., 52–53) may, on occasion, appear on only one of those pages.

Note: Tables and figures are indicated by *t* and *f* following the page number